WOOD & WATER

WOOD & WATER

The Story of SEABOARD Lumber and Shipping

E.G. Perrault

Douglas & McIntyre
Vancouver/Toronto

To the loggers, millworkers, foresters and entrepreneurs who have laboured to share British Columbia's forest harvest with the world.

Copyright © 1985 by E.G. Perrault

85 86 87 88 89   5 4 3 2 1

Douglas & McIntyre Ltd., 1615 Venables Street,
Vancouver, British Columbia   V5L 2H1

Canadian Cataloguing in Publication Data

Perrault, E. G. (Ernest G.)
     Wood and water

Includes index.
ISBN 0-88894-471-3

1. Seaboard Lumber Sales Company — History.
2. Seaboard Shipping Company — History. 3. Lumber
trade — British Columbia — History. 4. Merchant
marine — British Columbia — History. I. Title.
HD9764.C34S42   1985   338.7'674'09711
                                          C85-091482-5

Unless otherwise credited below, all photographs, map and Seaboard advertisement courtesy Seabord Lumber Sales Company Limited.

Founders and Their Environment/Vancouver Public Library: 1, #3937; 2,
     #5781; 4, #5268; 5, #4118   Humbird Papers: 14,15,16
A Walk Through the Office/Humbird Papers: 12, 18, 19, 20, 21, 22, 23
Vanguard to the Present/Crown Zellerbach Canada: 6

Design by David Lim
Typeset by Typeworks
Printed and bound in Canada by D. W. Friesen & Sons

CONTENTS

ACKNOWLEDGEMENTS

The author could not have attempted this book without the assistance and co-operation of an uncounted number of people, some active in Seaboard at the present time, others who have been in retirement for a considerable number of years. Relatives of Seaboard personalities now deceased extended themselves to search out and supply information. Hours of taped interviews with past employees, associates of Seaboard, and retired members of lumber associations, some of them octogenarians, resulted in an assembly of human interest material which added another dimension to the book.

Perhaps the single most important source of accurate information was supplied by Mrs. Virginia Dickie of Medford, Oregon. Daughter of Seaboard Lumber Sales' president John Humbird, she had come into possession of her father's meticulously detailed journals covering the ten years of his presidency. Her thoughtfulness in donating these volumes to Seaboard's archives is acknowledged with gratitude.

Violet Pritchard, one of Seaboard's first employees, demonstrated an almost photographic memory in supplying names of the company's first management and staff, together with personal recollections which compensated for missing early company records. Mr. Reg Barclay's constructive efforts as a liaison between the writer and Seaboard personnel past and present, and his thorough comprehension of Seaboard's operations, are greatly acknowledged.

Moving beyond the information resources supplied by Seaboard's staff and associates, sincere thanks must go to staff members of the Vancouver Public Library, the Library of the University of British Columbia, the British Columbia Provincial Archives, the Council of Forest Industries, retired members of the B.C. Lumber Manufacturers Association, and others who placed resources and skills at the author's disposal. Special mention must be directed to the extended research efforts of Margaret Campbell who worked closely with the author at every stage of the book's evolution.

PROLOGUE

Seaboard Lumber Sales Company Limited has been described as a company that defies logical explanation. At the time of its first formation in 1928 there were those in the business community who prophesied that a company managed by a committee made up of competitors could never work, and their point was well taken. Earlier attempts to establish similar sales organizations both in the United States and Canada had met with failure.

The early mill owners who comprised Seaboard were all rugged individualists accustomed to a rough-and-tumble struggle for survival in the troubled infancy of the forest industry. The demands made on them by one of the world's most difficult and overpowering market environments compelled them to rely on their own strengths, inventiveness, endurance and business sense. Competitors in the most dogged interpretation of the word, some were large and relatively well-financed, others small and operated close to the line.

The Seaboard structure was not an example of lions lying down with lambs in an act of mutual co-operation, but more a case of large and small independent entrepreneurs pulling in harness, suppressing individual feistiness and competitive machinations in order to achieve a common goal. And that goal was born of absolute neccessity. The lumber industry, as it emerged into the twentieth century, possessed a potential both in terms of forest resources and manufacturing capability that far surpassed the lumber demands either of the province or of the Canadian nation. The only sales opportunities remaining lay in the overseas markets, and the hard fact was that the British Columbia mills were latecomers in export marketplaces that were entrenched, complex and highly competitive.

In order to compete profitably in this new environment, the mills were compelled to join forces to realize the economies of large volume sales and shipment, to ensure that costs between the mills and the customer were as lean as possible, and to share the cost of the promotion of product and the establishment of grade standards acceptable to overseas customers.

Two distinct and disparate entities proceeded to address themselves to the overseas lumber export markets: one was Seaboard Lumber Sales Company Limited, a consortium of British Columbia sawmills; the other was MacMillan Export Company Limited headed by H. R. MacMillan whose preferred strategy it was to own mills and control lumber supply. These two powerful entities would remain in conflict for years, each reacting to the other's manufacturing and marketing innovations, thereby forcing one another into new positions of strength. H. R. MacMillan in later years stated that without the perpetual challenge of Seaboard he would never have been forced into the position of owning mills, thus strengthening his hand enormously.

It cannot be taken for granted that every reader is aware of Seaboard's position in world trade. The understandable tendency is to think of British Columbia's forest industry in terms of its domestic impact. The province's forests have made a substantial contribution to the construction of housing across Canada; its rail ties and bridge timbers have helped to support the ribbons of steel that span the nation; its planks have shaped the hulls of an immense flotilla of vessels, and its pulp and newsprint have supplied the presses of every province.

In fact, Canadians are surrounded, supported and sheltered by the products of B.C.'s forests, though it is unlikely that many give that fact a passing thought. Even less likely is a general appreciation of the amount and variety of forest products shipped from British Columbia to the rest of the world in any given year. Few indeed know that Seaboard Lumber Sales Company Limited has for many years been one of the largest exporters of lumber in the world. Soon after its formation it was acting as the export sales organization for almost 80 per cent of British Columbia's sawmill production. Today it remains the province's single largest lumber export organization. In this fifty-year history of a truly great export company many changes and crises are recorded. But in one respect nothing has changed. Long before British Columbia became a province the first timber hewn on this coast was slated for export.

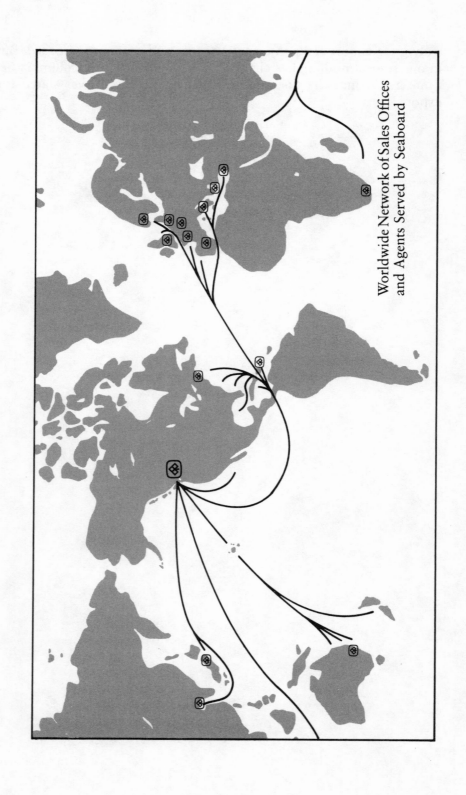

Worldwide Network of Sales Offices
and Agents Served by Seaboard

·ONE·

HOW IT BEGAN

Captain Cook's voyage of discovery into the waters of what is now British Columbia occurred in 1778, and was well chronicled by the captain/navigator and his officers. Records describe endless forests blanketing mountains and valleys. The trees in that rain forest were of a size and excellence to inspire awe; and before moving on, Cook refitted his ships, the *Resolution* and the *Discovery*, with masts and spars taken from stands at Nootka on Vancouver Island.

This, of course, was hardly a timber export transaction, since Cook had served his own purposes at no cost. However, the taking of the masts and spars might be considered the first instance of timber promotion on this coast. Certainly Captain Cook and his crew must have sung their praises because a few years later, when the British Navy established a Pacific station at Valparaiso, Chile, it arranged to obtain masts and spars from the nearest British territory, which happened to be Vancouver Island—the land of superlative timber.

One of the first instances of a timber export transaction in the territory to become known as British Columbia was conducted by Capt. John Meares, a British fur trader sailing from the China coast. His business was to collect pelts of the sea otter, then abundant in Pacific Northwest waters; but in 1788, in addition to this rich treasure, he took on a deck cargo of spars and other hewn timbers destined for the China trade. Both pelts and timbers commanded handsome prices.

Not all dealers in timbers were as fortunate as the intrepid Meares. Capt. William Brotchie in 1849 embarked from London, England, aboard the *Albion,* carrying with him written authority to cut spars for the British Admiralty as well as for the Hudson's Bay Company. Not far from his destination, the ship ran aground on a reef, later named appropriately "Brotchie Ledge," just outside of what is now Victoria harbour. Extricated with difficulty, the *Albion* was anchored in American waters, and Brotchie went ashore to cut spars. The operation proceeded smoothly—too smoothly. In a relatively short period of time a cargo of forty-two spars was loaded, some of the items measuring 96 feet in length, 26 inches square. Captain Brotchie had reason to feel satisfied . . . until an American cutter appeared on the scene. The *Albion* was seized and her crew imprisoned for logging in American territory without authorization. After months of difficult international negotiations conducted across thousands of miles, both ship and crew were cleared, a somewhat pointless gesture because the ship and its cargo had been sold long since.

Brotchie, a man of courage and determination, then journeyed to Fort Rupert on the northern edge of Vancouver Island, where he set up spar cutting operations, enlisting the labour of local Indians. This involved teaching the totally unskilled work force to square and trim huge timbers to specified dimensions. With 102 magnificent spars ready for shipment, Brotchie waited for transport that never arrived. Difficulty of communications, official apathy and, finally, a change in Admiralty policy conspired to defeat him. In 1857, eight years after the beginning of his venture, he received word from the Lord Commissioner that spars from Vancouver Island were no longer required. Brotchie was ruined and his spars, one of which measured 116 feet in length, were overtaken by the forest that gave them birth. In ensuing years, others would fail in their attempts to establish a forest products export trade, but Brotchie's effort remains the most ironic and poignant of all.

The first sawmill in the British territory was built by the Hudson's Bay Company at the head of Esquimalt Harbour near the present city of Victoria on Vancouver Island. Water powered, it was operative in 1848 and was used initially to supply lumber and sawn timbers for structures in Fort Victoria and the immediate surroundings.

A modest export trade commenced in 1849 when records show a

shipment of 42,270 feet of lumber* to San Francisco, to supply a demand for building materials generated by the California gold rush. Another cargo went to the same destination in January 1850, commanding the unusually high price for that day of $80 a thousand feet (compared to $300 in a 1985 market). Later still this same mill shipped lumber to Hawaii, as well as a number of other cargoes to San Francisco. All of this business came to a halt in 1854 when a spring freshet destroyed the mill's water wheel and major works.

By that time a second mill had been established on Vancouver Island by the first colonist to arrive there under the terms of the Royal Grant of 1849. The grant commissioned the Hudson's Bay Company to undertake a program of colonization. The entrepreneur was Capt. W. Colquhoun Grant, late of the 2nd Dragoon Guards, whose initial purpose was to locate both his mill and his habitation close to Fort Victoria. The company was unable to settle him conveniently, and he ended up some twenty-five miles away at Sooke where he installed his small, water-powered sawmill. Production began in 1850 but with small success. Local demand for lumber was satisfied for the moment, export demand had dwindled and it is to be suspected that the Hudson's Bay Company, unwilling to encourage colonists to enter its lucrative fur trading domain, provided little encouragement. Frustrated and bitterly disappointed, Captain Grant sold out to John Muir and Sons in 1853 and left the colony forever.

In due course the Muirs moved the mill to a more accessible location at the entrance to Sooke Harbour and there converted the millworks to steam. This enterprise succeeded where Grant had failed. Despite the fact that American sawmills not much farther south in Puget Sound, motivated by the California gold rush, were more advanced and productive, and further advantaged by a 20 per cent protective tariff, the Hudson's Bay mill and the Muir mill were able to compete. Records show that in 1853, nineteen lumber ships sailed from Sooke or Victoria to San Francisco, and at least one other sailed to Valparaiso with a cargo of spars, intended undoubtedly for the British Navy's Pacific station. Captain Brotchie, toiling over his superspars at Fort Rupert, must have raged when he learned of this. It might be said that he was British Columbia's first of many victims of competition in the forest industry.

While records of the Muir sawmill activity are spotty, there is an

---

* The term used by the lumber industry to quantify lumber is FBM, or foot board measure. In this book we have elected to use the term board feet or simply feet as being more familiar to the general reader.

1859 account of the barque *Euphrates* sailing from Sooke to London loaded with 157 spars and 40,000 feet of lumber. The Muir's fortunes rose and fell from that time until 1892, during which period they sold the mill, regained it, witnessed its destruction by fire in 1875, rebuilt it on another site, and finally closed it down. A pattern of lumber export had been established. The two Vancouver Island sawmills had penetrated markets in San Francisco, Shanghai, Australia, Hong Kong, the Sandwich Islands, South America and England. And from 1858 on, other mills on Vancouver Island and the mainland, known at that time as New Caledonia, shared in this trade.

The magnet that attracted sawmills to the mainland was the discovery of gold in the sand bars of the Fraser River in 1856–57. The California gold rush had run its course and the word of Fraser River gold went out when Governor Douglas, perhaps inadvisedly, sent 800 ounces of gold to the San Francisco mint. Within a few months the California argonauts had gone north overland and by sea to invade Fort Victoria. More than 20,000 miners, adventurers and inexperienced greenhorns descended upon Victoria in 1858, many funnelling through the Fort and then across to the mainland and the Fraser River workings.

At Fort Yale and downriver from that trading post, 5000 miners scrambled for gold. Timbers and lumber became an absolute necessity. The Land, Fleming & Company mill, erected at Yale in 1858, may not have been the first on the mainland but it is the first one recorded, and it was surely welcomed by miners otherwise reliant on axes, adzes and pit saws.

No need for this mill to concern itself with export. Local sales must have been phenomenal while the gold fever lasted—which was not long. A few other mills were installed on the mainland in this period, none of which are germane to this narrative since none of them engaged in lumber export with the exception of the Messrs. McDonald mill located at Douglas on Harrison Lake, a waypoint en route to British Columbia's interior. The *Columbian* newspaper published an account of this mill shipping 58,000 feet of white pine lumber to California in 1861, an item of particular interest because American lumber was now making inroads into the British colony. But Vancouver Island and mainland mills could not keep up with local demand, and the more numerous and productive Puget Sound mills, deprived of the dwindling California gold rush, were delighted to come to the rescue. In 1859, 3,539,500 feet of lumber arrived in Vancouver from Puget Sound and this amount was further augmented by 287,206 feet from San Francisco. The Puget Sound price was right at $18 a thousand feet. The British Columbia mills could not better this, all of which makes the McDonalds' sale to California something of a conundrum.

The argonauts, frustrated by the difficulties of having to explore the bars of the rampaging Fraser at high water, pushed on farther into British Columbia's interior. By 1860 the Cariboo gold rush was in full swing. With this event to encourage them the entrepreneurs began to build sawmills again, this time making larger investments and planning on a more generous scale.

Capt. Edward Stamp, an English sea captain, had visited Vancouver Island in 1856 and was sufficiently impressed by what he saw to enlist the resources of a British syndicate in a venture of considerable size. He negotiated with the Colonial government to erect a steam-powered sawmill at the head of Barclay Sound where Port Alberni now stands. By 1861 a sawmill boasting an assembly of saws capable of cutting 18,000 feet of planks a day per shift was in operation contiguous to residences for management, habitations for mill workers and a company store.

The first export shipment was to Callao, Peru, aboard the brigantine *Marcello*, followed by the *Starr King* with 700,000 feet destined for Australia, and then the *Sheet Anchor* to the Sandwich Islands. The beginnings were, by all appearances, auspicious, and the year 1862 lived up to expectations. Exports from Alberni in that year were 8,074,000 feet of which 7,804,000 was rough lumber.

Captain Stamp, irascible and overbearing at the best of times, had a terminal difference of opinion with his principals in 1863 and turned his attention to opportunities on the mainland while Gilbert Malcolm Sproat took over Stamp's management position.

There was no letdown in trade in 1863. The bills of lading read like a world atlas: the *Monsoon* to Shanghai, the *Arno* to Sydney, the *Early Bird* to Manila, the *Esk* to Sydney, the *Rising Sun* to London, the *Vancouver* to Callao, the *Buena Vista* to Melbourne, the *Alberni* to Honolulu. And so it went into 1864 with total exports for that year of 10,947,956 feet. On any given day there were at least five vessels at the company's wharf. Then, as January 1865 arrived, the saws halted, never to cut another foot.

Ironically the mill had exhausted its log supply, this in spite of the fact that vast timber resources surrounded the little community just beyond the reach of the oxen and horses. Until the steam donkey and railroad came along, many other mills would fail in the same manner, starved for logs on the edge of a forest just out of reach. Rugged individualists and fierce competitors emerged from ordeals such as this.

Over on the mainland, on the water's edge of what is now North Vancouver, the T. W. Graham & Company Pioneer Mills began to turn out lumber for New Westminster, Victoria and Nanaimo markets in 1863. In December of the same year, six months after startup, the owners admitted failure and put the mill up for auction. The new owner, feeling perhaps that a change of name might bring a change of fortune, called his new possession Burrard Inlet Mills; and it was from this mill, not far from Seaboard's present assembly and loading wharf in North Vancouver, that the first export cargo departed from Burrard Inlet.

The vessel was the *Ellen Lewis*. The cargo was 277,500 feet of lumber and 16,000 pickets destined for Adelaide, Australia. Because Burrard Inlet was not yet an official point of entry, the *Ellen Lewis* entered and cleared at New Westminster. Although this was an event of some historic interest, and though Burrard Inlet Mills struggled bravely to achieve success, the mill was on the auction block once again within a year.

This time Sewell Prescott Moody was the successful bidder, and he was to make the mill prosper where others had failed. An American hailing from the state of Maine, he was a successful businessman with a reputation as a "sharp Yankee trader," though not in a derogatory sense, for he was a popular figure, much the opposite of Captain Stamp who was soon to set up business across the inlet. Moody was a born patriarch whose employee preference was for abstemious married men. A hundred or more mill people lived in his settlement, which became known as Moodyville, now Port Moody. There was a school, and a library and church services, and a feeling of permanency to which earlier settlers had never been accustomed.

A Deputy Collector of Customs was installed at the Burrard Inlet Lumber Mills, thus facilitating the entry and clearance of ships. In late March 1865 the barque *Glimpse* began to load a cargo for Sydney, Australia; on 26 April she cleared the inlet carrying 290,000 board feet. Compare this with a modern Seaboard vessel's capacity of 20 million feet. In that year two cargoes went to Australia and two to Mexico, in addition to steady shipments directed to New Westminster, Victoria and Nanaimo. Moody further assisted his fortunes with the establishment of a retail yard in New Westminster. By 1866 he had exported some 5 million feet. Between January 1867 and June 1868 thirty-three vessels carrying a total of 5,832,000 feet of lumber and a quantity of shingles had sailed for such destinations as China, Peru, Australia, Mexico, Ireland, New Zealand and San Francisco.

When "Sue" Moody was drowned in the tragic sinking of the S.S.

Pacific in 1865, he was mourned by the entire community. Most remembered him for his sharp wit and his shrewd trading manoeuvres, which had become part of local legend. But businessmen of the day and historians now are in accord: he was a true pioneer who brought stability and permanence into a wilderness and advanced the lumber industry dramatically.

The second sawmill on Burrard Inlet was masterminded and constructed by Captain Stamp, unbowed by his stormy exit from his first sawmill enterprise at Alberni. Once again he was able to find backers in England, possibly by suggesting to them that overseas markets, previously served by United States mills, would now turn to Vancouver Island and the Colonial mainland. The American Civil War was at its peak and export production was either at a standstill or under blockade.

The company was registered as the British Columbia and Vancouver Island Spar Lumber and Sawmill Company. Captain Stamp made a first attempt to locate the mill just inside the First Narrows in what is now Stanley Park. It was an unwise location for at least two reasons: first, its intrusion into a long-established Indian village; second, the turbulent riptides rushing through the narrows which made the mooring of sailing ships and the storage of log booms virtually impossible. It is to be suspected that the second reason rather than the first prompted Stamp to look for a better situation. He found it on the south side of Burrard Inlet at a location now occupied by Centennial Pier.

Despite Stamp's choleric nature, there can be no doubt that he was a formidable achiever and a visionary. Under his goad all obstacles were overcome and the mill went into production in 1867. The first ship, the *Siam,* arrived June eighth and departed July twenty-fifth carrying 700,000 feet for Australia. Eight more ships were loaded that year.

Stamp's mill and Moody's mill kept pace with one another during that period. In 1869 twenty-four vessels loaded at Moody's mill while twenty-one loaded at Stamp's. The majority of cargoes went to South America, Australia and San Francisco, while England, China and the Hawaiian Islands took lesser quantities.

Inevitably Captain Stamp quarrelled with his partners; he retired from the company and launched a crippling lawsuit which finally was settled out of court. Regardless, the mill was known as Stamp's Mill until it passed into other hands in 1870 to be renamed Hastings Mill. Most people today remember it by that name—a familiar and busy landmark on the Inlet until it ceased operations in 1928 when it was purchased by the National Harbours Board.

Stamp, like Moody, must be regarded as a genuine pioneer and a founder of British Columbia's forest products export industry. Both mills established a worldwide reputation for timbers and lumber of the highest quality, a reputation upon which mills in the future would be able to build and expand.

One other mill must be mentioned in this brief outline of the pioneering colonial period. In fact, this mill cannot be omitted because it was to become one of Seaboard's strongest members. Small and water powered, it had humble beginnings at Horseshoe Bay on Vancouver Island, not far from the present town of Chemainus. Built in 1862 by A. G. Elliott, it was purchased in 1864 by ex-goldminer T. G. Askew, whose aspirations seem to have been modest measured against those of some of his competitors. The cut was an honest 2000 feet a day on an eleven-and-a-half hour shift. Later Askew petitioned to operate the mill throughout the year by leading additional water to his wheel from a nearby creek.

Although his mill equipment was rudimentary, he was still able to participate in export trade mainly through the production of spars. In 1868 he petitioned for a 500-acre timber lease in the immediate area; on the strength of this he improved his plant somewhat only to be dashed to despair when his lease was terminated and absorbed into the 3000 square miles of prime Crown grant timberland ceded to the Esquimalt & Nanaimo Railway as an inducement to construct a line from Victoria to Nanaimo.

Askew died in 1880, leaving the management of the mill to his widow, who struggled courageously to make a success of it; but circumstances forced her to sell out to Henry Croft and his partner, Henry Severne. Croft's involvement in the transaction is of interest in that he was closely associated with Robert Dunsmuir, the successful Vancouver Island coal mining magnate and the wealthiest man in the province.

Dunsmuir had the financial stature and international connections to undertake the construction of the E & N Railway in exchange for $750,000 and a strip of Crown land 20 miles wide extending from Victoria north to Courtenay. Croft and Severne upgraded the Askew mill with steam power and a wider and more efficient range of manufacturing equipment. Severne sold out to William Angus, and Croft and Angus laboured to supply the advancing railroad with lumber and ties, cutting 50,000 feet a day to fill the orders. Askew's widow must have watched all this with regret and bitterness.

When the railroad was finished in 1886, the Croft and Angus mill continued to produce lumber for other markets, using the E & N track both as a logging railroad and as a means of shipping lumber to Victoria and Nanaimo. Although this arrangement had all the appearances of efficiency and transportation advantage, Croft and Angus were losing money and were obliged to sell out to Dunsmuir in 1889.

Dunsmuir in turn sold 100,000 acres of splendid forest land in the Chemainus and Nanaimo valleys to a U.S. syndicate headed by J. A. Humbird. Another member of the syndicate was the U.S. lumber tycoon Frederick Weyerhaeuser, a friend and supportive associate of Humbird's. Humbird's personal background and United States business associations could scarcely have been improved upon; but these were not his sole credentials. An able and energetic businessman in his own right, he applied himself zealously to his sawmill venture.

The terms of the agreement called for a mill cutting 100,000 feet a day. Humbird complied, first investigating a site near Victoria, and then deciding in favour of Chemainus, where he replaced the Askew cum Croft and Angus mill with a behemoth almost 500 feet long. For years it remained one of the largest on the Pacific coast of North America. The name of the mill was the Victoria Lumber & Manufacturing Company; more will be said of it and the Humbird dynasty in later chapters.

The Crown colony of British Columbia became a province and a member of Canadian Confederation in 1871, encouraged in part by a federal government promise to push the Canadian Pacific Railway through to a western terminus at Esquimalt on Vancouver Island. Not until 1886 did the steel arrive at the head of Burrard Inlet, soon to continue on to Coal Harbour, skirting the busy perimeter of Hastings Mill. In 1905 the Canadian Pacific purchased the E & N Railway, thus fulfilling the promise of an Esquimalt terminus, although Victoria citizens would debate the validity of that promise for years.

In the period between entry into Confederation and the arrival of the CPR, British Columbia's lumber industry made slow progress. The year before provincial status was achieved there were fifteen mills in operation: three in New Westminster, two on Burrard Inlet, two between Hope and Lytton, two at Clinton, and one each at Lillooet, Kootenay/Columbia, Williams Creek, Lightning Creek, Quesnel and Nanaimo. The total export of rough and dressed lumber in that year was 9,886,976 feet, plus 841,000 shingles, 200 bundles of lath and pickets, and 832 spars. The Moody and Stamp mills on Burrard Inlet were the only two engaged in export of any magnitude. Domestic demand was limited mainly to Victoria, Nanaimo and New Westminster where the majority of the colony's 9000 population was centred.

It should be pointed out that American mills in Puget Sound and Oregon were formidable competitors. They had a ten-year lead on the

mills of British Columbia, enjoyed a comparable forest resource, were
larger, more numerous, more mechanized, and were closer to export
markets.

At the same time, American protective tariffs made it difficult for the
early B.C. mills to export south at a profit. Their recourse was to trade
as effectively as possible offshore. Evidence of this is to be seen in the
declared value of British Columbia's lumber exports in 1871. The
largest sale was to Chile in the amount of $59,671, representing the
cargoes of ten ships, whereas sales to the United States were $258,
amounting to part of a deckload.

*   *   *

British Columbia's arrival at provincial status, while a historic landmark, did not impact immediately or significantly on the lumber industry. On the other hand the arrival of the Canadian Pacific Railway did,
first of all through its own enormous requirements for ties, bridge timbers and lumber for all manner of construction, and second because it
opened the door to a domestic market which ultimately consisted of all
of Canada.

The first wave of sawmill expansion had been created by a small
export demand for timbers and spars. The second wave, stimulated by
the gold rushes, encouraged entrepreneurs to expand and improve small
mills, or to build larger, better-equipped ones. The third wave can be
attributed in large part to the railroad and the domestic markets it
opened up. Another catalytic force was the young provincial government intent on gathering in revenues by whatever practical means.

When President Theodore Roosevelt, committed to introduce con-
servation and safeguard the American wilderness, at the turn of the
century assigned 148 million acres to a protected National Forest, U.S.
lumbermen and speculators began to look elsewhere for cheap and
available timber. They found it in British Columbia, where for a few
years it was virtually given away by government decree.

Just as Sewell P. Moody, the New Englander, had surfaced in the
second wave of lumber entrepreneurs, men like Minnesotan John A.
Humbird were the precursors of the third wave. Experienced loggers
and sawmill operators from the dwindling forest stands of the Midwest
migrated first of all to the Pacific Northwestern states looking for new
prospects. From the Canadian Maritimes, Quebec and Ontario, equally
assiduous and aggressive professionals conducted a similar search for
new trees. Canadians and Americans met at a crossroads distinguished
by a seemingly inexhaustible forest in the province of British Columbia.

Across the border came men like John Humbird, the Cameron

brothers, Frank R. Pendleton, Henry J. Mackin, E. J. Palmer, Harold and Joseph Foley, Sidney Smith, T. B. Merrill and many others. Hailing from Eastern Canada were John Hendry from New Brunswick, J. G. McCormick and William Irving from Ontario, J. G. Scott, another Ontario native, J. G. McConville from Kingston, Ontario, via Oregon, J. D. McCormack from Prince Edward Island via Minnesota, James Maclaren from the Ottawa Valley, John Hanbury, an easterner via Manitoba, Aird Flavelle and Robert Thurston, just to name a few.

Many of these and others from points beyond North America arrived in the third wave to take their chances in the forest industry of British Columbia, and ultimately to become involved in the formation of Seaboard Lumber Sales. Almost all of them were men of means and ability, gifted with business and management skills which carried them to the top, taking advantage of whatever the economy, the government and the environment made available. The railroad and the ocean gave them access to domestic and offshore markets. The provincial government gave them entrée to the extremely large forest tracts they needed to feed their large, increasingly mechanized sawmills.

A comment on those times and the false security engendered by the immense and uncharted forests was the feeling that timber on the stump was worth virtually nothing. An attitude prevailed that although trees in the form of spars, lumber and shingles represented a potential profit, in the main they were an uncommon nuisance, particularly large trees calling for a herd of oxen or an overworked steam donkey to clear them out of the way for settlements, towns and cities.

In 1903 the British Columbia government, placing small value on the forest resource, threw open its Crown lands on terms so attractive that sawmill operators and speculators large and small rushed in to obtain leases and timber licences. In the few years before the government reconsidered its policy and curtailed their issuance, 15,000 leases and licences had been handed out in a "forest rush" that rivalled the earlier gold rushes. Some companies and syndicates acquired as many as 30,000 acres each. Large American corporations, in particular, recognizing the true value of prime timber, invested in the bonanza with little thought of logging or sawmilling. In later years they were able to sell to mill operators at staggering profits.

While John Hendry's arrival in British Columbia predates the arrival of the railroad by fourteen years, he, more than any other lumberman of that period, led the way to a larger industry concept. In fact, his efforts resulted in the first true forestry complex in the province, a model to be emulated by Seaboard's members in later years.

He began by going into partnership with David McNair to build and

operate a sash-and-door factory in Nanaimo, moving the entire operation to New Westminster in 1878 and renaming it the Royal City Planing Mills. Few mills at the time were equipped to manufacture finished
lumber and finished lumber products. Royal City filled a real need and
flourished as a result. Although this success might have been sufficient
for others, it just marked the beginning for Hendry, whose dream was
to raise the export of lumber to a new plateau.

Proceeding methodically from strength to strength, he prospered
further with the arrival of the CPR and was able, late in the 1880s, to
negotiate for and purchase Hastings Mill, then immersed in a construction boom as the city of Vancouver grew around it, and as other towns
and cities became established. He united the Royal City Planing Mills
and Hastings Mill under the management of the British Columbia
Mills, Timber and Trading Company, and consolidated his position by
modernizing and enlarging the plants, supporting them with an infra-
structure of superlatively equipped logging camps and a fleet of tug-
boats. In the early 1900s he purchased Hastings Mill's competitor and
the second of British Columbia's big export mills, the Moodyville Sawmill Company, and thus set the pattern for integrated forestry operations on a major scale.

Fraser Mills was established by James Maclaren—born in Scotland,
raised in Ontario, and a lumber magnate in his own right. Maclaren,
with his partner, Frank Ross, acquired large timber holdings in the
Fraser Valley and on Vancouver Island, securing them with two sawmills, one of which was Fraser Mills on the edge of the Fraser River not
far from New Westminster. The mill was in production and exporting
lumber in 1891, then ran into a series of setbacks, and after a year,
closed down. It was purchased in 1902 by an American group which
became overextended and was forced to sell to a group of Canadian
businessmen with more than ordinary capabilities. Two of them, William Mackenzie and Donald Mann, were the masterminds behind the
Canadian National Railways. Another, David Hanna, became president of the CNR, and Robert Montgomery Horne-Payne, a London
financier with a magic touch, who is credited with raising much of the
money for his lumber company partners' railway achievements, put this
same talent to work on behalf of Fraser Mills.

Under the direction of this group, and with generous transfusions of
money, Fraser Mills was transformed into the largest sawmill in the
British Empire. Equipped with the most advanced machinery of the day,
its output in one ten-hour shift was as much as 400,000 feet. At first the
mill was manned principally by French Canadians, most of them skilled
millhands. A group of 500, many with families, were transplanted from

Quebec to a townsite adjacent to the mill. Today it is the established community of Maillardville. Fraser Mills and its top management were to figure prominently in the development of Seaboard Lumber Sales Company.

The Canadians and Americans in the third wave, encouraged and rewarded by a sellers' market reaching throughout North America, and most enjoying a healthy export business, made major investments between 1900 and 1913. The financial commitment at the turn of the century was approximately $2 million and this would grow to something in excess of $150 million of which considerably more than half was American money.

R. H. H. Alexander, then manager of the B.C. Mills, Timber and Trading Company, addressing a forestry convention in 1906, stated that when the Moody and Hastings mills went into production, export trade averaged 25 to 30 million feet annually. When the Chemainus mill began to cut, the yearly export average rose to between 50 to 80 million. "This year [1906]," he said, "the Fraser Mill has joined the export shippers and foreign shipments will probably reach 85 million feet, the largest volume since the inception of the trade."

Rail transportation together with sail and steam transportation had caused a tremendous acceleration in the lumber trade. He acknowledged the technological evolution in shipping. "In the early days of trade a vessel which carried over 400,000 feet was a large one," he observed, "and to supply a cargo of 1,000,000 feet was an undertaking so colossal as to make a mill manager stand aghast, while now it is a difficult matter to obtain a vessel carrying such a small quantity, and steamers carrying 3,000,000 [feet] are not uncommon. Coincident with the increase in the size of ships, the mills have naturally had to increase their capacity and improve machinery over mills of the early days, and have risen from 50,000 feet to those of a capacity of 200,000 feet."

To further demonstrate how conditions had changed in a decade or two he stated that at the time when the Hastings and Moody mills were the only ones with timber leases, the government was paid one cent per acre without any further obligation—an amount that could not have exceeded $600. In 1906 new regulations and the increase of mills generated revenues of $600,000 or more.

Something to keep in mind, however, is that no matter how buoyant the export market may have seemed, British Columbia was still reliant on United States mills and brokers for almost all of its export business. Hastings Mill had overseas agents, and Chemainus had informal working arrangements with U.S. agents. Later, Hillcrest and a few other mills would arrange to supply one or two specific overseas customers on a regular basis. But, in the main, from 1900 into the early 1920s the export marketing of lumber on the Pacific Coast of North America was centred in San Francisco, Portland and Seattle.

The mills of Washington and Oregon, working through marketing organizations in San Francisco, had better access to buyers, could negotiate more quickly and satisfactorily, and had several days' sailing advantage to most offshore destinations. Generally speaking, the mills of British Columbia had an opportunity to quote on business the American mills didn't want or were too busy to supply. This situation would be rectified in due course through a process leading to the formation of Seaboard Lumber Sales.

In the meantime the mills of British Columbia for the most part did well enough in the period between 1900 and the outbreak of World War I. Records reveal that in the period around 1912, 250 sawmills were operating in the province, with the principal export mills located in the Lower Mainland and Vancouver Island. Many of these would eventually become members of Seaboard Lumber Sales.

Thurston-Flavelle Lumber Company began its successful climb when it leased an existing mill at Port Moody from P. D. Roe and Robert Abernethy. These two men had a half interest in this mill originally constructed by an American, J. S. Emerson. Roe and Abernethy owned and operated the Canadian Pacific Lumber Company mill, which showed all the signs of becoming one of British Columbia's leading forest complexes until a combination of unfortunate financial circumstances forced it into liquidation in 1914.

While these partners were still enjoying success they purchased from the same J. S. Emerson a small mill, situated west of the Marpole bridge at the north end. The name of the mill was Eburne Lumber Company. Some years later, Eburne would serve as the launching pad for one of Seaboard's strong and influential members—Canadian Forest Products Ltd.

The roster of mainland and Vancouver Island mills at that time is too long to list here. Among them was Pacific Coast Lumber Company, moved to its new location in 1902 on the site now occupied by the Bayshore Hotel. A string of highly productive mills on False Creek included Alberta Lumber Company, Rat Portage Lumber Company, B.C. Fir & Cedar Company, Pacific Box, Vancouver Lumber Company, John Hanbury's marvellous "push button" mill, and Robertson & Hackett Sawmill Company. Elsewhere in Vancouver were the prestigious Hastings Mill, the Peers & Anderson Shingle Mill from which the Anderson Brothers Lumber Company would derive, and a variety of other plants of various sizes and production capacities.

In New Westminster could be found Fraser Mills, M. B. King Lumber Company, Timberland, Brunette Sawmills, British Columbia Manufacturing Company and at Haney the Maple Ridge Lumber Company. Located at Barnet was the North Pacific Lumber Company and at Port Moody, the Thurston-Flavelle Lumber Company and the Canadian Pacific Lumber Company.

On Vancouver Island, equally productive mills proliferated in and around Victoria: Cameron Lumber Company, the Sayward Mill, Canadian Puget Sound, and Moore-Whittington Lumber Company Limited. At Chemainus the eminently successful Victoria Lumber & Manufacturing Company was producing 100 million feet a year. The Straits Lumber Company at Nanoose Bay, founded by Frank R. Pendleton, would one day become a leading proponent of Seaboard Lumber Sales. The Cowichan Lumber Company was located at Genoa Bay at Cowichan. Situated at Koksilah near Duncan was the Stone and Henderson Mill out of which the Hillcrest Lumber Company would emerge, and from which Carlton Stone would stride to take up the Seaboard cause.

·TWO·

MILLS, MILL MEN AND A FORESTER

The owners and managers of British Columbia's early mills were the product of a harsh physical and economic environment. Many of them had moved from more organized and settled situations to a province just emerging from a pioneering state. Their decisions to make this move could not have been arrived at easily in the light of the risks they knew they would be taking and the conditions to which they must become accustomed.

The lumbermen of the day were typically aggressive, forthright and resourceful. Out of necessity they were hardnosed and physically and mentally tough, more inclined to be suspicious than trusting of their competitors. Relentless hard work was the accepted order of the day and this was combined with an impressive degree of invention and innovation in order to save wear and tear on man, beast and equipment. Although there were the beginnings of lumber and forestry fraternities that would ultimately become useful organizations, the overriding concern was personal survival in an industry marked by many failures.

The business of earning a living from the coastal rain forests called for physically wearing and often heartbreaking encounters with trees standing 200 feet high or more in steep or rough terrain retreating beyond the reach of oxen, horses and primitive yarding machines. It involved battles with tides and fires, with mechanical breakdowns, with an inadequate and untrained labour force, with unsympathetic bankers and financiers, and with customers served by poor communications on the other side of the country and the world. The early forest industry was a formidable crucible in which the mill owners were either tempered or destroyed. They were not "joiners" in any significant sense of the word, except for the allegiance some paid to lodges and orders . . . yet many of these mill operators were destined to unite as staunch members of Seaboard Lumber Sales, an organization based on close co-operation.

The mills discussed in the following section are merely representative of the more than thirty that joined forces when Seaboard was first organized. They were of every size and degree of efficiency and production capability, and it would be safe to say that virtually the only common denominator was their determination to improve their position in world trade and to become masters of their own destinies in the offshore markets.

The Cameron Brothers

The founders of the Cameron Lumber Company are a case-in-point. James Oscar Cameron and Donald Officer Cameron were brothers with a spirit of adventure, willing to try their hands at anything that might turn a profit. Newt Cameron, son of Donald, identifies his father's and his uncle's birthplace as Sparta, Tennessee, and recalls that his Uncle James was ranching in New Mexico when he heard of the forestry opportunities in British Columbia. "Neither my father nor my uncle knew anything about the lumber business," Cameron revealed. "It could have been a case of fools going in where angels fear to tread. All they knew was that acquaintances had established themselves in a logging and sawmill operation on an island in the far western corner of Canada. They had heard stories of big trees and big money. My uncle came here first and then sent for my dad."

James Cameron arrived on Vancouver Island in 1906, followed shortly thereafter by Donald. The mill was the Taylor-Pattison Mill Company in Victoria's inner harbour; the logging operation was at Port Renfrew. The trees and terrain were bigger than either of the brothers had ever dreamed of, but they had not come all this way for their health, and they began by purchasing a share of the Taylor-Pattison company.

"Apparently the partners didn't get along too well," Newt Cameron said. "It didn't take too long before a decision was made to part company. My father and uncle acquired the sawmill business, while the other partners took over the logging business at Port Renfrew." The name of the mill was changed to the Cameron Lumber Company, specializing at first in fir crossarms to supply the burgeoning telephone, telegraph and hydro industries. Some business was developed with buyers in the Prairie provinces, but there were more bad times than good in those first years.

"They sold quite a lot of lumber locally," Newt Cameron recalls. "Victoria was growing at a good rate and the mill had a large inventory which I suspect was not very well balanced. My dad told me of the time they were stuck with thousands of feet of one by six only to be saved when a prominent sports promoter built an ice arena in Victoria calling for all the one by six Cameron Lumber could supply."

Local and out-of-province domestic trade was not enough to keep the company consistently solvent. Newt Cameron said there were times when the two brothers rode the length and breadth of Victoria on bicycles trying to collect on unpaid bills.

The need for involvement in offshore trade was more than apparent and, to that end, the Camerons decided to invest in a mill near Cowichan Bay, the Genoa Bay Lumber Company. The year was 1912. Newt Cameron describes it as an export mill. "Ships would tie up at the dock and the lumber, mostly timbers, would go right on board. The first load of B.C. lumber to go through the Panama Canal was shipped from that mill."

In 1914 the outbreak of World War I caused the world economy to collapse, with devastating repercussions in the British Columbia lumber industry. Export markets were disrupted; the German naval blockade compounded the problem. Payments could not be made, money for loans was restricted, and in Canada and overseas, banks started to foreclose. Even the largest mills found themselves in perilous circumstances. Fraser Mills, the biggest in the province, had to make special arrangements with London creditors in order to stay in business. Canadian Pacific Lumber Company was not as fortunate; overextended and cut off from lucrative overseas markets, this company which had shown so much promise was forced into foreclosure and disappeared from the B.C. scene.

The Camerons managed to cope rather well during those troubled times. Few of the mill men would deny that the B.C. offshore lumber trade was in a shambles. Fewer still were in a position or a frame of mind to do much about it. But the Camerons were in the forefront of a group of lumbermen who lobbied for a shipbuilding program to supply vessels for the lumber trade.

With the passage of the Shipbuilding Assistance Act in 1916, Cameron Lumber Company and Genoa Lumber Company together financed a company to build a fleet of wooden-hulled motor sailers, each with a 1,500,000-foot cargo capacity. Other companies were similarly involved on Vancouver Island and the mainland. The Cameron venture resulted in the construction of six vessels, with the Camerons withdrawing as direct participants part way through the program because of financial duress. They did, however, continue to supply shipbuilding materials until the end of the war, as did a number of other mills.

In 1918 they were in a sound enough position to construct a new mill on the Genoa Bay site, one of the largest and most modern on the Pacific coast. The new plant went into operation just in time to enjoy the profits of the postwar boom . . . and then to close its doors when the boom came to an abrupt end in 1921.

One thing was clear to the Camerons: the British Columbia lumber industry was too vulnerable, too dependent on the whims of San Francisco and Portland brokers, too liable to collapse when overseas markets went sour, too easily damaged by shortages of shipping, not sufficiently organized as a bargaining unit. How was it possible for 200 to 300 fiercely independent sawmill owners to present a united front?

The Mariner from Essex

The Cameron brothers came to the province with abysmally little knowledge of logging and sawmilling and absolutely no concept of the gigantic rain forest in which their destiny would take shape. This lack of forestry experience was shared by many lumber entrepreneurs of the day. Business acumen seemed to make up for professional and technological shortcomings, though in some cases even business proficiency had to be learned on the spot.

Such was the case with Carlton Stone, born in Essex, England, a merchant mariner accustomed to the ways of the sea and the care and handling of ships to the exclusion of virtually any other kind of experience. Stone's reason for settling in British Columbia was simply to escape the hardships of a mariner's life after three arduous voyages around the world in England's Merchant Service. He was fond of stating that his decision to trade the joys of tempests and maggot-ridden ship's biscuits for the unknowns of B.C.'s forests was one of the most fortunate moves he ever made.

Fortunate or not, his ascendancy to a position of prominence in the lumber industry was not achieved quickly or easily. He started as a labourer in sawmills on the mainland and then on Vancouver Island. Here, at least, he was able to learn the workings of a mill and the rudiments of logging; also he became proficient as a carpenter which

enabled him to assemble enough cash to enter a partnership in the
company of Stone & Henderson at Koksilah near Duncan on Vancouver Island. The year was 1912 and this was his internship in the
lumber business.

Those were the days of team and wagon logging; manpower and
animal power were the main forces at work among the trees. Skilled
labour was at a high premium and in short supply, and equipment was
crude and jerry-built. The mill, a conglomeration of machinery salvaged
from earlier plants, was subject to frequent breakdowns. Carlton
Stone's long day consisted of rushing from crisis to crisis, mending a
shackle at the forge, sharpening the teeth of a circular saw blunted on a
rock-imbedded log, organizing a firefighting crew, administering crude
first aid, and serving in whatever other capacity the moment demanded.
Not only was he involved in logging and sawmilling, he was also
obliged to find markets for his lumber, starting from scratch and developing local, regional and overseas clientele by slow degrees.

Stone laboured and learned on the job, until the inevitable event
occurred, precipitating his decision to strike out on his own. He and his
partner ran out of trees at Koksilah and went their separate ways, Stone
electing to start his own mill in the Sahtlam area not far from the town
of Duncan. With a flair for the dramatic and the evocative, he named
his new mill Hillcrest, a designation which was adopted by the region
called Old Hillcrest today. That year, 1917, marked Stone's total commitment to the business of sawmilling.

At Koksilah his labour force had consisted of himself, his partner
(who later chose a less physically strenuous career as a minister) and
two Chinese. The Hillcrest operation was more ambitious. In order to
transport logs purchased from Canadian Pacific (originally the Esquimalt & Nanaimo forest tract), Stone introduced a logging railway
typical of his ingenuity and resourcefulness. His "locomotives," of his
own design, were little more than gasoline-powered wooden trucks on
rails, geared to handle the steep logging grades.

His oldest son, Hector, remembers Carlton Stone as a tireless pow-
erhouse whose mind never stopped working. "No matter how efficient
the mill was, or how good the product was, Dad was always trying to
improve on the situation," he states. "I think he was a frustrated inven-
tor." Hector claims that his father's wooden "locomotives" were less
expensive to operate than a steam locomotive.

Restless by nature and determined to remain competitive, he demonstrated a degree of foresight which won him the admiration of his
contemporaries and attracted many imitators. Hillcrest's first market of
any importance comprised the Prairie provinces and Ontario. The local

market never accounted for more than 10 per cent of the total business, and the principal overseas market, by choice, was the United Kingdom where Stone exerted his energies to develop an important export trade.

He made it a point to acquaint himself with U.K. lumber requirements and then set about to supply forms and dimensions familiar and acceptable to U.K. builders. In order to do this he installed the first Swedish gang saw on the coast of British Columbia, a piece of equipment with multiple blades that, in one pass, sliced a log into a variety of dimensions. When dried, this dimension lumber was precisely the desired size and it soon won Carlton Stone a loyal customer list in the U.K.

Contemporary word has it that Pacific Coast hemlock was first introduced to overseas markets by the Koerner brothers just prior to World War II. Historically, this is not the case. Carlton Stone was convinced of the merits of hemlock virtually from his first days in the lumber business. He could see no reason why it should not, or could not, compete with Baltic softwoods upon which U.K. customers relied at that time. Stone preached the merits of hemlock with messianic fervour and he succeeded in his mission, remaining content to build a good market in the U.K. for the hemlock output of his own mill, and helping to break trail for the Koerner's much larger hemlock marketing program later on.

At its peak, the first Hillcrest mill at Sahtlam employed a work force of 500 including loggers, road and rail builders and millhands. For twenty-five years, until the logs ran out, the mill produced and exported lumber, weathering the storms and calms of the Canadian and world economies. In 1942 the entire operation was moved to Mesachie Lake, four miles west of Lake Cowichan on Vancouver Island; and here an entire company village was established.

"Dad was a family man in every meaning of the word," Hector Stone recalls. "For openers he sired five sons, and in the larger sense he regarded the entire Hillcrest community as his family ... with my mother as matriarch, he the patriarch."

Hillcrest consisted of fifty family dwellings, available for rent or conditional purchase on terms made reasonable because of company subsidy. There was comfortable accommodation for single white millworkers, and adjacent dwellings for East Indian and Chinese workers, including cooking and living arrangements compatible with each group's ethnic preferences.

A rustic, multi-denominational church, St. Christophers, was the scene of many marriages, christenings and funerals over the years. The people of the Hillcrest community created their own recreational programs, and few felt compelled to seek more excitement outside the community.

Hector Stone remembers his early days in that setting with considerable warmth. He and his four brothers—Gordon, Peter, Paul and Norman—were all raised in that environment and all took on management responsibilities when they came of age. Hector became president after his father's retirement; but today, in his own retirement, he admits that Carlton Stone was one of a dying breed. "I couldn't fill his shoes," he states, "but, of course, by the time I took over, there was no need to fill his shoes. New things were happening in the lumber business. A technological revolution had occurred and new marketing techniques had been introduced by a new generation of entrepreneurs.

"My father was a self-made, self-sufficient, successful lumberman of his time," Hector Stone asserts. "He was, in many ways, lord of his own domain and I am sure that there was a time in his life when you could not have convinced him that an organization like Seaboard would be of any advantage to him whatsoever."

That time was to change and Carlton Stone was destined to become one of the staunchest crusaders for the Seaboard idea.

Pendleton of Red Gap

Historians intent on telling the story of all the mills in production from 1900 through to the post—World War I period, would face a formidable task of research, and the frustrations of incomplete records and considerable hearsay. The result would be a volume of outsized proportions. For our purposes, in order to portray the conditions of the day and the style of operation in contrast to what prevails now, we have chosen to focus on a few representative mills and introduce some of the personalities who were to figure in the formation of Seaboard.

Many of those mills, successful at the time, noisy with activity and the cacophony of machinery worked to the limit, have passed into time for one reason or another. Hillcrest silenced its saws for the last time in 1968, finally starved for lack of trees at an economic price, having escaped a similar fate on two other occasions. In fifty-one years the company had manufactured more than 3 billion feet of lumber for Canadian and world markets.

Along the Vancouver Island Highway, between Nanoose Bay and Lantzville, the remains of another sawmill community have been accorded the recognition of an historical marker and a nearby traveller's rest stop. The mill was the Straits Lumber Company and the community was Red Gap.

Frank R. Pendleton, grandson of the founder of Straits, has made it his hobby to act as historian for the mills owned or managed by his grandfather, father and uncles. He recalls that the company mill was built originally by a colourful, high-energy French-Canadian with the unlikely name of Joe McKercher.

McKercher's methods were somewhat unorthodox; he would manufacture and stockpile lumber when prices were low, then when prices went up, shut down the mill and peddle his stock. Apparently the system worked. Pendleton states that McKercher went into ultimate retirement a moderately wealthy man, raising budgie birds on a mainland estate. Both in business and retirement he dressed in cowboy garb complete with Stetson.

His little mill went into production in 1914. A year later a touring car pulled up in front of what passed for a sales office and three Englishmen emerged to have a business discussion with Joe McKercher. They were interested to know if the mill was for sale. McKercher, in his typically forthright manner, informed them that anything he had was for sale if the price was right. In a matter of an hour or so a transaction had been completed to sell the mill for a generous $280,000 to be paid in four equal installments. The three English gentlemen were negotiating on behalf of the Newcastle Lumber Company and the Merchant Trust Company. McKercher received three payments precisely at the times agreed upon. And then, for reasons unrecorded, the new owners fell upon troubled times and were unable to make the fourth payment. Joe took back his mill and was wealthier by $210,000.

Soon another personality appeared on the scene. Frank R. Pendleton was born in Okonto, Wisconsin, in 1864 and learned something about logging in that state before moving west with his older brother, Ira, in 1896, to go into logging near Everett. It was a horse and wagon show successful enough to encourage him to look north into Canada for similar opportunities. Pendleton found what he was looking for near Gordon Pasha Lake not far from the present town of Powell River. It was 1906. Hard work and a nature both abstemious and frugal was paying off; with a base in Washington and a logging operation successfully launched in British Columbia, he and his brother continued to build their resources and assets, relying entirely on their logging expertise until 1916 when Pendleton decided to cast his net a little wider. Once more he went in search of a sawmill.

In due course he discovered Joe McKercher and his mill at Nanoose Bay and decided to make an offer. Conversation between these two must have been fascinating; Joe's expletives and figures-of-speech were colourful, to put it charitably, while Frank Pendleton shunned profanity and unseemly discourse. It can only be supposed that the important thing these two had in common was a proven reputation for hard work and a demonstrated ability to succeed.

Pendleton struck a surprisingly good deal with McKercher, considering what the French Canadian had succeeded in extracting from his previous sale. He obtained the mill for $60,000 with $10,000 cash down and the rest payable at 6 per cent. What he got for his money was a basic mill with a crew of ten Chinese, ten Japanese and eight East Indian millhands. There were fifteen houses half-hidden in a nearby gulch, renting for $8 a month including electricity, heat and water. Indoor plumbing cost $7 extra. Into this community he moved his wife, brother Ira, and a brother-in-law, Elmo Haskell, also a knowledgeable mill man who in due course became manager.

Pendleton lived at Nanoose Bay with his wife for two years, long enough to see the mill transformed and expanded before he returned to his base in Everett. The community received its name shortly after Mrs. Pendleton arrived and set up house. She was reading the novel *Ruggles of Red Gap* at the time, and the gulch in which the housing was located begged to be identified. Red Gap it became and Red Gap it remained, ultimately to receive a certain distinction as a postal station.

At its peak the Straits sawmill was producing 150,000 feet a day on one shift. Other refinements had been added including dry kilns and planers. Out in Nanoose Bay, ships from a dozen offshore ports anchored in wait for mill barges to shuttle the lumber cargoes to them. The bay was too shallow to permit ships to tie up alongside the mill wharf, a factor that would work to the mill's disadvantage when times became difficult.

Times were not too difficult when Joe McKercher relinquished his ownership. Neither he nor Frank Pendleton could have know the far-reaching effect that the opening of the Panama Canal would have on British Columbia's lumber export business, and no one could have predicted the calamitous Tokyo earthquake of 1923 which effectively levelled the great city and surrounding communities, creating a huge demand for B.C. lumber. Straits found its resources taxed to the limit supplying a quota of lumber for the reconstruction of Tokyo, but it was a fortuitous entrée into the Japanese market which became one of the mill's biggest customers. The Japanese were particularly fond of the company's fir timbers, two feet square with two clear faces. "There was a time when my grandfather must have thought the only way to do business was to square a log and ship it," Frank Pendleton observed.

He has told the story many times, and always with amusement, about Joe McKercher's irritation when he was paid off long before he expected to be. "Joe could see himself collecting six per cent for the next twenty years," he said. "My grandfather was free and clear in five years. Joe used to run into him at logging get-togethers. He would turn to his friends and say, 'This is the guy who stole my mill from me.'"

The mill at Red Gap was the heart and energizing force of the entire community and its surrounding area. British Columbia writer Arthur Mayse, in a newspaper article, described the scene during one of the busy periods: "The mill is working overtime these days. As we pass, the shriek of saws and the hiss of escaping steam is deafening. Great, dripping logs crawl endlessly up the chute to disappear in the busy dimness behind. On the other side, between the rails and the highway, are the houses of the Chinese workers, each with its small, gay garden of flowers and vegetables. At the Hindu boarding house a picturesque wellsweep dips its wooden bucket creakingly beside a chicken coop painted white and pink and blue to scare away the devils."

Frank R. Pendleton was not a big man, but his five-foot eight-inch frame carried much authority, and his personal discipline and attention to business commanded respect among those who worked for him as well as from his colleagues in the lumber business. He found time to father seven children—five boys and two girls—all but one of whom worked at Straits at one time or another. One of his daughters drove a taxi between Red Gap and other Island communities.

His sons remained prominently associated with the lumber business and played their own roles in the Seaboard story. Pendleton senior started another mill in 1924, Mohawk Lumber, on the mainland. Straits Lumber's manager, Elmo Haskell, transferred to Mohawk in 1928 while Pendleton's sons shared the management of the original company. No matter how the responsibilities were distributed, Pendleton remained very much in charge. Without fail, he made a circuit of the mills once a week, departing his office in Everett for meetings at Red Gap, then over to Mohawk on the mainland, then for Board sessions at Seaboard Lumber Sales, where he was influential for some years.

"He was Southern Pacific's best customer between Portland and Vancouver," his grandson reported. "My grandfather was a strongly religious, morally dedicated man. He never drank, smoked or swore. I suppose the closest he ever came to profanity was the day his son Wayne called him from Straits to tell him they had managed to put out a destructive fire at the mill. This was at a time when Straits was in terminal trouble because World War II had eliminated the all-important

Japanese market. At the other end of the phone my grandfather considered the news that the fire had been extinguished. Finally he said, in a
very tight voice, 'What danged fool put it out?' "

In Brotchie's Footsteps

Earlier in this narrative the sad story was told of Brotchie and his
magnificent spars and timbers left to moulder at the water's edge on
Vancouver Island. Both Brotchie and his timbers passed away un-
wanted, the victims of bad timing. In the case of J. G. Robson and the
Timberland Lumber Company, timing was impeccable and was rewarded with success. As with so many other lumbermen of the day, he
entered the business knowing little about logging and sawmilling but
with a solid grounding in business methods.

James Goodfellow Robson was born in Ayr, Ontario. It is to be
suspected that, from the outset, the personality he projected when
negotiating a business transaction was a combination of salt and steel.
Those who worked with him paint the picture of a short, square-set
gentleman marching ramrod-straight through the towering maze of
sawn timbers, impeccably dressed in dark suit and vest, a spotless fe-
dora squarely aligned on his head and a silver-mounted walking stick
swinging restlessly in his hand. His eyes darted everywhere and missed
nothing. Many a six-foot millhand, caught in some breach of performance, stared down at J. G. Robson abjectly and took the tongue-
lashing in silence. Robson ran a tight ship.

He began as the manager of a grain elevator in Manitoba but early on
observed the monetary rewards being earned by the local lumber yards
as farm buildings and towns began to rise across the Prairie provinces.
He reasoned that more money was to be made in lumber than in grain,
and without hesitation packed his bags and headed for British Columbia's West Coast.

The year 1907 saw him functioning as shipper for the Maple Ridge
Lumber Company at Haney, a position he held just long enough to
learn some of the ground rules of the lumber industry. Within a year he
had become a partner in a shingle mill, and two years after that he was
bankrupt with $19,000 in debts, $17 in his pocket, and an incurable
infusion of sawdust in his bloodstream.

In the same year of his bankruptcy he became manager of a mill
located near Craigs, six miles south of New Westminster on the B.C.
Electric Railway. It was a new operation started in 1909 and it took its
name from the nearest postal station—Timberland. Under Robson's
direction the mill lived up to its name to the full extent of the meaning.

When he claimed that he cut "the biggest sticks in the world," few mill men would contest the statement.

By 1912 he had obtained controlling interest in Timberland, and in 1918 he moved the entire operations to the edge of the Fraser River, a stone's throw from the site of the Pattullo Bridge and across the river from New Westminster. There he proceeded to establish a worldwide reputation as a specialist in the cutting of big timbers; in the process he built a substantial personal fortune.

Robson understood the importance of good public relations, and succeeded in drawing world attention to Timberland on a number of occasions. He supplied the world's tallest flagpole for erection in front of Kew Gardens in Surrey, England, another 186-foot flagpole for the grounds of the Canadian National Exhibition in Toronto, the timber for the huge, festooned maypole used to celebrate the coronation of Elizabeth II, the masts and spars for the replica of the Mayflower used in a Hollywood movie . . . just to identify a few of his out-of-the-ordinary accomplishments. Each of these undertakings earned him generous newspaper copy which, in turn, attracted new business.

Nor was there anything conventional about his mill. The outsized logs delivered from his own stands of prime, first-growth timber could not be lifted to the saw by means of the usual jack ladder; they were hoisted by cables to the carriage level. A 75-foot log called for the addition of another trailer to the carriage. Anything longer required two additional trailers. Timberland's carriage and trailers could carry logs up to 110 feet in length.

A tour through the mill's timber deck and storage yard under Robson's guidance was a memorable event. Row upon row of big timbers were stacked 20 feet high, and Robson seemed to know the story and the destination of every giant stick. Local deliveries of timbers like these required a police permit and a motorcycle escort to precede the truck on the way to its destinaton.

Today Timberland's big sticks are to be found in bridge spans, factory girders and supports, even in the framework of cathedrals. Robson was justifiably proud of his product. Very few mills could cut timbers of that size, and none made a regular practice of it. J. G. Robson, in effect, cornered the market for truly big timbers; he was one of a kind in a class by himself, until the time came to link the destiny of his mill with Seaboard.

One last footnote to the story of unfortunate Brotchie. Records reveal that the longest of his hand-hewn timbers exceeded Timberland's by 10 feet.

Anderson of Prince Edward Island

Arthur D. Anderson was one of a large contingent of Canadians who
severed their roots with eastern Canada to seek their fortunes on Canada's West Coast. Anderson, and later some of his brothers (he was one
of six), travelled from one of the nation's farthest Atlantic reaches to
become established on the shores of the Pacific. As with so many others,
the story began with unremitting toil.

Arthur Anderson, familiarly known as "A. D.," arrived in British
Columbia in 1899 at the age of seventeen and managed to set himself up
in a one-man logging operation a year later, employing horses and oxen
to wrestle with the formidable first-growth timber still standing on
Vancouver's North Shore. Until 1912 he busied himself one way or
another with a variety of logging, lumber mill and shingle mill enterprises, saving as much money as he could in readiness for the right
enterprise. He created his own opportunity by going into partnership in
1914 with Ross Peers in a shingle mill venture at the foot of Eton Street
in Vancouver. The business prospered to the extent that by 1918 he and
his partner were able to pay in excess of one million dollars for the
flourishing Brunette Sawmills in New Westminster. The sale of this mill
in 1922 to Southern Pine, a U.S. firm, earned the partners a substantial
profit, this in spite of the fact that the mill had suffered a serious fire in
that same year.

Perhaps the setback of the fire together with the fortuitous sale of the
mill were the principal factors that led Anderson into a new
enterprise—construction. Vancouver was burgeoning. The population
was increasing rapidly, partly as a result of veterans of World War I
electing to take their discharge in the West Coast city, and partly because of the decision of many immigrants to settle in and around the
port. It was the beginning of a "boom and bust" period characterized
by tremendous business successes. Historian Margaret Ormsby, in
British Columbia: A History, describes the frenetic activity of
downtown Vancouver as a noisy, smoky mélange of boats, trains, sawmills, flour mills, breweries, food processing plants, shoe factories and
clothing factories. "Just how busy the sawmills, iron plants and
machine factories in the False Creek district were, every roomer living
in the now shabby and smoke-stained frame houses of the West End
was only too conscious," Ormsby writes. "Sometimes, by a shifting of
the wind, the great activity at the Eburne and Marpole Sawmills was
also drawn to the attention of the wealthy resident living in timbered
mansions near the old McCleery farmhouse on Marine Drive . . . the
city was now held fast in the toils of industry—industry constantly

expanding to satisfy the apparently insatiable demands of the export markets."

Vancouver had a stock exchange, head offices for banks, insurance and trust companies. New suburbs reached out in all directions, each with its rows of new homes for people of every economic level. Entrepreneurs and speculators made fortunes or near fortunes; by the end of the boom in 1929 at least eighty-four millionaires had been created in this environment.

A. D. Anderson immersed himself in this industrial melee with total energy and determination. Together with Vancouver developer Col. Ed Ryan, he constructed several of the early buildings at the University of British Columbia, including the central section of the library; he built British Columbia's first lavish spa/resort, Harrison Hot Springs Hotel, and was president of the hotel company from 1926 to 1949; he built the Crystal Pool, the present Vancouver City Hall, and the present Hotel Vancouver, just to name some of his more outstanding structures. In 1928 he began the construction of the new Hotel Vancouver armed with a $4-million contract from the Canadian National Railway. The Great Depression struck in 1929 and Anderson found himself sorely tested to continue with the project. It took him ten years to finish the hotel, and he lost money.

In that interval he got back into logging and lumbering, starting with a somewhat spectacular shingle bolt operation at McNab Creek at the head of Howe Sound. He transported the chunks of cedar, destined to become shingles and shakes, by means of a flume seven miles long reaching down the creek to the ocean. In 1933, together with his brothers Ernest and Leith, he organized what was to be his last enterprise, the Anderson Bros. mill, constructed at the foot of Ontario Street. A modest mill by comparison with others operating at that time, it cut 50,000 feet a shift and employed fifty men. A. D. Anderson remained its president until 1973, but very early on, in common with other mill owners and managers in the Lower Mainland, this man of considerable individual achievement was led by evolving circumstances to throw in his lot with the Seaboard organization.

If space permitted, it would be interesting to chronicle the life and times of William Moore and Ernest Whittington, founders of Moore-Whittington Lumber Company, once one of Seaboard's larger member mills and one of Victoria's thriving industries which combined a logging operation, sawmills, a sash-and-door factory, a builder's supply retail outlet and a home construction division.

Launched modestly in 1892 with the signing of a document between

Moore and Whittington to join forces in the construction of a house, the company grew by slow degrees, and not without opposition from Victoria's townsfolk who resisted the partners' declared intention to expand their operation into a joinery factory and lumber yard. Moore and Whittington stood up to the well-organized public protest and established their rights to build on the property they had purchased. They celebrated their victory with a prominent announcement in the newspaper which stated in part:

> Will you kindly permit us to publicly express our thanks to the prominent city officials living on Yates Street, and two or three others who by their efforts to discourage enterprise and industry have been the means of advertising our business. . . .
>
> We hope the time is not too far distant when the street on which we are established will be adorned with handsome structures and we can consider clearing the land, as we did a few months ago, of its accumulated brush and rubbish to be the first step to that end.

Their printed statement was prophetic since they went on to build many residences in Victoria as well as expanding into logging and lumber manufacture. Their sons, Ron Whittington and Stan Moore, followed in their footsteps and were prominent in the lumber trade for many years.

Stan Moore has a scrapbook with newspaper clippings and other memorabilia that go right back to the beginning. One clipping reads: "The Chemainus mill shipped 6 million board feet overseas to Germany. In the past few days Hayward refused a contract for a large amount to San Francisco. Moore-Whittington shipped its first consignment last night on the *Marie* to Fiji and will continue this trade indefinitely. They have taken a contract for regular shipments to Hong Kong by every steamer that leaves this port although only about 40,000 feet will be contained in each consignment." The two points to be noted are that this was the mill's first export shipment, and that its output was minuscule compared to the giant Chemainus mill; both would become Seaboard members.

In support of the fact that the lumber business was highly and aggressively competitive, there is another set of clippings in Moore's book reporting on a lawsuit brought by the Cameron Lumber Company against Moore-Whittington. The latter mill was charged with stealing logs and the defence was that logs found on the beach were common property.

Both Cameron and Moore-Whittington would set aside their differences when they became members of the Seaboard organization. Stan Moore, remembering back to the first days of Moore-Whittington's entrée into the export market, gives us a clue to the role export was going to play. "We were cutting too much lumber for the local market," he said. "It was costly and we weren't getting our money back quickly enough. We had a negative cash flow situation and we had to find business which would allow us to sell lumber, ship it, get our money and keep revolving the cash we had. Back in the thirties we were always short of money."

To terminate this swift flight through the roster of mills, 1900–1918, it is appropriate to mention one which began, as many did not, with a bona fide lumberman at the helm. M. B. King was born into an established lumbering family in Chipman, New Brunswick. Logging and sawmilling was a thriving industry in the Maritimes when British Columbia was still the fur trapping domain of the Hudson's Bay Company. Shipments of logs and sawn lumber were moving out of New Brunswick ports to Britain and other overseas destinations long before the world knew that Douglas-fir, native to B.C., existed.

M. B. King was raised in the family business, and when he left Chipman in 1898 with his brother, K. H. King, he was better equipped than most to make a success in the lumber business as practised in British Columbia. His brother established a medical practice in the province and later became prominent in B.C. politics. In that same interval M. B. King found his first operational location in the interior of British Columbia near Cranbrook. By 1900 he was operating the first of two sawmills, later adding a planing mill in that region. Business was brisk. By all measures he was enjoying success, and his grandsons are not certain why he decided to exchange his business in the interior for a new start on the coast. Perhaps transportation was not entirely reliable. More likely the lure of big timber in the coastal rain forest overpowered him.

He moved to a new mill site at Dennison in the Fraser Valley in 1912, then moved again to Newton in 1914 where he was to manufacture lumber for the next sixteen years, drawing his logs from a magnificent stand of forest at Green Timbers, a few miles outside of New Westminster.

The last log was removed from Green Timbers just as the Depression descended on the land. Not until 1933 was M. B. King, assisted now by his two sons, M. D. and G. C. King, able to assemble the resources required to start another mill in North Vancouver on the shores of Burrard Inlet. And it was just about that time that Seaboard member mills were regrouping and surfacing from the depths of the Depression.

The Arrival of the Forester

In the previous sections, to indicate the human mosaic that comprised the lumber manufacturing fraternity of the day, we were introduced, however briefly, to a lawyer/rancher, a merchant mariner, two horse-and-wagon loggers, a grain merchant, two carpenter/joiners and one lumberman raised in the tradition. Now into this narrative comes another personality summoned by the changing times and fortunes of the province.

For some time the provincial government was becoming increasingly aware that the forest resource must be managed to protect a public heritage. The findings and recommendation of a Royal Commission launched in 1909 drew attention to the accelerating destruction of the forest resource on the one hand and the revenue potential of that same resource on the other. This led in 1911 to the formulation of a Forest Act which for the first time came to grips with the endangered welfare of the provincial forests.

Almost overnight a province, badly armed with desultory regulations related to land tenure and cutting rights and an almost toothless Land Act enacted in 1891, became a national precursor in the care and management of the forest. The British Columbia Forest Service came into being, staffed by professionals rather than political appointees, dedicated to the welfare of the trees.

Order and regulation were introduced into the sale of timberland; forest mensuration became a serious matter conducted meticulously and expertly, with the results employed to calculate royalty payments accurately. The tables were reversed from a time when settlers and developers set fire to the forest as though it were a weed in order to clear the land for farming and habitation; now an enforced system of fire prevention and the combat of forest fires was introduced and administered by the Forest Service.

This awakened concern for the trees would find further expression in reforestation programs and the establishment of tree nurseries acknowledging the principle that trees are a renewable resource and that the forest industry depends entirely on a calculated and assiduously administered program of renewal. The key word was then, as it is now, "perpetuation." Rather than being preserved, the forest was to be perpetuated in an ongoing process which involved the safeguarding of it against fire and disease, the harvesting of mature trees for processing by the mills, and the planting and natural regeneration of new trees at a rate that would allow forest products to be manufactured and marketed commensurate with the regeneration of the forest. Thus both the forest and the forest industries would be perpetuated.

This difficult balancing act could not be achieved by politicians or business men. It called for the special talents of foresters trained in the methodology of the day. The Minister of Forests, the Honourable W. R. Ross, combined idealistic traits with demonstrated political skills and he took seriously his mandate to stimulate and perpetuate a flourishing forest industry. What he wanted, and what he looked for, was a Canadian with a degree in modern, scientific forestry. Knowledge of British Columbia's forest resource would be an obvious advantage. The qualifications were demanding, particularly since the reservoir of Canadian foresters was meagre indeed, there being only thirteen Canadian graduate foresters in the country.

Ross, encouraged and advised by his mentor, Martin A. Grainger, compiler of British Columbia's first Forest Act, approached a young forester who had what appeared to be a satisfactory record of performance. He was a product of the Ontario Agricultural College at Guelph, a top graduate—and one of the youngest—from the Yale University Forestry School with practical and professional experience as a federal forester in Ontario, Saskatchewan and Manitoba. Furthermore, he had tasted British Columbia's forest environment in the spring of 1907 when he conducted a timber cruise in the Powell River area.

His name was Harvey Reginald MacMillan. At the time of the B.C. government employment offer he was working for the Federal Minister of the Interior's forestry branch as an assistant director of forestry. Ross's invitation to come to British Columbia as chief forester was too attractive and challenging for him to refuse. In 1912 he left Ottawa with his bride of one year and took up his new duties in Victoria.

MacMillan lost little time putting the Minister of Forests' plan into action, beginning by dividing the province into forest regions, each headed by a graduate forester empowered to carry out fire-prevention and fire-fighting programs, as well as to conduct forest inventories. World War I brought all this to an end. MacMillan's team of foresters enlisted while he, exempted from military duty because of a long but successful battle with tuberculosis, received a surprising appointment, considering the situation of a world at war.

From the earliest years British Columbia's lumber export trade was subject to the dictates of the lumber industry in the Pacific Northwest states. Mills in Washington and Oregon had several years' lead time in establishing overseas markets. U.S. lumber brokers on the Pacific coast were aggressive and canny in their negotiations, quite naturally favouring American mills over those of British Columbia. The lion's share of export production was supplied by Washington and Oregon. In fact, there were times in the early years when these two states had exported lumber to British Columbia at prices considerably less than the province's mills could supply.

Colonial mills were accustomed to ship their export production primarily through the offices of San Francisco brokers, and this stricture seriously limited their export involvement which seldom exceeded 30 per cent of the total from the Pacific coast. At the time of H. R. MacMillan's appointment, the province's export market share had dwindled to 17 per cent, almost all of it sold through U.S. lumber brokers. The Americans had taken over British Columbia's traditional markets in Australia, New Zealand and Great Britain, representing B.C. lumber as American. A few mills such as Hastings, Victoria Lumber & Manufacturing and Hillcrest had established their own customers in overseas markets, but these were rare exceptions and, even in these cases, their penetration of markets was limited and exclusive. Simply stated, British Columbia's export status was vulnerable at all times to the controlling forces of the U.S. Pacific Northwest lumber traders.

The situation in British Columbia was duplicated in other Canadian provinces in varying degrees to the extent that the federal government was moved to improve the Canadian lumber export position by whatever means. MacMillan's appointment was as special trade commissioner to conduct a one-man survey of world markets for Canadian lumber. In the light of what would happen, it is interesting if not ironic to note that one of British Columbia's prominent lumber men, E. J. Palmer, then manager of the Victoria Lumber & Manufacturing Company, exerted himself to persuade MacMillan to take the commission. If a precise turning point can be identified in the progress of British Columbia's lumber industry, it might well have occurred with the meeting of MacMillan and Palmer: MacMillan who would become the absolute head of an integrated forest products corporation, and Palmer who was one of the first proponents of an export association of autonomous mills.

Palmer borrowed his idea from an earlier model, the Douglas Fir Exploitation and Export Company of San Francisco, which was particularly active in the Northwestern states, even to the extent of an incursion into British Columbia in 1914 under the name of the Canadian Trading Company. This company had the mandate to pay going market prices for all the export lumber British Columbia could supply.

Palmer was prepared to sell Victoria Lumber & Manufacturing export production through this company; so were Vancouver Lumber, Cameron Lumber, Genoa Bay and Canadian Western. With mills of this size and influence, it is quite possible that the Canadian Trading Company, a façade for an American lumber export association, could have gained a strong and even dominant foothold. This was not to be: the advent of war brought lumber export from the Pacific Coast to a standstill, and the idea died.

The irony, in retrospect, is that Palmer strongly endorsed the appointment of British Columbia's Chief Forester as a federal trade commissioner to search out new lumber markets. After all, the training and concerns of a forester were in no way in conflict with those of the province's lumber entrepreneurs. MacMillan, objectively and with no vested interest, would find export business not only for the mills of B.C. but for all of Canada.

E. J. Palmer's expectations, shared by others in the lumber fraternity, were amply realized in respect to MacMillan's ability to stimulate new export business. The hope that the itinerant trade commissioner would remain an objective, disinterested forester was to be dashed. MacMillan's task, as he stated himself, was "to get the export of Douglas fir from British Columbia, and spruce and pine from eastern Canada, started as soon as possible, and to get it into Canadian hands."

It took eighteen months before H. R. MacMillan succeeded in persuading the United Kingdom Board of Trade to purchase government supplies directly from Canada, circumventing the United States. In British Columbia there was no broker or exporter of sufficient status with which to deal. The only recourse was to name the British Columbia Forest Service as the official negotiating body. For the first time, independent sawmills worked through a central agency to sell their products to offshore buyers. The seed of an idea had germinated.

The forester cum trade commissioner succeeded in obtaining orders for Douglas-fir from France, South Africa, India, Australia and New Zealand. As he prepared to make an exploratory sweep through Japan and China, instructions arrived summoning him back to a new Trade and Commerce post in Ottawa. MacMillan returned, but for various reasons based mainly on his lack of confidence in many of Canada's and British Columbia's overseas trade representatives, he rejected offers of this and other government positions. He was disturbed by the poor attempts made by trade representatives to establish Canada, in particular British Columbia, as important suppliers of superior forest products. This opinion, among many others, he incorporated in his report to the federal government—a report which was to receive little or no acknowledgement. World War I had turned the government's mind to graver considerations.

Irony compounding irony, he rejected an offer from the University of British Columbia to head the Faculty of Forestry, resigned his post as Chief Forester, and placed himself in a kind of apprenticeship to learn everything he could about the manufacturing and marketing of lumber products.

The overseas market junket had achieved two things: first, export sales increased materially, much to the satisfaction of British Columbia's lumber entrepreneurs; second, H. R. MacMillan's eyes had been opened to the potential that existed in the establishment of a Canadian lumber export agency. With methods typical of him, he turned knowledge into strength. He knew the forest and he knew the potential of the overseas markets. What he did not know was how to convert the forest into lumber and market it. Who but E. J. Palmer gave him the opportunity to complete his education. MacMillan accepted Palmer's offer to come to Victoria Lumber & Manufacturing as assistant manager. Both his decision and his choice of mill could scarcely have been better.

Victoria Lumber vied with Fraser Mills and a few others as a large-production, modern, efficient operation with direct connections to overseas markets, a thriving domestic business supported by a chain of lumber yards, and control of some of the best and largest timber tracts in the province. He could not have discovered a more practical training ground.

Perhaps he wished his indoctrination could have lasted longer, but he and Palmer began to have differences of opinion, undoubtedly the result of two strong and opinionated personalities in conflict. Palmer was, in all respects, more powerful than MacMillan. He had the advantage of position and years, and he was accustomed to running his show in his own way. The story of MacMillan's departure from Victoria Lumber has several versions now bordering on myth, but depart he did in the summer of 1917 with a year of hard work and accumulated experience to his credit. Some say he was fired, vowing to return one day as owner of Victoria Lumber. He was to state later on in life that he saw the axe about to fall and took his leave before the blow was struck. One thing is certain, he did succeed, several years later, in acquiring Victoria Lumber in a business coup which will be described later on.

His apprenticeship was over. He worked with the Imperial Munitions Board until the end of the war, expediting the production of Sitka spruce in British Columbia for aircraft construction; but this was merely an interval in which he was able to formulate and refine his own plan. Essentially it was drawn from the recommendations in his neglected report to the federal government on Canada's proper role in the world lumber trade. He had called for Canada to gain control of its own destiny in the export of lumber. Now he took his own advice and established his own lumber export company in partnership with Montague L. Meyer, one of Britain's leading timber importers.

MacMillan had first met Meyer in London on the initial leg of his world market mission. Meyer was timber buyer for the British Government at the time and he welcomed the opportunity to establish direct lines of communications with British Columbia, with MacMillan acting as intermediary. The two men met at precisely the right time when both had needs to be served. When H. R. MacMillan was ready to launch his export business, Montague Meyer was looking about for ways to supply a predicted building boom in England. If MacMillan could assemble the lumber for U.K. export, Montague Meyer was excellently positioned to sell it.

In July 1919 they went through the formalities of forming a partnership under the name of H. R. MacMillan Export Company Limited. British Columbia's lumber export trade was on its way to becoming master in its own house. However, four months earlier, partly under the goad of MacMillan's unexpected entrée into the lumber export business but largely because of other developing circumstances, better than thirty autonomous B.C. mills decided to attempt to work in harness.

·THREE·

CONSOLIDATION & DISSENSION

There is little doubt that H. R. MacMillan's actions influenced to some degree the formation of the mills' consortium. For that matter the mills' joining of forces must have spurred MacMillan to accelerate the establishment of his export company. However, where the mills were concerned there was no single catalyst or precedent for their decision to amalgamate.

As far back as 1869 in the United States, lumber entrepreneurs had attempted to combine their resources. In that year the Chicago Lumbermen's Exchange was formed in an effort to control production and price. It failed because of lack of mutual interest. For the same reason the National Association of Lumbermen established in 1874 proved ineffective. The Northwestern Lumber Manufacturers' Association formed in 1881 was marginally successful, but once again the unwillingness of the participants to commit to essential agreements was a stumbling block. Ten years later, drawing from these earlier unsuccessful attempts at amalgamation, the Mississippi Valley Lumbermen's Association was founded primarily for the purpose of setting and maintaining uniform prices. Almost immediately it discovered that the establishment of standardized grading rules would have to precede the establishment of price. The Association applied itself to these matters with considerable efficiency and energy until it was indicted in 1893 for suspected price-fixing under the Sherman Antitrust Act of 1890. Nothing came of the lawsuit, but it created an understandable setback.

In the last decade of the 1800s there were attempts made by the mills in Washington and Oregon to set up joint sales organizations. Invitations were extended to British Columbia mills upon occasion. In fact, Hastings Mill became a member of one of these groups and stayed with it for the short time it took to fail because of internecine differences. Not until 1913, with the formation of the Douglas Fir Exploitation and Export Company in California, was any degree of co-operative success demonstrated. The company was established to obtain orders for its members as well as to promote the use of Douglas-fir and to find new markets for that product. Within three years it had succeeded in recruiting a membership consisting of more than half the producing mills in the U.S. Pacific Northwest.

In British Columbia, the mills, more or less independently, were seeking for ways to improve their sales efficiency and gain entrée to new markets. The Camerons had tried to construct a fleet to carry their lumber offshore. Hastings Mill had joined an unsuccessful U.S. association. There was an abortive attempt by the Board of Trade in the Vancouver Island town of Duncan to establish an assembly wharf at Victoria's Ogden Point for use by an association of Island mills engaged in lumber export, but the inertia of the mills was too strong to overcome. E. J. Palmer, manager of Victoria Lumber & Manufacturing, appears to have been one of the most active in the promotion of the association idea. He was keenly aware of the Douglas Fir Exploitation and Export Company concept and he sought to emulate some of its activities in B.C. His correspondence with provincial government representative R. E. Gosnell in 1914 is recorded: "My idea is that the British Columbia lumbermen should get together and sell through one agency, each mill binding themselves to the amount they will furnish," his letter said in part. Typically the mill men listened but were slow to respond. Their individualism remained a barrier, and their provincially insular attitude made it difficult for them to comprehend the intricacies of the export trade. Few had ever travelled to any of the overseas markets. They had no concept of the uses of lumber products in these markets, or of the standards demanded by offshore builders. They were not accustomed to the fine points of price regulation or of dealing in a dozen different foreign exchanges. Above all they were not attuned to the idea of co-operating with other mills in a working association.

Not until H. R. MacMillan, on his federal trade commission trip to England and other overseas countries, generated a startling amount of new business were the mill men jolted into full awareness of a market potential which had never been properly exploited. Orders for more than 20 million feet of lumber to England alone had to be regarded as attractive incentive. The possibility of an association gained more support and the broad outlines began to take shape.

As the war came to a close, the expectations of the lumber industry were high. British timber controls would be relaxed; Europe, devastated by the destruction of war, would have to be rebuilt; ships no longer seconded to war service would be released to carry lumber. An editorial of the day affirmed that "with 1919 comes a new era, one of hope renewed and of a period of prosperity that will eclipse anything that has yet gone before." The lumber industry prepared for a period of boom which did not materialize as expected.

The first four months after the war were disappointing, and were adjudged as such by MacMillan in the March 1919 issue of *Pacific Coast Lumberman*. He stated that Britain's need for lumber seemed to be less than anticipated. It must be kept in mind, however, that he was well aware of the British Columbia mills' growing demonstrations of solidarity and he may have wanted to dampen their enthusiasm somewhat, particularly since he was about to launch his own business.

Of course, British Columbia had no monopoly on the British market. North European countries made substantial inroads into the British lumber market, and with considerable advantages. A shipment of lumber from Sweden took six days to arrive at an English port compared to two months from British Columbia. Moreover, many a North European vessel went back with a cargo of British coal. An advantage for British Columbia was that it could ship twelve months a year, including periods when Scandinavian and Russian ports were icebound.

B.C.'s Lumber Commissioner in Britain at the time, L. B. Beale, reported that not only would British Columbia have to exert itself to overcome the twin handicaps of time and cost of transportation, but it would also have to demonstrate that the mills could fill large orders reliably. It was quite apparent that a credibility gap existed between the British Columbia mills and potential buyers overseas. British Columbia had not been sold effectively in the marketplace.

Beale's report recommended the establishment of "a producing and selling organization to include such mills as are desirous of participating in the export trade. In Britain, a marketing organization to obtain orders and deliver goods to various importers would also be required." He went on to say that he doubted if prospective business could be handled satisfactorily by individual mills dealing with individual importers. What was required was an organization that would tend to stabilize and standardize production and FOB prices, as well as to negotiate the lowest rates of transportation while taking every advantage offered by the market situation.

His statement, carried in the May 1919 edition of *Pacific Coast Lumberman,* was concurrent with another motivating event. The British Timber Control Board, influenced, it might be suspected, by the British government timber buyer Montague Meyer, gave British Columbia the opportunity to take a contract for a large order of ties and crossings for use by the British Railways. The order was very large by the standards of the day: 70 million feet of fir and 1,770,000 feet of hemlock—enough to cause many B.C. mills to pause and consider, and certainly enough to raise doubts in the minds of the British that British Columbia could deliver.

In order to fill a contract of that magnitude, the production capacity of virtually every mill on Vancouver Island and the mainland would have to be tapped, and more than one mill man was forthright in his opinion that the business should be declined. These dissenters, however, were overruled by those who had fostered the idea of a mill association, particularly those who had warmed to the concept after they had tasted the volume of business generated by H. R. MacMillan's trade commission trip.

E. J. Palmer, of course was one of those in the forefront of the move to amalgamate. "Old Hickory" Palmer, an ex-Weyerhaeuser man with a reputation for removing barriers, human or inanimate, would have been a difficult man to argue out of a fixed opinion. He was joined by men of equally strong personality and power such as F. R. Pendleton, J. D. McCormack, J. O. Cameron, R. H. Alexander and H. J. Mackin.

J. D. McCormack was vice-president and manager of Canadian Western Lumber Company at Fraser Mills. Another Weyerhaeuser man, he first saw the light of day in 1859 in Prince Edward Island, got an early start in the lumber business as a Weyerhaeuser employee, becoming manager of Rutledge Lumber Company in Minnesota before moving to British Columbia in 1907 to take over as manager of the Columbia River Lumber Company at Golden. In 1910 he was invited to join Canadian Western as assistant to Gen. A. D. McRae, then the company's vice-president and manager. A man with singular leadership qualities and a thorough knowledge of the lumber business, he was president of the B.C. Lumber and Shingle Manufacturer's Association (BCLSMA) seven times and head of the Timber Industries Council of B.C. in its most active period.

J. O. Cameron was one of the enterprising Cameron brothers we met earlier. The Camerons were dedicated to the establishment of a viable lumber export system by whatever means. The extent of their determination was evidenced when, in 1915, they organized Cameron-Genoa Shipbuilders Limited.

Richard H. Alexander was the son and namesake of a redoubtable Scot who trekked across the Rockies on foot to become one of the principal founders of the lumber industry. He owned Hastings Mill, and young Richard learned the business there as well as espousing his father's belief in the need for quality control and a standard grading system in the lumber business. The senior Alexander had heartily endorsed the formation of the Pacific Lumber Inspection Bureau in the United States in 1903, and had much to do with its introduction into British Columbia. Richard Alexander was equally active in this respect, and in the formation of the B.C. Lumber and Shingle Manufacturers' Association of which organization he was the first secretary. In this capacity he laboured to standardize lumber grades particularly through the establishment of lumbermen's education classes. Another of his concerns was the elevation of safety standards in the mills.

Henry J. Mackin was a businessman/lumberman with the strength and tenacity of a bull terrier. Hailing from Portland, Oregon, he first worked for Standard Box Company in that city, moving to Vancouver in 1908 to become sales manager for Fraser River Lumber Company. When Canadian Western bought out Fraser River, Mackin remained as sales manager, proceeding through several executive promotions to become assistant to James McCormack, and succeeding him as vice-president and managing director when McCormack died in 1935. Mackin was an achiever of the highest order, short on words and strong on action. By 1939 Canadian Western Lumber was generally recognized as the largest lumber producing company in the British Empire, much of this due to Henry Mackin's perception and leadership qualities. He was active in every aspect of the lumber industry, including the formulation and production of standard grades through the Pacific Lumber Inspection Bureau, of which he was the first president elected from Canada.

These, then, were the men who pressed for and achieved the formation of an amalgamation of sawmills for the purpose of supplying large overseas lumber orders, a move made expedient by the inducement of the 70-million-foot British Timber Control contract. When these determined promulgators exerted their persuasive powers, things moved with amazing speed, although the *British Columbia Lumberman* quotes James McCormack as saying that a group of lumbermen had been discussing the idea for some months. If they had, then it is apparent that they had their game plan well thought out because it took exactly forty-eight hours to organize the meeting that led to the formation of British Columbia's first mill export consortium.

On 27 March 1919 a meeting of these lumber magnates was held in the offices of the Cameron Lumber Company in Victoria. The objectives of the proposed amalgamation as presented by McCormack to the Vancouver *Daily Province* were to "increase the exports of the province to the world's markets . . . particularly the Pacific Coast which offered the best inducements owing to cheaper freight rates. Efforts would be made, therefore, to capture some portion of the trade in Australia, China, South America and other Pacific countries."

Elections took place at the same meeting, with James D. McCormack being nominated and elected as president; James O. Cameron, vice-president, and Richard H. Alexander, secretary/treasurer. The first executive board of directors consisted of Edward C. Knight, Vancouver Lumber Company; Bruce M. Farris, M. B. King Lumber Company; Henry J. Mackin, Canadian Western Lumber Company; Edmond J. Palmer, Victoria Lumber & Manufacturing Company, Frank R. Pendleton, Straits Lumber Company and William W. Harvey, Dominion Creosoting. Even the matter of a head office was dealt with. Office space was arranged in Vancouver's Metropolitan Building and was quickly staffed by six employees under the management of Charles E. Huddart. The Associated Timber Exporters of British Columbia Limited was in business—and not a moment too soon.

Part of the reason for the precipitate formation of Astexo, as the company came to be known, was the visit in May 1919 of the British Timber Controller Sir James Ball, accompanied by the ubiquitous Montague L. Meyer, timber buyer for the British government and friend and confidant of H. R. MacMillan. Astexo rolled out the red carpet for Sir James and Meyer whose expressed purpose was to finalize financing and shipping details for the big lumber order, and whose covert purpose was to put their minds at ease as to British Columbia's ability to supply so large an order on time and up to specified standards.

The first day was spent with members of the newly formed association. Eric Hamber, general manager of thriving Hastings Mill, took them on a tour that did much to convince them of the productivity of a B.C. operation. Hastings Mill was an excellent first choice not only because of its size and modern equipment but also because of its ideal location on the edge of the Port of Vancouver.

Next J. D. McCormack led them through the noisy maze of Canadian Western Lumber in company with assistant manager Henry Mackin. This mill was at least as impressive as Hastings and production of both was known to the visitors because both mills had developed a certain amount of export business to the U.K. independently over the years. Officials of the Pacific Lumber Inspection Bureau were presented, as were key individuals with the B.C. Lumber and Shingle Manufacturers' Association. There was a reception and the best dinner the prestigious Vancouver Club could provide, followed by a five-day trip to Vancouver Island where some of the star mills of that region were put on display including the International Timber Company at Campbell River and, of course, the Victoria Lumber & Manufacturing Company at Chemainus.

Sir James and Meyer were shown magnificent stands of first-growth timber, living proof of the province's seemingly inexhaustible forest resource. It was a well-staged, carefully planned tour which left little to chance. There was nothing specious about it in any respect: the selected mills were the best on the North American continent; the timber resource was beyond belief; the hosts were the leaders in the industry, and the Honourable Duff Pattullo, B.C.'s Minister of Lands, together with M. A. Grainger, now provincial Chief Forester, assured the British representatives that the lumber industry of British Columbia would prove itself in every respect.

Sir James Ball was not to be dazzled by this show of strength and enthusiasm. At the conclusion of his visit, in commenting on what he had seen and heard, he combined praise with criticism, first applauding the industry for establishing an export association, albeit untested and about to come to grips with a 70-million-foot contract. But then he went on to rebuke B.C. lumbermen as a group for "sitting on your doorsteps in the expectation that orders will come your way unsolicited. They will not," he continued; "the competition to be overcome is keen and continuous." He was referring not only to established American competition but also to the consistently serious competition imposed by the Baltic countries and Russia. He recommended, as the newspaper reports put it, "in the strongest possible way that B.C. lumbermen should not lose an hour in maturing their plans for the systematic invasion of the world's markets." He was not about to leave B.C.'s lumber industry with the impression that it had a clear road ahead.

While he was at it he scolded the industry for the enormous and profligate wastage of good timber by fire, and for what he believed to be the unfortunate practice of leaving good downed timber in the wake of logging operations that concentrated on nothing but the best. His observations would be echoed by others in years to come.

J. D. McCormack countered with the observations that the large order for Douglas-fir and the small one for hemlock, while gratifying, was also indicative of one of British Columbia's problems, in that the export markets wanted a selective 30 per cent of the total cut for special purposes such as sleepers and ties, and remanufacturing. Markets must be found for the remaining 70 per cent of merchantable and common lumber, which he referred to as side lumber.

What he was saying, possibly without realizing it, was that overseas markets were unacquainted with British Columbia's variety and quality of sawn lumber, or the uses to which these could be put effectively and economically. Within a few years a program of education would begin in those markets.

All considered it was a positive and useful visit which undoubtedly contributed to the effort the B.C. mills made to fill the British order. Fill it they did, on time and to the satisfaction of the British authorities. Astexo manager C. E. Huddart was reported in the April 1920 issue of *Pacific Coast Lumberman* to the effect that the order had been filled by the end of February of that year.

J. O. Cameron, in an address to the Canadian Forestry Association convention in 1921, brought up the problem of sparse utilization of B.C. sawn lumber grades in the export markets. At the same time he was pleased to point out that overseas and out-of-Canada sales were on the increase since the establishment of Astexo. Before that organization began operations, not much more than 5 per cent of the province's lumber was exported. Cameron reported the export of 93 million feet in 1918 as compared to 108 million feet in 1919 after the formation of Astexo. By 1929, 27 per cent of B.C.'s lumber was being exported, increasing to 66 per cent in 1933.

In view of events that would occur in ensuing years, it should be pointed out that Astexo's member mills elected to sell their lumber on an FAS (Free Along Side) basis, which meant essentially that they contracted to deliver the correct amounts and grades of lumber to the dock, for which they received payment from the exporter within a stipulated period of time. After that it was the exporter's responsibility to arrange the freight. The Astexo mills felt more comfortable with this arrangment although it resulted in less profit, as they were to discover. They felt that shipping was not their business.

John A. Humbird, namesake and grandson of the founder of Victoria Lumber & Manufacturing, who was to become president of Astexo in due course, kept a detailed diary of the workings of both Astexo and Seaboard. He records that the articles of Astexo allowed for selling only on an FAS basis and did not permit the company to charter or own vessels. In fact, he states that some of Astexo's more prominent members, including J. D. McCormack and E. J. Palmer, were unalterably opposed to having anything to do with ocean freight and were convinced that engagement in ocean freighting would eventually break up the co-operation that had been stimulated in FAS selling. This opinion was not shared by all, and later attempts to enter into a form of export selling to California and the East Coast of the United States, while overruled by the majority, gave evidence of a second school of thought. This divergence of opinion would have much to do with the establishment of Seaboard.

*   *   *

The mill men were playing their new export role as responsibly as they were able. More than lip service was paid to the matter of education in the marketplace and to the task of establishing standard grading rules for the industry.

In 1922 the Forest Products Market Extension Bureau was set up by the industry to secure and expand existing markets and to develop new ones. The declared aims of the Bureau were: the investigation of new markets; assistance to salesmen and manufacturers through practical work in existing markets; promoting the value of B.C. lumber products through general publicity, exhibits, information brochures and personal communication and consultation; combatting propaganda aimed by steel, concrete and roofing manufacturers at denigrating timber as a good construction material; advising manufacturers as to the improvement of grades and the introduction of new lumber products, or types of lumber commonly used in the offshore markets; establishing an information pool and a news service for both the manufacturer and the consumer; analyzing market possibilities and changes for the timberholders; assisting logging operators in the most efficient and profitable ways to cut logs for grade and length.

It is significant to note that men like Henry Mackin and John Hendry, superintendent of Hastings Mill, were prominent on the board of trustees. There was very little delegation of authority; the men at the top were carrying the load—or making certain that it was carried to their satisfaction.

As to the establishment of standard grading rules, and a system that would maintain quality of manufacture, many of the mills were now subscribing to the standards laid down by the Pacific Lumber Inspection Bureau, following the example of U.S. Pacific Coast manufacturers. This system was formalized with the establishment of the B.C. Lumber Inspection Association in 1923, formed to appoint and train competent lumber and shingle inspectors. Once again Astexo men such as F. R.

Pendleton, president of Straits Lumber Company, and P. D. Roe, Eburne Lumber vice-president, were prominent.

And what did H. R. MacMillan think of this demonstration of solidarity in the traditionally disparate ranks of the B.C. mills? For a man within weeks of launching his own lumber export organization, he made a curious statement reported in the March 1919 issue of *Pacific Coast Lumberman:* "The small volume of lumber exports from B.C. has occasionally been improperly ascribed to a lack of exporting organizations prepared to purchase lumber in B.C. for export. This is, of course, a mistaken view. Although trade would undoubtedly benefit by an increase in the number of active trading companies represented in Vancouver and Victoria, there are several experienced and competent exporters doing business in the province, some of whom have excellent connections and reputations in the most important overseas markets."

Obviously this opinion did not dissuade the Astexo mills from forming ranks, better than thirty strong, though the objective to sell direct to markets in Australia, China, South America and other Pacific countries was set aside, for the time being at least.

In July 1919, hard on the heels of Astexo's formation, H. R. MacMillan Export Company Ltd. came into being, combining the talents and assets of MacMillan and Meyer. MacMillan would manage the export side of the business in Vancouver, obtaining, principally from the Astexo mills, the lumber needed to fill orders obtained largely by Meyer. The negotiating arm of H. R. MacMillan Export in London was the CANUSA Trading Company, managed by Montague Meyer. Astexo for a number of years was apparently content to sell most of the export production of its member mills to Vancouver wholesalers and exporters, the largest volume by far going to H. R. MacMillan Export as time went on.

For the first year MacMillan ran his new firm by himself until expanding business led him to employ W. J. Van Dusen as manager, releasing MacMillan to nurture relations with existing and potential markets. Astexo and H. R. MacMillan Export found themselves occupying almost adjacent premises in Vancouver's Metropolitan Building—MacMillan with a total staff of four, and Astexo with a staff of six now managed by a professional lumberman who commanded the respect of the entire industry.

Jack G. McConville was another Canadian who had cut his teeth in the lumber industry in the United States. Born in Kingston, Ontario, he was introduced to the lumber industry when he went to Oregon in 1907, moving to the Victoria Lumber & Manufacturing Company four years later where he served for eight years in a variety of management capacities. When he took over as manager of Astexo, he had earned a reputation as an authority on virtually every aspect of lumber production and marketing as it was then practised.

The close physical proximity of Astexo's and MacMillan's offices had its advantages in the years when Astexo was almost entirely concerned with selling the export production of some thirty mills in the easiest, quickest way within the framework of profitability; and H. R. MacMillan was entirely occupied with securing orders from offshore buyers and shipping those orders effectively and profitably.

Astexo sold the export output of its member mills on an FAS basis. Its responsibility was to deliver the right quantity and the right grade of lumber at the ship's side on the date contracted for. Upon presentation of documents confirming that this had been done, Astexo received payment on behalf of its supplying mills. An "Equalization Plan" was established whereby Astexo paid the mills a flat price of $30 per thousand for merchantable grades. Astexo absorbed any difference. Later, any surplus in the fund was paid to the mills on a pro rata basis to their quarterly shipments. For this and other services rendered Astexo charged a 2½ per cent commission. Again, any surplus after expenses was refunded to the mills pro rata. This equalization system was used until 1925 with the base price changing from time to time as conditions dictated.

Astexo sold its export production FAS while MacMillan, and other exporters and brokers, sold to overseas buyers CIF (Cost, Insurance and Freight). This meant that MacMillan had the responsibility to arrange the freight and insurance for the buyers' accounts. Thus a buyer was covered for any damage or loss of lumber until it was landed at port of discharge. With the presentation of proper documents, the export broker was then entitled to payment from the overseas buyer, on completion of loading of the vessel, usually by drawing on a letter of credit established by the buyer. The broker received a commission on the FAS value.

Under this arrangement the two neighbours in the Metropolitan Building were to coexist in a satisfactory manner for some time with Astexo adding substantially to the success of H. R. MacMillan Export. There were a number of other factors contributing to this symbiotic relationship, not the least of which was the final opening of the Panama Canal, an event that was to change the whole face of Pacific Coast lumber exporting dramatically and for the better.

Although completed in 1914, the canal was not an immediate success largely because of a serious earth slide which made it inoperable during 1915 and 1916. When the official opening occurred in 1920, it triggered an enormous increase in shipments to the Atlantic seaboard, further assisted by a 33⅓ per cent rise in rail rates imposed in 1921. In that year 25 million feet of lumber were shipped to the U.S. from British Columbia, mostly to California. However, by 1926 shipments to the U.S. totalled 400 million feet, of which 95 per cent went to the U.S. Atlantic Coast market.

Through 1919 and 1920 Britain continued to be British Columbia's best export customer, but it was a situation that could not continue indefinitely, for pressure from the Baltic countries and Russia was powerful and seductive. Their lumber was good, their prices were right and shipping times were relatively short. For these reasons Britain's allegiance to Canadian lumber exporters wavered and went into deep hibernation.

Were it not for the healthy trade enjoyed with other British Empire countries, Far East markets and the United States throughout the 1920s, the B.C. lumber industry would have found itself in desperate straits. Japan took over as British Columbia's best lumber market in 1921, demonstrating an almost exclusive preference for 24″ × 24″ timbers devoid of defects. These "Japanese squares," as they were called, were destined for remanufacture in Japan.

Healthy though trade with Japan was in 1921 and 1922, a natural disaster tripled lumber shipments to that country in 1923 when a major earthquake levelled many of her cities and towns. In four months Tokyo purchased 430 million feet of lumber, three times as much as the annual consumption. Even after the period of reconstruction, Japan continued to be a strong customer, importing 177 million feet in 1926.

As well, China showed promise of becoming an important market in the first years of the twenties. In 1921 alone she imported close to 40 million feet of B.C. lumber, but this bubble was to burst, pricked by more convenient markets and better prices to be commanded elsewhere, particularly in the United States. By 1926 imports to China had dwindled to 4.5 million feet.

Business with Australia and New Zealand was comfortable, with 37 million feet going to Australia in 1926 and 16 million to New Zealand in the same year, these figures indicative of a steady annual trade. Business with South Africa, South America, Egypt and India was encouraging but more spasmodic and was hindered to some extent by the uncertainties of freight space.

It was to become typical of the export lumber business that when one market or a series of markets became slow or closed down, for whatever reason, others would strengthen or a new market would open up. This was acknowledged by H. R. MacMillan when he told the Vancouver *Daily Province* in 1921 that "four sections of the earth are now buying. Rarely more than two or three are purchasers at the same time." He indicated that his company's markets were Australia, China, Japan, New Zealand and, to a lesser extent, the United Kingdom. McConville confirmed this on behalf of Astexo, and went on to say that the U.S. market was opening up under the stimulus of the new Panama Canal access.

The difficult conundrum of securing a substantial share of the British market had to be dealt with, and to a large extent the problem was seen to be a lack of understanding and education on the part of the British buyers. In Canada, particularly in British Columbia, the wholesale use of lumber as the principal building material was an accepted fact. Building codes were developed around the use of lumber. Wooden houses worked. At their best they were mansions the equal of any anywhere; in their most modest form they were warm, comfortable and within the financial means of the population. As far as Canadian manufacturers and builders were concerned, wood construction was a way of life, and it had never really occurred to them that wood construction was not a widely accepted custom in Britain. In that country bricks and mortar were the traditional building materials. Lumber was a secondary material to be used for roof timbers, flooring, sash and doors, and trim. Furthermore, when wood was used, it was more likely to be pine or a hardwood species than the softwood Douglas-fir from faraway British Columbia.

Education was needed, and forthwith a program of education was initiated, spearheaded by the Canadian government, and actively supported by the B.C. industry, of which Astexo was the single largest entity within the framework of the B.C. Lumber and Shingle Manufacturers' Association. In May 1924 the Canadian government sent a major exhibit of Canadian woods and wood products to the Empire Exhibition at Wembley Park in Middlesex. One of the outstanding elements of the exhibit was the British Columbia display supervised and managed by B.C. Lumber Commissioner Loren Brown. The focal point was a two-room bungalow built on the site from B.C. woods. MacMillan's overseas entity, CANUSA Trading Company, contributed a timber display, and Brown succeeded in obtaining prestigious publicity in British publications such as the *Architects' Journal* and *British Builder* dealing not only with the Wembley Park exhibit but with an architect-designed house at Hampstead constructed almost entirely of B.C. Douglas-fir.

Although Loren Brown's efforts as Lumber Commissioner were beyond reproach, when he returned to Canada in 1926 he had few positive results to report. Newspaper editorials deplored the failure of the Canadian government and Canadian exporters to capitalize on the interest the Wembley exhibit and Brown's other promotions had engendered. Quite obviously the B.C. lumber industry had much more to learn about selling in the overseas market.

This then was the state of affairs in the export lumber trade by the mid-1920s. A forester had turned from the business of managing a forest resource to the business of selling the products of the forest to world markets. A group of thirty mills had joined forces for mutual benefit in the export of lumber. H. R. MacMillan and Astexo had elevated the B.C. lumber business to a new plateau and appeared to be working in tandem, the Astexo member mills labouring to fill export orders obtained and placed by H. R. MacMillan Export and other brokers.

But beneath the surface a ferment was occurring as aggressive mill men learned more about the export business, and as strong personalities began to assert themselves in this enterprise. Out of this subsurface agitation would emerge a new concept which was still without a name and was too embryonic to require management.

* * *

Shortly after the termination of World War I, a reconstruction boom occurred not only in the war-ravaged countries but also in North America and the Dominions where the material demands of the war had curtailed normal housing development and other forms of peacetime construction. The housing boom in the United States was singularly ambitious, buoyed by a healthy economy. On the Eastern Seaboard the call went out for lumber in enormous quantities. The depleted timber resources of eastern North America were not equal to this sudden demand and the huge timber reservoir of the Pacific Northwest became the mecca of U.S. eastern builders. British Columbia shared in this thriving new market, with H. R. MacMillan enjoying a good share of the export, and Astexo benefitting from sales to MacMillan and other brokers.

Another factor contributed to this profitable state of affairs. The Jones Act, passed by the United States in 1920 to benefit American shipping, worked to the advantage of foreign shipping lines as well. Under the terms of the Act, foreign vessels could not move from U.S. port to U.S. port; they were restricted to loading cargo at one U.S. port and then moving on to other foreign destinations. This restriction was no imposition whatever to British Columbia's export trade to the U.S. East Coast because almost all lumber cargoes were full shiploads, destined for any one of several eastern U.S. ports. The Panama Canal was functioning smoothly at last. A world surplus of tonnage had dropped freight rates substantially. Chartered foreign vessels arrived at British Columbia ports, took on full loads of lumber and went on their way. So lucrative was this trade that in 1925 H. R. MacMillan opened an office in New York to solicit additional business and to facilitate shipments.

We will leave him in this fortunate situation for the moment, remembering that Astexo mills were sharing in his good fortune, even though some of the Astexo leaders felt that their share could have been improved upon. Our scene shifts to the American state of Washington where Tacoma-born Charles Herbert Grinnell, a Commerce graduate from the University of Washington, and a young war veteran who had served with the U.S. Quartermasters Corps, was applying his training and talents to the lumber business. He was a partner in the firm of Heidner & Grinnell and was engaged primarily in the movement of lumber cargoes to the U.S. East Coast. There is reason to believe that his enterprise did not work to his satisfaction at a time when the lumber business was an invitation to relative prosperity. In 1925 he accepted a position with the American firm of Brady & Ketcham, with the directive to open a branch office for this broker/wholesaler in Vancouver, British Columbia.

American lumber exporters and brokers were not about to be hoist by their own petard. As well as using American vessels to carry the shipments of U.S. mills under the provisions of the Jones Act, some of the more enterprising firms became extremely active in the purchase of British Columbia lumber at the right price, carried in foreign bottoms at attractive freight rates. They even sent American vessels north to B.C. ports to pick up cargoes of lumber. Brady & Ketcham was one of these, and Charles Grinnell was their chosen emissary. His physical arrangements in Vancouver were not elaborate. He established a desk in the Merchants Exchange Building at the corner of Hastings and Howe streets, sharing office space with Andrew Graham and his associate, Lorne Richardson, whose responsibility it was to administer the affairs of the Anglo-Canadian Shipping Company.

Anglo-Canadian was launched in Vancouver by Melville Dollar of the San Francisco Dollar Steamship Lines dynasty. Apparently he had serious differences of opinion with the family and struck out on his own to establish the Canadian shipping company. (A modern mill, the Canadian Robert Dollar Company, was erected in 1916 on the north shore of Burrard Inlet near Deep Cove; it was managed by Alexander Dollar, but this business was quite apart from Melville Dollar's shipping operation.)

Founders &
Their Environment

1 Lumber shipping at the turn of the century. Three sailing vessels take on
lumber at Hastings Saw Mill, Vancouver.

2 Log storage on the Fraser River at Canadian Western Lumber Company,
New Westminster, 1913.

1

2

3

3
Carlton Stone, the Essex-born mariner who came ashore to found
Hillcrest Lumber Company, one of Seaboard's first members.
4
In 1926 B.C.'s forest giants were a formidable challenge for the hand
logger with axe and crosscut saw.

5

5
The headrig at the Robert Dollar mill, North Vancouver, 1928, slices boards from a magnificent Douglas-fir cant.
6
A U.K. trade delegation in company with Seaboard representatives at B.C. Manufacturing Company's mill, New Westminster, 1938.
7
Millhands and office staff stand behind a Douglas-fir timber. Such timbers, up to 110 feet long, were sawn at the Timberland mill on the Fraser River at New Westminster.
8
Millhands on a timber deck prepare Japanese squares for shipment.

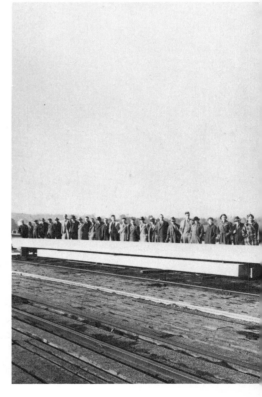

6

7

8

9

9
Spruce Woods takes on a Seaboard lumber cargo bound for the U.S. Atlantic Coast, 1956. The barges carry parcels of lumber from L & K Lumber Company on the North Vancouver harbour front.
10
Seaboard delivered Canada's first lumber cargo to Spain. S.S. *Syra* discharges a full cargo for Messrs. Ismael Mateu at Barcelona.
11
Onboard S.S. *Western Park* in 1944 are (*l to r*) A. Davis, C. J. Culter, Captain Hansen (*Dunlop Park*), T N. Phillips, Captain Young (*Westend Park*), A. H. Carson, J. G. McConville, H. J. Mackin, J. A. Humbird, C. H. Grinnell, J. G. Robson, William McDonnell, W. C. Robinson, E. Glaspie and A. F. Menzies.
12
M.V. *Seaboard Queen*, once a wartime Park vessel, discharges 4.5 million feet of lumber at Cardiff, Wales, 1944. Over 1 million feet was carried on deck.

10

11

12

13

13
For the coronation of Elizabeth II, Seaboard donated a maypole sawn at Timberland and presented as a gift from the City of New Westminster. Lt.Col. N. Edwards, mayor of Westminster, accepts the gift from B.C. trade commissioner Douglas Roe. George R. Taylor (*r*) represents Seaboard.
14
Attending J. G. (Jack) McConville's 1946 retirement dinner are (*l to r*) William Burke, G. Robin Hackett, J. G. McConville, J. G. Robson and Arthur D. Anderson.
15
James P. O'Hagan, Astexo assistant manager, *c.* 1946
16
Left to right: Bruce M. Farris, John A. Humbird, Henry J. Mackin and John H. McDonald at McConville's retirement dinner.

14

15

16

Carriers to the Markets

1 M.V. *Nordhval,* built in Denmark in 1924 and owned by Norden, carried lumber from the Pacific Northwest to Japan in 1926.

2 M.V. *Coronation Park.* During World War II Seaboard Shipping managed ten of this class of ship for the British Ministry of Supply. Seaboard later purchased six Park vessels to form its own fleet.

3 Seaboard supercargo, Dick Witts; captain of *Dorothy Ann,* C. K. Woo, and Seaboard's marine superintendent, Capt. William Rion. 1967.

4 M.V. *Skaugran* with one of the first full cargoes of packaged lumber for the U.K., *c.* 1964. The name has been passed on to a Seaboard Ro/Ro vessel now in service to Japan.

1

2

3

4

5

6

5
Capt. William Ellis, manager of s.i.t., Wray Howard, manager of ship operations, and Dick Bonney, marine superintendent, examine packaged lumber in prestow racks before loading on Johnson Line vessels M.V. *Suecia* and M.V. *Pacific, c.* 1973.
6
Before construction of Seaboard International Terminal (s.i.t.) in North Vancouver, lumber was usually loaded from barges alongside ship. Packaged lumber is lifted to the deck of M.V. *Demosthenes.*
7
Gantry cranes on vessels like M.V. *Pacific,* handling packaged lumber prestowed in racks at s.i.t., improved loading time substantially, *c.* 1973.
8
M.V. *Pacific* departs Vancouver with 13 million feet of lumber.
9
M.V. *Pacific Defender* was the first vessel to carry Seaboard's new corporate symbol. 1968.

7

8

PACIFIC DEFENDER

9

10

10
Murray Mather, assistant manager of Seaboard Shipping, with Ronald Safe, captain of *Silvercape,* who holds a Captain Vancouver plaque marking *Silvercape*'s first voyage to the port of Vancouver in 1967. This vessel later tested a central loading facility; she loaded 11 million feet of packaged lumber in five days at Ogden Point assembly wharf in Victoria—half the normal loading time.
11
In 1968 M.V. *Chennai Ookem,* 42,530 tons, arrived in Liverpool with the largest lumber cargo ever carried to that time—20.5 million feet—all supplied by Seaboard mills.
12
C. Y. Tung, owner of M.V. *Pacific Defender,* Capt. Y. W. Feng and Vassall G. Forrester, vice-president of Seaboard Shipping Company. The Seaboard insignia combines ancient craftsman marks for wood and water.
13
M.V. *Nordpol,* Seaboard's first ten-year charter, was built in Japan for the Norden Company of Copenhagen to Seaboard's requirements and is still in service.

11

12

13

14

14
Seaboard's Ro/Ro vessel, M.V.
Skeena, at s.i.t. The 42,000-ton
vessel was delivered in 1983 to
service the Japan market.
15
M.V. *Skaugran,* delivered in 1979,
was designed primarily for trade
with Japan, carrying lumber there
and returning with automobiles and
other cargo.

15

In addition to his own enterprise, Melville Dollar was president of a company set up in Vancouver by American lumber exporter/ship operator W. L. Comyn. This ambitious and successful businessman, like Brady & Ketcham, had established an arm of his company in British Columbia to take advantage of low freight rates and attractive Canadian lumber prices to increase his profits from U.S. Atlantic seaboard business. Charles Grinnell found himself representing Brady & Ketcham, but in the daily company of individuals closely associated with W. L. Comyn & Company

Grinnell's business was sufficiently brisk to justify the addition of another person—someone reasonably well-connected, familiar with the Vancouver lumber industry scene, and sufficiently experienced to be able to handle a lumber sales transaction intelligently. He found his man in the person of Claude Effinger, twenty-five years of age, born in eastern Canada but raised and educated in Vancouver. Although he had worked in the lumber business both as a manual labourer (during school holidays) and in sales for a number of years, he also had attended university which possibly gave him an edge at a time when higher education was experienced by a relative few. Grinnell introduced Effinger to the intricacies of the export trade, particularly as it was practised in the U.S. markets. When he deemed his employee to be ready, he sent him to New York to set up an office on behalf of Brady & Ketcham.

This was Claude Effinger's first taste of travel and living in the heart of a major marketplace, and he found it satisfactory in every respect. He adjusted to the routine with little effort and acquired a taste for selling in strange places that was to stand him in good stead throughout his entire career. His New York office was in the Shelton Hotel, and from there he went out to meet the lumber wholesalers, many of whom were existing customers or contacts supplied by Grinnell or by the company principals, Hugh Brady and Henry Ketcham. The modus operandi, then and later, was for Effinger to act as representative, calling on new customers and following sales leads often generated by Grinnell back in Vancouver. Grinnell liked the stability of the home office. Effinger thrived on travel. He dealt on a daily basis with such prestigious wholesalers as Shepherd & Morse, Cooney-Eckstein (Cooney was a Harvard University friend of Henry Ketcham), J. Herbert Bateman, Blanchard Lumber Company, Gurnsey Westbrook and Dant & Russell.

The business procedure, as laid down by Grinnell, was unvarying. There were telephone conferences at set times each day. Effinger dealt directly with the customers and took their orders, or acquainted them with special lumber availabilities and prices supplied by Grinnell. Orders phoned or cabled to Grinnell in Vancouver were relayed from there to Brady & Ketcham in Seattle for final confirmation. The Seattle office arranged for space with various shipping lines. Effinger's recollection is that only American vessels were used: Grace Lines, Luckenbach, Weyerhaeuser, Calmar, American Mail, Pope & Talbot. If the Jones Act imposed any restrictions, he is not aware of them. "The American ships came from the East Coast loaded with cars and structural steel for California and other U.S. Pacific Coast cities," he recalls. "Then they came up to Vancouver and the Vancouver Island ports to pick up lumber for the East Coast."

To this day, Claude Effinger is mildly bemused when he describes what happened next. He had been covering the New York wholesalers satisfactorily for several months, and the Brady & Ketcham arrangement seemed to be working well; "then Chuck Grinnell called me one day and told me that we were no longer with Brady & Ketcham," he states. "We had swung over to W. L. Comyn & Company. I asked for the reasons, but Chuck never gained a reputation for saying more than he wanted to say. I never did get the whole story. I know that Chuck and Ketcham never spoke to one another again; and I know that when Seaboard came into being, Brady & Ketcham was one of the few companies we could never deal with."

As it turned out, Grinnell's decision to move to W. L. Comyn was well-considered. W. L. Comyn & Company was a large lumber firm with headquarters in San Francisco and an office in Seattle. An added advantage was that the company owned and operated its own ships, deploying them to all parts of the world. It had offices in China, Japan, England and Australia, enjoying a particularly thriving business in Australia.

Under the new management, business became considerably simpler. The need to negotiate for ships' bottoms was virtually eliminated. Comyn's fleet could handle most, if not all, of the lumber cargoes for the U.S. East Coast. In order to strengthen its shipping position, Comyn time-chartered two more vessels for the fleet, both Canadian flag with Chinese crews and British-Scots officers. The *City of Victoria* and the *City of Vancouver* were carryovers from Canada's wartime merchant fleet.

Claude Effinger remained in New York, his allegiance now directed to W. L. Comyn & Company in a relationship he grew to enjoy considerably. He and Charles Grinnell became close friends with the company's namesake, described by Effinger as possessing the ability to work meticulous and profitable lumber sales and shipping deals on the back of an envelope. Isolated as he was 3000 miles from home office, Effinger was never close to the inner workings in Vancouver. His immediate superior never told him one iota more than he needed to know to represent the company effectively. Less than a year after joining Comyn, he was subjected to another unexpected directive. Grinnell called and advised him that he was leaving the employ of W. L. Comyn to join H. R. MacMillan. His request to Effinger was that he remain in New York to represent MacMillan's interests there. Claude Effinger had been somewhat torn when he was asked to leave Brady & Ketcham for Comyn. He was even more disturbed now to be asked to desert Comyn for MacMillan.

What lay behind this apparent chess game Grinnell was playing? Granted, the move to Comyn was a step up and in the right direction. There was good reason for Effinger to believe that the move to MacMillan might be equally efficacious. But at what point did a person become committed? When did it become wise to put down an anchor and declare permanent allegiance to a reputable firm?

"Chuck's mind was made up," Effinger says. "As far as Grinnell was concerned his own arrangements were signed and sealed, and he wanted me to stay with him under the MacMillan banner. While he talked, I thought hard." Effinger's decision was to stay with W. L. Comyn. "Comyn's been damn nice to me," he told Grinnell. "I can't leave him like this. Under the circumstances I'm coming back to Vancouver."

He admits that Grinnell could be stubborn and persuasive. "They were two traits that he used very effectively in his business activities," he said, "and he used them on me that day on the telephone. He wanted to talk to me personally, to spell out all the advantages there would be with MacMillan's. I told him I was coming home, and he must have been studying the railway timetable while I talked. Chuck was about to take a business trip to eastern Canada. He told me that the least I could do was to meet him half way on the journey home. The schedule showed that both our trains would cross and stop at Medicine Hat, Alberta . . . and that is where I agreed to meet him."

At this juncture it is interesting to speculate on what drove Charles Grinnell to join the MacMillan forces. Many have advanced their own opinions, ranging from those who suggest Grinnell's own spiralling ambitions to those who ascribe more complicated and Machiavellian motives. Certainly H. R. MacMillan would have had excellent reasons for wanting a man of Grinnell's experience and training. First of all he would have wanted to increase his personnel to take full advantage of the soaring East Coast lumber demand. The increase in British Columbia sales from 1920 on had been impressive.

In 1920 Oregon and Washington mills shipped 50 million feet by water to the U.S. Eastern Seaboard. That same year British Columbia shipped 650,000 feet. The following year, American West Coast mills quadrupled their shipments to 200 million feet while British Columbia's shipments increased to more than 5 million. In 1923 the U.S. West Coast shipped 800 million feet to the East Coast, and British Columbia's shipments were up to 153 million. Ocean freight rates were so low that it was profitable for East Coast wholesalers to take delivery of shipments from the West Coast and backhaul by rail as far west as Ohio.

H. R. MacMillan had capitalized on this state of affairs to the best of his ability, even to the extent in 1924 of establishing his own shipping subsidiary, Canadian Transport Company Limited. Now he was in a position to profit not only from astute sales manipulations but also from a control of freight.

Grinnell's position, as representative of W. L. Comyn in Vancouver, ran parallel to MacMillan's organization on a smaller scale. He was working with a company involved in both sales and shipping, and he thoroughly understood the machinations of the East Coast lumber trade. MacMillan hired Grinnell to manage the company's Atlantic Coast sales. It made sense. MacMillan, with a canny eye for human potential, had strengthened his organization with the acquisition of Charles Grinnell. The acquisition of Claude Effinger would have been useful as well.

In February 1927 two trains departed from opposite sides of the continent, one travelling east carrying Charles Grinnell, one travelling west with Claude Effinger aboard. The two trains converged at Medicine Hat, and the businessmen disembarked to meet in the town's best hotel. "Chuck was in no hurry to talk business," Effinger remembers. "The hotel had a mezzanine floor with potted plants and a piano. Chuck could play the piano by ear, and he played very well. We spent an hour or so on the mezzanine while he experimented with various tunes, and I waited to get down to the reason for our meeting. It was a pleasant interval; we were both tired from travel."

The outcome of the meeting changed nothing. Grinnell presented eloquently on behalf of the move to MacMillan, and Effinger remained adamant on his commitment to W. L. Comyn. "It never became an argument," Effinger emphasizes. "We merely acknowledged that we were parting company each for our own reasons."

In fact Grinnell never gave Claude Effinger his own reasons for joining the camp of the most powerful individual in British Columbia's lumber export trade. He simply wanted Effinger to join him, and spelled out the advantages that would accrue if he did so. Next day Grinnell went east and Effinger went west, with no expectation in Effinger's mind that they would ever be together again in a business enterprise.

Some of those who attribute convoluted motives to Grinnell's joining MacMillan suggest that he had a master plan in mind which could only be achieved after personal experience with the MacMillan group. Others say that he was singled out by one or more of the members of Astexo, in particular Henry Mackin, to infiltrate the MacMillan camp, confirm suspicions that MacMillan was selling the Astexo mills short, and then emerge with a battle plan. The truth will never by known, although it is more likely that Grinnell and the Astexo proponents had a meeting of minds, possibly shortly after Grinnell went to work for MacMillan.

Effinger had expected to take over Grinnell's abdicated position with the W. L. Comyn Company but discovered when he reached Vancouver that Comyn had hired someone else. He could have stayed in a lesser capacity, but he elected instead to phone Comyn in San Francisco to tell him he was quitting. "I'm getting married," he said.

Claude Effinger did get married within a few weeks of his departure from W. L. Comyn. His wife, Helen, was a newspaper journalist who would ultimately become womens' editor of the *Vancouver Sun,* a position she held with distinction for a number of years.

The couple honeymooned at Harrison Hot Springs Spa. A. D. Anderson, the logger cum mill owner who had built Harrison Hotsprings, happened to be there on the honeymoon night, as were a number of others of the lumber fraternity, including Melville Dollar and his wife, who were up for the weekend. It is to be suspected that the newlyweds were accorded little privacy. Effinger learned from Dollar that W. L. Comyn was in Seattle and was eager to meet with him, which may have been the reason that Claude Effinger and his new wife found themselves in Seattle on the next leg of their honeymoon being royally entertained by the company's owner.

Overnight Effinger was reinstated with the Comyn group in Vancouver. (The new man had not worked out.) It was March 1927, and Claude Effinger, just married and now promoted, could not have been in a much better situation. He handled Comyn's Canadian transactions smoothly enough until 10 May 1928, when Charles Grinnell telephoned him. "I'm leaving MacMillan," he announced. "We're setting up a company with Astexo mills to sell CIF to the U.S. Atlantic seaboard. I'd like to have you with me."

It was a concept that both excited and challenged Effinger. He agreed to join, on the understanding that he could make suitable arrangements with Comyn. This he was able to do amicably. And when the new, upstart company, Seaboard Lumber Sales Limited,* began business on 1 June 1928, Charles Grinnell and Claude Effinger were together again.

* This was the first company's name. The present company's name is Seaboard Lumber Sales Company Limited.

·FOUR·

INSURRECTION & THE AFTERMATH

Dissatisfaction was surfacing. Power was beginning to resent power. There were those in the Astexo group who openly expressed their feelings about H. R. MacMillan. The man, in their opinion, was an interloper, a Johnny-come-lately who had dared to cross over from academe and public service to invade and conquer the world of their business. What galled them even more was that he had, by reason of prior knowledge and impressive foresight, leapfrogged over their established ways of doing things and gained a firm grip on British Columbia's export markets. It mattered little that the Astexo mills, through their sales to H. R. MacMillan Export over an interval of nine years, had profited more than modestly. It mattered much that H. R. MacMillan might be taking a lion's share.

We must remember that one of the reasons for Astexo's formation was ultimately to deal direct in overseas markets. This intention had been lost sight of in the first rosy years, when it was convenient to sell to MacMillan, allowing him to obtain the orders and arrange for shipment, while they could pick up their cheques without delay immediately upon delivery of lumber to ship's side. Under this arrangement, more than thirty mills, most of them for the first time, were manufacturing lumber for export and making a profit. Why rock the boat?

And then Astexo's key figures began to take stock of the situation. The Astexo member mills' main dealings were with H. R. MacMillan Export, although there were a number of smaller exporters and brokers in business at the time. It was MacMillan's role to obtain orders from the overseas markets, mainly the United Kingdom and the United States. He then purchased lumber principally from the Astexo mills to fill these orders. (He bought some lumber from Washington and Oregon also.) As well, it was MacMillan's responsibility to arrange for shipment. In the first years he derived his profits from his ability to extract a high price from the overseas importers, and to purchase lumber from the Astexo mills at as low a price as he could manage. It was good business.

In 1924, possibly taking a page from the book of W. L. Comyn, MacMillan established his own shipping subsidiary, Canadian Transport Company, and thus positioned himself to control not only sales to the importer and purchases from the mills but to take advantage of freight rates as well. This, it seemed to Astexo mill men like Mackin, Pendleton and Cameron, was clearly a licence to steal. Astexo was not privy to the prices MacMillan commanded from the importers nor had they any control over the freight rates charged by his shipping company. Furthermore, they had considerable reason to believe that Mac-Millan's procedure was to accumulate overseas orders and hold them until the mills were hungry enough for business to sell at lower prices. As Claude Effinger expresses it: "It was not good. I was present at many formative meetings when the Astexo executive members held forth. Much of what they relied on was hearsay, partial fact and intelligent guessing; but it added up to anger and a decision to do something about it."

MacMillan, on the other hand, was not entirely happy with Astexo's performance. Some of the large member mills such as Canadian Western, Victoria Lumber & Manufacturing and Hillcrest had established regular customers overseas, and these they continued to supply directly without recourse to H. R. MacMillan Export. It would have been much neater and more logical, in MacMillan's estimation, to channel all export business through his company. He stated publicly that the direct dealing of these mills could only serve to confuse agents and importers in the overseas markets. In Effinger's personal opinion, a man with a good idea—Charles Grinnell—appeared at a time when Astexo was looking for a way out of a dilemma. "Grinnell was not happy at MacMillan's," he states. "He could see what was going on, and he could see that if the mills joined ranks they could circumvent not only MacMillan but all the other exporters. His plan was to deal direct with the market he knew best—the U.S. Atlantic Coast."

No doubt a similar scheme was forming in the minds of the Astexo leaders. "Some spent most of their time planning the overthrow," Effinger remembers. "The active ones were [H. J.] Mackin, [C. J.] Culter, [J. G.] Robson, [J. H.] McDonald, F. R. Pendleton, Carlton Stone, the Cameron brothers, John Humbird, Bruce Farris; those were the ones I remember most clearly. They all agreed that MacMillan had gone too far, buying low, selling high and controlling freight rates. Three profits were too much."

Seaboard Lumber Sales Limited started business on 1 June 1928, occupying a small office in the Metropolitan Building. Grinnell and Effinger shared a double desk and directed their energies to the development of U.S. and Canadian East Coast business, as well as to the recruitment of additional member mills. First president of Seaboard was F. R. Pendleton of Straits Lumber Company. Members of the Board were: Henry Mackin, Canadian Western; F. E. Reid, Barnett Sawmills; J. D. Kissinger, Canadian Puget Sound Lumber Company; John H. McDonald, B.C. Manufacturing, Westminster Shook, Maple Ridge Lumber; G. Robin Hackett, Robertson & Hackett Sawmill; John A. Humbird, Victoria Lumber.

The express purpose of the company was to sell the export production of Astexo and other member mills to the U.S. Atlantic Coast market on a CIF basis, taking advantage of the disparity between U.S. rail and international charter freight rates. U.S. rail rates were inordinately high and there was no through rate across the United States. Under the Jones Act, U.S. lumber buyers paid American shipping companies an Intercoastal Conference rate that compared with U.S. rail charges, and was considerably higher than international charter freight rates. B.C. lumber exporters, and now Seaboard Lumber Sales Limited, could make tremendous profits by chartering foreign flag vessels at the lower rates and charging the U.S. buyer the U.S. intercoastal freight rate based on the rail rate.

Seaboard Lumber Sales assembled a staff quickly. Grinnell, no doubt, had his people in mind well in advance of any formal announcement. Claude Effinger, of course, was an obvious choice by reason of past association. He knew the business and he knew the market they were about to move into. Also, these two had learned to work together efficiently and without undue friction.

Executive secretary Louise Marchesi followed Charles Grinnell from H. R. MacMillan's. Her considerable talents included her skill as a typist; she was the current Canadian speed typing champion. Also persuaded to leave MacMillan's were Madge Scott and Violet (Prendergast) Pritchard. H. E. (Hap) Solloway, with a proven record in the shipping business, was hired to take charge of the company's shipping requirements and the booking of space. Shortly after that, Lloyd Ford, recommended for his ability to expedite the movement of lumber from mill to vessel, was brought from a sawmill at Fort McNeil and put in charge of the traffic department. Rube Scotcher came from Hastings Mill to take charge of the documents department. Stewart Slater was hired to keep the books. Rounding out the staff were Frank Pendleton, Arthur Anthony, Ronald Gordon, Steven Kingley, Frank Hemming and Hazel Black. And then there was the obvious need to man offices in the marketplace. Charles Grinnell, drawing from his previous experience and contacts in the United States, appointed an American, G. D. Anderson, to take charge of Seaboard's New York office. To Boston he sent W. F. Tucker Battle, American born but raised and educated in British Columbia.

Mill members at the time of Seaboard's formation were: Barnett Lumber Company Ltd., B.C. Manufacturing Company Limited, Canadian Puget Sound Company Ltd., Canadian Western Lumber Company, Dominion Mills Company Ltd., Mohawk Lumber Company Limited, Rat Portage Lumber Company Ltd., Robertson & Hackett Sawmill Company, Straits Lumber Company Limited, Timberland Lumber Company Limited, Victoria Lumber & Manufacturing Company Limited, Alberni Pacific Lumber Company and J. Hanbury & Company Ltd.

Seaboard was launched, staffed and prepared to make inroads into the frenetic and buoyant markets of America's Eastern Seaboard. The years 1928 and 1929 would raise the hopes and the expectations of the Seaboard mills to the maximum. The mills functioning through Astexo continued to sell lumber to MacMillan and the other exporters for all other markets, but there can be no doubt that a new pattern had been set with the creation of Seaboard.

In 1928 and 1929 B.C. sales to the U.S. Eastern Seaboard continued to escalate, with Canadian domestic sales accounting for 55 per cent of total sales, 18 per cent to overseas markets, and 27 per cent to the United States by rail and particularly by water. Then October 1929 saw the onset of the Great Depression, an event that the countries of the world were ill-prepared for, coming as it did out of an apparent boom. Like many other major industries, the British Columbia lumber industry failed to appreciate the severity and universality of the Depression, or to foresee its longevity. In the spring of 1930 the *British Columbia*

Lumberman announced proudly that the exports of sawn lumber for the first three months of that year were the largest in recent years.

Another demonstration of unfortunate optimism, perhaps, was the Astexo mills' decision to form a shipping company primarily to control the movement of lumber to the East Coast, as MacMillan was doing with his Canadian Transport Company. On 24 February 1931 Marine Shipping Company was incorporated. The Board of Directors consisted of F. R. Pendleton, Ross Pendleton, H. J. Mackin, C. J. Culter, J. G Robson, J. D. Kissinger, G. R. Hackett and J. H. McDonald. F. R. Pendleton was elected president and John A. Humbird, vice-president.

The specific reasons for taking this action are difficult to determine in the light of what these astute businessmen knew then, and what was soon to occur. The Depression was a grim reality, and other storm clouds were clearly evident above the horizon. First of all, the U.S. railways, in an effort to regain some of the freight business they had lost to intercoastal and foreign flag shipping, made their rates more competitive on a transcontinental basis, which succeeded in attracting many mills back to rail. Secondly, the ravages of the Depression caused the United States lumber industry to close ranks in an attempt to keep its own mills and labour force working. As early as 1929 the United States, intent on protecting the lumber industry in Washington and Oregon, was threatening to impose a tariff on B.C. lumber and shingles.

British Columbia millowners did not remain passive under this attack but protested vigorously that 80 per cent of the shingles they produced were high grade, bearing no resemblance, and threatening no competition, to the flat-grained, low-priced shingles which were the main product of U.S. mills. J. H. Bloedel, with mills in both British Columbia and Washington state, argued vehemently against such tariff threats. He pointed out that there was very little difference in production costs, and that British Columbia was not indulging in price exploitation in supplying a U.S. demand for quality shingles and other lumber products. H. R. MacMillan, speaking to the United States National Foreign Trade Council in Baltimore in April 1929, declared that "there is considerable opposition to [the proposed tariff] across the boundary, and practically every retail lumbermen's association handling Canadian materials has declared strongly against it."

On the whole, however, Canada maintained a reasonably controlled stance in the face of the growing U.S. tariff threat, choosing to make its case formally through government channels and trade associations. This attitude was not imitated by the Americans. The U.S. press made much of the Canadian threat to the U.S. lumber industry and trade, arguing with some accuracy that British Columbia was profiting from advantageous ocean freight rates. More than one journalist claimed that B.C. was able to keep its lumber prices down by exploiting cheap immigrant labour, failing to observe that the U.S. lumber industry drew from a substantial immigrant population as well.

B.C. journalists countered with the accusation that the U.S. lumber industry was the instigator of its own dilemma through large-scale overproduction resulting in prices so low that mills were being driven out of business. This parry and thrust at the press level did little more than fan the flames. Millowners in the process of being crushed by world forces few of them understood clearly struck out at the apparent enemy.

The U.S.-based West Coast Lumbermen's Association lobbied vigorously for a 50 per cent increase ($1.50 a thousand feet) in import duty on Canadian lumber. In 1930 a bill to this effect was narrowly defeated by Congress, and in May 1932 the tariff battle came to a conclusion with the passage of the Smoot-Hawley Act, which imposed the prohibitively high tariff of $4 a thousand feet on lumber entering the United States from Canada. With U.S. buyers able to purchase lumber domestically at $10 to $12 a thousand feet, the $4 tariff on Canadian lumber made it impossible for B.C. mills to compete in the U.S. market. Shipments of $360 million in the late twenties dropped to $12 million in 1934.

The effect of the depressed economy coupled with the imposition of the U.S. tariff placed many of the Seaboard mills in jeopardy and sent some into bankruptcy. A number of them, as well as some unattached mills, stopped their saws, never to activate them again. Others, with the resources to carry them through the bad times, ceased operations and waited anxiously for any sign of an improving economy.

MacMillan, in the meantime, had consolidated his corporate position by restructuring the H. R. MacMillan Export Company to qualify as a federal company entitling it to capitalize surplus earnings without being taxed. With the U.S. market virtually closed, he exerted great efforts to build up business in Australia and New Zealand, and he was far from alone in this endeavour; the B.C. Lumber and Shingle Manufacturers' Association launched a trade extension program in 1929 aimed initially at Australia and extending to New Zealand.

These overseas markets, combined with fluctuating trade happenings in the United Kingdom, kept MacMillan in reasonably solvent condition as a broker, and enabled some of the Astexo mills to keep their doors open. The concerted action on the part of a large group of U.K. importers to purchase 800 million feet of Russian timber was cause for real alarm, not to be assuaged by the marked reduction of the U.K. rail tie business.

In spite of these setbacks, or perhaps because of them, MacMillan assumed a position of strength, seeing the opportunity to discourage his opposition for good and all. As the Depression gathered momentum in 1929, he stated categorically that "this company [H. R. MacMillan Export] is still by the far the best instrument in existence for its purpose, and Canadian business will not be furthered by breaking it down, particularly as business we lose passes out of control by going to 100 per cent American firms, there being no other Canadian firms combining the necessary components of staff experience, finance and single-minded devotion to foreign trade." The members of troubled Seaboard must have studied these words with mixed emotions and when, a few years later, after the imposition of the Smoot-Hawley tariff, he attributed that unfortunate event to the Seaboard mills, he could not have increased his popularity to any extent.

MacMillan is on record in correspondence as stating that Seaboard's entry into the U.S. Atlantic Coast market had begun conventionally with the established wholesalers in that region. Gradually the wholesalers were dispensed with as Seaboard began to sell direct to their customers. "This," he contended, "finally earned for the Seaboard Sales the hostility of the wholesalers."

Then, in his estimation, Seaboard further antagonized established American business. "As the strength of the Seaboard Sales developed," he wrote, "the management discovered in their hands a great power in control over freight, which power they used almost entirely against the interests of the Conference American InterCoastal [Shipping Lines] by continuously chartering below Conference rates and making almost negligible employment of American vessels, thereby bringing the American Shipowners' Association into the field as strong, aggressive enemies." This, in fact, was an accurate description of his own tactics.

The United States' strong and protective action against the import of Canadian lumber was, of course, a direct reflection of its own depressed lumber trade. John Humbird, in his journal, states that Astexo's condition was so serious and the sales positions of its member mills so threatened that an effort was made in 1931 to unite not only with equivalent organizations in the United States, but with major exporters as well in an attempt to find strength through unity and co-operation on a much larger scale.

He reported that conditions had become so bad in 1931 that an effort was made to get together the four main mill selling agencies (Associated

Timber Exporters, Douglas Fir Exploitation and Export, Grays Harbour Export and Dant & Russell) with the three larger exporters (H. R. MacMillan Export, J. J. Moore and Balfour Guthrie) in an organization known as the United Lumber Export Association. Mackin, McConville and Humbird were named to represent Astexo. A form of contract between exporters and selling agencies was drawn up but eventually fell through because one exporter withdrew support. Humbird's journal does not reveal the name of the one exporter, but the result was that the association failed in its objectives, and Astexo found itself hard-pressed to remain in business.

Under the circumstances, the Astexo shareholders decided to suspend company operations of both Seaboard Sales and Marine Shipping rather than to close them permanently. A convenient and useful repository for the two companies was found with Grinnell Export Lumber Company Ltd., formed by C. H. Grinnell when Seaboard ceased to function. While Grinnell would attempt to conduct export business on his own behalf, he would also undertake to represent the interests of the two latent companies.

His procedure would be, as the *British Columbia Lumberman* reported in March 1933, "to work with and for the mills, and to make a special effort to move those items which previously were taken by markets which, unfortunately, for the time being at least, are closed to us. The firm intends to concentrate on the United Kingdom, Australia, China, and Japan markets, and to bend every effort to obtain a larger volume of business at better prices for the mills from these important markets." He would take commissions and fees for this service and, in the case of Marine Shipping, for the consideration of one dollar a month would take care of whatever rudimentary paperwork or administration that might be called for.

He set up an office at 831 Marine Building, Vancouver, and moved in a staff to generate business in any lumber market available to him. His people were recruited mainly from the ruins of Seaboard. (Claude Effinger joined Grinnell's enterprise for a brief period and then left for a sales position with the Shell Oil Company.) Tucker Battle returned from Boston to take charge of Eastern Seaboard business from head office. G. D. Anderson, Seaboard's man in New York, now became Grinnell's man in the same city. A. S. Penketh, manager of the Douglas Fir Exploitation and Export Company in Seattle, opened an office in that city for Grinnell. And in September 1933 Wilfred Mitchell, formerly manager of H. R. MacMillan Export's U.K. department, joined Grinnell in Vancouver, an acquisition of considerable significance since he brought with him experience and insight into the British marketplace that had eluded Grinnell up until then.

Wick Gray, hired as a junior clerk and switchboard operator, and now a timber executive in his own right, states that Grinnell lost little time in establishing solid sales connections not only in the United Kingdom but in other markets as well including the Far East where he gained entrée to China through the China Import and Export Company in Hong Kong. He had always been attracted to Australia as a market worth nurturing and he soon established sales contacts with the tough traders in that country. In the U.K. he secured close associations with Duncan Ewing, Denny, Mott & Dickson, Boyson Neame, Churchill and Sim, among others, including Hunt Leuchars, a firm with valuable trade contacts in South Africa. The Astexo mills that had not succumbed to the Depression and the ravages of the U.S. tariff were dependent once more largely on sales of lumber to the other overseas markets.

Now some of the Astexo mills had been through their first, albeit unsuccessful, skirmish in direct selling, ending in the temporary defeat of Seaboard. They had gained more knowledge of export procedures and had gleaned more information from the overseas markets as to the specific needs and preferences of the buyers. They had begun to establish an image overseas through the market extension efforts of the BCLSMA and had learned the tremendous value of periodic visits to the marketplaces. Most important of all, Astexo mills had gained an appreciation of their true bargaining position. All of the pieces were in place for the next major move.

* * *

The overriding and far-reaching damage of the Depression, followed by the punishment meted out by the Smoot-Hawley tariff, spelled the end for many British Columbia mills without the resources to ride out the storm. On the other hand, these world disasters served as a catalyst to the British Columbia lumber industry as a whole. Threatened with the very real prospect of an industry-wide shutdown or setback extending over years, millowners, lumber associations, exporters and governments joined forces to stimulate sales in existing overseas markets, as well as to seek out new markets. It was apparent that Seaboard's having relied on one market was a weakness.

While Seaboard and Marine Shipping were dormant, the surviving Astexo mills were among the most active in this fight for survival. The prospect of failure was the adrenalin that motivated them all and fuelled their struggle to survive. Headlines in Victoria's *Daily Colonist* on

24 May 1932 read, "Canada may lose trade worth $28 million last year with lumber duty increase . . .," and articles on retaliation began making their appearance. One suggestion was the exclusion of U.S. hardwoods, a trade worth about $20 million annually to the U.S. The *New York Lumber Trade Journal* pointed out that Canada's curtailing the import of hardwood lumber from the U.S. would hurt many eastern mills.

Vancouver's *Province* spoke of "the rising tide of indignation in the world" against tariff policies that threatened the material welfare of the world. Canada had been forced to make "a different kind of budget." Great Britain was being forced to abandon her free trade policies because the U.S. wanted to "sell its own goods everywhere but buy its neighbours' goods not at all." The result, the *Province* writer concluded, would be the paralysis of world trade. The *British Columbia Lumberman* editorialised that many U.S. lumbermen and economists were actually opposed to the tariff, and pointed optimistically to historical precedent which showed that any tariff against Canadian lumber products was always abolished in a very short time because it was never to the advantage of anyone in the long run.

Despite the huge impact of the Smoot-Hawley tariff, Canadian reaction seems to have been relatively restrained. An editorial in the *British Columbia Lumberman* in June 1934 commented that throughout the tariff squabbles, B.C. demonstrated tolerance, recognizing "the driving hardships in the U.S. fir industry brought on by unparalleled depression. . . . rather the lumbermen of B.C. were bewildered by the fearsome height of the barrier [that was imposed in 1932] and the suddenness of its erection, and were stunned at the loss of what was their most important market during the hardest times in their history."

The British Columbia Lumber and Shingle Manufacturers Association, later called the British Columbia Lumber Manufacturers Association, had learned a great deal about market extension tactics since its formation in 1903. Knowledge is one thing, but the capacity and desire to benefit from that knowledge is quite another. The BCLSMA had gathered considerable information on the lumber preferences and accepted standards of the overseas customers, and it had been urged by such assiduous and hard-working representatives in the United Kingdom as Loren Brown to adopt these preferences and standards. Brown and others had urged, as well, a program of education and indoctrination to make overseas customers more aware of B.C. woods, their qualities and their accepted dimensions and uses. Not all of these recommendations were taken seriously or acted upon in the prosperous twenties. Now the time had come for some serious reconsideration and a frontal attack on market extension.

In 1929 the BCLSMA launched a trade extension program in co-operation with the provincial and federal governments. Their first big effort was in Australia, and in the fall of that year a "party of business executives" (J. H. McDonald, T. T. Gadd and J. G. Robson) left for that country. Maj. L. R. Andrews, B.C.'s lumber trade commissioner for Australia, was also very active in market extension work, and the result of their combined efforts was the signing of a treaty between Canada and Australia that came into effect in July 1931. It enabled B.C. to boost its share of the Australian softwood market from 50 per cent to 83 per cent.

Both Andrews and the delegation also visited New Zealand where they found less favourable response. But in 1931, after a major earth-quake in which the collapse of brick buildings caused many deaths, the advantages of timber construction became more apparent and accepta-ble. However, the effects of the Depression were just beginning to be felt deeply in New Zealand. This in addition to high lumber import duties limited market extension possibilities for B.C.

The U.S. tariff made new markets imperative, and the logical place to turn was Britain. In June 1931 Loren Brown, joint B.C. government and lumber industry trade commissioner in England, was in Ottawa for consultations and assured lumbermen that he would spare no effort to secure preferential treatment and improve British attitudes to B.C. lumber. He lobbied hard in London, helping to pave the way for the Imperial Economic Conference held in Ottawa in August 1932. Brown had already advised B.C. that a strong "trade within the Empire" sen-timent was detectable in Britain but pointed out that the one major obstacle he was encountering was the frequent lack of unassailable evidence that lumber being sold from B.C. actually originated there. A letter from the Honourable Nels Lougheed, Minister of Forests, to all mills early in 1932 urged them to brand all lumber consigned to the U.S. Astexo mills would use that name as their identifying mark, but all others were asked to use the mark CAN—TIM, which had recently been registered by the BCLSMA.

While this and other product-identifying, image-building measures initiated by B.C. government and the industry were undoubtedly efficacious, nothing could work positive changes to compare with the action taken by the United Kingdom. In July of 1932 prime ministers of all the Dominions, each supported by committees and advisers, con-vened in Ottawa to work out an agreement that would counter the

effects of the U.S. Smoot-Hawley lumber tariff on the one hand and on
the other, protect the trading positions of the Dominions for all commodities. The final document was titled the Imperial Preference Agreement, and it was to be a life-restoring transfusion for the Canadian
lumber industry.

The "trade within the Empire" sentiment dominated the Economic
Conference and saved the day for British Columbia's lumber industry.
McDonald and Robson of Astexo, H. R. MacMillan and Major Andrews were among the lumber delegates to the conference. On behalf of
Canadian lumbermen they requested a 20 per cent preference in Britain's softwood market and a quota system that would ensure Canada
one-third of the softwood business, the balance to be delivered by quota
with other softwood countries, Russia being given the minimum quota.
At this time, depressed business and currency conditions in Baltic countries made their timber so competitive that only a quota would assure
Canada a share of the market. Members of the British Timber Federation who were in Ottawa as unofficial delegates did not oppose the 20
per cent preference or the proposal that Canada receive one-third of the
business, but they strongly opposed government quotas or restrictions.
Britain had been a free trade nation for over 100 years, and this tradition was hard to break.

The conference covered all British Empire countries, and Canadian
delegates were busy negotiating for 10 per cent preferences with the
member countries. Of course, they had already settled trade conditions
with Australia and New Zealand. South Africa, one of the few countries
still solvent in 1932, was a promising possibility. The U.K. signed
treaties with Canada, Australia, New Zealand, South Africa, India,
Newfoundland and Southern Rhodesia, and bilateral pacts were apparently signed between these members of the Empire. However, for
Canada the pact with Britain was to be by far the most important.

The agreement that was finally signed gave Canada an increase of 10
per cent lumber preference (making the overall preference 20 per cent)
for a period of five years, and protection from Russian dumping. Article
21, which covered the dumping, was intended to prevent a repeat of the
spring 1932 action of the Soviet government in shipping 800 million
feet of lumber to Great Britain and selling it at uncompetitively low
prices. In that instance Britain's own free trade policies had hamstrung
every effort to combat the dumping, despite indignant outbursts in the
press against the indentured labour conditions at Soviet mills and the
unfairness of the Soviet dealings. However, Article 21 stated that Britain
intended "hereafter to take measures to prohibit the entry from such
foreign countries directly or indirectly of such commodities into its

country for such time as may be necessary to make effective and to maintain the preferences hereby granted by it."

There must have been some Canadian dissatisfaction with the outcome of the conference because in October 1932 *British Columbia Lumberman* ran an editorial attacking the critics of the conference for "looking a very serviceable gift horse in the mouth." It pointed out that Britain's abandonment of its free trade policies was an extraordinary step in itself, and that those who hoped to see immediate results were being unrealistic—the export trade would have to be built up and worked at, but the potential was unlimited."

The industry's first step in building up export to this new protected market was to send a delegation to the U.K. led by H. J. Mackin who was accompanied by J. G. Robson, F. R. Pendleton, M. A. Grainger (British Columbia's Chief Forester) and C. H. Grinnell. They sailed in October, and on the same day Major Andrews sailed for China on a similar mission of trade extension and goodwill.

The delegation visited London, Liverpool, Manchester and Glasgow. It is referred to in speeches in England as the British Columbia Timber Delegation, and is described in *British Columbia Lumberman* as being "thoroughly representative of the B.C. lumber industry," but the exclusive Astexo composition is significant. The intention was to become more knowledgeable on the requirements of the British market and to explore every possibility of increasing trade. The men inspected the huge housing development of the London County Council which had used B.C. timber, sawn to B.C. standard sizes, exclusively.

Several speeches delivered by the Canadian delegates conceded that the visit should have come much earlier. Mackin said that until this visit they had not understood, for instance, that timber used for construction in the U.K. had so little machine work done on it and was used unplaned (rough cut). They also met an indignant Scottish merchant who for years had bought 26-foot lengths in order to cut them himself into 13-foot lengths, ignorant of the fact that B.C. sawmillers were eager to sell the shorter lengths at lower prices.

Robson made an important speech to the Building Division of the British Standards Institution in London concerning B.C. "scant" sizes one-quarter inch under the true dimensions after passing through the sizing machine. Despite the scepticism of some British buyers, research at the Forest Products Labs of both countries had proved that there was actually greater strength in B.C.'s "scant" timbers than in the "full size" Baltic timbers. Also the sizing meant that the lumber was absolutely uniform, which the Baltic timbers were not. Of course, the advantage to B.C. was that scant sizes gave substantial freight advantages to offset the cost of greater distance. The U.S. market had already accepted B.C.'s scant sizes, and the delegation emphasized that it was an important part of the mission to have these sizes accepted.

Despite much goodwill and lavish hospitality, the mission failed to negotiate a contract for bulk sales of softwood, primarily because North European (Russian) prices were so low. The Anglo-Soviet trade agreement did not expire until April 1933, but after that Britain invoked Article 21, and imports from Russia were embargoed for two months and then cut substantially. Canada picked up much of the benefit.

The delegation did succeed, however, in winning recognition of Canadian lumber standards by the large departments of the governments—the city of London, the great municipalities and other public bodies—as well as by major contractors and prominent architects. Loren Brown reported in September 1933, for instance, that B.C. fir paving blocks had been purchased by the London Metro Boroughs of Holborn, Islington, Finsbury and Hackney, by Middlesex County Council, by the City of Bristol, by the City of Hull, and that fir carcassing stock had been ordered by various post offices and telephone exchanges. The City of Bristol also agreed to allow the use of B.C. scant stock in the building of a 3000-home development. In 1934 a house built entirely of Empire timber (90 per cent of it from B.C.) was featured at the five-day Royal Show in Ipswich and widely advertised; Loren Brown had his London office panelled in B.C. red cedar and produced two booklets advertising red cedar and red cedar shingles. Brown organized exhibits at all shows, notably the Building Trades Exhibition at London's Olympia exhibition centre at which more than a dozen B.C. firms were represented.

The delegation also recommended that an assistant to Brown be appointed. This led to a second man being sent in 1933 and a third in 1934, plus a shingler to teach British craftsmen how to shingle houses. By 1934, 450 million feet of sawn lumber alone was supplied to Great Britain, more than had ever been shipped to the U.S. Atlantic Coast or California in any one year to that date. Market extension work was energetically continued. During the first six months of 1934 the total volume of overseas business exceeded the total for the whole of 1929—and this despite a worldwide Depression.

Major Andrews' mission to China was quite successful too. He reported in the November 1932 issue of *British Columbia Lumberman* that "during the past 15 years B.C. has shipped nearly 400 million feet of sawn lumber to China . . . 25 per cent in 1930–31." The volume of trade was steadily improving, with China the fourth largest overseas market, mainly because they would take low grade material, the disposal of which was so necessary to the equable distribution of the log cut. In January 1934 Major Andrews was sent to Australia by Astexo to "straighten out a few kinks" despite the fact that B.C. lumber was dominating that market at this time.

On 20 September 1934 a B.C. Lumber Trade Mission left for South Africa, travelling via Ottawa and London. Members were J. H. McDonald, at that time chairman of the export committee of the B.C. Lumber Manufacturers Association and managing director of B.C. Manufacturing Company, a shareholder of the dormant Marine Shipping Company, as well as a director of the equally latent Seaboard; A. T. Robson, sales manager of Timberland; P. Z. Calverhall, B.C.'s new Chief Forester, and R. B. Cherry, president of Sterling Lumber. At this time South Africa was importing only 9 per cent of her softwoods from Canada (compared to 75 per cent from Russia and Baltic countries and 16 per cent from the U.S.). The delegation found that Canada was considered to be a supplier of long length lumber only, and they corrected this impression. They also succeeded in having Canadian lumber accepted as standard for all public works and railway work, and successfully negotiated an effective rate on lumber on the subsidized steamship service to South Africa, and an equalization of rail rates on lumber to Johannesburg and other points. The concessions amounted to $100,000, almost twice the amount appropriated by the provincial government in 1933 for market extension work all over the world.

All was not smooth sailing, however. On 19 July 1935 Japan placed a 50 per cent surtax—virtually an embargo—on all imports of B.C. lumber as a result of unequal trade balances. This meant a $6-million loss of trade in timber products for the industry. In the same year the silver purchase policy of the U.S. injured the credit of China (a silver standard country) and reduced its purchasing power, so British Columbia lost most of that trade too. Because of these losses, in one year 25 per cent of its export market disappeared.

In June 1935 Loren Brown retired from his position as B.C.'s lumber commissioner in the United Kingdom. As an interesting aside, some of Astexo's leaders in 1933 attempted once again to enter the U.K. market on a CIF basis, running in the face of the majority of mill members. At that time, because of Loren Brown's outstanding effort in the U.K. and the respect with which he was regarded in that country, he was offered the position of manager of an Astexo office in London. The feeling was that Brown's involvement might overcome the opposition of the Astexo majority, but this did not happen, and the office never opened.

Concurrent with these marketing forays were a number of related shipping activities, both national and provincial, which affected the

West Coast lumber industry. In the early twenties the Canadian government merchant marine opened up sales outlets in Australia and the Orient. As we have already seen, H. R. MacMillan's Canadian Transport Company was formed in 1924 and the Marine Shipping Company was organized in 1931.

In 1929 representatives of B.C.'s lumber exporting firms applied for a subsidy from the Canadian government for a freight service from B.C. ports to the Commonwealth countries. Although the Vancouver manager of the Union Steamship Company of New Zealand protested that some of his ships had room for lumber, both Astexo and MacMillan claimed that they had frequently been told no room was available on that company's ships for such cargoes.

In May 1932 Ottawa reviewed its subsidies for shipping and elected to reduce them by 25 per cent. Among other actions it cancelled a $92,000 subsidy to the ABC Shipping Company for maintaining a freight service to China. H. R. MacMillan's shipping company and shipping subsidiaries suffered from the cutbacks, and he joined other shippers and exporters in a strong organized protest which ultimately produced the desired results. An article in the February 1933 issue of the *British Columbia Lumberman* reported that the subsidy on shipping had been renewed. The same publication, in January 1934, mentions that Vancouver was sending a vessel a day overseas with a load of lumber, and that the ports of New Westminster, Victoria, Chemainus and Port Alberni were surpassing all records for waterborne shipments.

It was this healthy state of affairs that encouraged the mills to take a direct interest in the overseas markets once more.

·FIVE·

REFORMATION

Although a number of the Astexo mills might have been disenchanted with the final outcome of their incursion into the U.S. East Coast markets, and though several failed to weather the combined punishment of Depression and tariff strangulation, the stronger mills and the more determined owners extended their energies and resources to save the industry through the expansion of existing markets and the creation of new ones.

Fortuitous happenings, such as the strength of the United Kingdom market and the opening up of the Japanese and Chinese markets in 1932, assisted substantially; as did the influence of product education and promotion. For the time being at least, the lumber exporters, H. R. MacMillan in particular, continued as the overseas export brokers. The Astexo mills had continued their traditional role as suppliers to the export companies. On the surface, the mill/exporter relationship was restored.

The apparent restoration of order was an illusion, of course. Nothing would ever be the same again. Severely bruised though the mills may have been, they had tasted a few years of success as direct exporters to the U.S.A. before disaster struck. They could not remove from their minds the memory of the satisfaction they had experienced as sellers and freighters no longer dependent on exporter middlemen in the U.S. trade.

The exporters were well aware of this increasing restiveness. H. R. MacMillan in particular must have felt deep concern when Astexo leaders joined with Charles Grinnell in the late summer of 1933 to test the export waters in the United Kingdom. R. H. (Bob) Edgett, who would rise through the Seaboard ranks to become one of its sales executives, tells the story.

MacMillan appeared to be securely ensconced in the United Kingdom market, teamed as he was with Montague Meyer, and thereby well-established with the agents, importers and government agencies. Meyer's decision, in 1927, to relinquish his partnership with MacMillan was motivated primarily by the possibility of embarrassment in dealing with Britain's lumber buyers. He could not wear two hats comfortably. Another suggested reason for the partnership dissolution was that MacMillan had made his first tentative moves into sawmilling, a policy which Meyer was thought to have opposed. In his opinion, their legitimate and exclusive business was the buying and selling of lumber products.

Disassociated in name but still closely involved, the two continued to conduct a thriving business through the smoothly functioning machinery of the CANUSA Trading Company. It was an extremely difficult fortress to breach. MacMillan, through the influence and the established reputation of Montague Meyer, had secured the inside track without breaking any of the traditional trading rules. The chance of any other Canadian export organizaton doing the same was very slim.

Edgett reports that the Astexo executives' restlessness was mounting, aggravated once more by the suspicion that MacMillan was accumulating overseas orders and holding them until the mills would accept lower prices. Nor was MacMillan alone; Vancouver was still headquarters for surviving lumber exporters enjoying what would be their last period of affluence at the expense of the supplying mills.

Astexo could deal with MacMillan, or try to make a better deal with smaller exporters. Either way was unsatisfactory. Astexo had been warned that some of the smaller exporters had side arrangements with MacMillan. One company in particular, Coast Mills Export, was suspected of being owned by MacMillan although it operated as a separate entity; could it be purchasing from Astexo mills to MacMillan's direct or indirect advantage?

Whatever the truth of the situation, troubling facts blended with dark rumour to produce a smouldering resentment in the Astexo ranks. This was sharpened by information arriving from the United Kingdom that

MacMillan and Meyer had secured a large rail tie order at a substantial price and had offered the order to the mills at a much lower price. This was the final straw. Astexo's leaders, notably John Humbird, spurred on by an irate Henry Mackin, decided to take direct action.

Humbird's family owned Victoria Lumber & Manufacturing and Mackin was a power at Canadian Western; they represented two of the largest mills in the province, both with their own export customers as well as their export arrangements through Astexo. It is to be suspected that principle as much as the need for new business prompted them to attempt an invasion of the U.K. market to break the stranglehold which MacMillan's and CANUSA had secured on the U.K. Rail and Admiralty business.

Edgett emphasizes the sacrosanct and time-honoured system prevailing in the United Kingdom at that time: in those days the British timber agents held the dominant position in the trading hierarchy. It was unheard of for exporters of whatever nation to do business with U.K. importers except through an established British agent. The one exception was H. R. MacMillan in tandem with Montague Meyer through CANUSA.

Astexo's strategy was to work with and through Charles Grinnell, now in the export business and representing Astexo mills on a sub rosa basis wherever he could find markets. What happened now would establish Grinnell's credibility with the mills beyond question. Grinnell had developed a close relationship with Denny, Mott & Dickson, one of the leading importers in the U.K. His contact (and later, personal friend) was Percy Harwood, the firm's softwood buyer who had good British Admiralty contacts. Grinnell's second strategic connection was with another timber importer, Burt, Boulton & Haywood, a company that combined lumber imports with water and rot proofing treatment of timber products. Railway ties required treatment, which brought the company close to the four major private railways operating in Britain at that time.

With contacts in place, and preliminary arrangements agreed upon, Grinnell and John Humbird journeyed to the United Kingdom where, in a short span of time, they broke the barrier surrounding the importers: first, they signed contracts with Denny, Mott & Dickson for rail ties and other lumber items, then they signed with Burt, Boulton & Haywood for a tie order exclusively. It was a bold stroke—a frontal attack on British business tradition which was not without its repercussions. Astexo's defence was to point to the MacMillan-Montague Meyer-CANUSA arrangement as a precedent which they felt justified in imitating. The outcome for the Astexo mills could not have been better.

Grinnell, with Humbird's official backing, was able to obtain the rail tie
orders at prices well above those being offered to the mills by H. R.
MacMillan. This was the kind of encouragement Astexo needed to
assert itself further.

While J. G. McConville's performance and status as manager of Astexo was never remotely in question, he was receiving increasing assistance from J. P. (Jim) O'Hagan (brother of Harry O'Hagan), who had
been hired by McConville initially as office boy in 1930. Jim O'Hagan
was a graduate of the University of British Columbia with a firm grasp
of mathematical processes and a flair for sales organization. He came
along quickly in Astexo and in January 1934 was appointed assistant
manager specifically responsible for negotiations with the mills and the
setting of prices. His presence as backup to McConville was a positive
force which enhanced Astexo's already buoyant position.

As 1934 proceeded Astexo assembled its forces, both real and
psychological, for a confrontation with MacMillan and other export
brokers. Its advantages consisted of a rapidly expanding U.K. and
Commonwealth market, its initial experience in the Atlantic Seaboard
markets and its recent victory in the U.K. rail tie negotiation. When an
Astexo delegation went to MacMillan and the others, it was not to
announce that Astexo would now deal direct with the United Kingdom.
Instead, the exporters were asked to agree to purchase 75 per cent of all
their export lumber from Astexo mills. Perhaps this was a final testing
of the exporters' strength; alternatively it could have been an indication
that Astexo was not yet ready to fly alone. Whatever the reasoning, the
exporters, MacMillan included, signed the agreement with reluctance,
thus advancing Astexo's position further.

If MacMillan and his fellow exporters hoped to put the Astexo mills
at ease with this agreement, they were to be disappointed. United Kingdom business was booming. Exports to Australia, New Zealand and
South Africa were on the increase. There was strong reason to believe
that normal trade with Japan would be revived in the near future and,
most encouraging of all, there were strong signs that the United States
was giving serious consideration to the reduction or complete removal
of the Smoot-Hawley tariff.

However, the Astexo directors were learning lessons in swift progres-
sion, many of them in emulation of H. R. MacMillan. Early on he had
learned the value of travel into the markets he served or was intent on
serving. In the final analysis, nothing could surpass the effectiveness of
one-to-one negotiations. The men who controlled Astexo's destiny, on
the other hand, came from a tradition of insularity. For years they had
been accustomed to do business over distances of thousands of miles,

dealing through brokers with a nebulous entity known as "the customer." The real customer did not have a face; his idiosyncrasies, attitudes and product preferences were unknown or were understood in the most general terms. Only in recent years, with the appointment of overseas lumber commissioners, had some attempt been made to become more thoroughly informed. One of the first recommendations made by commissioners like Loren Brown was the need for the British Columbia lumber industry to make frequent and personal contact with the buyers.

Humbird's and Grinnell's first visit to the U.K. was followed by a second visit in the latter part of 1934 but for a somewhat different purpose. Export market indications were such that Astexo's urge to float alone had reached compulsive proportions. There was a need to secure sufficient indications of support from U.K. agents and importers to ensure a successful move to autonomy.

This time Charles Grinnell and John Humbird were joined by Henry Mackin. In their meeting with the principals of the lumber trade both in the private and government sectors, they were able to arouse sufficient interest in their concept of a co-operative type of sales organization. While they received few endorsements in writing, they received many in principle. The visit was intended to test the business climate, and the climate appeared to be most receptive.

As 1934 came to a close H. R. MacMillan and the smaller exporters, well aware of Astexo's excursion to the United Kingdom, and pressed by their agents and importers in that market, began to express their feelings of apprehension openly. MacMillan described the time as one of great tension and speculated that Astexo would persist in its "coercive measures." Not too surprisingly, he was correct. Sooner than he might have guessed, Astexo made its next move. John Humbird and Henry Mackin, representing two of the largest mill suppliers as well as Astexo interests, confronted him in Vancouver. The two businessmen reported the decision of Astexo to commence exporting directly, not only to the U.S. Atlantic Seaboard when tariff restrictions were lifted but also overseas, to the United Kingdom. The method of transaction would be CIF, similar to MacMillan's and other exporters. As a result of this decision, acknowledging H. R. MacMillan's position in the industry as a precursor and innovator, the two-man Astexo delegation offered him 15 per cent of the total export volume to the United Kingdom into the foreseeable future.

It was an historic moment in the Canadian lumber trade, and it would have been an interesting confrontation to witness. MacMillan, massive and craggy-browed, his brilliant blue eyes piercing the countenances of the Astexo spokesmen, searching for some kind of weakness or a bargaining position. Henry Mackin, in particular, short and stocky with the mien of a terrier, withstanding MacMillan's cold, somewhat unbelieving scrutiny. It was a standoff that was resolved within a few days; MacMillan refused the offer, opting to stay in business on his own terms, which, in view of the size of the U.K. market at that time, meant that he must reorganize his sources of export lumber supply by whatever means.

The day of the ultimatum was memorable in that it forced MacMillan to expand into sawmilling in order to survive. On the other side of the coin, an amalgamation of British Columbia sawmills had decided to expand into direct exporting—a decision that would result ultimately in the development of one of the world's largest lumber export organizations.

Although Astexo did not make an official statement until the second week in March 1935, alluding to the formation of Seaboard Lumber Sales Company Ltd., Vancouver's *Daily Province* published its evaluation of the move on 2 March. This was a departure from Astexo's sixteen-year practice of selling FAS to exporter brokers who then took care of space and freight and quoted a final CIF price to British and continental markets, the paper reported. "The net position would appear to be that the lumber manufacturers are trying to eliminate the lumber merchants in their export business. The Seaboard Lumber Sales, it is understood, will at the outset, confine its activities only to the British and continental markets, and will not operate in the markets of China, Japan, Australia, South Africa etc." Astexo would deal with these markets through exporters and direct.

On 1 April 1935 Seaboard Lumber Sales Company Limited was incorporated; on 3 April it was doing business. It will be noted that the word "Company" was now added to the original name as advised by legal counsel. The April 1935 issue of the *British Columbia Lumberman* describes the resurrection of Seaboard:

> In view of the rapid growth of B.C.'s lumber trade with the U.K., and of the importance of further increasing the already large business with this market, it has been decided by the leading export mills of the Province to form a separate organization for the handling of British and European business.
>
> In consequence, a substantial portion of the sawmills in B.C. have formed Seaboard Lumber Sales Company Ltd. through which they will sell all of their lumber for U.K. and European destinations. The new

company will have the sole use of the "Astexo" trademark for these markets.

The management of the new organization wish to state that the present channels of trade will be utilized to the fullest extent.

The justification of this step by the export sawmills is made evident by the fact that in 1934 considerably over 50 per cent of the total export lumber shipments from B.C. were shipped to the United Kingdom.

The Associated Timber Exporters of B.C. Ltd. will continue to handle orders in other world markets on the same basis on which they have heretofore operated.

The Astexo/Seaboard move made major news in the business pages for days to come. Both MacMillan and the new mill co-operative had their supporters and detractors, but MacMillan was the target for the larger portion of commentary. In the minds of many, his success and his aggressive business techniques in world markets had made him some kind of capitalist stereotype. He was a formidable moving force which had been outmanoeuvred by the hard-working, put-upon sawmills of the province—an image which, while popular, was not entirely accurate or unbiased.

A retrospective article on H. R. MacMillan, published in the *Vancouver Sun* in May 1966, describes the impact of Seaboard's formation this way:

> In 1935 a group of producers representing about 80 per cent of B.C. lumber producers decided to form their own marketing agency and freeze MacMillan out.
>
> MacMillan's answer to the freeze was to light the hottest fire the industry had ever seen.
>
> While in certain circles people rubbed their hands in glee at the wishful prospect of a MacMillan Export Ltd. on the rocks, H. R. was marshalling his forces and launching his counter-attack.
>
> Mustering the firm's entire resources and assets, as well as the assets of its leaders, he launched an all-out expansion program designed to give it the timber and production facilities to supply its traditional markets and meet the demands of the new markets it was about to go after.

In a later article dealing with the same period, the *Vancouver Sun* states: "It was at this time—perhaps not for the first time and certainly not the last—that he was called a buccaneer. 'Sure,' he responded. 'I sink them all.' "

To put the record straight, and in no way to detract from his later accomplishments, H. R. MacMillan's first retaliatory broadsides failed to sink anything or anybody. In a sense they were shots that rebounded against him. As reported in Donald MacKay's *Empire of Wood*, one of his top executives, Ralph M. Shaw, stated:

> They [Seaboard] had made their declaration that they were not going to supply the H. R. MacMillan Export Company with lumber, and we said, "well, we'll fix them, we'll take all the business." So the H. R. MacMillan Company kept on taking orders and filling our black book containing the order sheets for lumber that had been sold for export but not bought yet from the mills, which was customary. You didn't always buy lumber the day you sold it and so we kept on taking all this business for sixty to ninety days, and Seaboard was getting desperate, and we were getting rather uncomfortable. We had all the orders. They did not have the orders, but they had the lumber. We had been counting on filling orders from mills in Washington and Oregon, but then the longshoremen in the United States went on strike, and that was the end of our cornering the market, because U.S. lumber was unavailable. Then Seaboard started getting their own order file filled up at better prices.

Seaboard Lumber Sales organized remarkably quickly, aided no doubt by its previous experience on the Atlantic Coast, as well as by careful planning on the part of Grinnell and the Astexo directors.

President of the new company, appropriately enough, was J. A. Humbird (Victoria Lumber & Manufacturing, Chemainus). Vice-president was Chris McRae (Alberta Lumber Company, Vancouver). C. H. Grinnell was elected secretary/manager. The mill member list consisted of the following limited companies: Alberni Pacific Lumber; Cameron Lumber; Canadian Western Lumber; Eburne Sawmills; False Creek Lumber; Bloedel, Stewart & Welch; Inlet Timber; R. B. McLean Lumber; Maple Ridge Lumber; Mohawk Lumber; Robertson & Hackett Sawmills; Sproat Lake Sawmills; Straits Lumber; Timberland Lumber; Victoria Lumber & Manufacturing; Hillcrest Lumber; Westminster Shook Mills; Alberta Lumber; Canadian Robert Dollar; Industrial Timber Mills; British Columbia Manufacturing; P. Bain, and Burke Lumber. By 1938 membership had increased by fifteen for a total of thirty-eight mills.

Grinnell, as a matter of interest, did not dissolve his own company but turned it over to the manager of his Seattle office, H. V. Simpson. He brought with him to Seaboard his secretary, Louise Marchesi (who had been secretary to the original Seaboard). Other old hands were

Stewart Slater functioning as accountant, Rube Scotcher in documents and Hap Solloway and Lloyd Ford in traffic.

This staff was augmented by others. Douglas Matthews, a proficient stenographer, joined Solloway and Ford in traffic and shipping. From the ranks of Astexo came Madge Scott to perform the duties of order typist, and Harry O'Hagan, who, like his brother, had started as office boy at Astexo, now became head documents clerk. Frank Hemming was hired to assist Slater in accounting. The switchboard was handled by Marie Gow who doubled as an order typist when Madge Scott and another typist, Noreen Geroline, became overloaded.

Claude Effinger was summoned from his position with Shell Oil as a fuel salesman to take over the United Kingdom sales department at Seaboard. He was pleased to return to the business he knew best, and he brought with him the contacts he had made with many of the Lower Mainland mills while working with Shell. Joining him in U.K. sales was another salesman, John Anderson.

Within a few months R. H. (Bob) Edgett joined the company as office boy and apprentice in the documents department. His memory of those first days is quite clear. "It was a constant struggle to adapt to increasing sales pressures," he recalls. "When I arrived, Johnny Anderson had been hired to handle U.K. cedar sales. H. E. (Hap) Solloway was dividing his time between shipping and U.S. sales. The documents department never stopped. Harry O'Hagan, Rube Scotcher, Jim Matthews and Boswell Whitcroft were pushing paper through day and night. My job was to help wherever I could and learn as much as I could."

This staff of seventeen, working on part of the eighth floor of Vancouver's Marine building, laboured to serve as the sales liaison between the more than thirty member mills and at least fifty agents and importers in the overseas markets.

* * *

A shift in power and business method of this magnitude could not help but create shock waves in British Columbia and in the traditional corridors of the British lumber industry. Agents and importers were at a loss to know where their confidence should be placed. Effective reassurance was needed. Consequently on 13 April 1935, just a few days after the formation of the company, John Humbird, Henry Mackin and Carlton Stone crossed Canada and embarked for England on a mission intended to set minds at rest.

Hector Stone, with some humour, recalls his father's story of that event.

The decision to go to London was made hastily. Frantic cables were coming in from all parts of Britain demanding clarificaton, asking to join Seaboard, launching accusations. Something had to be done.

My dad packed his bag in a matter of minutes, caught the Victoria ferry to Vancouver and joined Mackin and Humbird in time to take the train. They were just beginning to catch their breaths when they boarded ship for London. According to Dad, they worked on strategy and prepared speeches and statements all the way across the Atlantic. What stories had MacMillan fed the industry? How would they counter them? What were MacMillan's remaining strengths and bargaining positions? How could these be matched and surpassed?

Their one source of satisfaction was that they were beating MacMillan to the punch. They would be able to meet with the British lumber industry first and tell the story accurately. They had five days on ship to rehearse and prepare.

When they disembarked at London, ahead of them on the gangplank was H. R. MacMillan, briefcase in hand and limousine waiting. Unknown to them they had shared the voyage with their chief adversary.

The Seaboard delegation may have been uneasy at the sight of MacMillan striding into the London traffic, prepared to do battle in an environment he knew well, but there could be no turning back; the issues were clear, and there was reason to believe that the agents and importers were beginning to see the situation in a new light.

The three men took turns in addressing groups and individuals, each dealing with those they had done business with over the years. Their choice as spokesmen had not been accidental. Of all the Seaboard shareholders, these three represented the mills that had, on a limited basis, dealt direct with preferred customers in the United Kingdom. At least they had a rudimentary basis for communication.

Their explanation to the U.K. lumber industry was persuasive. In essence it was this: The mills of British Columbia, for a number of years, had been the targets of criticism directed by British agents and importers. It was true that lumber prices fluctuated wildly, often to the detriment of the buyers; but the mills were just as vulnerable to price manipulation over which they had no control. The Seaboard delegation laboured to convince its listeners that onerous prices orginated not in the mill offices, but after the companies had completed their FOB transactions with the exporters. At that point the exporters, speculating on freight fluctuations and keen to make the maximum profit, charged the most the market would bear, taking advantage of the Commonwealth Preference Agreement. Seaboard, on the other hand, represented an organized effort on the part of the mills to stabilize prices while ensuring a reliable supply of lumber products. This would be achieved through the new sales company, which would be the marketing arm for mills accounting for from 70 to 80 per cent of the province's export production.

Sales would take place on a CIF basis and Seaboard, because it would be dealing in large volumes of lumber, would be able to control freight rates at a manageable and acceptable level. Both the mills and the buyers could not help but benefit from this arrangement. The same basic procedure prevails to this day.

Naturally the Seaboard triumvirate pointed out to agents and importers alike the changed nature of the lumber supply. Export brokers would no longer have access to their major source of product, and this loss could work hardships on any British importer or agent who failed to secure a lumber supply from whatever source—the obvious one being Seaboard.

MacMillan and Meyer argued eloquently that nothing would change. MacMillan was already reorganizing his sources of lumber supply, partly through his connections with Washington and Oregon mills, partly through B.C. mills outside the Seaboard organization, and partly from the production of small mills he had acquired.

The U.K. agents and importers of B.C. lumber were presented with a dilemma. On the one hand, they could continue their relationship with the established export brokers, of which MacMillan was the largest and most prestigious, with a proven record of performance. On the other hand, Seaboard's announcement that its mills would no longer supply the exporters, including MacMillan Export, forced them to take sides in a revolt in which they were unwilling victims.

Seaboard's objective was to assemble as broad a list of committed agents as possible in order to ensure complete market coverage and to secure trade financing. To be accepted by Seaboard, an agent had to pledge that he would deal exclusively with it for Pacific Coast lumber products. Some British agents made the move without hesitation. When Seaboard officially and firmly bade farewell to the British Columbia exporters, the exodus to the new company accelerated, and when MacMillan, in spite of his promise to maintain the status quo, was forced to delay deliveries and try to renegotiate contracts, the rush was on.

William Brandts, who had been the sole U.K. agents for Grinnell Export Company, became Seaboard's first agents. The two importers who had first dealt with Grinnell in negotiating the British Rail tie sale—Denny, Mott & Dickson and Burt Boulton & Haywood—were

Seaboard's first importer accounts and they were dealt with direct without recourse to the usual agent middleman. In a matter of days Seaboard acquired some thirty-five U.K. agents without showing any preference or according any exclusivity. This impartial attitude resulted in the loss of some agents who felt they were entitled to special terms, and for the next two or three years Seaboard's agent list was in a state of constant flux.

Some agents chose to stay with their established exporters in the hope that independent mill supply would keep them alive. For some such as Lloyd, Duncan and Duncan Ewing this decision proved disastrous; others like Foy, Morgan were greatly damaged. Balfour, Williamson chose to ride two horses for a time, representing Seaboard as well as Balfour Guthrie through the stratagem of employing C. Leary as sub-agents. Pharoah Gane managed to attach itself to Seaboard by forming a separate agency designated Canadian American Wood Agencies. Munro, Brice and Alfred Dobell, in the Liverpool area, joined Seaboard and demonstrated their usefulness from the outset.

At the beginning of 1936, Seaboard's agent roster, still undergoing changes, consisted of the following companies:

Balfour, Williamson	Gordon, Watts & Co.
Denny, Mott & Dickson	Great Eastern Timber
Berner & Nielsen	Andrew Elliot
William Brandts	James Dowie
Boyson & Neame	Dorman & Company
Scantlebury & Hemingway	Wright, Graham
E. H. Hearnden	R. Hendwerk & Company
Munro, Brice	U.S. Trading Company
Churchill & Sim	Lyneve
Alfred Dobell & Company	C. V. Haerem
Duncan Ewing	L. Banberger
Hunt Bros.	Cousland & Browne
Lloyd, Duncan	Edmiston & Mitchells
Thomas Simson	C. Noel Legh
Farnworth & Jardine	Robert Coltart
Bryce, Junor & Jellie	Home Builders
Spencer, Lock	Theodore Beaton
Flatau, Dick	Foy, Morgan

Of these the majority were London based, some with offices in other U.K. cities such as Liverpool, Manchester, Hull and Bristol. Andrew Elliot, James Dowie, Wright, Graham and Edmiston & Mitchell were based in Glasgow; Dorman was an Irish agent. In addition, Seaboard conducted direct business with importers and agents supplying to the British Railways, War Office and Admiralty. These included: Burt, Boulton & Haywood; Gabriel Wade & English; Denny, Mott & Dickson; Balfour, Williamson; May & Hassell; Gordon, Watts, and Scantlebury & Hemingway. Business with the above list of agents and importers in a period from 1 April 1936 to 31 March 1937 amounted to just short of 477 million board feet, a sizeable undertaking for a new export company.

Within a year, John Humbird, Seaboard's president, was entertaining various formulas for the reduction of the agents' list in order to simplify sales negotiations. Jack Hood, the company's representative in London, recommended that the list be pared down to twelve including a London group: Balfour, Williamson; Berner & Nielsen; William Brandts; Boyson & Neame; Scantlebury & Hemingway; E. H. Hearnden, Churchill & Sim, and Alfred Dobell. In Liverpool Hood's choice was Munro, Brice and Duncan Ewing; in Scotland he favoured Andrew Elliott and Calder, Henderson. At the same time he recommended the dismissal of Hunt Bros.; Lloyd, Duncan; Thomas Simson; Farnworth & Jardine; Bryce, Junor & Jellie; Spencer Lock; Flatau, Dick; Gordon, Watts; Great Eastern; James Dowie; Lyneve, and Wright, Graham. As we will see in later chapters, not all of Hood's recommendations were acted on.

As for the export brokers, the formation of Seaboard Lumber Sales Company spelled the end for many of them within a short period of time. H. R. MacMillan, of course, had most to lose, but there were other exporters and lumber brokers as well who had first felt the loss of Astexo mills in the U.S. market and were now deprived of their lucrative U.K. and continental European markets.

The established firm of Borland and Melville chose to go out of business shortly after Seaboard cut off their main source of export lumber. Capilano Trading Company was a partnership of two men experienced in export: Lloyd Edgett and Clarence Fraser. Deprived of their export supply, they tried to make other arrangements and finally parted company. Nelson Spencer Limited had been quite prominent in the export trade until the advent of Seaboard. Alexander Sereth at that period had a thriving U.S. East Coast business which he tended to operate with considerable financial panache. Pressure from Seaboard, together with internal financial crises, placed the company in distress. Heaps & Sons was a smaller operation struggling to compete with MacMillan and Sereth; cut off now from the Seaboard mills, it faded away. P. H. Barnett was an active exporter who reacted to the Seaboard export lumber drought by switching to the rail wholesale business and log trading. There were many others, but the point to be made is that, for the second time, a group of mills had banded together in a concerted effort to control their own destinies in exports sales. This time they commanded a much larger market.

* * *

Meanwhile, back in British Columbia a difficult juggling act was in progress. It involved the consolidation of the existing Seaboard membership, the recruitment of additional member mills, and the all-important filling of orders for export at the right price, on time and of correct grade and quality.

Essentially, Seaboard is an export consortium, specifically, an export marketing organization for a group of wood products manufacturers. By combining forces, manufacturers can ensure that their products are marketed effectively and be certain they receive a fair price for them. All aspects of the exporting process are expedited with maximum efficiency, from the initiation of the sale to the manufacture of the specified product. This includes arranging documents, credit, foreign currency exchange, insurance, finance and all the other administrative activities necessary to deliver a shipment of lumber to its destination—on time, at the agreed price and quality, including paying the manufacturer promptly.

With this access to a large volume of lumber and plywood for shipment to overseas markets, Seaboard was, and still is, armed with a powerful competitive instrument—economy based on scale. Ocean freight rates could be negotiated directly with ship owners on the basis of full cargoes, and ships could be chartered on a trip or period basis. Such a large capacity provided a wide range of specifications to a varied customer base in an expanded market. This has been the key to Seaboard's stability: the ability to provide regular and continuous sales for its member mills to a worldwide market.

Significantly, the company's basic policies and operational procedures laid down in 1935, and with roots extending back to 1928, are basically the same today. The ideas which worked then have weathered the test of time.

One of the basic tenets of the initial company was to have a contract called a Mill Agreement with each member. Any company making application for membership must sign this agreement, which among other things gives Seaboard Lumber Sales the exclusive right for sale of the member's products in overseas markets. This generally means lumber, plywood, shingles and shakes and it does not include pulp and paper. The agreement also stipulates the terms of membership including payment terms, purchase of shares, recognition of quality standards, transfer of title and termination procedures. The purpose of the company can be summarized by the first few paragraphs in the agreement as follows:

> The Company was formed by its members for the purpose of action to their mutual benefit as an organization to acquire, market, and sell in export markets, certain forest products such as all types of lumber as defined, sheet materials as defined, manufactured in the Province of British Columbia by its members, of increasing the demand for lumber and sheet materials and of establishing uniform sales practices for the benefit of both its members and buyers.
>
> Through its various offices, agencies, contractual arrangements and selling organization the Company has facilities for the marketing and selling of lumber and sheet materials in the areas and in the manner hereinafter mentioned, and the member is desirous that such facilities should be used for the distribution of lumber and sheet materials in such areas.

Seaboard does not sell in Canada by reason of its organizational structure. The markets served by Seaboard on behalf of its membership are defined as overseas markets. This then by definition includes all markets served by water including the U.S. Atlantic Coast and Gulf of Mexico ports. However, historically the company has always treated the California market and the United States rail market as special. While Seaboard has serviced these markets from time to time through the years, such service has always required special agreement of the directors.

Seaboard was born in an atmosphere where members were concerned about hidden profits in the distribution chains from mill to customer. The mills knew that if they were going to have a future as an industry, the costs in the distribution chain had to be as lean as possible and the return to the mills as profitable as possible. Thus from its start Seaboard's objective has been to maintain the best possible mill return for its member mills consistent with selling the volume available for export. The focus in Seaboard has been to build close and lasting relationships with buyers by serving their needs for quality and specification required, shipment within contract terms and reliable performance. At the same time Seaboard management has made every effort to continuously reduce the cost of distribution while maintaining performance. Over the years this has manifested itself in working with ship owners to design and build ships especially suitable for carrying lumber products.

Lumber is now packaged with sticker attached for efficient handling, and marked for ready identification of specification.

Seaboard's pride has been its excellent sales representation overseas with customers. In the early days agents of the highest calibre were appointed. In recent years the trend has been for Seaboard to establish its own representation companies in major markets so that Seaboard products receive priority sales attention, and any surplus of revenue over cost resulting in large volume sales will accrue to the company and its shareholders.

Each company joining Seaboard must purchase shares in both the Lumber Sales and Shipping companies. The number of shares purchased is relative to the member's annual shipments so that each member holds shares in proportion to the company's total annual shipments. Redistributions are undertaken from time to time to ensure that this relationship is maintained. Members receive a 7 per cent dividend on the capital investment. In addition, debentures or preferred shares are issued from time to time in return for special capital expenditures.

The basic company procedure is to charge the mills a 2½ per cent sales commission. For this commission, mills receive a full marketing service. All of Seaboard's costs are applied to this revenue and any surplus is refunded at the end of the year to each mill pro rata to their participation during that period. Over the years this refund has varied but by and large the normal refund is about 1¼ per cent. In the early days of the company—1938, 1939 and 1940—this percentage was much higher since at the beginning there were many more opportunities for savings. The Shipping Company also applies a service charge to the freight to cover its administrative costs which include co-ordinating the movement of the goods to ship's side, loading the vessel, the vessel voyage, and discharge at the contracted destination. Whereas shiploading may seem to be a routine function, it is in fact a very complicated procedure requiring years of experience and a complete knowledge of vessels. Inefficient and incorrect loading can result in damaged goods and disastrously high costs. Again, the practice is to refund any surplus generating in the Shipping Company accounts to the member mills pro rata to their participation during the period. Since Seaboard's inception, only rarely has the company not covered its costs, and most often the refund to members has been substantial. Because the freight market is a commodity market, subject to volatile fluctuations, in some years the windfall profits have been substantial.

Probably a key element in maintaining the company has been the opportunity for each member to contribute to policy. Each member has a representative elected to the board of directors each year. The president of Seaboard is also a member of the board. From the board, an executive committee is elected composed of directors from a mix of large and small companies, and the president. This committee meets regularly with management to discuss policy matters arising from day-to-day business. From its inception, the Seaboard directors have provided active support to management leadership in matters pertaining to their best interest. This has required excellent communication skills by management. As a result, decisions are not always made quickly, but at the same time, the organization stands for stability and continuity. Because of their participation, members know what costs are and know also that any surplus developing is refunded to them pro rata to their participation in both Lumber Sales and Shipping companies.

One of Seaboard's more enigmatic processes is the way it handles the distribution of sales enquiries among its members. For lumber products, this is not as complex as it looks. Each mill produces a different specification of lumber which varies according to wood species, width, length and grade. Since no two mills are alike, Seaboard is able to distribute enquiries to take advantage of each mill's strengths. Because the marketing objective is continuity and stability, with a regular flow of orders from markets all around the world, a pattern is established so that this flow to individual mills develops quite naturally. In times of market upheaval, where continuity and stability disappear, distribution of orders becomes more difficult, but members realize they must work together and share the more easily provided specifications with the more difficult. This situation often requires considerable negotiation on the part of Seaboard management and its members to arrive at a successful conclusion.

As has already been noted, effective communication between Seaboard management and its shareholder companies has been a key ingredient in the success of the company. Thus Seaboard management is highly dependent on excellent communication with overseas markets. Situated in Vancouver, the head office of the company is the centre of daily telephone and telex contact around the world. Agents and subsidiary sales offices are required to report daily on events that can affect the demand for Seaboard wood products. In the early days this information was obtained on a personal basis and communicated in the same way. While the personal contact is still important, modern business science has also provided reports on economic trends and forecasts which are all part of the daily input and which are fed to the shareholder companies either on the basis of daily conversations or in more formal reports concerned with planning the following year's operations.

Customers demand, and are entitled to expect, a high level of quality predicated on internationally recognized grading rules. From the outset, Seaboard mills were called upon to produce to grade, and regular mill inspections were conducted by company representatives to ensure this. One of the first actions undertaken by the first board of directors was to set up a committee of directors to deal with claims and grade standards. This reflects the importance that the membership placed on supplying a grade to the standard. Now skilled grading inspectors visit mills on a regular basis and check stock delivered to shipside to ensure that grade of product is to the acceptable standard.

In outlining the Seaboard structure and its reason for being, the narrative has moved between the past and the present, in order to indicate a certain evolutionary process. The key point to reiterate, however, is that Seaboard's original and basic structure has remained intact. Any changes to the structure that have taken place have been in response to world events, economic challenges, technological innovations and other factors which demanded appropriate action. And these changes have been in the nature of neccessary additions rather than replacement of the company's foundations.

*   *   *

During the first days of the company's formation, when it was labouring to consolidate its position under formidable pressures, agents were clamouring for association, importers were demanding reassurance in the matter of lumber supply, British Columbia exporters were pressing to negotiate some kind of continuing relationship and member mills were anxious to know their roles in this new association, and what the mechanics of the operation would be.

Of overriding concern was the need to conduct business in an efficient and expeditious manner. Nothing would reverse Seaboard's position faster than an observed inability to honour contracts. Lumber *must* be delivered on time, in the quantity and at the price contracted for. The company was under the closest scrutiny, and any display of weakness or incompetency would have been magnified out of all proportions.

In Vancouver, manager Charles Grinnell was faced with the difficult task of staffing the new organization. There were any number of lumber experts to be had, men who understood the workings of a sawmill and the many ingenious ways a log could be converted into lumber products. And there were some who combined this expertise with a knowledge of lumber sales, but almost always in local or domestic markets.

Few there were who had gained a sufficiently thorough knowledge in export trade.

The reduction of U.S. tariffs from $4 to $2 a thousand feet occurred in November 1935, thus justifying Seaboard's return to United States Atlantic Coast trade and creating a need to open at least one office in that market. H. E. Solloway was quickly dispatched to establish a branch office in New York. Claude Effinger was assigned the United Kingdom and European continent departments (which included the Mid-East) and he immediately set about looking for a sufficiently qualified candidate to represent Seaboard in the U.K. He found what he was looking for in the person of Jack Hood, sales manager of Industrial Timber Mills at Youbou on Vancouver Island. Shortly after year's end Hood arrived in London to open a Seaboard office. "Jack Hood was one of the best lumber men in the business," Effinger says today. "We loaded him with tremendous responsibilities. He had to learn the export business almost overnight, and he had to deal with a pretty sophisticated and entrenched group of agents and importers, some of whom were not too happy with the new arrangements."

Effinger recalls the clamour that arose in the U.K. market when Seaboard dispensed with the export brokers. "The U.K. agents had no other alternative but to come to us for their Pacific Coast lumber orders. In a matter of a few months we picked up the agent lists of fifteen or twenty exporters in Vancouver. It sounds fine on the face of it—but really it created problems."

He confirmed that Seaboard had better than thirty-five U.K. agents on its lists at one time. "The trouble was that we couldn't service that many agents efficiently," he said. "Not only had we picked up many of MacMillan's agents, we had picked up those of the other exporters as well. There were just too many. One of our first tasks was to reduce the list to a workable number."

The criteria used to make a final selection of agents were size and geographic location. "Obviously it made more sense for us to deal with big agents and importers than with small ones," Effinger said. "Large, well-established firms like Denny, Mott & Dickson and William Brandts were what we preferred. The ideal situation was a network of large or medium-sized agents covering every major or potentially productive market in the United Kingdom. The few small agents we retained on our list were kept because of their strategic geographic location."

Effinger in Vancouver guided Hood's undertakings in London, and Harry O'Hagan was taken out of the document department and given the U.S. desk, developing the business Hap Solloway handled out of the New York office. Bob Edgett became assistant to Claude Effinger in U.K. sales. John Anderson left Seaboard within a few months and was replaced by Albert Head who took over cedar sales until he was assigned larger first-line duties.

Still there were not enough useful bodies to cope with the business at hand, and Grinnell cast his net wider. The Grinnell Export Company, which he had turned over to H. V. Simpson, and which now operated as General Export Lumber Company, was a dependable source of trained manpower. Ironically, General Export was as vulnerable as any other export company now that Seaboard was in business. Clearly it made much sense for its personnel to team up with the dominant organization. From General Export came Simpson, its manager, another of the Solloway brothers, F. G. (Pott) Solloway, Wick Gray, and several of the stenographic and clerical staff, all of whom were thoroughly familiar with the lumber export business.

Wick Gray was installed in the miscellaneous department. "I had been somewhat upset when Seaboard formed again in 1935," he recalls. "I was not included in the initial staff of the company and I wondered why I had been left out. Grinnell was simply being cautious. He didn't want to hire people until enough business had developed." The miscellaneous department was a catchall which included such markets as South Africa, China, Ceylon, Egypt, South America, and later the West Indies and South Pacific.

Gray states that South America was a difficult market to penetrate because most of the trade was controlled by an American shipping line headquartered in San Francisco. "Whenever I was able to put together a full cargo for any of these markets I was awarded a new hat," he remembers. "I collected a few hats over the years."

As for the essential matter of shipping services, Seaboard Lumber Sales relied, as it had once before, on Anglo-Canadian Shipping to arrange for its charters. This would not be for long, but while it lasted, it was a most useful and workable arrangement. And it is to shipping that we now turn our attention, since Seaboard's policy in this regard, though sometimes stormy, has had much to do with its competitive position.

*   *   *

From the outset, Seaboard's self-appointed mandate was to sell CIF to waterborne markets exclusively. In this respect the company differed significantly from Astexo, which had been founded on the principle of selling on an FAS basis. It is important to remember that some of Astexo's prominent members were strongly opposed to any involvement in ocean freighting on the premise that it would have a disruptive effect, to the extent of breaking up the co-operation that had been carefully nurtured in FAS selling. This difference of opinion explains in part why Astexo and Seaboard operated in tandem for several years.

Shortly after Seaboard Lumber Sales Limited was formed in 1928, a shipping arm, Marine Shipping Company Limited, was incorporated. By 10 May 1932 the following sixteen limited companies had become shareholder/members: Maple Ridge Lumber Company; Rat Portage Lumber Company; Westminster Shook Mills; Eburne Sawmills; Dominion Mills; Alberni Pacific Lumber Company; B.C. Manufacturing Company; Timberland Lumber Company; Canadian Western Lumber Company; Canadian Puget Sound Lumber Company; Hammond Cedar Company; Mohawk Lumber Company; Robertson & Hackett Sawmills; Barnett Lumber Company; Victoria Lumber & Manufacturing Company, and Wilfert Lumber Company.

Marine Shipping had barely put its organization to the test when the U.S. government's Smoot-Hawley Act squeezed it into submission. In Seaboard's earliest stages, before Marine Shipping became operationally solid, the company had relied on the services of Anglo-Canadian Shipping Company to freight lumber to the East Coast, so that the time span between phasing Anglo-Canadian out and Marine Shipping in gave the latter company little time indeed to prove its worth.

On 12 January 1933 the minutes of a Marine Shipping directors' meeting record a resolution to the effect that the company be terminated. At a general shareholder's meeting on 21 February 1933 the resolution to conduct a voluntary liquidation was carried. However, an extraordinary general meeting held on 13 March of that year reviewed the situation, and the decision was made that "in view of the change in market conditions, no action be taken on the resolution."

Marine Shipping remained in limbo until 13 June 1933. Seaboard was no longer operating and Grinnell had formed his Grinnell Export Lumber Company Ltd. in an attempt to do some kind of business with certain overseas markets. On this date Grinnell was appointed to operate Marine Shipping. A note opposite this entry in the minutes, signed by Charles Grinnell, reads "at one dollar a month."

By 1934 and into the spring of 1935 a few of the mills, in particular Canadian Western and Victoria Lumber & Manufacturing, ventured into the United Kingdom with token lumber shipments sold on a CIF basis outside the Astexo organization. Much to their gratification they realized returns considerably better than selling FAS through Astexo.

Mills that had never seen sufficient advantage in belonging to Astexo before were strongly attracted to this new way of thinking. Alberta Lumber Company and Canadian Robert Dollar were two of these. The logic was simple enough; if there were demonstrable advantages in selling CIF, and if Astexo was not permitted under the terms of its charter to sell CIF, then a company must be formed that could do this.

The new corporate entity was Seaboard Lumber Sales Company Limited. A year later, on 2 July 1936, the name Marine Shipping Company Limited was changed to Seaboard Shipping Company Limited. While the reason for this change is not to be found in any of the records, it would be reasonable to suppose that this name was more obviously associated with the controlling company.

And controlling company it was beyond all doubt. The agreement between Seaboard Lumber Sales and Seaboard Shipping stated that the two companies had been incorporated for the purpose of acting co-operatively for the development of sales of British Columbia timber products in foreign markets. The agreement made it clear that the shipping company existed to serve the sales company, and that it should neither retain profits nor sustain losses. Shipping profits would accrue to Seaboard Lumber Sales and losses would be reimbursed by the same company.

Seaboard Shipping Company Limited became operational in June 1936 under the management of Alec Martin, and almost immediately found itself in serious trouble. In retrospect, the experience must be regarded as the growing pains of a company not entirely decided on its principal modus operandi. John Humbird, then president of Seaboard Lumber Sales as well as of the shipping company, recalled in his diary that 1936 had been an active sales year in a rapidly advancing freight market. Seaboard Lumber Sales filled orders aggressively and with great zeal, only to discover that it had sold more lumber than Seaboard Shipping could supply space for.

It was a critical time for the young company. This is not to say that Seaboard Shipping was the only one to be bruised by the sudden rise in freight rates and a shortage of ships, but the company in its formative stage was more vulnerable to this shipping crisis than most. In some cases rates went up by 250 per cent. On the Vancouver to Sydney run, for instance, rates escalated from $7 to $10 per thousand feet of lumber to $20 per thousand feet. Now Seaboard was forced to book the space at a higher rate than had been quoted to the buyer, and substantial losses were incurred.

Every exporter who had promised to deliver lumber without first contracting for freight found himself in trouble. It is difficult to place heavy blame on the exporters, although an experienced few were able to read the signs and take preventive measures. The first big jump in freight rates in more than a decade simply took exporters by painful surprise.

Many of them delayed shipping their lumber in the hope that rates would ease within a reasonable time; but freight continued to climb, and the exporters found themselves paying penalty charges in addition to inflated rates. Rumours were flying that the market was being manipulated by a cleverly hidden monopoly and that profiteering was being conducted on a massive scale, but nothing could be proven. Exporters either weathered the storm or went under.

Charles Grinnell turned to his long-time friend Andrew Graham, who put Anglo-Canadian Shipping's resources to work. The necessary bottoms were found, but the price was not cheap. Humbird describes this crisis as the first serious test of the member mills' solidarity. The mills stood behind management, agreeing to finance the freight deficit at the rate of $1 per thousand feet of lumber shipped, until the loss had been made up. Fortunately, by the end of 1937 sufficient profits had been accumulated to more than compensate for the freight deficits.

A valuable and expensive lesson had been learned; from now on, Seaboard Lumber Sales would take every precaution to avoid getting into an oversold position. Charles Grinnell was particularly sensitive to the speculative pitfalls of freight negotiations. He had been severely hurt in a similar experience while operating Grinnell Export. This, together with Seaboard Shipping's narrow escape, was to put him on guard against freight speculation from that day forth.

It was clearly evident that if Seaboard was to function efficiently and profitably in the overseas market it must manage its shipping arm with utmost professionalism, in competition and in company with the long-established, experienced shipping companies of the world. It needed reliable information on movements in the tramp market as well as accurate reports on supply and demand in world shipping. The appointment of a manager with extensive shipping experience was essential, and an intensive search for the right man was begun. Potential candidates were interviewed in Vancouver, Seattle, Portland and San Francisco, but all fell short of the qualifications Seaboard was looking for. Early in June 1937 John Humbird and Charles Grinnell transferred their search to England.

While the appointment of a suitable shipping manager was paramount, a second objective was to establish a good chartering connection in England. As a result, interview sessions were interspersed with visits to a considerable number of shipping and brokerage offices, among them Tatham Bromage, Heatly's, Mitchell Cotts, Morell, Muir

Young, Basil Mavroleion, Brown Jenkinson, Rigg & Thue, Mathews Wrightson, H. Clarkson & Company, Reardon Smith, Furness Withy, Rethymunis & Kulukundis. As though this business itinerary were not enough, the two men made the opportunity to meet with sixty individuals, representing some thirty lumber agencies either on Seaboard's list, anxious to place themselves in that position, or concerned that they might be removed from that position.

Humbird's practice to write in his diary virtually everything that happened to him in the course of a day gives considerable insight into his personality and method of doing business. He left few details unattended, and absolutely nothing open to chance. A score or more of shipping manager candidates were interviewed, many of them on more than one occasion; careful notes and ratings were kept on each interviewee. Humbird's personal opinions were succinctly appended: "Seems to have information on tap and knows game from owners' side. His handicap is that he doesn't know our side of the game." Or "He has experience in general chartering, but not much in the North Pacific. The man is not worth fussing with." Or "Believes he is worth 2,500 pounds (per annum) to us. I don't agree and neither does Grinnell."

Among the chartering and brokerage firms visited was Eggar Forrester & Verner. Extracts from Humbird's notes indicate that this company, the second largest charterer of sugar cargoes in the world, had solid Pacific Coast connections, as well as being a major charterer of lumber from Eastern Canada.

"These people make a very good impression," Humbird writes. "Both Vassall Forrester and [W. C.] Robinson live wires and by far the best we have seen yet outside of N———. Am not sure they won't shape up just as well. Forrester to be married Saturday. We will try to see them tomorrow and have suggested, as they figure on sending one of their principals to Vancouver to familiarize them with the business we require, that he make this his honeymoon trip. Might possibly work it. Very favourably impressed and believe these will be brokers we finally pick."

Humbird's June twenty-third entry tells the story:

Returned to Eggar Forrester & Verner offices at 4 o'clock. They are agreeable to let Forrester come to Vancouver and agreeable to Solloway [Hap Solloway, Vancouver office] to come here for six months. We to pay Forrester at the rate of 1,500 pounds a year, and they to pay Solloway's salary while here. Each firm pays expense out and back of their own man.

Can imagine shock to his fiancée, few day before wedding, to find plans all changed and to leave immediately. He is to bring her up to Mayfair at five tomorrow to meet us. Thinks it won't be quite so strange to her if she meets someone from B.C. before going out there. She tells him change quite O.K. with her just as long as he doesn't try to leave her behind.

Once the matter of a shipping manager had been settled, Humbird turned his mind to other business. The very next day he was lunching with the managing director of Price and Pierce, one of MacMillan's agents, in a guarded effort to persuade him to swing to Seaboard. The lunch was friendly but to no avail. Price and Pierce remained loyal to MacMillan, even though the director wrote out a favourite recipe for a Golden Cocktail for Humbird, acknowledging the Seaboard president's known appreciation for good food and appropriate spirits. In addition, the Price and Pierce man picked up the bill which, Humbird noted, was the equivalent of $19 for three people. "Too steep for my blood," he observed.

John Humbird was greatly respected in the timber trade, and his effectiveness as a businessman was proven conclusively on a number of occasions. Business before pleasure was an unwritten rule with him, but when the business had been transacted, he was able to enjoy life's pleasures as he saw them to be. His diary describes in appreciative or critical detail many lunches and dinners. The beauty spots of England and Scotland do not miss his eye, and at all times he was prepared to demonstrate his considerable skill as a sleight-of-hand artist.

In Vancouver he belonged to the Magic Circle, a club whose membership was comprised of skilled amateur magicians. He is said to have been among the more proficient of them, and often used his skill to relieve the tension in a difficult business session, or in a luncheon recess when he was in the process of attracting new business associates. One of his popular tricks was to split a one pound note into two. Among the agents and importers in England and elsewhere were a few who shared his way with magic, and whenever he visited, there would be an exchange of the latest illusions.

The trip to England and Scotland had been successful, ending in the selection not only of a shipping manager but also of a brokerage firm to serve Seaboard's interests in the British Isles. It appeared that Seaboard Shipping would now proceed on a more solid footing, in part because freight rates dipped by as much as 25 per cent in late 1937, and undoubtedly because Vassall Forrester, under the now sensitive scrutiny of the shipping company directors, was managing Seaboard's shipping affairs with great care and assurance.

Seaboard Shipping records surrounding this period reveal a steady increase in chartering. Seaboard chartered three ships in 1935. In 1936 ten were chartered to the United States and thirty-six to the United Kingdom. In 1937 five went to the U.S. and fifteen to the U.K. In 1938 twenty went to the U.S., sixty-one to the U.K., twenty-one to Australia and two to Eastern Canada. And in 1939, as war threatened, sixteen went to the U.S., ninety to the U.K., thirty-one to Australia, three to South Africa and three to the Far East. All these sailings were without mishap, and with freight profits returned to the Seaboard member mills every year but 1936. The CIF sales strategy was proving to be successful.

SIX

THE END OF ASTEXO & THE EVE OF WAR

Seaboard re-entered the lumber market in 1935, just in time to benefit from the best years of the thirties. The company's lumber exports from 11 March 1935 to 31 March 1936 totalled 319,060,563 board feet, and the same period the following year saw an increase to 466,110,519 board feet. The totals for the ensuing two years were slightly lower but were still a gratifying improvement over the drought of 1932 to 1934.

The improvement in British Columbia's lumber trade was due largely to the expansion of United Kingdom and Commonwealth markets. Certainly the U.S. East Coast market had not recovered significantly, though the reduction in tariff from $4 per thousand feet to $2 per thousand encouraged Seaboard to consider another try at that market.

The effort to expand Commonwealth trade was intensified. Between 1935 and 1936 the British Columbia government, in co-operation with industry, established timber commissioners in the United Kingdom, South Africa, the British West Indies and Australia. Douglas Roe, with family roots in Eburne Sawmills, served as timber trade commissioner in the U.K., working tirelessly to promote the use of B.C. timber products in the British Isles.

The forest industry made its principal contribution through the B.C.

Lumber and Shingle Manufacturer's Association whose membership consisted mainly of Seaboard mills. Funds to be used for overseas lumber promotion were accumulated by means of a levy of two cents per thousand feet of lumber exported.

It should be observed that H. R. MacMillan, and the mills he began to assemble under his banner, remained aloof from the association, perhaps for understandable reasons. During that period he had no reason to believe that he would have been in salutary company in that group. Instead, he was responsible for the formation of his own organization, the Western Lumber Association, which performed trade extension activities on behalf of his mills as well as certain independent mills outside of the Seaboard perimeter.

When British Columbia timber trade commissioners were appointed to take up duties in Australia and the West Indies, it was not surprising to see two Seaboard employees receive the assignments: Ralph Smith went to Australia and Charles Schultz to the West Indies. Both were thoroughly familiar with the export trade and the capabilities of the member mills. William Johnson opened a trade commissioner's office in South Africa, while, back in the United Kingdom, Douglas Roe's promotional efforts warranted the appointment of an assistant in the person of John Berto, an expert in the manufacture and use of red cedar. The B.C. forest industry was making a considerable effort to elevate its profile in the export markets.

In November 1935, the economic climate in the United States having become more favourable to lumber imports, Seaboard proposed to its member mills that it once again take over sales of forest products to the U.S. Atlantic Coast. The membership agreed to this, and an office was opened once again in New York under the management of G. D. Anderson.

Astexo, under the agreement previously mentioned, continued to sell to British Columbia and U.S. brokers on FAS terms for all export markets other than the United Kingdom and the United States, but changes were in the wind. On 23 July 1936 a somewhat subtle alteration occurred in the company name. Associated Timber Exporters Ltd. was incorporated, taking over, on 11 August, the assets and business of the Associated Timber Exporters of B.C. The reasons for this modification of the original name are not entirely clear, but the action presaged coming events.

It will be recalled that a number of Astexo's principals had been opposed to the inclusion of a shipping function in the company's operations. In addition, the mandate of the original Astexo and its successor did not allow selling on a CIF basis. Seaboard, on the other hand, was demonstrating considerable success dealing CIF and employing the services of a shipping arm. The natural question in the minds of many of Seaboard's directors and members was "Why restrict this manner of doing business to the U.K. and the U.S. when every market should respond to it with comparable success?"

The situation had its sensitive aspects. Astexo's manager, J. G. McConville, had handled the company's affairs assiduously. He was highly regarded in the industry and enjoyed the confidence of Astexo's member mills without exception. As well, there were some in Astexo who shared his strong belief that the company's principal purpose was to co-ordinate the production of the mills for FAS sale to bona fide exporters, of which Seaboard was now the largest. He and his supporters were in the minority however, and there were some, like his second-in-command, James O'Hagan, who felt that Astexo should spread its wings a little farther and become less dependent on the exporters and brokers.

The compromise action was to attempt a direct sales incursion into an overseas market. This was done in October 1936 when Astexo entered the Australian market, selling direct to buyers in that country. By January 1937 an office had been established in Sydney, under the management of L. S. Anderson, and business began to accelerate. In 1937 mutually satisfactory trade agreements between Canada, Australia and New Zealand were renewed, setting the scene for a further expansion of business for Astexo, and motivating an exploratory visit to Australia and New Zealand by McConville and two of his Astexo directors, R. McFarlane of Eburne Sawmills and J. H. McDonald of B.C. Manufacturing and Westminster Shook Mills.

McConville in particular was encouraged to make the trip, and he had every justification to do so under the circumstances. The Astexo membership could rest assured that he would spare no effort to present the case for Astexo and the superior qualities of British Columbia lumber products. While he and his companions were away on their trade mission, however, Seaboard's directors, almost all of whom were interlocking with Astexo's directorate, began to move the pieces that would lead to the demise of Astexo and the ascendancy of Seaboard.

At a board meeting of Seaboard Lumber Sales Company held on 21 October 1937, the first formal discussion of Astexo's viability was recorded, including a motion that the two companies be consolidated under Seaboard's banner. A committee was struck to study the pros and cons and to report back as soon as possible with a recommended course of action. At a meeting of Seaboard directors held 30 November 1937, John Humbird outlined the details of the committee's recommendations which supported the consolidation of Astexo and Seaboard under Seaboard's name. He then outlined the somewhat complicated formula of share exchanges and disposition of cash and assets by which the consolidation would be carried out. A motion to accept these recommendations was passed and the wheels were set in motion to merge Astexo's identity into Seaboard's. While the dissolution of Astexo was now assured, the legal procedures leading to that end continued for better than a year.

On 15 November 1938 a motion was passed at a Seaboard meeting of directors calling for an informal assembly of key representatives of the member mills of both Astexo and Seaboard Lumber Sales Company. This would take place during the Christmas season, and it would be an occasion to discuss common problems and exchange ideas. In the pages of John Humbird's diary is found a note to the effect that the evening's entertainment was provided by a professor from the University of British Columbia who gave a dissertation on the by-products of wood, showing samples of medicines, plastics and other materials all derived from trees. The presentation could scarcely have been more appropriate.

In effect, that Christmas get-together was the farewell to Astexo. On 24 January 1939 the Seaboard minutes read: "That the books of Associated Timber Exporters Ltd. and Seaboard Lumber Sales Company Ltd. be consolidated, and that the assets and liabilities of the Associated Timber Exporters Ltd. be transferred to the books of Seaboard Lumber Sales Company Ltd., and that Seaboard Lumber Sales Company Ltd. be authorized to take such necessary acts to transact all necessary business in the name of Associated Timber Exporters Ltd., and the president and management be authorized to take such acts as are necessary to put into effect the provisions of this resolution, and that all the above shall be effective as of January 1, 1939." That was the end of Astexo as a functioning sales entity, and the final move in the changeover to CIF sales for all waterborne markets. The phasing-out process was conducted with appropriate care and timing, though new member mills continued to sign contracts with both Seaboard and Astexo for a period of time.

In August of the same year Charles Grinnell recommended that wherever and whenever possible, shipments should be marked with *Astexo Canada*. Astexo over the years had built a solid reputation for itself in the overseas markets, and it was just good business sense to continue to use its name until such time as Seaboard had developed the same credibility. In short order, Astexo's imprint was appearing on export lumber in company with Seaboard's mark. Then, on 8 October

1940 the decision was made to begin the elimination of Astexo's name from export lumber parcels. It took the better part of three years to achieve this, with Seaboard gaining in prominence as Astexo faded away.

At a Seaboard member mill assembly held on 5 January 1943, John Humbird asked for a show of hands approving the complete discontinuation of the use of the Astexo trademark, contingent on the successful registration of the Seaboard trademark as the company's official symbol. Twenty members were in favour of discontinuing the Astexo mark, with two opposed. By May 1943 the Astexo mark was gone, replaced by a registered *Seaboard Canada* trademark, the name in bold letters enclosed in the end section outline of a piece of timber.

Astexo's key people were absorbed into Seaboard without delay. J. G. McConville became vice-president in the Seaboard organization with specific responsibility for the Australian and New Zealand markets, having already established suitable business connections in those countries. James P. O'Hagan was named manager of the Astexo FAS department within the Seaboard structure. The final stages saw Astexo's direct involvement in Australia narrowed to the exclusive sales rights for the export of logs supplied by Crofton Export Company Ltd., Goodwin Johnson Ltd. and Nelson Spencer Ltd. A Seaboard man, Albert A. Head, was sent to assist manager L. S. Anderson in the Astexo office in Sydney, Australia. When Charles Grinnell visited Australia in June 1938, he initiated the action that resulted in the transition of Astexo to Seaboard in that market. Albert Head became manager, and Anderson returned to British Columbia.

The managerial strength and determination of Charles Grinnell are apparent at all stages of the company's formative period. Although he was surrounded by an equally determined board of directors, he was able to communicate his beliefs and convictions to this group. He saw no reason for Seaboard, or any other assembly of mills such as Astexo, to deal through middlemen exporters. His impatience with McConville's strict adherence to the Astexo marketing formula was thinly concealed. In his estimation, if Seaboard was to succeed then Astexo was redundant, and with the ultimate support of men like Humbird, Mackin and Stone, he was able to achieve his ends.

The set-up was such that Grinnell answered to the member mills and was subject to his board of directors, but was in no way subservient to them. He had a plan for Seaboard, he knew what his position was in that plan, and he knew that without the total support of the member mills the plan was little more than a pipe dream. It would have to be said that Charles Grinnell was an innovator of the highest calibre, as well as an accomplished salesman. He was able to sell the Seaboard plan to a group of mill owners who were groping for a stratagem. Also, he was able to sell himself to the same controlling group as the manager of a new and better way to sell lumber products in the overseas markets. Finally, he seems to have positioned himself in such a way that the member mills felt secure in their position of control. He was trusted, respected and listened to.

Time would reveal his preference to manage Seaboard's affairs from home base in Vancouver. Business trips were not his favourite form of activity, although in Seaboard's formative years, as we have already seen, he travelled as much as was necessary to negotiate critical agreements with agents, to become acquainted with new markets, and to set up new branch offices wherever his presence seemed to be essential.

Other Seaboard representatives, particularly John Humbird, continued to show the company flag in the marketplace. Vice-president and treasurer C. J. Culter visited the U.K. and met with Seaboard's newly acquired agents in 1935; J. O. Cameron and Carlton Stone went to the U.K. in 1938; John Humbird and Seaboard's secretary, Harold V. Simpson, travelled to the U.K. in 1939. This personal attention to the United Kingdom was in direct response to the business emerging from a market that represented by far the largest volume on Seaboard's books.

Nor was travel all one way. In August 1938 a large British delegation of importers, thirty-four in all, arrived in British Columbia. The group had been assembled under the chairmanship of E. P. Tetsall of William Brown & Company, Ipswich. Canadian members of the delegation, representing British Columbia, were Agent General W. A. (Bill) McAdam and Timber Trade Commissioner Douglas Roe, both of whom were held in high regard by the timber traders in the U.K. Although the delegation was hosted by the province of British Columbia, Seaboard played a substantial role in the entertainment and indoctrination of its members. One of Seaboard's gestures of hospitality was to entertain the delegation at a banquet in the Hotel Vancouver on August twenty-third, followed by a visit to a baseball game.

As might be expected, the members of the delegation were divided among British Columbia's principal export lumber firms, of which Seaboard and MacMillan's were the two largest. Seaboard was particularly involved with the following:

E. P. Tetsall	Wm. Brown & Company, Ipswich
J. N. Craig	Craigs Ltd., Widnes
George Mackie	Garland Rogers, Leith

C. M. O'Kelly	Irish Lumber Importers Association, Dublin
W. R. E. Phelps	John Bland & Company, Cardiff
H. H. Goddard	H. Goddard, Liverpool
I. J. O'Hea	W. H. Colt & Company, Glasgow
J. E. Forrest	Brownlee & Company, Glasgow
Mrs. Hemingway	Scantlebury & Hemingway, London
Norman French	Timber Trades Journal, London

No effort was spared to show the group British Columbia's logging and lumber operations in a favourable light. Tours were conducted to the most productive logging and sawmill operations on the mainland and Vancouver Island. With few exceptions, the visitors, viewing this kind of logging and sawmilling for the first time, expressed their amazement at the scale of the operations. Massive trees called for massive machinery at every stage of the harvesting and manufacturing process, and a first introduction to this was impressive.

More than one member of the delegation commented on the apparent waste and destruction created in the logging operations. This would be repeated in other years by other visitors to British Columbia's logging scene. Hemlock was not afforded the respect it receives today, and was often left behind as an uneconomic residue of logging. In fact, the visit of the 1938 U.K. delegation provided an opportunity to promote a greater use of hemlock and western red cedar, neither of which had gained the complete confidence of U.K. agents and buyers. Samples of well-manufactured, properly dried hemlock lumber were displayed at several of the mills, including hemlock-framed structures and examples of joinery. It was pointed out that Australia, in 1937, had formally accepted Canadian hemlock as a suitable material for the construction of butter boxes not only because of its structural strength and stability but also because it did not impart a "flavour" to the butter it contained. This did not result in a sudden conversion to hemlock on the part of the U.K. delegation, but it made an impact.

At the same time, as part of the education process, the delegation was presented once more with the arguments for the use of one-quarter inch scant Douglas-fir, for example, a 2″ × 4″ stud planed four sides to produce a finished product 1¾″ × 3¾″. This recommendation had first been made in 1932 during the visit of the B.C. mill men to the U.K. Henry Mackin had been the principal spokesman on behalf of the scant formula, pointing out that quarter scant Douglas-fir was as strong as full size lumber, and in every way as useful and versatile. He noted that the savings would be considerable because shipping by water is calculated on volume rather than weight. The effort to persuade the U.K. to accept the quarter scant product had continued from that time on, the argument being pressed vigorously by British Columbia's agents general and trade commissioners. The 1938 British delegation heard the story once again without committing itself one way or another. After its departure, John Humbird observed that two of the delegation in particular, Messrs. E. P. Tetsall and I. J. O'Hea, had extended themselves to promote B.C. wood by means of talks to timber trade groups throughout Britain. O'Hea filmed many of the highlights of the trip to be shown to these audiences. Beyond these comments, Humbird was not prepared to go further in the way of positive evaluation. It must have been deeply satisfying to him therefore to hear from Agent General McAdam, shortly after his return to England, that the timber trade had formally accepted the quarter scant formula. Education was making an impact.

In the same year affairs took a more positive turn in the United States with the signing of a tripartite agreement among the U.S., the U.K. and Canada. The U.S. tariff at this time still remained, although it had now been reduced to $1.50 per thousand feet. It appeared that this deterrent to Canadian lumber sales in the U.S. was about to be removed, but actually the tax was retained for two more years. British Columbia's lumbermen were disappointed, but they did not protest too strenuously. United Kingdom trade could scarcely have been more buoyant, compensating nicely for the restricted business in the United States. The British acceptance of quarter scant made the U.S. tariff imposition much easier to tolerate.

* * *

In Europe, Adolph Hitler's sabre rattling was becoming worrisome. The possibility of war was something most Canadian businessmen preferred not to think about. Seaboard was not alone in its optimistic determination that all would be well and that attention to the export markets in a continuing peaceful environment was the paramount consideration. It was business as usual.

In the U.K. Seaboard's Jack Hood was experiencing some difficulties. An excellent mill man and a lumber expert, he had functioned impressively in a British Columbia environment; however, he was having trouble adapting to new customs and procedures in the British business world. Under more stable circumstances his situation would have been secure, but it was a critical period, and the decision was made to replace him as soon as another appropriate position could be found for him.

Claude Effinger was selected as Hood's replacement. "It was a traumatic situation," he recalls. "Jack Hood had been my appointment. To this day I don't think I have met a better lumberman, and it was a matter of real concern and acute embarrassment to me to have to take over his job. I went to London by way of San Francisco World's Fair. My wife went that far with me together with the Solloways. Then I took a train to New York, boarded the *Queen Mary* and braced myself for the scene in England." Ostensibly Effinger was in England to open and manage an office in Liverpool. It was January 1939, and the Liverpool office never came to pass. Shortly after his arrival, Claude Effinger took over in the London office on Canon Street, and Jack Hood went to work for Munro, Brice, one of the English agents.

When Effinger was transferred to the United Kingdom, a replacement had to be found for him in the Vancouver office. The man selected was Clifford Crispin, an experienced and capable lumberman who had come up through the ranks, starting with Fraser Valley and New Westminster mills. He worked for J. G. Robson at Timberland for a few years; then was lured to the Bloedel-Donovan mill in Bellingham, below the border in Washington state. Robson persuaded him to return to Timberland, and it was while he was there that one of H. R. MacMillan's lieutenants hired him away to take a position at newly formed Canadian White Pine.

This was the period when MacMillan was struggling to fill tie orders for the U.K. railroads. Seaboard had cut off his major source of supply and he had launched into the acquisition of mills and signed contracts with mills to fill a large backlog of orders. Fred Manning, a Seaboard director for Manning Lumber Mills from 1939 to 1949, recalls as a tie mill operator the great pressure H. R. MacMillan exerted to ever increase production. Crispin was given the job of managing several tie mills on Vancouver Island. This he did with considerable efficiency, establishing a reputation for system and reliability. When MacMillan's export supply crisis had been overcome, Crispin was instructed to return to Canadian White Pine where, to his chagrin, he was given the job of manager of the company's sawdust retailing division. Charles Grinnell learned of Crispin's disenchantment and made him an offer which was accepted immediately. Clifford Crispin moved to fill the vacancy created by Claude Effinger and became manager of U.K. sales in the Vancouver office. In due course, he went on to even more prestigious undertakings.

If the possibility of war had made a deeper impact on the company's consciousness, it is doubtful that Effinger would have been sent to

England. Likewise, John Humbird's business trip to the U.K. in May 1939 to further cement relations with Seaboard's chosen agents and to continue the pruning of the agent list largely ignored the approaching conflict.

Humbird travelled via New York where he had a brief meeting with Seaboard's East Coast representatives, George Anderson and Harry Martin. Then he boarded the *Queen Mary* on the same sailing as Claude Effinger's wife, Helen, now going to join her husband. Also returning to England were a Mr. Lodge of Lloyd Duncan and a Mr. Ward of Edward Chaloner. Humbird notes wryly that "in view of the fact that we had already cut off Chaloner's as agents, and were intending to cut off Lloyd Duncan on this trip, this wasn't so good."

For Seaboard in the United Kingdom these were the best of times. Business was flourishing. The month of May was the first month in which Seaboard sales in the United Kindom achieved 100 million board feet, and it was an occasion to be celebrated. Claude Effinger, the incumbent Seaboard man in the U.K., received an accolade from Humbird in the form of an umbrella with the month, date and the footage engraved on a gold plate. Effinger still has the umbrella, its present excellent condition explained by the fact that he refused to use it in the rain and treated it most tenderly.

He and John Humbird made the rounds of many of the agents (sixty-six representatives of thirty-one agencies in a twenty-three-day period). Among them was a Czechoslovakian refugee attached to Foy, Morgan. His name was Walter Koerner, and he would figure prominently in the British Columbia lumber scene in years to come. Humbird's notes on him are of interest:

Koerner is brother of the Czech who has bought International Wood Products at New Westminster. Peter Schonnenchien, Koerner's nephew [whom Humbird and Effinger met at the same time], is the sales contact man for them for Koerner's Polish mills. In peculiar position. When Austria was taken over by Germany he elected Czech citizenship. When Czecho-Slovakia was taken over, his passport and citizenship were cancelled and he is presently a man without a country.

The Koerners have two mills in Poland and a hardwood beech mill in Hungarian Czecho-Slovakia. The government was taken over and they are firing all Jews in employ. This family consists of four brothers. Theodore, located in southern France, is older and apparently the leader of the family. He is retired. Walter, now in London, was originally head of state forests in Czecho-Slovakia. Leon, now in British Columbia, also had some government appointment. Otto, also in British Columbia. . . . Leon Koerner is well spoken of but Walter is supposed to be the operator while Leon handles the finance.

As usual, Humbird was able to combine serious business with lighter moments. He records a meeting with one of the U.K. traders: "Beach quite a sleight-of-hand man. Learned a couple of new tricks from him and gave him the split note one. He was tickled and fell all over himself."

On the more serious side, the weeding-out of agents continued apace, and a diary entry dated Friday, 2 June attests to this:

Took the 8:45 A.M. train from Paddington Station to Cardiff. Breakfast on the train with Hal [Simpson] and Claude. Discussed cutting out further agents. Looks now as if we would discontinue with Hunts Bros., Farnsworth and Jardine, and Baird at Glasgow. Due to the fact that Lloyd Duncan have just gone to the expense of having Lodge out to B.C., will continue with them for the time being, but believe we will have to cut them off in a comparatively short time. Andrew Elliot in Glasgow will now be the only resident Scottish agent, so don't feel we should discontinue them.

In this notation is one of the few references to the possibility of war.

Foy Morgan attitude not right for sale of B.C. lumber. If it were not for their connection with proposed control schemes in case of war, would feel like discontinuing with them also. We should get just as much volume with fewer agents. In the case of Farnsworth and Jardine, it is possible we may have some kick back from Harold Lees and Lamb Bros., but the volume this firm produces is not sufficient to justify keeping on. These changes should be made in Liverpool, Monday or Tuesday.

There is a happy note with reference to Jack Hood in his new position: "Jack Hood and Allen Frost of Munro Brice came in at 11:30. Agreed that lumber marking should consist of a red 'Seaboard' on the end of each lumber piece plus an individual mill mark if neccessary, and by all means leave and use Astexo mark on the top of each piece. Jack has done very well this month on sales, particularly hemlock."

And evidence of internecine discontent is to be found in an entry dated 8 June 1939. Claude Effinger, it seems, was not entirely happy with his lot:

Had lunch with Claude at the Sackville Club. His point-of-view on treatment by Seaboard is not right, and he will have to snap out of it or he will be due for a shift. He feels abused that Charles [sic] Crispin took over his job at more money than he was getting, also that he is receiving less money than Jack Hood did when he left. I will see him again before we go. Have told him frankly that if I had a man working for me at Chemainus who felt the way that he does toward his job, that if I knew it I would fire him. I explained to Claude that thinking he was abused would not get him anywhere except eventually a chance to look for something else. He has a chance to make a real job of this if he digs into it.

It would appear that Effinger took the discussion to heart. Many years later he was to become vice-president and managing director of Seaboard.

The only other serious reference to Seaboard's concern with war is found in an account of a meeting John Humbird had with one of the principals of Gabriel Wade & English. Humbird had been advised that Christopher Gabriel would likely occupy one of the main positions in the British Timber Control in the case of war, and he was eager to remain on a good footing with these people. The company's executive advised him of the following probabilities:

"European countries will all be short in timber supplies this year and Canada will have to take up the slack. If peace is secured there will be a world boom in lumber. If peace continues to be uneasy, the British government will continue to buy in substantial quantities. If war comes a large stockpile of lumber products is a good thing to have. Whatever happens, European countries can't take up any slack in demand before next year."

Humbird must have made this entry with some satisfaction. Everything pointed to continuing good times for Seaboard. He returned to North America aboard the newly commissioned *Mauritania* and, shortly after, he presented his report to Seaboard's directors in Vancouver, painting what could only be a positive picture of the company's expectations. At the same time the announcement was made of the removal of Lloyd Duncan, Farnsworth and Jardine, Hunt Brothers and Foy, Morgan from the list of Seaboard agents.

As the thirties reached their close, Seaboard, ever careful to keep all markets active and to develop new markets wherever possible, decided that Eastern Canada was deserving of attention. The country's largest concentration of population was in the East. British Columbia lumber products had gained acceptance there and were in demand. Delivery could be made more cheaply by water than by rail. The reasons for opening a Seaboard office in eastern Canada were at least as good as for maintaining an office on the U.S. East Coast. True, comparable volumes did not exist in eastern Canada, but on the other hand there were no restrictive tariffs to discourage sales.

Charles Grinnell managed to persuade the member mills of the advantages of an eastern Canadian office. In January 1939 Harry O'Hagan arrived in Montreal with a mandate to represent Seaboard in eastern Canada and Newfoundland. In other times and circumstances this move might have worked, but war was closer than most wanted to believe.

In retrospect, Harry O'Hagan, now retired, states that the omens of war were becoming oppressive. "The signs were all there," he recalls, "but none of us were prepared to admit it. It was a kind of ostrich mentality. There I was in Montreal, doing my best to develop some kind of waterborne trade. I remember I was promoting mining timbers in particular. It was a hopeless exercise because there were no ships to be had. British and Canadian bottoms had all been taken by the U.K. government hurrying to stockpile before the first shot was fired."

O'Hagan's brief term in Montreal was anything but productive for his stated reason. The office was closed in August 1939, and he returned to Vancouver. The most positive occurrence in that eight-month period was that he met Carmelita, the girl who would become his wife.

The Seaboard scene on the eve of war has been set. In the first months of 1939 the export lumber trade was buoyant and the future looked very good indeed. Newspaper editorials of the day repeated the theme that "war can be avoided." Virtually everyone had adopted an optimistic stance, in spite of Harry O'Hagan's admission that the signs of war were becoming oppressive.

Typical of the "business as usual" attitude was the visit of H. V. Simpson to South Africa in 1939 to explore the opening market potential in that country which had been effectively stimulated by William Johnston. Johnston became B.C. Timber Trade Commissioner to South Africa in 1936 and began an uphill struggle to elicit some interest in B.C. lumber. Traditionally South Africa was an importer of Baltic wood and by and large was quite satisfied with that source of supply. Johnston, by dint of hard work and persuasive talent, had convinced the South African buyers to double their purchases of Douglas-fir, as well as introducing them to hemlock and cedar. It remained now for Seaboard to capitalize on the commissioner's effort. Simpson's report to the directors that South Africa warranted a Seaboard office was not acted upon at that time because of the interference of the war.

Likewise, good things were happening in the Mid-East. In 1939

W. W. Harvey was appointed British Columbia's special timber commissioner assigned to investigate markets for creosoted timber particularly in Ceylon, India, Egypt and Palestine. His efforts were successful enough to generate two cargoes of creosoted sleepers for the Ceylon Railway, and Claude Effinger flew to Alexandria to meet with Harvey not only in the conclusion of this business but also in the sale of another cargo.

Not until the end of August is there any significant record of Seaboard's girding for the possibility of war. On the twenty-ninth of the month Humbird reported to the directors that because of generally unsettled conditions due to the political situation in Europe the company was unable to sell additional business. Exchange rates were fluctuating wildly and it was impossible to obtain tonnage to carry further commitments. "In general," John Humbird said, "anticipating the possibility of war being declared, all of our contracts, charters, and so forth, have been reviewed with our solicitors, with a view to seeing what our position would be in the event of war being declared . . . with the further thought of putting ourselves in as good a position as possible."

At this meeting, one of the directors, a retired colonel, congratulated management on its precautionary actions even though they would prove to be unneccessary. In his opinion there was no more danger of war being declared than there was "of the Metropolitan Building sprouting wings and flying away."

War was declared on 3 September 1939. Thirty Seaboard member companies and an administrative staff,* in Vancouver and overseas, wondered what role they would be called on to play in a period of world conflict, the length of which could not be guessed.

* See Appendix A, page 282.

SEVEN

WORLD WAR & A CORPORATE BATTLE

On 19 September 1939 Humbird appointed a War Council consisting of himself, C. J. Culter, J. H. McDonald, J. G. Robson, B. M. Farris and H. J. Mackin. This group was authorized to act in emergency on behalf of the board and membership. Not much later the B.C. Lumber and Shingle Manufacturers Association struck a similar War Council with Seaboard's Council members performing in a dual capacity.

At this time the following cable, signed jointly by Seaboard and MacMillan Export Company, was sent to the United Kingdom Trades Federation:

WE WISH TO ASSURE YOUR ORGANIZATION OF OUR FULLEST JOINT CO-OPERATION IN ANY PLAN EVOLVED BY THE TIMBER INDUSTRY OF THE UNITED KINGDOM TO MEET THE PRESENT EMERGENCY STOP ARE CONFIDENT BRITISH COLUMBIA CAN SUPPLY A SUBSTANTIAL INCREASED QUANTITY OVER PRESENT COMMITMENTS PROVIDED TONNAGE IS AVAILABLE.

The final sentence was the loaded one.

The first impact to be felt by the lumber industry was the shortage of ships. Just before the outbreak of war, 70 per cent of all British Columbia's waterborne exports were moving in British ships. Almost overnight this tonnage was diverted to operations with a different and higher priority, making it extremely difficult for the mills to adjust to the bottlenecks that were created. Most mills began to stockpile.

In the United Kingdom under wartime conditions, all lumber products were purchased through the Timber Control Department of the British Ministry of Supply. There was no doubt whatever that Britain needed Canada's lumber. The war had cut off all sources of supply except Canada, and the deployment of ships was threatening to reduce delivery from that source to a trickle.

Seaboard's Bruce Farris together with H. R. MacMillan travelled to Ottawa to work with government and rail authorities on a system for moving lumber across the country by flatcar at a cost mutually satisfactory to the lumber companies and the railways. Their success was evident as lumber soon began to make the long trip from the Pacific to the Atlantic by rail, transferring to ships in Montreal, Halifax and other eastern ports serving the United Kingdom. Even after order was restored to shipping in a few months, the trans-Canada shipment of lumber by rail was maintained, continuing for most of the war. In all, 20 per cent of British Columbia's export shipments were delivered in this manner during World War II—an impressive achievement when it is realized that 60 per cent of British Columbia's total lumber output went overseas in that period.

Not that Seaboard did not attempt to solve the shipping problem. The newspapers reported Charles Grinnell's speech in April 1940 in which he stated that the institution of a shipbuilding program would be Canada's most useful contribution to the war. It was a hot topic of discussion in government circles, and ultimately that kind of thinking resulted in action, but not in 1941. The B.C. Lumber and Shingle Manufacturers Association's formal proposal in that year to begin the construction of wooden ships was rejected by the federal government.

Shipbuilding aside, Canada had taken on some gargantuan tasks, not the least of which was responsibility for the British Commonwealth Air Training Plan. This included the construction of 100 completely equipped air fields and training bases, all of which relied heavily on the use of B.C. wood. In addition, operational army, airforce and naval establishments were needed for Canada's own defence. Wood was the logical material for the construction of barracks, drill halls, warehouses, even aircraft hangars requiring huge areas of clear space. British Columbia's long timbers were the answer for hangar spans and trusses.

In order to introduce system and logistics into this truly formidable task of lumber supply, C. D. Howe, federal minister of supply, appointed a Canadian Timber Controller. His choice was H. R. MacMillan, and it was a good one. Both men had a propensity for hard work and for finding the most expedient means to achieve their ends. They worked well together until politics and bureaucracy drove MacMillan to frustration and he and Howe came to a stormy parting of the ways. But while MacMillan was Timber Controller he moved mountains of wood.

He took over his post in July 1940 and wasted no time in asserting his authority, making it clear that the lumber industry in wartime would not be an occasion for profiteering but rather an occasion where industry, labour and government shared the losses. In every lumber producing province he set up an advisory committee to assist in the extraction of maximum production.

In British Columbia the committee consisted substantially of Seaboard mill men. General problems and overriding issues would be dealt with by J. G. Robson, president of the BCLSMA; C. Dewey Anderson, president of the B.C. Loggers Association, and W. J. Van Dusen, president of the Western Lumber Association (the parallel body of the BCLSMA). Export problems would be the concern of Seaboard's C. H. Grinnell, L. R. Scott of MacMillan Export, and Harry B. Dollar, Canadian Robert Dollar Company (trading directly with the Far East). Problems in domestic supply were the responsibility of J. R. Murray of Canadian Western, C. J. Culter, Hammond Cedar Company (and a Seaboard vice-president), and R. W. Steveston, Canadian White Pine (a MacMillan mill). Sitka spruce production would be under the eye of Fred Brown, B & K Logging, and Aird Flavelle, Thurston-Flavelle.

The production of spruce became a high priority item with the development of the renowned Mosquito bomber with its spruce frame and plywood skin. In 1942 a federal Crown corporation, Aero Timber Products, was established to further expedite the production of airplane spruce. R. J. Filberg of Comox Logging and Railway Company was president and J. H. McDonald of B.C. Manufacturing Company was vice-president.

It is rather extraordinary that Canada's, and in particular British Columbia's, lumber production in the war years was as high as it was, taking into account the departure of so many loggers and millworkers to the armed services. Early on, C. D. Howe declared logging and lumber manufacturing essential war industries, but this did not alleviate the labour shortage. Some 7000 men served in the Canadian Forestry

Corps during the war; most of these went overseas and trained as combat troops as well as foresters. So critical did the need for competent loggers and mill workers become that ten Canadian Forestry Corps companies (2000 men) were returned to Canada in 1943 to attempt to improve the situation.

At Seaboard's head office a number went into uniform or into other war service. Bob Edgett, Tom Ferris and Dick Silbernagel joined the RCASC. Frank Solloway ended up as a captain in an RCA anti-tank battery. Vassall Forrester was seconded to the Ministry of Transport in Montreal, his position in Vancouver filled by W. C. Robinson, one of the top executives with Seaboard's U.K. chartering agency Eggar Forrester & Verner in London.

John Humbird's twin sons joined the U.S. army. Charles Grinnell had two sons in the services: Charles Junior was in the U.S. Army Air Force and son James was in the Royal Canadian Naval Volunteer Reserve. Henry Mackin had a son and daughter in the RCAF. Murray Mather joined the Canadian Navy, and undoubtedly there were many others who left Seaboard for active service but whose names are not available in existing records.

An interesting aside related to the war experiences of Seaboard personnel has to do with F. G. Solloway who was struck down by an automobile during a London blackout. As he was being lifted into the ambulance, he noted a plate on its side with the inscription: "Donated by Mr. and Mrs. R. B. Cherry, Vancouver, B.C." Cherry was at that time head of Sterling Lumber Company, a member of Seaboard.

As one contribution to the war effort, Seaboard volunteered for a rehabilitation project involving the safety of a group of children from the United Kingdom. At the outbreak of war the decision was made to make accommodation available locally for British children escaping the English cities targeted for strategic bombing. On July fifth Seaboard minutes record an arrangement with the Fairbridge Farm School on Vancouver Island to pay for the construction of additional accommodation including the construction of a six-bed infirmary. At the same time twenty-eight mill members accepted John Humbird's invitation to accept the responsibility for the upkeep of twenty-eight of the refugee children. Later eight more refugees were added to the list.* As well as donating money, each subscriber would be expected to take a personal "parental" responsibility for a child.

Each "parent" agreed to keep in contact with the wartime wards while they were at the school and to take them into their own homes, or

* See Appendix C, page 284.

to locate them suitably when they were out of the school. The response to this solicitation was so positive that Claude Effinger was instructed to contact Seaboard's agents and principal customers to discover if any of them would like to send their children to live out the war in the homes of Seaboard members.

Effinger assembled a list of seven boys and girls within a few days, and the decision was then made to extend a similar invitation to the entire membership of the Timber Trades Federation in the U.K. A committee was set up to take charge of this project. Homes were found for 200 more children, but before these could embark for British Columbia an event occurred which prompted the British Government to curtail programs to send children out of England. The *City of Benares* was torpedoed and sank with many British children on board.

* * *

In 1940 an event occurred which, while related to the exigencies of war, was indicative as well of the aggressive and competitive atmosphere that prevailed between Seaboard and MacMillan regardless of the concern the principals of these two companies had to lend to the war effort. The British Timber Control Board, directed by Maj. A. I. Harris, a gentleman whose tireless and efficient performance has won generous praise from war historians, was extending itself to acquire large supplies of lumber for bomb damage repair and reconstruction. Labour shortages in Canada, combined with the uncertainty of shipping lumber cargoes, created a need for close personal negotiations. Telegrams and the mails were not good enough.

In January MacMillan and Humbird met in Vancouver to discuss the problem of supplying British Timber Control, and it was decided that a trip to the U.K. was called for. A delegation of four consisting of H. R. MacMillan, Ralph Shaw (then MacMillan's sales manager), John Humbird and Charles Grinnell would undertake the mission. The agreement was that they would meet with the British Timber Control people as a delegation and negotiate contracts together. As it happened, MacMillan had other business to attend to in Britain, related to his fisheries interests, and he elected to go with Shaw to England a few days before Humbird and Grinnell departed.

The two Seaboard men embarked from New York on 27 January aboard the S.S. *Manhattan;* they landed in Naples, entrained to Rome and then went on to Paris where they were grounded because of an extended period of bad weather. They had to content themselves with passage to London on a cross-Channel boat from Calais to Folkestone, all of which created delays and contributed to mounting impatience. While they waited in Paris, a disturbing cable arrived from MacMillan.

> JOHN HUMBIRD,
> RITZ HOTEL, PARIS.
> AFTER HAD BEEN LONDON FEW DAYS IT WAS OBVIOUS AFFAIRS WERE NOT MOVING OUR DIRECTION, CHIEFLY VESSEL SCARCITY AND LARGE PRODUCTION SEEKING MARKET, THEREFORE WHEN UNEXPECTED OPPORTUNITY AROSE TO FIX PRICE ABOUT TWO DOLLARS HIGHER THAN SEPTEMBER SALE FOR FURTHER SIX MONTHS I DID SO, REALIZING IMPOSSIBILITY OF COMMUNICATING WITH YOU, DANGERS OF WAITING WEEK, AND IMPOSSIBILITY OF GETTING MORE, BUT ON UNDERSTANDING MAKE YOU SAME OFFER—STOP—WILL AWAIT YOU SAVOY.
>
> H. R. MACMILLAN

John Humbird's reaction to this communication, while it may have revealed a trace of paranoia, was not entirely unjustified. His diary entry speaks for itself: ". . . cable received here from H. R. M. at Bristol. This is certainly a facer when we have come all this distance on his assurance that he would not only not have any negotiations with the Control but would not go near them until we could go together to talk price, amounts, shipments, etc. It was on this assurance that we have undertaken the whole trip and now to be let down like this is a hell of a note. Will be interesting to see what feeble excuse it takes for him to break his word like this."

Time and circumstance had obscured the details of this incident until Humbird's written account came to light. Mill men to this day conjecture on what happened when the heads of Canada's two largest lumber export companies struck sparks in London and Bristol better than four decades ago. Humbird writes about his meeting with MacMillan in the Savoy:

"Had breakfast and called H. R. M. who came to my room. He reiterated the advice he had cabled to Paris and said he had sold 150,000 standards* for April/September shipment. Also repeated what he said in cable that this had been done on the undertaking [Humbird's underline] that the Control would make us the same offer. All above absolutely contrary to his definite assurance that he would not approach Control in any way until our arrival and that we would make this approach together. . . . Decided to get down to Bristol and find out what was going on."

---

* A British standard is approximately 2000 feet board measure of lumber.

The British Timber Control was headquartered in Bristol, as was Seaboard's U.K. office. Claude Effinger had made the move when war was declared, wanting to be as close to Timber Control as possible. On 13 February Humbird and Grinnell met with Major Harris:

> We were taken to Cyril David's office [David was in charge of part of the Timber Control's softwood purchasing agency]. Very cordial, but could begin to feel the bad news. We were told that MacMillan was first come first served. For him 120 to 150 thousand standards; and for us 75 to 100 thousand standards at the same price, but with further cancellation privilege for the Control after three months. This was the joker after our understanding with MacMillan before we left home, and his breaking this and feathering his own nest. We were advised it was either this or drop the whole thing and discuss again in April or May. We asked for time to consider until next day, which was granted.

Negotiations and meetings within meetings proceeded to an extent that it is not necessary to record here, but Humbird's final precaution was to frame a detailed statement for both Claude Effinger, as Seaboard's representative, and for Paul Williams, the British Timber Control Board's representative, in order to put the record straight. (See Appendix D, page 285.) The rights or wrongs of this incident are not at issue here. No doubt, H. R. MacMillan, had he seen Humbird's account of what happened, would have placed his own earnest interpretation on this transaction with British Timber Control. The final outcome, of course, was a handsome contract for both companies in which Seaboard received the larger order but relations between MacMillan and Humbird, which had never been cordial, became further strained.

It was fortunate that the need for lumber in the United Kingdom was so desperate in this period, because business in other overseas markets was on the decline. Australia and New Zealand imposed import restrictions in order to protect their currency, thus causing Canada's exports in this direction to drop by 50 per cent. In South Africa in and around 1937 a recession had forced the reduction of Canadian lumber imports, no matter how favourably disposed the buyers were to the product. When the country's economy had recovered in 1940, and its traditional source of lumber supply from the Baltic countries had been cut off by the war, South Africa was more eager than ever to obtain Canadian lumber. This, of course, was virtually impossible because of shipping shortages. British Columbia's Timber Commissioner in South Africa, William Johnson, tried every official channel available to him to set up a supply line, succeeding in 1941 in obtaining two ships to carry lumber to South Africa—a pittance measured against the country's need.

In the Far East, the invasion of China by Japan had wiped out the lumber export trade to that market. Even though Japan's 1935 trade embargo had been removed in 1936, lumber export to the country had not regained its former momentum; and then, of course, Japan's entry into World War II put an end to all trade. The doors to those two markets were closed, at least until the end of the war.

Business to the West Indies was in jeopardy as well, once again because of the dearth of ships. It was decided in January 1941 to send a Seaboard representation to that market to meet with the agents and study the market firsthand. A trio made up of John Humbird, Charles Grinnell and James O'Hagan landed in Port of Spain, Trinidad, on 26 January where they met with T. Geddes Grant, Seaboard's West Indies agents. Meetings were held with eight of Seaboard's largest buyers there. Complaints were listened to, the universal one being the uncertainty of lumber delivery and the difficulty of obtaining vessels. Seaboard's delegation could do little more than share the frustration of this group—and it would go through the same exercise in Bridgetown, Barbados and Kingston, Jamaica. The value of the West Indies trip could be measured largely in terms of goodwill. Certainly it did nothing to improve lumber delivery or materialize shipping. By 1942 export to the West Indies had almost ceased.

The United Kingdom demand for lumber was so great that the loss of other export markets could be tolerated. Some of the U.K. lumber market was eroded after June 1941 when Germany attacked Russia, and Russia was suddenly on the side of the Allies. Convoys struggling across the North Atlantic with vital war supplies for Russian ports occasionally took on cargoes of Russian lumber on return trips to the United Kingdom. While this made inroads into Canada's and Seaboard's share of the U.K. market, another event occurred at the end of 1941 which would more than compensate for the drop in U.K. lumber orders. Japan attacked Pearl Harbor on 7 December, and the United States threw its full weight into the war. Very soon the U.S. demand for lumber began to accelerate dramatically.

After Pearl Harbor a small irony was created out of general apprehension that Japan might attack the West Coast of North America. Certainly the submarines were there, for one of British Columbia's Vancouver Island lighthouses was shelled. One of the first vessels torpedoed off the U.S. West Coast was carrying a full load of lumber.

Military precautions including blackouts were the order of the day. British Columbia mills tried an experiment with three consecutive nights of blackout, only to discover that production dropped by 25 to

30 per cent at a time when demand was soaring. The experiment was abandoned, and the mills equipped and trained themselves to create instant blackout in the event of attack. Until that happened production would continue twenty-four hours a day.

While Seaboard's operation was predicated on waterborne shipments exclusively, it is worth noting that on 17 March 1941 the directors approved Seaboard's entering into contracts with the member mills utilizing rail to ship lumber to the eastern United States on an exclusive basis. Because shipping was not available to this region from British Columbia, it was felt expedient to supply East Coast buyers by rail for the rest of the war if necessary, or until a reliable supply of vessels could be secured.

By May 1941 it had been officially established that lumber sales to the United Kingdom would be an automatic procedure conducted through the offices of the British Timber Control Board working with designated lumber importing agencies. Under these circumstances, Seaboard's office in Bristol was redundant. Claude Effinger was recalled to Vancouver, an order which he must have welcomed because it returned him to a condition of stability he had not enjoyed for some time.

The company's thoughtful gesture to bring him home for Christmas 1940 had led him to near disaster. The ship Seaboard had booked for his return was torpedoed with no survivors. Fortunately Effinger had switched his booking to another ship at the last moment.

In Effinger's absence from the U.K., Seaboard's affairs would be taken care of by a company set up for the purpose, comprised of all the remaining agents on Seaboard's U.K. list. Because British Timber Control would only recognize one agent for each shipper it was necessary to combine Seaboard's agents into one official entity, Associated Seaboard Agents, or "Seagents" as the company was more commonly called. (Humbird, in his first reference to this organization, had erroneously but more jauntily referred to them as "Sea Gents.") For the balance of the war, and until decontrol occurred in the postwar period, Seagents would handle Seaboard's business in the U.K., a procedure that consisted of little more than processing the orders received from British Timber Control and collecting the commissions.

Seaboard's ten agents at the beginning of the war were Balfour Williamson, Baird, Berner & Nielsen, William Brandts, Canadian American, Churchill & Sim, Alfred Dobell, D. Dorman (Ireland), Andrew Elliott (Scotland) and Munro, Brice. The chairmanship of the new company was rotated among the agents, the first chairman being Tad Wilson from the firm of Balfour Williamson. The responsibilities of Associated Seaboard Agents were relatively undemanding. George Taylor, who joined Seagents in 1949, had no illusions as to the agents' fortuitous position. "At the end of each quarter," he recalls, "the books would be checked by the auditor and the profit (commission) shared out among the member agents pro rata to the proportion of Seaboard's business they were handling when Seagents was formed. It was usual for a general meeting and lunch to be held at the Grosvenor House or the Dorchester at which the commission cheques were distributed with a great show of bonhomie and back-slapping. No wonder! When you consider they did absolutely nothing for it. They didn't even negotiate the original sales."

The Timber Control method of taking care of the agents during the war is of interest. The Control paid standard commissions on all buying to all agents concerned; however, 50 per cent of this commission was deposited in a pool to be participated in by all agents on a percentage basis calculated on their volume of business in the last three prewar years. It is said that the average commissions of eighty-eight prewar agents in softwoods alone was £629,000 annually, and of these agents the top eighteen were responsible for 70 per cent of the imports.

While 1942 saw the return of Claude Effinger to Vancouver, it also saw the sudden passing of George Anderson, longtime manager of Seaboard's New York office. Anderson was in Vancouver for a short leave and was making the rounds of the member mills when he suffered a heart attack and died. In those times of uncertainty, Seaboard did not want to incur the expense of hiring a man to replace Anderson; instead the company's secretary, H. V. Simpson, was assigned to the New York office. Also in the interests of economy, the Sydney, Australia, office was closed. Australia's import restrictions had reduced timber imports drastically with no improvement expected in the immediate future. Manager Albert Head was transferred closer to home, taking over Seaboard's Seattle office.

In the first seven months of 1942 rail sales to the East Coast amounted to 109 million, amply reflecting the upswing in the U.S. market. In that year the bulk of Seaboard's sales was to British Timber Control and the government of the United States, 58 per cent going to the U.K. and 38 per cent to the U.S.

In spite of British Columbia's formidable effort to supply the U.K. with its lumber needs, that beleaguered country continued to press for more. Canada's new Timber Controller, A. S. Nicholson, together with Major Andrews, first began applying pressure at the beginning of 1942, visiting British Columbia to issue the word that Canada's lumber industry was now on a "total war footing," a statement which bemused the mill men somewhat because that is precisely the position they felt themselves to be in. Nicholson, however, was referring more to the need to hold prices than to increase production. He also made it clear that Canada's war requirements were to be met first, followed by those of the United Kingdom and then the United States.

In September T. L. Lees, Assistant British Timber Controller in charge of transportation, came to Vancouver and addressed a full meeting of Seaboard members on the urgent need for more timber in the United Kingdom. This exhortation disturbed and frustrated men like John Humbird and Charles Grinnell who would have been delighted to supply more timber if the ships could be found to carry it. Other U.K. transportation authorities had made it very clear and firm that munitions and food took precedent over timber, particularly now that German submarines were making serious inroads into the supply convoys. The message seemed to be: "Give us more timber even though we cannot give you more ships." It was a conundrum.

There was no doubt as to the urgent need for lumber, nor the extent to which the British were prepared to go to obtain it. At one point serious consideration was given to assembling giant ship-contoured rafts of Canadian lumber, installing engines at the rear of these floating masses and propelling them across the Atlantic—an experiment which was shelved.

In December, hard on the heels of Mr. Lees came the British Timber Controller himself, Maj. A. I. Harris (who would be knighted for his tireless and efficient efforts to keep the U.K. supplied with lumber). His message was the same as his predecessor's, but harder hitting. The United Kingdom's lumber reserves were exhausted and British Columbia's stockpiles seemed to be dwindling. British Columbia would have to try harder, he said. He virtually demanded that Canada and the United States set aside their own domestic needs for lumber and channel that lumber to the U.K. Whether or not his visit was the catalyst, British Columbia in 1943 shipped 40 per cent of all its lumber and 40 per cent of all its plywood production to Britain. This was more lumber than had been shipped to that market in any of the previous three years, in spite of logging camps running at 40 per cent of their normal complement and mill labour drastically depleted. From Seaboard's position this meant that 74 per cent of its member mills' total export volume went to the U.K. that year, a situation made possible in part by a drastic reduction in United States orders, down from 38 per cent in 1942 to a disconcerting 6 per cent.

While the heat of war continued unabated, a tribute to the far-sightedness of British Timber Control must be paid. In 1943 the Control Board had begun to plan for the end of hostilities and at that time made first enquiries as to Seaboard's reaction to a twelve-month contract to supply lumber after war's end. Seaboard's members had little difficulty in approving the idea in principle, but held back on taking specific action, feeling that it was much too soon to fix prices and delivery schedules for the day after an armistice which could be a long way off.

On 15 and 16 June 1944 stronger evidence of British postwar planning was displayed when a delegation from the British Ministry of Supply and Cyril David, Deputy British Timber Controller, came to Vancouver seeking a contract with Seaboard for postwar lumber shipments to the United Kingdom over a two-year period, commencing twenty-eight days after the cessation of hostilities. No firm contract was entered into at that time, but by 18 July an agreement had been drafted committing the member mills to a minimum of 423,300,000 FBM and a maximum of 734,000,000 FBM over two years. By December the amended agreement was in the hands of the members for final perusal and acceptance.

In 1944, 72 per cent of Seaboard's total volume went to British Timber Control, with the balance going to Australia, New Zealand and the South Seas (12.3 per cent), United States rail (11.3 per cent), South Africa (4.1 per cent) and the West Indies (1.7 per cent).

On 20 March 1945 Lees was back in Vancouver, this time to report that Britain had but three months' supply of lumber left. He stated that the present essential rate of consumption and the existing rate of shipment would reduce that figure to a one-month supply by year's end, and he pleaded for more production.

On 15 May C. D. Howe, Minister of Supply for Canada, issued a request for the services of Clifford Crispin who had been managing Seaboard's United Kingdom Department with considerable effectiveness. Charles Grinnell could ill-afford the absence of Crispin, but was able to make an arrangement with the federal government for the military demobilization of Bob Edgett to compensate for the gap left by Crispin. Claude Effinger took over U.K. sales and Edgett became manager of U.S. rail sales.

With hostilities in Europe all but over and with the British Ministry of Supply and British Timber Control pressing for the implementation of the postwar sales agreement it became essential and expedient for final negotiations to be concluded in the U.K. where effective dates, cost change formulae, division of orders and other matters could be ironed out. To this end John Humbird left for England on 16 May 1945, travelling from Montreal on a British bomber destined for Prestwick, Scotland.

Claude Effinger and MacMillan's Ralph Shaw followed a week later to be present with Humbird at various conferences with the British Timber Controller (now Sir Archibald Harris) and his several deputies and assistants. These meetings ended with a memorandum of interpretations of the postwar contract, which was signed on behalf of the British Timber Control Board by the Assistant Timber Controller, Paul Williams. The effective date of the postwar agreement was established as 6 June 1945 with delivery to begin within twenty-eight days of that time. Seaboard's final commitment was to deliver to the U.K. a minimum of 450 million feet and a maximum of 734 million feet within two years of the commencing date. For a survey of possible or probable suppliers to British Timber Control, see Appendix E, p. 289.

The aftermath of war was making great domestic demands. Seaboard and MacMillan, it would seem, had made a smooth transition from war into peace. There was little need to worry about competition from other suppliers; they had all the business they could handle.

* * *

We have said a great deal about the shortage of shipping during World War II and the considerable frustration created by Seaboard's inability to find vessels for the lumber the United Kingdom needed so badly. It might be natural to suppose that Seaboard Shipping was inactive during the war years, but this was far from the case. The company was in charge of the agency handling the British Timber Control boats assigned to carry Seaboard lumber, and also continued freighting business to other markets wherever an order could be filled and a ship could be found.

In 1939, for instance, phasing into the war, Seaboard Shipping loaded 131 vessels under their own charters, serving forty-nine ports throughout the world. In addition to this, four vessels were loaded for British Timber Control, twelve vessels were chartered through the B.C. Shipping Agencies for lumber cargoes to Australia, and one vessel was chartered through the North Pacific Shipping company for the West Indies. Another West Indies vessel and a vessel for Alexandria and Haifa were chartered in 1939 for loading in 1940. The chartered vessels called at twenty-three ports, ten in Australasia, eight in the U.S. Atlantic and Canada and six in South Africa.

This was a year of indoctrination for the new management of Seaboard Shipping. H. E. (Hap) Solloway spent three months in England with Eggar, Forrester & Verner, taking time out to study shipping procedures in Sweden and other parts of the Continent. Altogether he visited forty different ports. Upon Solloway's return to Vancouver, Vassall Forrester travelled to England for a five-month period while W. C.

Robinson, a director of Eggar's, moved to Seaboard's Vancouver office for the same period of time to acquaint himself with the company's systems and personnel.

But by 1940 the war was in full swing, creating some marked differences in Seaboard Shipping's activities. Seaboard handled the vessels as agents to the British Ministry of Shipping, supervising the loading of the ships in close co-operation with local representatives of the Ministry. Eighty-three full cargoes were dispatched to the United Kingdom; eleven charters went to Australasia, eight to the U.S. and the Canadian Atlantic Coast, four to the West Indies, three to the Mediterranean and five to South Africa. Altogether in 1940 Seaboard Shipping chartered 114 full cargoes plus large and small lumber parcels on 156 outside vessels and liners.

Because New York was becoming increasingly the entrée for any available free tonnage, in particular ships flying the Panamanian flag, which seemed to possess more immunity to the vagaries of world governments, Hap Solloway was sent to New York to survey the shipping scene. As a result of his findings he was assigned to New York on 3 January 1941 with the mandate to secure a reasonably steady supply of ships for as long as was neccessary.

The years 1941 and 1942 were not happy years for Seaboard Shipping. Early in 1941 a few ships moved from Canada's West Coast, but after that lumber movements were largely by rail to eastern Atlantic ports for shipment by vessel to the U.K. The United States/Japanese war in the Pacific painted a gloomy prospect for the future. Parcel space business for Australia, the South Seas and the West Indies was gravely threatened, and Seaboard's chances of being able to charter for these markets appeared remote. Under the circumstances, because Seaboard Shipping's role had become minimal, Vassall Forrester was seconded to the British Ministry of Shipping in Halifax to help expedite shipping from the East Coast to the United Kingdom, and there seemed little reason to fill his position at Seaboard.

While waterborne shipments were slowing to a standstill, the shipping company remained busy servicing Seaboard Lumber's shipments by rail to the Atlantic seaboard. Little improvement was experienced in 1943. British Timber Control business that year saw 27 per cent of all lumber orders moved by water from the West Coast, while 73 per cent moved by rail across Canada for loading aboard ships on the East Coast. However, one significant change occurred which would affect Seaboard Shipping and carry through to its postwar operations. The Canadian government was now well into wartime shipbuilding and had set up an agency, the Park Steamship Company, to handle the deployment of these vessels for the delivery of war materials and for other world trade. Its policy was to use this growing fleet to service the United Kingdom, South Africa and Australia, with first priority given to the U.K. Selected Canadian shipping companies were allocated one or more of these ships and given the responsibility to manage them according to Park Steamship's instruction. In 1943 Seaboard was informed that it would receive three of the Park vessels. One was commissioned and assigned to Seaboard immediately. The other two were still in the shipyards in various stages of completion, one to be delivered in March 1944 and the other in June. While the management of the Park fleet would make new demands on the shipping company, the additional expense and effort would be more than compensated for by the fees and expense allowances paid by the Park organization.

Seaboard's first Park vessel was assigned to the British Columbia/ South Africa trade, and little time was lost in putting the new vessel to work. By January 1944 the ship had taken on a full cargo and was on its way to South Africa. Although the acquisition of the Park vessels was welcomed, Seaboard remained alert to the possibility of making closer and more productive arrangements with other shipping companies to serve as the agent for other vessels.

In 1944 Seaboard Shipping handled only three vessels for the British Ministry of Supply, and its parcel business was down from the previous year. There were two direct charters to the West Indies, but apart from that very little opportunity presented itself to charter to any market. Fortunately Seaboard's rail shipments and the Park Steamship arrangement generated steady business. Up to the end of 1943, Seaboard had received the management of three Park vessels. In 1944 the allocation was increased to ten vessels, eight of which were put into operation during the course of the year; the other two remained to be completed for delivery in February and July 1945. This brought the company into parity with top Canadian operators, many of whom had been in a more preferred position when the distribution of vessels began. John Humbird attributed this gratifying position to the lobbying skills of Bruce Farris, a Seaboard vice-president who had twice accompanied Charles Grinnell to Ottawa to petition for the allocation of more ships.

Now in possession of ten 10,000-ton vessels, Seaboard Shipping was truly active again and in need of a competent shipping manager. Because of a personality difference with Charles Grinnell, Seaboard's former shipping manager Vassall Forrester had decided not to return to his place but had recommended a shipping colleague, William Hurford, for the position. Hurford was a seasoned shipping man who had learned his business in the United Kingdom and had been attached to the British Ministry of Shipping in the United States when vessels were being requisitioned for the D-Day invasion. He took over as manager of Seaboard Shipping in May 1945, ushering in a significant period for the company.

Rounding out the story of Seaboard during the war years is an incident that is not directly related to the war. It has to do with John Humbird and his mill, Victoria Lumber & Manufacturing Company, one of the flagship mills on the Seaboard member list.

Victoria Lumber had always been one of the largest and most productive mills on the West Coast. After a devastating fire in 1925, it rose from the ashes, as large as ever and even more efficient, thanks to advancing technology. John A. Humbird was the third in line in the Humbird dynasty. His grandfather had been the mill's founder and first president, and following his death, the company's destiny was largely in the hands of its manager, E. J. Palmer, the man who had hired and then rejected H. R. MacMillan. When Palmer died unexpectedly, John A. Humbird stepped into his position as president and managing director, determined to keep the mill productive and profitable.

His capability can be measured by the fact that he was able to manage Victoria Lumber with a tight rein while at the same time functioning as the working president of Seaboard in its formative period. Had John Humbird been in total control of Victoria Lumber, he likely would have continued to operate it indefinitely. The business had become his life. However, he had to answer to others. The mill's owners, including his father, T. J. Humbird, were aging and anxious to put their affairs in order to avoid the erosion of death duties. An additional thorn in their sides was what they considered to be an unfair forest tenure system that imposed a tax on the purchase of timber which, in their own books, had been written off long ago. Their decision was firm and unyielding: Victoria Lumber & Manufacturing Company must be sold. John Humbird had no alternative but to start the proceedings. The one proviso he insisted on was that Victoria Lumber would not be sold to H. R. MacMillan. The antagonism between these two men persisted, and the experience Humbird had gone through with MacMillan and the British Timber Control in 1940 was still fresh. Sell the mill he would—but not to H. R. MacMillan.

In the fall of 1942 he received encouraging overtures from one of Canada's most successful businessmen, E. P. Taylor. When the Toronto business tycoon went as far as to inspect Victoria Lumber and its forest holdings in that year, Humbird's curiosity was aroused because Taylor had never evinced an interest in forestry before. But when Humbird tried to discover if Taylor was acting on his own behalf or in company with others, he was told in effect that this was not his concern.

Taylor took his time to make a final decision. In the interim, he had the company's plants, logging operations and timber holdings carefully evaluated. One of the ironies is that he asked Wayne Pendleton, one of Seaboard's staunchest supporters and a lumberman of great knowledge and experience, to assess the Victoria Lumber empire. Taylor could scarcely have received a better evaluation. The description of the sawmill was impressive and commended the company's townsite and prevailing community spirit. He summed up his report with these words: "This is, without a doubt, the finest property in B.C. and with their vast timber resources behind them will no doubt be in this position for many years to come."

Taylor did purchase the property. He describes the conclusion of the deal: "Humbird came to my suite in the Vancouver Hotel and I made him an offer—I remember saying, 'This is my final offer. Take it or leave it.' " The offer was for $9 million in debentures and several million in cash. Apparently Humbird had gone to the meeting expecting a considerably smaller amount. He was prepared to trade up to a price which would still have been less than Taylor's. Under the circumstances he accepted quickly.

In the early summer of 1944 H. R. Macmillan became mill managers and agents for Victoria Lumber for a fee of $250,000 a year which was merely the first stage in acquiring full ownership. For MacMillan this was a successful conclusion to his reported promise when he left the employ of Victoria Lumber that "the next time I walk through this door I'll own the place." It is to be supposed, however, that he was much more intent on acquiring one of British Columbia's best and biggest mills than he was on enjoying revenge.

As for John Humbird, the double deal must have seemed the ultimate betrayal. MacMillan had used his friend E. P. Taylor as intermediary to obtain the mill. It was a business transaction on a grand and devious scale. Thus the little war between two strong and determined lumbermen came to a conclusion within a few months of the termination of World War II. It was now time to adjust to the return of peace.

EIGHT

CORPORATE
COUNTERPLAYS
& MARKET EXPANSION

Seaboard's entrée into the lumber export business initiated a corporate tug-of-war between H. R. Mac-Millan and Seaboard to attract and secure lumber production. The competition was intense, with advantages gained and lost on a regular and often unpredictable basis.

MacMillan had entered the private sector as a businessman involved exclusively in the export of B.C. lumber products, and probably would have been content to continue in that capacity if Seaboard had not effectively eliminated the major source of his export lumber supply. He was then obliged to acquire his own mills and to supplement his lumber supply from the few independent, nonaligned mills left in the province.

His first incursion into the business of lumber manufacture was the purchase of Pacific Cedar Company in 1926, prior to breaking with Astexo. This purchase resulted in the dissolution of his partnership with Montague Meyer, who felt that lumber export entailed enough risk without the added hazards of lumber production. He next acquired a small number of rail tie mills on Vancouver Island which enabled him to supply British Rail orders, particularly after Seaboard's supply was no longer available to him. But in 1936 an acquisition of real significance occurred which elevated MacMillan to a major lumber producer.

A Walk Through the Office

1 Charles H. Grinnell,
one of the instigators and the first manager of the
Seaboard companies. He was prominent for seventeen years in the
development of Seaboard and its world markets, retiring in 1952.

2
A reception aboard M.V. *Skaubord* on its maiden voyage to Vancouver, 1979. *Front row (l to r):* Ken Milton, Capt. P. Traagstad (ship's master), Art Fullman, Jack Cunningham. *Back row (l to r):* Murray Mather, Harry Berry, Capt. W. Ellis, George Smith (L & K Sawmills), Jack Brigden, Bill Whiles, Dick Silbernagel, Vassall Forrester, Ken Sloat, Tom Ferris, Bob Sayle.

3
Seaboard House, the companies' head office (1948–78), at the corner of Burrard and Hastings in Vancouver.

4
Kit Candler (*l*), Seaboard's European representative, hosts reception aboard M.S. *Swift Pool,* Rotterdam, 1961, for Seaboard's agents, Altius & Company, and brokers.

5
R. to l: B. L. (Dick) Silbernagel, Seaboard's Australia sales manager, H. McKenzie, an Australian importer, and Frank G. Solloway, Seaboard's Sydney office manager, 1952.

6
R. D. (Doug) Reid joined Seaboard in 1952 to develop an export market for plywood.

4

5

6

7

7
J. K. (Ken) Sloat, Seaboard's New York representative for almost twenty-three years. He retired in 1974.
8
W. Laird Wilson was with the company for thirty-four years, associated mainly with U.S. sales as sales manager and later in the Japanese market. He retired in 1982.
9
W. O. (Bill) Whiles started with Seaboard in 1952 as sales manager, first for the Caribbean and later for Pacific Rim markets. He retired in 1973.
10
T. W. H. (Tom) Ferris joined Seaboard in 1939 and was prominent in South Africa sales. Later he was the company's U.K. representative. He retired in 1975.
11
H. Lloyd Ford, Seaboard's first traffic manager.
12
Seaboard Shipping secretary-managers H. E. (Hap) Solloway, 1950–54, and W. L. (Bill) Hurford, 1947–49.

10

11

12

13
Charles Hatfield of Flatau Dick, W. E. (Pat) Burns of
Pacific Veneer and R. D. (Doug) Reid, manager,
plywood sales.
14
G. Dudley Darling started with the company in 1939
as an accountant and rose to general manager,
distribution. He was active in establishing Seaboard's
shipping terminals.
15
Harry P. O'Hagan and Harry A. Berry, c. 1946.
16
R. H. (Bob) Edgett and Claude Effinger, c. 1946.
17
Al Gardner (r), Seaboard's Sydney office manager,
and John Stiles, Canadian trade commissioner to
Australia, examine timber supplied for construction
of Australia's America Cup entry, *Dame Pattie*, in
1967.

15

16

17

18

19

20

21

22

18
Mitzi McCulloch, executive secretary, *c.* 1952.
19
Minerva Potter, documents, *c.* 1952.
20
R. M. (Rube) Scotcher, one of Seaboard's first
employees in documents and accounting.
21
H. E. (Herb) Stacey, documents, *c.* 1952.
22
Ella Sim, accounting, *c.* 1952.
23
Grace Eccleston, "the voice of Seaboard" for
more than thirty years.

23

Denny, Mott & Dickson, a leading lumber importer, had some years previously purchased a large and well-equipped mill—Alberni Pacific—at the head of Alberni Canal on Vancouver Island. The company also handled a share of MacMillan Export's sales to the U.K. Measuring its mill's high productivity (125 million feet a year) against the life expectancy of its timber holdings, the company became justifiably uneasy and decided to sell out. Not only was H. R. MacMillan privy to this decision, but he was also well aware of a superb forest property, the Rockefeller tract, adjoining Alberni Pacific's holdings, and now up for sale. He was further aware that Bloedel, Stewart & Welch, one of British Columbia's largest timber holders as well as a top lumber producer, was negotiating for the Rockefeller tract. Bloedel, Stewart & Welch's mills were members of the Seaboard organization.

Securing the tract would give MacMillan the impetus to make an offer on Alberni Pacific. In negotiations with Rockefeller's representatives in Vancouver, preceding literally by minutes the offer made by Bloedel, Stewart & Welch's Sidney Smith, MacMillan concluded the deal. Shortly after that he travelled to England to complete his purchase of Alberni Pacific. He was now the satisfied owner of a large mill with twenty or thirty years of prime timber to keep it in production. Now, in 1946, he effectively became owner of one of Seaboard's most important member mills, Victoria Lumber.

The acquisition of Victoria Lumber was not only a major coup; it was the latest move in an ongoing program to acquire the mills MacMillan needed to make him a leader in lumber production, and to back up those mills with timber holdings that would guarantee production for years to come.

E. P. Taylor had taken the hook. Before he became involved in H. R. MacMillan's carefully orchestrated strategy to obtain Victoria Lumber, Taylor had never paid the lumber industry more than a passing glance. His lucrative entrepreneurial interests had been in other directions. The Victoria Lumber transaction brought him face-to-face with the lumber industry in B.C. and the potential that industry possessed. He decided to get into the business himself, and he wasted little time doing it— assisted wherever necessary by H. R. MacMillan.

In 1946 E. P. Taylor and his associates set up a major, new company—British Columbia Forest Products (BCFP)—which was the umbrella for a number of sawmill and logging companies. Sitka Spruce Lumber Company was purchased from Matt Sutton. Cameron Lumber Company was obtained from D. O. Cameron (his brother J. O. Cameron had been one of Seaboard's strong supporters until his death in 1943); Hammond Cedar Company Ltd., and Industrial Timber Mills

Ltd., both C. J. Culter's companies, went to BCFP. Culter was obliged to cross over and become a vice-president. All the Camerons' subsidiaries and joint ownerships were purchased including Hemmingsen-Cameron Company Ltd., Osborne Bay Timber Buyers Ltd., Renfrew Holdings Ltd., Cameron Investment and Securities Ltd. and Cameron Bros. Timber Company Ltd. Almost overnight, Seaboard found its mill membership reduced to a disconcerting degree.

British Columbia Forest Products contracted with MacMillan Export to handle their waterborne business. All the Seaboard member mills obtained in the transaction were lost to Seaboard, and losses like this meant that Seaboard not only was denied access to substantial lumber supplies but also that strong and constructive personalities were removed from the mill membership.

Then too there was the erosion of mill members, by reason of economic distress, the depletion of timber reserves, or simply the decision to go out of business to put estates in order, or to resign membership. This happened on a regular basis. No year went by without the loss of at least one or two member mills, and this had to be balanced by a ceaseless effort to enroll new mills.

Not every unaligned mill qualified as a Seaboard member. If production capacity was too small, if an inspection tour of a mill revealed poor management and antiquated equipment, or if an examination of a mill's performance record indicated unreliability of delivery or poor grading standards, application for Seaboard membership was rejected.

On the other hand, Seaboard was not always successful in its solicitation of mills well qualified to become members. Some of these clung stubbornly to their independence, resisting Seaboard's attempts to persuade them that their export volume and profits would be enhanced through this co-operative system. Others were satisfied to base their trade on domestic and U.S. rail, seeing little need to get into waterborne delivery. Still others had over the years established contacts with a small list of overseas buyers and were accustomed to doing regular business with them, utilizing liner space and sharing freight space with other exporters. In addition there was a small group of independent mills that chose to export through MacMillan. Time alone, and the continuing warm endorsement of Seaboard member mills broke down the resistance of some of the qualified standoff mills, and eventually many applied for membership and were accepted.

Indirectly, the rise of Adolph Hitler set up a chain of events that delivered a number of strong member mills to Seaboard during and after the war. This influx of the European contingent would compensate handsomely for the loss of mills to MacMillan and British Columbia Forest Products. Companies like Canadian Forest Products and Alaska Pine became giants in the B.C. forest industry. Other mills like Pacific Pine and Bay Lumber, while not as large as these first two, were highly productive and delivered lumber of top quality. These mills were put into place when Hitler's war drove their founders from their homelands to British Columbia.

The principals of what would become Canadian Forest Products arrived in Vancouver, British Columbia, four months after the Nazis invaded Austria in 1938. John Prentice and Poldi Bentley, brothers-in-law and business associates, had been in a successful textile manufacturing enterprise with mills in Austria and Czechoslovakia. The Nazi regime uprooted them overnight.

Poldi Bentley recalls that their main assets in those first days in Vancouver consisted of their business training and experience, a little cash and some accounts receivable they had been unable to collect from accounts outside Germany. A meeting with a Hungarian refugee, John Bene, put them on the right track to earning a living. Bene's business had been the manufacture and merchandising of veneers for use in the furniture industry. His knowledge and experience in a wood-related field was more attuned to British Columbia than was their expertise in the textile trade. "We were totally ignorant of the lumber business," Poldi Bentley states, "but we believed correctly that business principles are the same, regardless of the enterprise. If you produce a good product cheaper and sell it for a little more, you are doing all right."

With a relatively small amount of capital they joined forces with Bene and incorporated Pacific Veneer Company Limited on 12 November 1938. A search for a suitable site ended on the banks of the Fraser River near New Westminster, and in April 1939 construction of a mill began. The mill went into production as planned, manufacturing furniture veneers from imported exotic hardwoods . . . but the market for the product was discouragingly limited. Then the advent of World War II transformed Pacific Veneer's efforts into an unexpected and outstanding success.

John Bene's United Kingdom import agent during his days in Hungary had been Leary's. When the British Ministry of Aircraft Production began to look around for new sources of aircraft plywood, the regular supply from the Scandinavian countries having been cut off, Leary's thought of Bene and his plant on the banks of the Fraser River in British Columbia.

Pacific Veneer contracted with the British Ministry of Aircraft Production to convert to the production of aircraft veneer to be used in the construction of Anson and Oxford trainers, and for the highly successful Mosquito bomber. Thousands of miles away from their homeland, now under the cloud of war, Prentice, Bentley and Bene had been visited by an incredible business windfall which allowed them to participate in the construction of one of the Allies' effective war machines. Bentley still recalls with satisfaction that "every Mosquito bomber which ever flew, except the prototype, had our wing leading edges and our plywood built into it."

The British wartime contract allowed Pacific Veneer to establish its identity and to prove its capability in a manufacturing process that was meticulous and demanding, and profitable. The company now had the capital it required to consolidate its position. "We had become the largest manufacturer of birch plywood anywhere in the world," Bentley states, "but we knew this was a situation that couldn't last, and we began to lay a groundwork for the future."

The first piece in the plan was to purchase Eburne Sawmills on the Fraser River at the edge of Marpole in Vancouver. The mill was in disrepair and in debt, but it did have at least one advantage to recommend it. Eburne had been a Seaboard member since 1935, and the new owners carried on that membership with the approval of Seaboard's directors. Eburne was refurbished and retooled to cut hemlock and balsam rather than fir, which had been its mainstay in the past. The next move was to establish a timber base.

"In those days you could still buy all kinds of wood on the open log market," Bentley says, "but we could see the tightening of the situation with the control of the good timber holdings going into firm ownership patterns with integrated companies. . . . we could see that without a wood basis, there was no use staying in business on the Coast. The key to all of it is to own your raw material base."

To establish this base the company made a series of purchases including Vedder Logging Company Ltd., Consolidated Timber Company Limited and Spring Creek Logging Company Limited, ultimately to be consolidated into Harrison Mills Logging Division some sixty miles from Vancouver. In the same year, 1943, Prentice and Bentley picked up Stave Lake Cedar Limited, primarily for the timber it controlled, but also to improve and run the mill. This is the same year that John Bene left the partnership in order to develop his own enterprise, Western Plywood. He was not around when Bentley and Prentice made the purchase that would not only strengthen their position markedly but would give them a new corporate name.

In 1944 Beaver Cove Lumber Company was bought from the Puget Sound Pulp and Timber Company, giving the company large tracts of timber in the Nimpkish Valley. The timber had first belonged to International Harvester, who purchased it in 1916 and placed it in the keeping of a company incorporated for the purpose—Canadian Forest Products Ltd. Later on, Puget Sound Pulp purchased the Nimpkish tract, and then Bentley/Prentice made their bid. Word was out that MacMillan was trying for it as well, but some of the principals in the deal were not sympathetic to MacMillan, and the sale went to Bentley/Prentice.

"The Nimpkish Valley was the best claim anywhere," Bentley says. "It contained the finest fir in British Columbia. What is more, the acquisition of Beaver Cove Lumber included Canadian Forest Products Ltd. We liked the name so much that we combined all our companies and holdings under it."

The demand for aircraft plywood had peaked by 1943. Britain, even in the midst of war, began to plan for peace and reconstruction, and Pacific Veneer became a part of that plan when in 1944 it received a contract for 100 per cent of its production for a two-year period if it would convert to the manufacture of Douglas-fir plywood. With new machinery and systems, and with a work force that had grown to almost 1000, the mill launched into the production of plywood to assist in the repair and replacement of Britain's war-damaged communities.

Pacific Veneer exported all its plywood through Seaboard. Likewise, Eburne Sawmills, another Canadian Forest Products Division, worked its export sales through Seaboard.

Another of the European contingent mills, Pacific Pine Company Ltd., headed by two brothers, Samuel and Paul Heller, joined Seaboard in 1945. They brought a modern and efficient Douglas-fir mill into the co-operative together with a familiarity with lumber production learned in their homeland, Poland. Polish custom and trade were rudely upset in the years leading up to World War II. When Soviet Russia occupied the country containing their forest estates, the two brothers were in England studying at Cambridge, but were still firmly dedicated to careers in the lumber industry. They made their way to Vancouver and established their mill on the north arm of the Fraser River near New Westminster. Paul Heller, with an engineering background, took charge of the plant and production while Samuel Heller handled the business end of things, including his member position with Seaboard.

Other mills owned and operated by Europeans displaced by the war, such as Alaska Pine and Bay Lumber, joined Seaboard a few years later. Each of these mills helped to compensate for the attrition imposed by departing mills.

In the period surrounding the war, between 1938 and 1946, the arrivals and departures of member mills is worth noting: Moore-Whittington Lumber Company joined in 1938 with W. S. (Stan) Moore serving as representative.* In the same year Manning Lumber Mills, which would later become Manning Timber Products, was accepted as a member. But at the same time Nelson Spencer, represented by Col. Nelson Spencer, resigned membership. Shawnigan Lake Lumber Company joined in 1938 and then resigned going to H. R. MacMillan Export in 1946. Sterling Lumber Ltd., represented by R. B. Cherry, joined in 1938 and left in 1945.

In 1939 False Creek Lumber Company Ltd. went into voluntary liquidation. Inlet Timber Company Ltd. departed, and Glaspie Lumber Company Ltd. joined, represented by E. S. Glaspie. Pacific Lime Company left in 1940. James O'Hagan, who had been one of the prime movers in Astexo and had joined Seaboard when Astexo was terminated, went to Glaspie Lumber in 1941, ultimately to become manager and mill representative with Seaboard.

In 1940 International Wood Products resigned membership. This setback was more than compensated for by the acquisition of B.C. Fir & Cedar Lumber Company Ltd., represented by Norman Burley, and by the addition of Timber Preservers Ltd. together with its subsidiary, Royal City Sawmills Ltd., represented by W. K. (Kim) Nichols and A. K. Leitch respectively. M. B. King Lumber Company Ltd. joined Seaboard in 1943, represented by M. B. King.

In 1944 one of Seaboard's first and most supportive members, Straits Lumber Company Ltd., owned by Frank Pendleton and managed by his son Wayne, closed its doors forever—a sentimental as well as a material loss to the Seaboard organization. The same year saw the acquisition of Anderson Brothers Lumber Company Ltd. represented by A. D. Anderson. Brownsville Sawmills also became a member in 1944 with R. McLennan as representative. North Shore Lumber Corporation Ltd. represented by Ralph Plant also added to the list.

In 1945, as was stated before, Pacific Pine joined, and in 1946 Wood & English Ltd. left, having been purchased by Canadian Collieries (Dunsmuir). In 1955 Canadian Collieries became a Seaboard member with R. M. Johnston as representative.

This coming and going over an eight-year period serves to indicate the continuous shifting which occurred and which was characteristic of Seaboard's operations during that time. In the main, the balance was in Seaboard's favour, with more mills joining than departing, particularly

* Each Seaboard member mill elects a representative annually to serve on the board of directors.

as it became apparent that export business conducted through Seaboard's system was more efficient and profitable than operating alone.

*   *   *

Seaboard Lumber Sales Company Limited began to write business in 1935, working in parallel with Associated Timber Exporters until 1939 when Seaboard purchased the shares of Astexo and took over management. World markets had been penetrated with considerable success only to be cut off or badly fragmented by four years of war. Now, with peace secured and a semblance of normality returning, Seaboard assessed its situation and made ready to renew and extend its position in the world markets.

The visit of John Humbird and Claude Effinger to the United Kingdom in 1945 had resulted in a postwar contract with British Timber Control that would keep the Seaboard mills busy for a two-year period. It was an encouraging way to emerge from the war.

Ongoing arrangements with the Seaboard agents were less clearly defined. It was difficult to foresee what would happen when trading returned to normal channels. All of the agents were making vigorous representations in the hope of re-establishing business on a postwar basis, but Seaboard was hesitant to commit itself too soon.

An unfortunate incident relating to the agents occurred on 13 June 1945, on the eve of Humbird's and Effinger's return to Canada. Gilbert Lundwall, incumbent chairman of the Associated Seaboard Agents, was killed in a train accident while travelling in Sweden. This was a great loss, not only to Seaboard but also to the entire agent group since Lundwall had been the motivating force of Seagents. He had made a number of trips to British Columbia before and during the war, and was regarded as the best informed of all the Seaboard agents.

At of the end of 1945, 177 million feet of lumber had been shipped under the British Timber Control contract, with a possible 557 million yet to be delivered, if the maximum amount of the contract was called for. At the same time, Seaboard's member mills had an additional 97 million on their books destined for other world markets. Within a few months, a concerted effort would be made to find suitable agents on the Continent and in other markets with the mandate to represent Seaboard and promote sales.

From its beginning in April 1935 until the end of 1945, Seaboard had shipped 6,186,282,000 board feet of lumber for its member mills. The advantages of exporting lumber in this orderly and efficient manner had been demonstrated beyond doubt. Any reservations the member mills might have had were dispelled by the refunds they received each year, after all of Seaboard's operating costs had been accounted for. In the first ten-year period, member mills received refunds totalling $6,007,848, which represented an average of 97¢ per thousand feet . . . a further measure of the effectiveness of co-operative marketing.

Successful or not, the pressure of business took its toll in various ways, mostly in terms of physical attrition. Charles Grinnell, whose self-demanding efforts had been commended by Humbird and his fellow directors on several occasions, became seriously ill in the final days of 1945, and was taken to the Rochester Clinic for abdominal surgery. He made a satisfactory recovery and, within six months, had taken up his management duties again.

And there was much work to be done. Handling the export interests of fifty-two sawmills large and small called for the integration of the efforts of a trained work force approximating 100 individuals, ranging from the heads of each of the market divisions through the sales force, documents department, accounting department and the staff of the Shipping Company. In April 1946 Paul Williams, representing the British Board of Trade, Timber Control Department, arrived in Vancouver with Ure Wilson to negotiate for additional quantities of lumber for the United Kingdom. Williams concluded an agreement with John Humbird, representing Seaboard Lumber Sales Limited, and with H. R. MacMillan, representing MacMillan Export Company Ltd., which was well received by the mills.

British Timber Control acknowledged the difficulty of trading with British Columbia under two price structures, one being the price laid down in the 1945 postwar agreement, and the other being the going price in the present market. To simplify the system, and to take into account the increased prices lumber could command, the department agreed to increase the basic price under the postwar agreement by $9 a thousand feet for all deliveries after 1 April 1946, and to pay the going rate for all purchases made outside of that agreement. In addition Seaboard and MacMillan agreed to support an application to the Canadian government ensuring a lumber quota to the United Kingdom of at least 35 per cent of the total production of the Coastal Area of British Columbia. Britain was continuing to be British Columbia's best customer.

Then quite suddenly, with no warning to the lumber industry, the Canadian Government made a disconcerting move which John Humbird describes succinctly in his diary: "Overnight the Canadian Foreign Exchange Control removed the 10 per cent premium on U.S. dollars and de-valued the pound sterling in equivalent Canadian dollars by 10 per cent from $4.43 to $4.00. Where you have lumber sold in U.S. funds on a basis of U.S. dollars, or where you have freight sold in the pounds sterling, this makes a considerable difference in your income. Also, with the devaluing of the pound sterling, the spread between our prices in the United Kingdom widens even though we have sold in Canadian dollars." What Seaboard had gained in its revised agreement with the United Kingdom was diluted by the unexpected move of the Canadian Foreign Exchange Control.

In July 1946 the company lost C. J. Culter and the Camerons when E. P. Taylor purchased Hammond Cedar Company, Industrial Timber Mills and Cameron Lumber Company with its several subsidiaries. Culter and the others had no alternative but to resign. All had been among Seaboard's original members, and Culter had been a vice-president for several years. He had served on the War Council and, all-in-all, had been one of Seaboard's most knowledgeable and productive officers.

John Humbird too had reached the end of his tenure with Seaboard. With his prestigious Victoria Lumber mill sold to H. R. MacMillan, his direct association with the lumber industry had been effectively concluded, and he turned his attention to other business interests. That he left Seaboard in a substantially healthy condition is attested to in his final report to shareholders dated 7 January 1947, part of which is excerpted here:

The amount of refunds returned to the mills in 1946, both in total dollars ($2,103,143.42) and in average amount per thousand feet ($5.03) is the highest in any year of Seaboard's operation. This is also true of the sales average ($51.92 per thousand feet), which, adding the $5.03 refund, makes an average return to the mills of $56.95 per thousand for their lumber shipped through Seaboard this year. This compares with an average through Seaboard of the previous eleven years of $23.27 per thousand, or almost 2 ½ times the eleven year average.

It is also interesting to note that the average price received by Astexo during the eighteen years in which they operated was $18.54 per thousand.

While it is never safe to prophesy what the future holds for us, we have on hand in our unshipped order file, 140 million feet, most of which is protected by irrevocable letters of credit, and at price levels which are approximately $35.00 higher than our 1946 averages.

This is in addition to orders from the U.K. for approximately 100 million feet at better than 1945 average U.K. prices. In addition, we have behind us six months of our new Shipping Company year, together with fixtures for the next two months which will assure a very substantial freight refund. It is therefore safe to assume that prospects for starting 1947 are very favourable for another successful year which might easily top 1946.

One of his last official duties in his final year as president was to honour W. A. McAdam, Agent-General for British Columbia in Britain. McAdam and his wife visited British Columbia in August 1946. On the fifth of that month a reception was held in his honour, prior to his return to London. Most of the members of Seaboard and the B.C. Lumber and Shingle Manufacturers' Association were in attendance. Of McAdam and his wife, John Humbird had this to say: "No country or province has ever had representation abroad which has done them more credit than have the McAdams in representing British Columbia. Particularly during the war years they did a grand job for our Armed Forces in the United Kingdom. Nothing has ever been too much trouble for Bill McAdam to do for Seaboard or any other personnel or friends while in England." Humbird himself was accorded a final tribute at a testimonial dinner held on 25 January 1947.

In retrospect, Humbird's contribution to the consolidation and growth of Seaboard in its formative years was remarkable. His personality, business philosophies and opinions intruded into every corner of the organization, often to the chagrin of Charles Grinnell who was not receptive to anything resembling interference.

Humbird's insistence on total involvement, no matter how irritating at times, worked to Seaboard's benefit. He would allow no disadvantage to remain uncorrected. He was an excellent businessman and administrator, able to represent Seaboard's interests confidently in the overseas markets, and he was a natural warrior when it came to confrontations with captains in the industry, including H. R. MacMillan. For those who followed as presidents of Seaboard, John Humbird was a formidable model.

The position of president of Seaboard was taken over by Bruce Farris, vice-president of marketing and sales for Bloedel, Stewart & Welch. Farris was born in New Brunswick in 1882 and came to the West Coast soon after he had completed his schooling, taking jobs in the lumber industry and learning the business from the ground up. He spent a number of years with Bay Lumber Company in Bellingham, Washington, before joining Ocean Falls Company in 1912 where he spent three years adding to his experience in manufacturing and sales.

In 1915 he joined forces with M. B. King to form the King-Farris Lumber Company, King having shifted his sawmill activities from

Cranbrook, in B.C.'s interior to the larger action of the coastal industry. Both men were thoroughly experienced in all aspects of their business and were sufficiently successful with their new mill to extend their sights further with the formation of Great Central Sawmills on Vancouver Island near Alberni. Great Central represented a much larger investment both in plant and timber holdings. In order to take on a project of this magnitude they enlisted the support of Bloedel, Stewart & Welch Ltd., a thriving forest industry started in 1911 by an American, Julius Bloedel, and two partners, Gen. John J. Stewart and Patrick Welch.

Julius Bloedel was the strongest of a strong triumvirate, convinced from the outset that the success of a company depended to a major extent on the timber reserves it controlled. He made it company policy to acquire good timber stands whenever the opportunity presented itself. Bloedel, Stewart & Welch backed the new Farris/King enterprise when it was launched in 1925, and Bruce Farris became vice-president and general manager; Bloedel was president. Later, in 1933, M. B. King having resigned to start a mill with his brother on the shore of North Vancouver, Great Central Sawmills merged with Bloedel, Stewart & Welch, with Bruce Farris taking the position of vice-president in charge of manufacturing and sales.

Farris did not limit his activities to his own company, but became actively involved in the entire industry. In 1932 he was elected president of the B.C. Lumber and Shingle Manufacturers Association and when Seaboard was re-established in 1935, he became a vice-president on the executive committee.

His activities with Seaboard and his contributions to its operation were impressive. For instance, it is generally acknowledged that he was largely instrumental in obtaining additional Park ships for Seaboard during the war years.

In 1946 he was again elected president of the BCLSMA, and when the presidency of Seaboard became vacant with Humbird's resignation, Bruce Farris was the popular choice to fill it, not only because of his proven record of service but also because Seaboard now owned a fleet of ships. In fact an associated group, Seaboard Owners, had been incorporated in 1946 to purchase a number of the Park ships. Farris was elected president of the new company. Seaboard's decision to become directly engaged in shipping made it all the more appropriate to place Farris in the position of president.

Bruce Farris inherited a number of problems which required to be addressed not only at Seaboard's level but also at the industry level affecting every mill in the province. It was false wisdom for any lumberman to believe that the U.K. could continue indefinitely to be British Columbia's largest customer. Russia and the Scandinavian and Baltic countries were beginning to export again and were prepared to price low in order to reinstate themselves in the export markets. British Columbia had disappointed some of its U.K. buyers in 1946 when, as a result of a crippling six-week lumber industry strike, 225 million feet of production were lost, and contracts could not be filled. If the British Columbia lumber supply was to be endangered in this way, then the U.K. could and would turn to other sources of supply.

Any thought that a burgeoning United States market would serve as a hedge against the reduction of sales in the U.K. was due for disappointment. The United States abolished timber controls in 1946 but reinstated the tariff on lumber imports.

As though this were not enough, the United Kingdom, early in 1947, announced the restriction of imports from dollar countries because of a severe dollar shortage. While British Columbia's contracts still had a year to run, the fear loomed large that the U.K. was soon to disappear as a significant customer. Alarmed representations were made to the British government, in particular the British Timber Control Board, for assurances of continued trade on a meaningful scale. Advertising campaigns were launched and editorials were elicited to remind Britain that Canada had supplied and supported her in her hour of need. The British Timber delegation that visited British Columbia in September 1947 was subjected to all of these sentiments and exhortations, but though members of the delegation were sympathetic, they were in no position to give Seaboard or any other exporter any guarantees.

Seaboard's recourse on its own behalf was to hasten to reopen previously active markets and instigate a search for new markets. At the industry level, principally through the resources of the B.C. Lumber and Shingle Manufacturers Association, it would support all lobbies and representations to the British lumber buyers. Accordingly, Claude Effinger was dispatched to the United Kingdom on the first leg of a journey to seek out new agents on the Continent. Associated Seaboard Agents was a useful way to gain entry into markets outside the U.K. because the members of this organization traded in all directions.

Chairman of the board of Seagents when Claude Effinger arrived was James Sewell, who helped align Effinger with the people who could be most useful in making the neccessary contacts. Niel Morison, who had returned to Brandts from distinguished service in the war, was also of great help because of his broad experience in the lumber trade. Ten years with Denny, Mott & Dickson had seasoned him thoroughly before he went to the agency side of the lumber trade in 1933, joining the firm of Berner & Nielsen, one of the agents who represented Grinnell Export during its short existence. He had met Charles Grinnell at that time and the two had made mutually favourable impressions.

In 1937 he was induced to join Brandts, one of Seaboard's principal agents, thus maintaining his connection with Grinnell as well as aligning himself with the Seaboard organization. When Claude Effinger arrived to go on his agent-seeking expedition, Morison recommended Rolf Berner of Berner & Nielsen as the best man to open doors on the Continent. Rolf Berner represented his own agency in Paris.

In company with Berner, Claude Effinger embarked for Paris via Cherbourg. Because of a rail strike in Paris, the two were obliged to travel by limousine from Cherbourg, a trip which Effinger remembers vividly. "Berner was a delightful person," he recalls. "He seemed to know every building and landmark on the road to Paris, and saw that I was cared for in every way. The hotel he selected for us in Paris had been used as a German army headquarters—which may have explained why it was in excellent repair. I interviewed several possible agents there."

His final choice of an agent to represent Seaboard in France was Ingemar Nordin, a decision which he describes as fortunate in every respect. "Nordin was a good businessman with a thorough understanding of the lumber trade," he said. "More than that, he was a gentleman and became a good friend." Later, Ingemar Nordin would become Seaboard's agent for Belgium as well.

From Paris, Effinger travelled to Amsterdam where he met Henry Brandt, as had been prearranged. Brandt assisted in lining up interviews with potential agents in Holland, the final choice of which was Otto J. Faber. Later, in 1957, Altius & Co., under the direction of Messrs. Manger and Thesen Ender, were appointed sales agent. He went with Effinger to Denmark and Sweden where the same interview procedures were conducted and appointments made.

"Selecting an agent was largely an act of faith," Effinger recalls. "We had to have enough faith in people like Morison and Berner and Brandt to put us in contact with reputable and reliable agents. After that it was largely a matter of instinct. Performance records were not always easy to decipher. I tended to make my final choice on the basis of agreeable or compatible personality. Today I suppose you would subject a prospect to a battery of tests."

In Italy, Effinger selected an agent without benefit of a Seagents intermediary. As far as the Mid-East was concerned, appointments had been made in 1940: Rosenburg and Company in Cairo, and Dizengoff and Company in Tel Aviv. Both of these were now reinstated and, for the moment, Seaboard's search for additional agency representation ceased.

While Claude Effinger continued with his search for agents on the Continent and elsewhere, Bob Edgett was instructed to learn all he could about the timber trade and end uses of wood products. This was the first time in a long time that anyone had moved into the trade beyond the agents. While the agents resisted his efforts, many of his importer friends assisted, such as Arnold Tait and Alf Priddle. During his three-month visit he accumulated information which led to a number of positive changes at Seaboard. He recommended the adoption of company end marking in red on every piece of lumber, combined with improved end trimming, having discovered that cleanly trimmed, distinctively end-marked lumber commanded better prices.

He also undertook a thorough study of the prevailing lumber grading standards as they applied to the U.K. and made a number of recommendations which, some years later, had much to do with the formulation of a new export grading rule, "R" List, more in line with the needs of the end users and more profitable for the mills. And aware that the B.C. lumber industry was experimenting with anti-stain treatment techniques, he crusaded vigorously for the increased use of hemlock, confident that anti-stain treatment would soon overcome one of the major objections to this species.

The efforts of Effinger and Edgett abroad were matched by those of Seaboard at home experiencing the joys and sorrows of owning and operating its own fleet of ships. And it is to the matter of ships and shipping that we now turn our attention.

·NINE·

THE SEABOARD FLEET
—A SHORT STORY

Not long after the beginning of World War II, when Britain and her allies were attempting to solve the problem of shipping, Canadian shipyards were asked to examine their capabilities. Dry cargo vessels of up to 10,000 tons were thought to be within the range of Canadian shipbuilders. A Canadian Crown company, Wartime Shipbuilding Limited, was formed to oversee the Canadian shipbuilding effort, which resulted in the construction of some 400 vessels including naval craft, tankers and dry cargo vessels.

This last category ranged from 300-ton China Coasters "C" Class up to the 10,000-ton categories of which there were three types: the North Sands, the Victory and the Canadian. Some of the ships were constructed in Canada for the United Kingdom under the United States Lend-Lease program, while others were delivered to the U.K. under agreements with the Canadian Government. Vessels built and operated by the Canadian government were paid for by Canada. As each vessel was completed and put through its sea trials it was turned over to either the British Ministry of Shipping or to Canada's Park Steamship Company.

Capt. J. S. Clarke, in an article in *Harbour & Shipping* on these vessels, tells how they received their names: "In order to assist Government Agencies, Port Authorities, steamship agents and others directly interested in the operation of the vessels, it was decided to name those operated under the Canadian flag after well-known Canadian parks, having the word "Park" included in the name, while those operated under the British flag were named after the famous forts of Canadian history and the word "Fort" was used as a prefix in the name."

At first Seaboard's involvement with the Park ships was purely managerial, acting as agents through the machinery of Seaboard Shipping. In January 1945 W. C. Robinson, who had been seconded from his British chartering company to manage Seaboard Shipping, returned to England and his position was filled by William (Bill) Hurford.

Hurford was a shipping man of long experience and no mean capabilities. He was able to provide eminently practical reasons why Seaboard should become ship owners, supporting his arguments with irrefutable facts and figures. Hurford's mind was not married to lumber exclusively. Although lumber would be given first priority, he could see the ships being used for a variety of cargoes. As ship owners, Seaboard would be able to hedge against shipping shortages and profit from freight advantages.

John Humbird was impressed by the argument that a company-owned fleet would have the ability to deliver lumber on time as well as operate at an increased profit. Although he was well aware that there were dissenters among the directors, he was in a position, and possessed the strength of personality, to sell the idea to the directors and mill members.

Charles Grinnell, for one, was highly sensitive to the vagaries and unpredictability of shipping. In his opinion, Seaboard was in business to export lumber for a group of member mills: nothing more, nothing less. And there were others who sided with him. Poldi Bentley appears to have been one of these, although one report indicates that at the outset he was in favour of owning ships. "We bought these ships very cheap and made a lot of money," he said, "but I felt all the time that there was a conflict between Seaboard's objective to get the maximum net mill price for its members and making money out of freight." Bruce Farris supported Humbird and took counsel from Bill Hurford; in fact, Farris was largely instrumental in negotiating the purchase of the Seaboard fleet.

On 22 February 1946 Seaboard Owners Limited was organized for the purpose of purchasing and chartering ships from the Park Steamship Company through the War Assets Corporation. Three vessels were purchased initially: the *Connaught Park,* which was purchased on 10 January and renamed *Seaboard Ranger;* the *Coronation Park,* purchased 14 February and renamed *Seaboard Star;* and the *Queens Park,* purchased the same month and renamed *Seaboard Queen.* At the same time, in the first five months of 1946, Seaboard Owners obtained an additional six Park ships on charter for one year. These included the *Westview Park, Westend Park, Kootenay Park, Tobiatic Park, Winnipegosis Park* and *Mohawk Park.*

Hurford lost no time in putting the ships to work. Capt. William Rion was the first master to be hired, followed by Captains Ellis, Baird, Hunt, Weiss, Quinn and Brown—others who came and went. Richard (Dick) Witts, who joined Seaboard Shipping in May 1945 to assist Bill Hurford, remembers the problems experienced in finding satisfactory masters.

"We had great difficulty in finding good masters for Seaboard," he said. "It was the same thing we ran up against in the Ministry when I was working down in the States. It was a fact that Britain sent out a lot of people they didn't want. They sent them to the U.S. and Canada as surveyors and in charge of this, and in charge of that, and they didn't pan out at all. You can bet your sweet boots they didn't send their best men out of Britain. Mostly we found satisfactory men to captain the Seaboard ships, but some of them couldn't handle it . . . and some died. Beefsteak Brown died. Harry Hunt just quit. He went fishing."

Witts had been with the British Ministry of Shipping during the latter part of the war, working out of New Orleans on the transfer of American ships to Britain for the Normandy invasion. He was a knowledgeable shipping man and had his master's ticket. He describes Hurford as a brilliant shipping man with ideas and objectives that went beyond those of Seaboard. "Hurford's idea was, and I think Mr. Bentley went along with it too, that there should be two separate identities: Seaboard Shipping Company and Seaboard Owners as one; and Seaboard Lumber Sales Company as the other. Seaboard Shipping Company would charter ships for the purposes of Seaboard Lumber transport. But Seaboard Shipping Company would also charter other vessels for other cargoes and become something big—which they could have or would have."

That Hurford was forthright and somewhat impatient in his approach, there can be no doubt. After all, he could point to his performance to support his recommendations. Seaboard's three-vessel fleet made money from the outset, and as far as Hurford was concerned, three vessels was too small a number. On 25 March 1946 he delivered a written rationale to John Humbird, supporting his strong recommendation that Seaboard purchase additional Park vessels while they were still available at attractive prices. He writes:

As Mr. Barker [a Park Steamship representative] told us Tuesday evening, there is a considerable demand from foreign buyers who are prepared to register Canadian companies. I understand that six of the vessels which were presently on bare boat to others have been sold. One of the reasons for this interest in Park vessels is the anticipation that depreciation in Canada will be more favourable and corporate taxes in Canada no less favourable than the U.S.

There is also the possibility that, although the Ship Sales bill has passed in the States, there will be months of haggling to establish the foreign building costs and pre-war building costs, which are two of the items in the formula used for establishing the sale price of Liberty vessels.

I do not yet know what MacMillans intend to do ... but for the purposes of this memorandum I am only thinking in terms of our buying two or three more vessels.

It does not seem necessary for the moment to reiterate the desirability of our having the hedge. Even five ships, representing say 18 cargoes per annum, does not seem too heavy. In fact if we were only left with five ships and the volume of our business were upon pre-war levels I would still be inclined to give serious consideration to time chartering sufficient tonnage over a relatively long period.

The advantage of purchasing two or three more vessels appears to be that we could hardly fail to make more money over the next two or three years, than if we only keep three after the expiry of the bare boat charters.

His powers of persuasion and his shipping logic were enough to achieve the result he wanted. On 17 April, less than a month after his communication to Humbird, three more vessels were purchased, selected from the group of bare boat charters. The *Kootenay Park* became *Seaboard Pioneer,* the *Westview Park* was renamed *Seaboard Enterprise,* and the *Tobiatic Park* was named *Seaboard Trader.*

The total price for the six vessels was $3,013,594, which represented an average cost per vessel of $502,265. The purchase agreement called for 25 per cent in cash at the time of purchase, with the balance to be paid over a period of seven years with 3½ per cent interest on deferred payments.

The ships were managed and deployed in the following manner: a contract was entered into with Seaboard Shipping Company in which it chartered from Seaboard Owners all nine vessels, comprised of six owned outright and three on bare boat charter. In return, Seaboard Owners received an amount for the first year equal to the 25 per cent depreciation allowed on the vessels, plus an amount to pay a 6 per cent dividend on the capital issued by Seaboard Owners together with an amount sufficient to pay the tax on this dividend, plus incidental organization expenses. Seaboard Shipping Company was to operate the ships, pay all running expenses, repairs, insurance and sundry expenditures. In exchange for its services the company would retain the balance of earnings over and above the amounts paid to Seaboard Owners as indicated above.

In 1946 the gross revenue realized from the operation of the six owned vessels and the three chartered vessels was $7,671,404 with earnings of $1,490,585. It would appear that Hurford's shipping strategies were more than vindicated and that he was riding a wave of success. The Seaboard Owners annual report for that year clearly states that "it has been very useful to Seaboard Lumber Sales to have these vessels to use as a hedge against freights in their forward selling. . . . These vessels also carry many other commodities besides lumber, and also lumber for other shippers besides Seaboard members. It is interesting to note that of the total cargo carried by our own vessels, only approximately 40% has been our own lumber and the balance has been made up of other commodities and lumber for other shippers."

In Hurford's time Seaboard Shipping acted as agents for more than forty different companies in Canada and other parts of the world, including Weyerhaeuser Limited and United Fruit—large companies with their own fleets. "We had a big staff," Witts said. "We had to because of the number of companies that were represented. We were busy every minute of the time. For instance, we had to put the Weyerhaeuser ships through their annual American survey up in Canada. They always had strikes down in the States. We would bring up a captain, an engineer, a coastguard representative and install them in a Vancouver hotel while the work went ahead in one of our shipyards. When the ship was ready we would fly in a crew. Weyerhaeuser was just one line: we had dozens of lines."

Seaboard Owners and Seaboard Shipping occupied a full floor in the Marine Building and overflowed onto half of another floor. Witts claims that there was never enough personnel even though the assignments were always finished on time. Vancouver then was one of the busiest ports on the West Coast of the Americas. (Today it is the busiest.) When activity was at a peak, Seaboard could have as many as six ships in port requiring a full range of services: victualling, crew replacements, arrangements for repairs and drydocking, the interpretation of the marine laws of a dozen countries and, of course, supercargoing, documentation and supervision of all Seaboard lumber cargoes going into ships' holds.

Busy and frenetic though it must have been, Hurford ran a relatively relaxed organization. There was an overriding good sense of humour prevailing in the office. Witts tells two stories indicative of this. One has to do with his first meeting with John Humbird:

> I didn't know who he was. I saw this great hulking big man waiting to get on the elevator. We had so many firemen, and seamen and masters coming in all the time and I decided he was one of these. I slapped him on the back and said, "Listen, Mac, if you want a job you'd better get in the elevator." I pushed him through the door and got in behind him.
>
> His eyes started to sparkle. When we got out in the hall, I passed him and went into my office and the big fellow followed me in. I said, "Who are you looking for?," guessing he was a fireman looking for a job.
>
> "I'm here to see Mr. Hurford." he said.
>
> "Nothing to do with ships?" I said.
>
> He said "No." So I told him how to find Mr. Hurford's office, wondering at the time what kind of business Mr. Hurford could have with a man dressed like that.

While Charles Grinnell, Seaboard's general manager, was not a martinet, he saw to it that a fair degree of discipline was maintained both in the sales and the shipping offices. Drinking on the job was simply not permitted, although mill members and directors could not be prevented from producing flasks during the course of a meeting (a practice which was not common). Grinnell himself kept a social bottle in his desk in the event that a mill member or a visitor was inconvenienced by thirst, but drinking among the staff was prohibited.

William Hurford was of the opinion that the taking of alcohol in reasonable amounts was part and parcel of the shipping business. In fact, he set aside a room where visiting masters could take their ease while documents were being prepared. There they could and did pleasure themselves with various kinds of alcoholic beverage. Dick Witts tells the story of how that room got Hurford into trouble.

> I used to get liquor from the ships. [Canada still had rationing.] I would put these bottles of V.O. and Gordon's in this little out-of-the-way room. It had an old, unused safe in it and a few filing cabinets, and it was the staff "snake pit." Not too many people knew about it and we never abused it. Sometimes, after a hard day's work, or before we went scrambling through a shipyard we'd go in and have a couple of drinks and talk things over. It wasn't bad medicine.
>
> One day a few of us were having a serious discussion in my office, no drinking, just serious talk about a few problems that were shaping up. All

of a sudden, Chuck Grinnell walked in and joined the conversation. He started to give us a pep talk to cheer us up and sort out some of the problems, and I am sure he thought he was doing us a favour when he called the office boy in.

"Go down to my office," he told the boy. "In the top drawer of my desk you will find an unopened bottle of rye. Bring it up here with a few glasses."

"You don't have to go that far for a bottle, sir," the office boy said with a happy smile. "I'll just go to the snake pit and get whatever you want."

He was gone before anyone could stop him and he came back with a 40-ounce bottle of good rye, expecting us to give him a round of applause. Well, that was the end of the snake pit; and I don't think the office boy lasted much longer either.

The story serves to indicate that a certain amount of friction might have been created by Hurford's lenient approach to doing business as compared to Grinnell's more disciplined code.

With established success on his side, Hurford had every reason to believe that he was dealing from a position of strength. He had been partly instrumental in persuading Seaboard to purchase its first three ships, and he had been largely instrumental in persuading the company to purchase its second three. Hurford was further commended by the Shipping Company for negotiating successfully around threatened longshoremen and maritime union strikes, and for finding other cargoes for the company vessels when a five-week IWA strike put a halt to the loading of lumber. And yet, in the face of what can only be interpreted as a successful shipping operation, a wave of opposition was building against Bill Hurford. The stated reasons for his fall from grace are many. Some may be apocryphal, others appear to have a logical basis, and at least one explanation has to do with the Shipping Company manager's individual manner of doing business.

Bill Hurford is described by most of those who knew him as an affable extrovert with a unique sense of humour. He was completely absorbed in the business of shipping, and much less concerned with social graces. For him the shipping business took precedence over the lumber industry. Lumber was a commodity to be carried in ships' holds; so was grain, or sides of beef, or kegs of rum, or ladies' girdles for that matter, as long as the maximum freight rate could be set and a good profit realized.

Hurford may have lost sight of the fact that he was working for a dedicated fraternity of lumbermen. Dick Witts describes the reaction of the mills to Hurford's strong suggestion that Seaboard Shipping could become a major profit centre in its own right: "A lot of the mills—many of the smaller mills in particular— said 'no way!' All they could see was lumber. Wood, wood, wood! They didn't understand how anybody else could survive without wood at all. Wood was their life's blood, you see. That was the only thing that made money. Sure, in their field of endeavour, it was, but the rest of the world doesn't live by wood alone."

Poldi Bentley expresses another opinion: "He was a very brilliant guy; that was my impression of Bill. Rightly or wrongly he made everybody feel that he was the only one who understood the shipping business, and he didn't want any interference. I think he was too independent."

His independence can be demonstrated through the words of Witts: "Bill Hurford was chartering ships that never saw British Columbia; trading in Africa and India and making all kinds of money. That was one of the big arguments. He was making more money at that particular time than Seaboard Lumber Sales could make. He didn't have Humbird to back him up now. Humbird was gone and Farris was in as president—a different kind of man."

If Hurford suspected that the climate was growing stormy around his shipping operations he gave no evidence of it. On the contrary, he began to press for the purchase of additional vessels, and once again his logic was sound. Included in the inventories of Park Steamships and the War Asset Corporation were a number of smaller vessels of a type that were extremely attractive to Bill Hurford. Witts refers to them as "China Coasters," which is probably not correct since the largest Park China Coaster "B" Class was in the 1200-ton category. Hurford wanted to acquire vessels in the 4000- to 5000-ton category which would have been either the Dominion or the Grey Type Park vessels both of which were 4000 tons.

He had wanted to include vessels of this size in the Seaboard fleet from the beginning, arguing the economics in a convincing manner. "To fill a 10,000 tonner," he pointed out, "you needed 8000 tons of cargo. To fill a 4500-ton ship you only needed 3800 tons of cargo. A small ship can go fully laden into ports that are not available to a 10,000 tonner, and it pays for itself with a profit left over. A bigger, 10,000-ton ship, half-loaded, doesn't pay for itself."

Hurford wanted Seaboard to acquire four 4700-ton Park vessels and he was aware when he made his formal request for purchase that two of these Parks were lying in North Vancouver waiting for a buyer. What could be more opportune?

Hurford was sufficiently confident that his recommendation would be given favourable consideration to make a business trip to Toronto and Montreal, expecting to discuss the proposed purchase of ships further upon his return. In Toronto, he received a disconcerting phone call from one of his colleagues. Seaboard had called a directors' meeting, not to decide on the purchase of the 4700 tonners, but to decide whether or not to sell the Seaboard fleet.

Hurford scrambled back by return plane, very likely to the chagrin of Charles Grinnell and those directors who were opposed to ship owning, for Bill Hurford had a way with words that could disarm those who did not understand the intricacies of the shipping business. However, this time he did not succeed. The groundwork of opposition had been carefully laid; the decision of the majority of directors was solidly entrenched and the arguments for the sale of the fleet were at least as telling as Hurford's reasons for keeping it.

First of all, there was the basic philosophy of the mill members as subscribed to and stated by Charles Grinnell: "We are not a shipping company; we are a lumber export company. If you are in the business of owning ships you are interested in high freight rates. If you are in the business of selling lumber, you are concerned to obtain the lowest possible freight rates. Under the present arrangement, we are in serious conflict."

Other objections were raised. Seaboard Shipping Company's papers of incorporation limited the profit it could make before becoming a separate identity for increased tax impositions. And then there was the matter of operating vessels under the Canadian flag. It was becoming expensive.

The Seamen's Union was beginning to press for higher wages and other benefits both in the United States and Canada. Strikes became the order of the day, and ships were getting caught in foreign ports when crews refused to sail. On these occasions demurrage costs (hire charges while ships waited in port) could amount to thousands of dollars, and lumber cargoes were long delayed in delivery. Labour unrest could create major frustrations, almost always expensive. Witts recalls: "We had strikes in Brazil, Paraguay, Peru. We even had a ship that was stuck in Tierra del Fuego. How can you get down to a place like that to solve the problem in a reasonable length of time? Planes don't fly there."

Some dramatic local infighting took place. When the wireless operators went on strike, Seaboard Shipping attempted to make a point by placing four of their masters aboard one of their vessels as mates. Captains Rion, Ellis, Weiss and Baird took the ship from Vancouver to New Westminster and back to Vancouver in a token gesture to prove that ships could be moved without seamen.

"We tried to get around the wireless operators' strike with a little help

from Marconi," Dick Witts said. "We discovered that the strongest
radio telephone available was on display in Vancouver. Marconi had
just introduced it. We could see how we could go from Vancouver,
British Columbia, to the United Kingdom without a wireless operator
on board, but it was going to be an awfully long voyage staying within
200 miles of coastline all the way, hugging Greenland and Iceland and
coming in through the back of the U.K. It was legal because we were
always within radio telephone range." The strike was resolved before
Seaboard could attempt that voyage.

The special meeting of Seaboard's directors resulted in a majority
vote to sell the fleet. In the midst of success, Hurford had failed. Seaboard's adventure in ship owning had lasted little more than a year. The
issue of the purchase of additional ships was merely the superficial
irritant which motivated the directors to dispose of the fleet. Dudley
Darling's recollection is that Hurford was dismissed largely because he
did not reveal soon enough the profits being made by the shipping
company. This not only disturbed Grinnell because of his insistence on
being privy to everything at all times, but it also embarrassed him with
the mill members, who resented the delay in receiving their share of the
profits.

Selling the fleet was not a difficult task, government regulations and
red tape being the main impediments. Foreign shipping companies were
on the lookout for serviceable vessels available in any country. Where
government policy permitted, they dealt direct with ship owners in the
purchase of ships; and where governments prohibited or discouraged
the sale of vessels to foreign interests, there were ways of circumventing
these restrictions.

Canada was a repository for a large number of vessels, in particular
10,000 tonners like the Park ships. The Greek shipping firm Goulandris
set up a Canadian company, presumably for the purpose of conducting
shipping operations from the Canadian East Coast, but obviously, in
retrospect, to avail themselves of any opportunity to purchase ships in
Canada. When the word went out that Seaboard's fleet was for sale,
Goulandris made the best offer. The deal was quickly consummated.

The transition took place smoothly and over a period of several
months. The ships stayed under the Canadian flag (Goulandris being a
Canadian company to all intents and purposes for as long as this arrangement was convenient) for some six months. Seaboard's captains
and mates stayed with the vessels for the transition period, and business
went on as usual, with the ships continuing to carry Seaboard lumber.

"We loaded them still," Dick Witts stated, "and it went on like that
for eighteen months maximum. Then one would disappear, then

another, and then they began to come back under a different flag. The man who took over from me was a Greek captain. I worked with him for a while, six months perhaps, while he learned the ropes . . . and then it was farewell and goodbye."

Bill Hurford departed the company almost immediately and joined Anglo-Canadian Shipping Company. While he might have failed in his objective to make Seaboard Shipping Company a recognized profit centre, no one in the business regarded him as a failure in any respect. He had, in fact, managed his company successfully and profitably. His only mistake, if it can be called that, was to allow his enthusiasm for shipping to run counter to Grinnell's single-minded objective to export lumber profitably, rather to run a successful freighting business.

Dick Witts stayed on at Seaboard Shipping as a supercargo and served in that capacity for seventeen years. Captain Rion, the first master to be hired for the Seaboard fleet, became head of operations, responsible for the assessment of ships for potential charter, and for the efficient stowage of Seaboard's lumber cargoes. Capt. William Ellis, another of the Seaboard ships' masters, remained long enough to be appointed first manager of Seaboard International Terminal in 1971.

Seaboard Owners realized a substantial capital gain on the sale of the six ships. If Seaboard chose to relinquish its shipping holdings, they could not have made the decision under more favourable circumstances—on a wave of success. And the company's environment became more comfortable now that it was back on familiar ground exporting lumber for its member mills in the most efficient way at the best price obtainable.

·TEN·

CLOSING THE FORTIES

In the closing months of 1948, motivated to a considerable extent by the need for more office space, and even more by an attractive real estate opportunity, Seaboard Lumber Sales and Seaboard Shipping moved into their own premises, a self-contained structure on the northeast corner of Granville and Burrard streets. Seaboard purchased the two-storey office complex and renamed it Seaboard House, installing sales on the main floor and shipping on the second floor in company with documents and accounting.

The building was completely renovated and redesigned, with the reception area, executive offices and sales offices finished in different B.C. wood species. It made use of various types of plywood panels and furnishings finished in a range of stains and paints intended to demonstrate the versatility of the materials. Member mills were more than pleased to supply the required wood products.

Here, in the freestanding edifice adjacent to the prestigious Vancouver Club and overlooking Vancouver's busy waterfront, Seaboard settled in to do business with the world markets. Over a period of years, Seaboard House in its prestigious location was "home" to a multitude of agents, buyers, prospective buyers, members of visiting trade commissions and others involved in the timber trade from every corner of the earth. As well it was the bustling crossroads for representatives of the member mills, almost all of whom visited Seaboard House several times a week (some of them every business day) to keep abreast of activities in the export markets and to avail themselves of sales opportunities.

While much of Seaboard's business with its member mills could be transacted by telephone and through the mails, there was need as well to discuss the details of export lumber transactions on a one-to-one basis with sales staff and department heads. Mill representatives beat a steady path through the halls of Seaboard House.

Mills that had operated independently found themselves in company with others who were traditional competitors in the domestic market. Small mills shared their export sales destiny with huge forest products complexes like Canadian Western. A certain mild paranoia existed in the minds of new member mill representatives that the big mills would be given first call on available export business, or that larger, established Seaboard mill members would receive the cream of the export business.

Bob Edgett can remember when Seaboard, in order to allay the suspicions of the member mills, kept a file of current mill orders on the front desk in the sales area. Mill sales managers could and did check the file regularly in the early years. "They would want to see who was getting what business," he said. "Then we would have to explain why, for instance, Hillcrest had received a certain order or why Timberland seemed to be favoured. There was always a logical explanation, and I can't remember an occasion when we were not able to supply a satisfactory explanation for the distribution of an export order."

Perhaps Poldi Bentley sums up the reason for the success of Seaboard in the simplest way: "What I always appreciated in Seaboard was the fair treatment in the distribution of business to the members. It was, and is, marvellous. Nobody in the world could understand how you could keep a group of so many people all happy. No mill, regardless of size, received an advantage. If anything, the larger mills acceded to the smaller ones."

In time, over a period of a year or two, the order file on the front desk ceased to attract investigation and it was removed without comment or protest from any of the mill members.

As business with the United Kingdom was slowing at this time, a concerted effort was made to increase and improve the promotion of B.C. lumber products in the overseas markets, particularly in the U.K. The most important move in this direction was to amalgamate the three lumber promotion associations in the province, an achievement approaching the impossible.

The earliest of these was the B.C. Lumber and Shingle Manufacturers Association, the first assembly of mills in the province for the purpose of promoting and educating overseas buyers on the qualities and uses of B.C. lumber, plywood shingles and shakes. The majority of this association's members were either Seaboard members, or were oriented towards Seaboard. Almost without exception, its officers and directors were drawn from Seaboard's ranks year after year.

Because of this bias in favour of Seaboard, H. R. MacMillan was understandably reluctant to join ranks with the BCLSMA. W. J. Van Dusen, MacMillan's closest business colleague and the company's vice-president, was quoted in *Empire of Wood* as saying: "The B.C. Lumber Manufacturers Association was backing Seaboard very strongly, going to the provincial and dominion government trade services to do all they could to get support for Seaboard's export effort. We objected to this, the lumber association of which we were members utilizing their powers to work against us . . . to run down the H. R. MacMillan Export Company in favour of Seaboard, which they were doing; we got it back from all over the world that this was going on. So, to counter that, we developed our own association."

The association engendered by H. R. MacMillan was the Western Lumber Manufacturers' Association, formed in 1935 with Chris McRae, head of Alberta Lumber, as its first president. (Alberta Lumber, it is interesting to note, had a restless involvement with Seaboard. It was a member for a period of time, then was asked to leave because of an infraction of the company's export regulations. Some years later, in 1960, it became a Seaboard member once more.)

Van Dusen became president of Western Lumber Association in 1939–40. Then Sitka Spruce Company's Matthew Sutton took over the position until 1948 when W. L. Macken of Collins Macken Lumber Company replaced him. The WLA was made up of most of the remaining independents outside the Seaboard pale, and it conducted a lumber promotion campaign which, while less well funded and more limited than that of the BCLSMA, ran parallel to it in terms of objectives.

The third force in organized lumber promotion was the Alaska Pine Company Ltd., which had undertaken on its own behalf to extol the virtues of western hemlock, the "weed" species of British Columbia's forests. It is at this point that we introduce another European group, the Koerner brothers, whose impact on the lumber industry of the Pacific Northwest can be described as revolutionary in the most positive sense.

The Koerner brothers—Theo, Otto, Leon and Walter—came from a family which had been prominent in forestry and forest products manufacturing for four generations in Czechoslovakia. They were born to the industry and the trade, and have been described by a Vancouver business editor as scions of Czechoslovakia's commercial aristocracy. In 1930 Walter was appointed Economic Director of National Forests in Czechoslovakia.

Over the years the family had developed strong associations on the Continent and had established firm export outlets in the United Kingdom, working through the services of the British agency Foy, Morgan. Had the Second World War not intervened, the Koerners would have continued to function with singular success from their established European base.

The advance of Hitler's armies forced them to find sanctuary, and their choice, more by accident than design, was British Columbia. Leon and Otto preceded Walter Koerner to British Columbia and they launched themselves in the business they knew best, purchasing a dilapidated mill in New Westminster (formerly owned by International Wood Products) which had once specialized in the manufacture of boxes to contain Kraft cheese. Soon after the outbreak of war, Walter joined them, and the brothers set about to make a new life for themselves and their families. (Their oldest brother, Theo, was now retired in Southern France.) Otto was the first president of their new company and Walter was in charge of marketing, a position he had held in the family business back in Europe. The year was 1939.

At first the Koerners had great difficulty penetrating British Columbia's close-knit lumber fraternity. Proficient though they were in all aspects of forestry, manufacturing and marketing, their methods and manners did not correspond with accepted practice on the Pacific Coast. Their courtly approach to doing business was eyed narrowly by the lumber establishment; and the fact that they were of the Jewish persuasion set up all-too-apparent barriers.

While this is to be regretted, the very difficulties that might have deterred the Koerners from persevering were the catalysts which led them to success. If they had attempted to compete with the established British Columbia mills in the production of Douglas-fir lumber products, they could conceivably have encountered serious difficulties. Leon Koerner commented tactfully that because the province's industry was based on Douglas-fir primarily, his company should not encroach on the resource claims staked by others.

So the Koerners looked elsewhere for a legitimate entrée into the market, and they found it, not too suprisingly, in a forest species that had been largely ignored by B.C. lumbermen. Western hemlock was, in the estimation of loggers and entrepreneurs alike, the pariah of the West Coast forests. Compared to the noble qualities of Douglas-fir it was a weed and an encumbrance. Fallers and buckers had to thread their way through a maze of hemlock to reach their Douglas-fir objectives, cutting it and leaving it to rot on the ground in order to make way for the extraction of fir logs. Few were the lumbermen who attempted to do anything with hemlock.

One of the few was Carlton Stone of Hillcrest Lumber Company, who succeeded in developing a small market for hemlock in the United Kingdom. Long before he joined Seaboard he was supplying limited quantities of hemlock to a small group of buyers, but he never attempted to expand his market for this species.

The other proponent for the commercial use of hemlock was John Haley McDonald, an aggressive lumberman who had made an indelible mark on the B.C. industry almost from the time he entered the lumber business. Glasgow-born in 1878, he was educated in Ontario and came to the West Coast in 1905 to apply his knowledge of forestry and lumber manufacturing in the larger setting of British Columbia. He was an active promoter of B.C. lumber and was largely instrumental in the formation of the first Trade Extension Bureau of the B.C. Lumber and Shingle Manufacturers Association. In 1912 he became managing director of B.C. Manufacturing Company in New Westminster and, not too much later, manager of Westminster Shook Mills and Maple Ridge Lumber Company, all of which were members of Seaboard. He was, in addition, president of Salmon River Logging Company and vice-president of Courtenay Lumber Ltd.

J. H. McDonald was an accomplished and highly regarded member of the B.C. lumber fraternity who could be counted on to advance the cause of the province's lumber in any market. He headed a lumber delegation to Australia and New Zealand in 1929, was one of the leaders of the B.C. delegation to Ottawa in 1932 to participate in the Empire Trade Conference, member of a B.C. lumber trade delegation to South Africa in 1934, and of a second delegation to Australia and New Zealand in 1937 (at which time the groundwork was set for the establishment of an Astexo office in Sydney). He was president of the B.C. Lumber and Shingle Manufacturers Association in 1936, and one of the shareholders in the first Seaboard—altogether a consummate spokesman for the lumber trade.

McDonald was a strong promoter of hemlock at a time when his colleagues must have questioned a devious twist of mind. When the British Timber Delegation came to British Columbia in 1938, McDonald, at considerable expense, arranged for a display of various types of lumber and joinery products manufactured from hemlock. He was largely instrumental in setting up a special hemlock committee through the offices of the BCLSMA. His perseverance did succeed in the acceptance of hemlock in Australia for the manufacture of butter boxes, since one of its qualities is that it is odourless and imparts no taste.

During the war, hemlock had been used in the United States as an alternative to Douglas-fir, but it received a mixed response. The green wood was wet and heavy and was subject to warping as well as to unsightly black staining which, at its worst, covered the entire surface of the lumber. Compared to Douglas-fir, the aristocrat of lumber, hemlock was a poor cousin not worth the time and energy of any sensible lumber entrepreneur.

Now the Koerners targeted in on hemlock exclusively. It reminded them of the whitewood species they had grown and converted to lumber in Europe, and they were convinced they could market it successfully if they could overcome its tendency to twist and discolour. They began to experiment, drawing from their knowledge of similar woods in Europe. The answer seemed to lie in the use of correct and uniform drying methods. Once they had mastered the technique, they were in business.

Although they now knew how to dry and machine hemlock into a product comparable to Douglas-fir lumber, they were keenly aware of the bad name hemlock had earned in the marketplace, and knew if they were to sell it successfully they would have to create a new image for it. Among the alternative names they discovered in their research they found the name Alaska pine. Although it was not a botanically accurate description of the species, it was catchy and avoided any association with hemlock. The question was, would they be allowed to market the wood under this new and disarming name. When the Koerners went to British Columbia's Chief Forester, Ernest Manning, seeking an official opinion, his response was forthright: "I don't care what you call it," he said, "as long as you sell lots of it."

Naming their mill Alaska Pine Company Ltd. gave their product credibility and a corporate identity. The Koerners' U.K. agent, Foy, Morgan, was able to open the right doors for them, and the war created a huge and steady demand for their product. Alaska Pine produced box shooks for food containers and ammunition boxes. In addition, the Koerners, being familiar with the U.K. market and buyer preferences, supplied lumber cut to accepted and traditional specifications rather than to the scant specifications which British Columbia was attempting to introduce.

Lumbermen remember that the Koerners' swift climb to success on the strength of hemlock did not endear the brothers to John McDonald. For long years he had crusaded on behalf of hemlock, only to be beaten to the bonanza by a European family who had combined doggedness with know-how and a marketing approach to achieve the objective he had singled out for himself. They were not encouraged to join the British Columbia lumber fraternity and thus chose to market their lumber independently, supporting it with an organized program of promotion.

The Koerners consolidated their position quickly, acquiring Jones Lake Logging Company Ltd. in 1942 to establish their own timber base. In 1942 they purchased Universal Lumber & Box Company, located at Marpole in Vancouver. The following year they took over the large logging operation of Pioneer Timber Company at Port McNeill. In that same period they formed a subsidiary company, Northern Timber Company Ltd., which acquired 20,000 acres of Crown Grant land at Port McNeill, as well as leasing Vancouver's Evans Products Company sawmill which was put to work immediately custom cutting.

Expansion continued in 1946 with their first incursion into the pulp and paper business at Woodfibre where a modernization program was initiated. In the same year they associated with the Carpenter Company, an Australian entity, to incorporate Western Forest Industries Ltd. and to purchase Lake Logging & Lumber at Lake Cowichan. In addition they obtained the saw and shingle mills and logging camps of Canadian Puget Sound Lumber & Timber Company at Jordan River. This would not be the end of their acquisitions.

When British Columbia's three major lumber promotion associations—BCLSMA, WLA and the Alaska Pine promotion department— amalgamated in July 1949, these three promotional groups set aside their differences for reasons of expediency and joined forces under the name of the B.C. Lumber Manufacturers Association (BCLMA).

H. R. MacMillan and, it is to be supposed, the Koerners saw good sense and savings in an amalgamation. Alaska Pine was now well-established in the B.C. industry. Many mills were now producing hemlock lumber thanks to Alaska Pine's pioneering venture. Any resistance to its inclusion in the amalgamation was of no significance. And so the new Association was formed—but not without the exercise of politics. H. R. MacMillan's proviso for joining was that his second-in-command, W. J. Van Dusen, be named vice-president, which placed him in line for president in 1951. It is said that pressure was exerted to depose the long-time secretary of the BCLSMA, Thomas Wilkinson, who had applied for a position with the new organization. Another of H. R.

MacMillan's people, Earl King, was appointed to the permanent staff. These conditions, taken in context, may not have been as unreasonable as some believe. Certainly Seaboard continued to be well-represented in the newly formed B.C. Lumber Manufacturers Association.

One of the first actions taken by the BCLMA was to form a new Trade Extension Bureau to upgrade and intensify the promotion of lumber exports in all markets, particularly in the tenuous U.K. market. Henry Mackin of Canadian Western was elected president of the Bureau, with MacMillan Export's Ralph M. Shaw as vice-president. Secretary-manager of the Bureau was G. Cleveland Edgett, brother of Seaboard's Bob Edgett. These men directed new promotion techniques towards the United Kingdom in particular in an effort to reinstate the share of market British Columbia had once enjoyed.

The United Kingdom Timber Development Association was urging its government to increase reciprocal trade with Canada in order to earn the dollars they needed to purchase additional Canadian lumber. When Harold Wilson visited Canada in 1949 in his capacity as president of the British Board of Trade, he spoke of a program for increasing sales to Canada, especially to the Canadian West. Later in the same year representatives of the B.C. lumber export trade travelled to the United Kingdom to discuss increasing Canadian sales. Included in the delegation were Charles Grinnell, H. R. MacMillan, Bruce Farris, Leon Koerner, Bob Edgett, Chris Dalton and Ralph M. Shaw. "We were dangerously close to running out of United Kingdom business," Bob Edgett states, "and we had to make an all-out effort to get the British Timber Control to start buying again."

Once in England, the delegation discovered that some of their work had been done for them by Canada's go-getter cabinet minister, C. D. Howe, who had opened negotiations with the Timber Control Board for a large amount of B.C. lumber. Howe's instruction to the delegation was to "tidy up the details."

"The politics of those negotiations were extremely interesting," Edgett recalls. "The Seaboard faction and the MacMillan faction kept within sight of one another at all times. MacMillan and Grinnell, with some involvement by Leon Koerner, negotiated the deal together, and Seaboard ended up with a generous contract for 602 million feet."

In addition, Bob Edgett generated negotiations for a large amount of hemlock door stock—an order which Leon Koerner wanted badly. "The business couldn't have worked out better," he states. "The order was so large that our mills couldn't handle it all. We traded the residue to Koerner for other lumber specifications, and everyone was happy."

These large U.K. contracts were windfalls not only for Seaboard but for the entire B.C. lumber industry. They would keep the mills busy for two years.

Mercurial though the U.K. lumber trade might have been, an event occurred in the United States midway through 1949 which helped to alleviate any diminution of export business to Britain. The passing of the Wagner-Ellender-Taft Act galvanized the United States housing industry into massive action. Described as "the world's biggest housing program," it resulted in an unexpected acceleration of demand for lumber that sent lumber export volumes to the U.S. soaring. Thus the fortunes of the lumber industry as the forties drew to a close were bullish.

* * *

H. R. MacMillan had been forced, primarily by Seaboard, to protect his position as a lumber exporter by also becoming a major lumber manufacturer. Actually, the acquisition of existing sawmills with their own timber resources was the only sensible course of action. Some of the larger mill complexes possessed enormous tracts of timber, and this was the key to a perpetuating timber trade. The best and most efficient sawmill on the coast was only as good as its timber reserves.

MacMillan knew this and so did the Seaboard faction. MacMillan's strength was that he was in command and could negotiate in any direction, and did so with audacity. Seaboard, by the nature of its organization, could only maintain its membership and obtain new members through persuasion. In the final analysis, each Seaboard member was obliged to serve its individual need, which might or might not conflict with Seaboard membership.

The coming and going of mills was not always deleterious to Seaboard, of course; there were sellouts and mergers which turned out to be beneficial. Powell River Company's move in 1951 is a case in point, although what it did at that time would ultimately play into the hands of H. R. MacMillan.

The Powell River Company got its start in 1910 when the large U.S. lumber firm Brooks-Scanlon Lumber Company purchased Powell River timber leases from the first owners, Canadian Industrial Company, and water rights from Pacific Coast Power. The two partner-owners, Dr. Dwight F. Brooks and M. J. Scanlon, were energetic and far-sighted entrepreneurs who had launched and expanded one of America's most successful lumber complexes. In British Columbia they developed the Powell River Company into the first, and for some years the largest, pulp and paper mill in the province. It was typical of the two men to take a personal interest in the enterprise. Its isolated location on British Columbia's coast required the construction of a townsite as well as a modern plant. In due course, Powell River emerged as a new, well-designed, excellently serviced industrial town with a mill that did large and profitable business in a world market.

Entering the fifties, the company interests began to look around for opportunities to diversify and integrate within the framework of the forest industry. They found their opportunity at the door of B.C. Manufacturing Company and its affiliates. J. H. McDonald, head of B.C. Manufacturing, Westminster Shook Mills, Maple Ridge Lumber and Salmon River Logging, had died in 1946; his position was now filled by Harold A. Renwick, who became the company's representative with Seaboard. Chances are that if McDonald had still been alive, the integration with Powell River Company would not have occurred, McDonald having been prominent in the cult of the rugged individualist. But Powell River purchased McDonald's property and timber holdings, thus combining the resources of two B.C. forest industry pioneers. Salmon River Logging brought a large tract of lumber into the company integration. B.C. Manufacturing, Westminster Shook and Maple Ridge remained Seaboard members, but the Powell River Company as an entity did not join Seaboard until 1960.

Concurrent with this amalgamation, another set of negotiations was culminated, administering a serious blow to Seaboard. Bloedel, Stewart & Welch Company, one of Seaboard's principal members accounting for at least 18 per cent of the co-operative's total annual shipments, had grown restless. Ironically, the company's vice-president, Bruce Farris, was also president of Seaboard. Another twist was that the second player in the scenario was H. R. MacMillan.

Bloedel, Stewart & Welch was one of the province's most prestigious and successful lumber companies, with roots going back to 1911 when Wisconsin-born Julius H. Bloedel, already a successful logging operator and mill operator in Washington state, acquired extensive forest lease and water rights at Myrtle Point, near Powell River. Failing to enlist United States partners in this venture, he joined forces with John Stewart and Patrick Welch, who were actively involved in Canadian railway construction. Bloedel held 50 per cent of the shares in the new logging company and his partners each held 25 per cent. The arrangement was fortuitous from the outset: Stewart and Welch were engaged in the construction of a section of the Grand Trunk Pacific Railway from Edmonton to Prince Rupert, and later a section of the Pacific Great Eastern Railway in British Columbia. They were in a position to secure contracts for the logging company run by Julius Bloedel.

There was no sawmill at first. Bloedel, Stewart & Welch supplied logs
to mills like Hanbury's on False Creek in Vancouver, and the sawn
lumber was delivered in due course to the sites of railroad construction.
Bloedel ran the operation almost single-handedly. Nearly fanatic in his
belief that timber reserves were the key to success and longevity in the
business, he took every opportunity to expand his timber holdings.

His lieutenant and manager-supreme almost from the beginning was
S. G. (Sid) Smith, a logger with instinctive management and business
sense, and an ability to run a logging show with an iron hand inside a
velvet glove. He was of the old school of logging and sawmilling but
had been able to make the transition into the new way of doing things.
He it was who put Julius Bloedel's policy of timber acquisition into
continuing practice.

Among the timber parcels picked up by the company were 275 million board feet at Union Bay on Vancouver Island in 1920 and 1.3
billion feet at Menzies Bay a few years later. The first incursion into
sawmilling began in 1924 when the company purchased a shingle mill
which had gone into bankruptcy. We have described earlier how
Bloedel, Stewart and Welch, in 1926, combined with Bruce Farris and
M. B. King to launch Great Central Sawmills Ltd. Julius Bloedel was
president, Bruce Farris was a vice-president and B,S & W held the majority share position.

In 1934 the company began construction of a modern mill on the
Somass River at the head of the Alberni Canal. When this was completed a merger took place between Great Central Sawmills and
Bloedel, Stewart & Welch with the former company coming under the
corporate umbrella of the latter. M. B. King by this time had moved on
to start his own mill in North Vancouver. Bruce Farris, although he had
sold his Grand Central shares, stayed on as vice-president and manager
of lumber manufacturing and sales. When the company joined Seaboard in 1935, Farris became the mill's representative. Sid Smith stayed
with the activity he liked most and understood best—logging and
timber acquisition for the company.

Julius Bloedel's son, Prentice, had joined his father in 1929. With a
business administration degree from Yale University he was eager to try
new techniques. His first major responsibility in the company was be-
stowed in 1935 when he took over as head of the Somass River mill.
Prentice Bloedel became president and treasurer of the company in
1942, though he continued to accede to his father on many issues. The
older man was of no mind to retire and continued for some years to be a
strong force in company decisions. In August 1947 a pulp mill, started
before the war, was completed and began the production of sulphate

pulp. Located adjacent to the Somass mill, it made immediate and efficient use of the chips produced there.

Logging operations expanded to a large spread at Sproat Lake in 1944, and to Sarita River in 1947. And at the other end of the scale, Prentice Bloedel was introducing new technology into the operations with such innovations as the conversion of wood wastes into a trademarked fuel log for fireplaces and stoves. A huge battery of dry kilns was installed at the Somass plant to overcome problems of lumber staining and warping, and to make hemlock more marketable. Bloedel, Stewart & Welch was the first company to engage in extensive pro-grams of seedling plantation for reforestation, and was the first to experiment with and install hydraulic ring barkers to remove bark from logs for woodchipping purposes.

In 1948 Prentice Bloedel demonstrated a determination to perpetuate the company when in a speech to employees he said in part: "Stand still we may not. To my mind, development during the next decade will be in the direction of further integration, diversification and refinement." Yet by 1950 he had decided to sell the company. At this time it consisted of five logging operations, two efficient sawmills, two shingle mills and a modern pulp mill. Most important of all, it owned or controlled well over 310,000 acres of prime forest. The factors and forces that caused him to change his mind 180 degrees within a few years will never be fully understood. He has stated several reasons and has implied others.

Sid Smith was opposed to the plan, and so, it is reported, was Julius Bloedel who, although in his eighties, remained interested and proud of the dynasty he had created. "What dynasty?" Prentice Bloedel could argue. He had no son to carry on the business. In terms of family control, the company ended with him. His officially reported statement concerning the disposal of the company was that Bloedel, Stewart & Welch, while a successful forest products company in its own right, would not be able to continue long in a changing world economy. Only the largest, most affluent and best-financed companies would be able to cope in the marketplace and adapt to enormously expensive new technology. Small mills would be gravely threatened. Medium-sized mills would either have to amalgamate into larger complexes or sell to the forest products giants. That was his opinion which he translated into a decision to sell . . . and the forest products giant he chose to approach was H. R. MacMillan.

It has been observed by many that this was one of those rare cir-cumstances where a company approached H. R. MacMillan with an offer to sell out. Almost always it was the other way around. Donald MacKay, in *Empire of Wood*, states that MacMillan at first was suspicious of Prentice Bloedel's motives. After all, he was being presented with a superb forest products complex on a silver platter. It took him some time and considerable investigation to decide that the offer was bona fide in every respect. Negotiations began and, after a few complications with shareholders and tax authorities, the deal was consummated in October 1951. The merger that created MacMillan & Bloedel Limited resulted in the largest lumber and pulp operation in British Columbia.

Seaboard bade a reluctant farewell not only to two mills and 18 per cent of its export volume but also to its president, Bruce Farris, who had no recourse but to resign and take a position with MacMillan Bloedel as a vice-president with no defined responsibilities. Sid Smith found himself in the same position, and within a year both men had resigned their positions as corporate officers.

An additional subplot involves Clifford Crispin. It will be remembered that Seaboard hired him away from MacMillan Export to take over Claude Effinger's position when Effinger was posted to the company's U.K. office. Later, Crispin was seconded to Ottawa as an assistant timber controller for British Columbia in wartime. He served in that capacity for three years and, with his duties fulfilled, returned to Vancouver to serve for a short period as B.C. Timber Controller. He then rejoined Seaboard, but not for long; H. R. MacMillan wanted him, and Crispin tells his story:

> H. R. had always said that Chuck Grinnell stole part of his flag when he got me. You know H. R. when he got the bit in his teeth. He was bound to get me back, and he invited me to have a talk with him.
>
> I met him at his house and I said, "I understand you're interested in hiring me back." He said he was and he offered me a hell of a good deal. Well, first of all I had to tell Seaboard what was going on so I phoned Chuck Grinnell.
>
> "I've been getting a little restless, Chuck," I said, "and I think H. R. is prepared to offer me a job. A good challenge . . . good money. What do you think you should do about it?"
>
> Chuck said, "Nothing."
>
> So I went back to H. R. and he hired me right off the bat. I went back to Seaboard and cleaned out my desk. That was that.

Crispin went on to become manager of Harmac, MacMillan's first pulp mill, and when MacMillan & Bloedel was formed, he returned to head office as vice-president in charge of the company's pulp and paper operations.

Once again an event occurred that would compensate Seaboard for the loss of an important member. In leading up to this, it must be observed that Prentice Bloedel's prediction that the trend in the lumber industry towards integration and amalgamation had other supporters. The *Financial Times,* in April 1951, stated:

The MacMillan-Bloedel transaction follows a pattern followed in British Columbia's forest industry by other companies in recent months. Abitibi Power & Paper Company, Toronto, recently completed arrangements for its integration with Alaska Pine Company and the purchase of the B.C. Pulp & Paper Company, both of Vancouver. Canadian Western Lumber Company and Pacific Mills, Canadian subsidiary of Crown Zellerbach Corporation, are partners in a new newsprint enterprise on Vancouver Island. Canadian Forest Products Ltd., another big Vancouver company which, like Alaska Pine, was organized by groups from Czechoslovakia and Austria shortly before World War II, has joined with Sorg Paper Company of Middletown, Ohio and Perkins-Goodwin Company of New York in restoring a pulp mill at Port Mellon.

Big corporations, many of them United States—based, were looking north to profitable enterprises. Alaska Pine's first merger was with Canadian interests rather than American, but when the Koerner interests, in company with Abitibi Power & Paper, purchased British Columbia Pulp & Paper Manufacturing Company Ltd., it was but the first of a series of moves.

The company formed by the merger was Alaska Pine & Cellulose Limited, and its holdings were not inconsiderable, consisting of British Columbia Pulp & Paper with pulp mills at Port Alice on northern Vancouver Island and at Woodfibre in Howe Sound together with timber properties and logging operations; the Alaska Pine group of companies including Alaska Pine Company Limited, Universal Lumber and Box Company Ltd., Pioneer Timber Company Ltd., Jones Lake Logging Company Ltd., Empire Machinery Company Ltd., Alaska Pine Purchasing Ltd., Canadian Puget Sound Lumber & Timber Company Ltd. and Western Forest Industries Ltd.

In 1952 Alaska Pine & Cellulose joined Seaboard. Claude Effinger recalls that Leon Koerner called on Charles Grinnell one day. "We have come to the conclusion," he said, "that it would be of benefit to us to become members of Seaboard." Effinger states quite candidly that there had been a time in the past when Seaboard would have entertained such a statement with small interest and no enthusiasm, but times had changed and Alaska Pine had become one of the moving forces in the industry. So the loss of Bloedel, Stewart and Welch was alleviated by this friendly and unexpected visit from Leon Koerner. While Alaska Pine's entry into Seaboard was of great benefit to the export company at a critical time, it was also a wise move for Alaska Pine.

"Alaska Pine was having difficulty in getting sufficient distribution through one agent in the United Kingdom," Effinger states. "In addition, it was difficult to secure enough reliable shipping at a reasonable rate in the open market. Seaboard's organization could and did solve these problems."

Effinger's memory of the event remains warm. "Shortly after Alaska Pine joined Seaboard, I travelled to the United Kingdom with Leon Koerner and his wife. It was what might be called a thoroughly enjoyable business trip. The Koerners were wonderful travelling companions and were well-connected in England. We established our headquarters at Claridge's and, in the next few days, I was introduced to the principals in Alaska Pine's agency, Foy, Morgan. In return I introduced Leon Koerner to our list of agents—each of whom insisted on entertaining us appropriately. We didn't resist these gestures."

Notwithstanding the acquisition of Alaska Pine, Seaboard remained justifiably uneasy in the face of MacMillan's aggressive campaign to add to his list of producing mills. Efforts were redoubled to increase Seaboard's membership. Alaska Pine's entry into the co-operative was an example to be followed by others. That same year, 1952, eight more mills joined Seaboard: Whonnock Lumber Company Ltd., L & K Lumber Company, North Shore Lumber Ltd., Farris Lumber Company Ltd., Silvertree Sawmills Ltd., McDonald Cedar Products Ltd., Oak Bay Lumber Ltd. and Collins-Macken Lumber Company Ltd. Bay Lumber Company Ltd. joined in 1953 and Anglo-Canadian Timber Products Ltd. in 1954. Three or four more came into the organization in the interval leading up to 1960.

The years 1951 and 1952, then, marked a period of intensive activity in the game of corporate chess, with both MacMillan and Seaboard emerging stronger than ever before. H. R. MacMillan was recognized as a very powerful entity in British Columbia's and Canada's lumber industry. Seaboard, on the other hand, was now ranked as one of the largest lumber exporting organizations in the world, drawing more than 1 billion feet annually from forty member mills.

ELEVEN

THE FIFTIES

Within the British Columbia forest industry the final years of the forties and the first years of the fifties were characterized in part by a dramatic repositioning of mills and what appeared to be an unavoidable and ongoing power struggle between two giants. Other things were happening as well. Many of the founders of Seaboard were preparing to take their leave or had already done so. They had been in harness for better than twenty years.

During that period, those who had weathered the storm of the Depression, the vagaries of the overseas and domestic markets and the punishing demands of technological change had been called upon to further adapt to all these changes and pressures. Individualists and independent entrepreneurs, they had to leave behind the rough-and-tumble of the early lumber industry and accustom themselves to more sophisticated methods of doing business.

Some managed to do this; others could not or would not and, as a result, were faced with either insolvency or the sale of businesses to larger, better-financed companies and corporations. No mill could stand still, stubbornly mired in a backwater of time, hoping that the old ways would see them through. This was the advent of mergers and the incursion of larger companies and corporations.

The *Journal of Commerce,* in August 1953, sums up Seaboard's position quite succinctly:

> Things have not been static in Seaboard. Changes have come and improvements have been made. Some of the old and well-known mill names, Robertson and Hackett, B.C. Fir and Cedar, Nanaimo, Mohawk are disappearing from the picture, but new mills are coming to take their places. In recent months such mills as L & K Sawmills, Oak Bay, Collins-Macken, McDonald Cedar Products, Farris and Silvertree have swelled production figures, and the entry of three large and modern Alaska Pine Company Ltd. mills last February was a major addition to the Seaboard organization.
>
> The sawn Douglas Fir, Pacific Coast Hemlock, Western Red Cedar and Sitka Spruce that have long been in demand by importers everywhere, are still forming the major items of production, appearing somewhat more "glamorous" with precision trimmed ends and bright Seaboard marks. Other commodities are finding enthusiastic acclaim in many markets; decorative plywoods and hardboard in many designs and for every purpose, Red Cedar shingles, door components and creosoted timbers (often cut to size or prefabricated), all these are establishing themselves as swiftly as exchange rates and import regulations will allow.
>
> Seaboard has come a long way since its beginning. Today, with 40 strong mills including two plywood plants, three shingle mills, a hardboard plant and a timber preserving plant in its membership—employing 12,800 persons—representing a total annual payroll exceeding $41,000,000, it plays a major role in the welfare of the province.
>
> There is every reason to believe that it will continue to play this role in the future sending the "Seaboard" mark around the world on the end of strong, attractive timber products.

Be this as it may, Seaboard applied itself aggressively and with great determination in the restless opening years of the 1950s. A fire had been lit under the organization with the shock of losing Bloedel, Stewart & Welch. MacMillan was proving himself to be a formidable adversary, determined to survive and strengthen his position by all legitimate means, no matter how audacious. Seaboard's attitude and performance could be no less aggressive and exploratory.

The United Kingdom market was a frustrating challenge in that a great need for lumber existed behind barriers inhibiting supply. The market was recovering only slowly from the effects of the war. Balance-of-payment problems obliged the government to maintain Timber Control until 1952, in the face of vociferous pressure from the timber agents and importers, and the exhortations of the Canadian lumber associations. Charles Grinnell, Claude Effinger and Bob Edgett made a number of trips to the United Kingdom, lending Seaboard's weight to that of the Seaboard Agents' Association in attempts to break the impasse. One reassuring situation prevailed: the United Kingdom represented a stable market with a potential for long-term contracts that could only work to the continuing benefit of the B.C. industry.

Although business with the United Kingdom did not surpass the sales of the war years, that market continued to be British Columbia's best single customer, taking 40 per cent of the province's total cut in 1952, with the United States accounting for 27 per cent and Canada, 30 per cent. The termination of the U.K. Timber Control Board in December 1952 should have meant an upsurge in business for B.C., but such was not the case. Baltic and Scandinavian lumber suppliers, selling at lower prices and offering traditional grades and dimensions, drained a considerable amount of the new business away.

The B.C. Lumber Manufacturing Association, working through its Trade Extension Bureau, attempted to counter the European competition with a number of product promotion campaigns including one in 1952 in joint sponsorship with British Railways to lay a mile of test track installed on hemlock ties in England.

In 1953 the BCLMA sent a prefabricated cedar hut as a gift to the United Kingdom Timber Association to promote the use of this type of structure as accommodation for military forces overseas. The Trend House promotion, introduced and administered by Cleve Edgett, had been first tested in Canada with singular success in 1952. Demonstration houses making use of B.C. woods were deployed in various Canadian centres and opened to public inspection. Models of these same houses were displayed at trade fairs where viewers were invited to visit the actual demonstration homes. Public response was immediate and positive, encouraging the Association to do the same thing in the United Kingdom. In that market, while an encouraging degree of interest was demonstrated, the ingrained feeling for bricks and mortar remained to be overcome. Still, the Trend House campaign was a far from futile undertaking. Undoubtedly it represented British Columbia's most effective overseas educational effort to that date.

The United Kingdom, of course, could not be Seaboard's only area of concern. Established markets had to be maintained and expanded, and new markets had to be explored and developed. As usual, Claude Effinger was the principal emissary. In 1951, travelling with Charles Grinnell's son, James B. Grinnell, he visited South Africa intent on renewing contacts and market advantages eroded during the war. The

Effinger-Grinnell junket to South Africa would lead to the opening of a Seaboard office in Johannesburg in 1954.

For the peripatetic Effinger the year 1952 was extremely busy. Not only was he involved in the recruitment of member mills but also in the acquisition of agency representatives in various world markets. That year he explored the business climate in Japan, hoping to restore connections severed in 1941. His observation was that the Japanese had been seriously overcutting their own forests throughout the forties and were now suffering the consequences.

Effinger reported that the Japanese were demonstrating interest in renewing the import of cedar squares and fir logs, the trade that had once sustained Straits Lumber Company, among others, leading to their demise when trade was cut off. Effinger's response, in accord with provincial policy and Seaboard's own interests, was to discourage the sale of logs and encourage the purchase of sawn lumber as well as plywood, pulp and paper. His opinion was that Japan's internal forest industry problems would probably force it to begin importing forest products again in 1953.

From Japan he went to Hong Kong, there to reinstate communications and to activate a Seaboard agent, Butterfield and Swire. Then he moved on to Bombay, Calcutta and Singapore, where he was unable to generate business of any significance. In retrospect, he later regretted that a greater effort was not made to establish an agency in Singapore. "At the time," he said, "we were not sufficiently aware of the market potential in that area, and we were not able to find the kind of regional advice we needed."

The establishment of markets and representatives in South America remained a sensitive consideration. Charles Grinnell had never felt easy trading in that part of the world, and his fears were borne out when Seaboard was severely burned in the delivery of a substantial lumber cargo to Caracas, Venezuela. A change of government resulted in no payment, and the Seaboard management of the day resolved to concentrate its attention on other world markets.

In 1951 the company had posted Frank Solloway to the Sydney, Australia, office, where he struggled to activate business. In 1952 Dick Silbernagel, head of Seaboard's Australia, New Zealand and South Seas markets, travelled to Australia to see for himself what might be done to increase trade. He reported that Australia had large stocks of lumber on hand and that no more than a trickle of business could be expected into the foreseeable future.

Hints of change were evident in the ranks of the Associated Seaboard Agents in the United Kingdom. Seagents, Seaboard's single representative during the Timber Control years, continued in operation until the Control Board's termination in 1952. In 1950 Niel Morison, who had been a principal with Brandts before the war, was persuaded to become managing director of Seagents, a position which he accepted and in which he served with distinction. George Taylor, Seagents' first accountant, has vivid recollections of those days. "In 1949," he remembers, "the office was in Piccadilly, directly opposite the Burlington Arcade. David Hardcastle [seconded from Brandts for a term as manager] was due to be relieved from Seagent duties and was anxious to return home to Liverpool. I suspect his heart was not in his work.

"At 5 P.M. every day the porter of the Burlington Arcade would stand outside and ring a bell to warn shoppers that the Arcade was closing; whereupon Dave Hardcastle would shout, 'Muffins!', close all the books with a slam and that was the end of work for that day."

Taylor relates that when the lease ran out at the Piccadilly address, they leased a suite of offices in the city near the monument at the corner of Pudding Lane. Soon after that another move took place to a building over the Mark Lane tube station overlooking Tower Hill and the Tower of London.

When Timber Control was dissolved, Seaboard was placed in the position of having to decide whether to continue with the Associated Seaboard Agents or revert to the old system of dealing with each Seaboard agent individually. Bob Edgett, manager of Seaboard's U.K. Department, pressed hard for the continuation of Seagents, but he was rigidly opposed by Charles Grinnell and Henry Mackin, who felt that the restoration of the old system would be healthier because of the competition thus generated among the agents. The individual agents, of course, were all for the old system, eager to see Seagents dead and buried. Furthermore, they banded together to insist that Seaboard would from now on discontinue dealing direct with Denny, Mott & Dickson for British Railways and Admiralty business, an arrangement that had prevailed since 1935. Seaboard agreed to this, with the understanding that any "tender" business issued directly either by the Railways or the Admiralty would be handled by Seaboard's London office.

Naturally this meant that Seaboard required a London office once more. Niel Morison's position changed from manager of the defunct Seagents to manager of Seaboard's London office, and one of his first moves was to invite George Taylor to stay on as his assistant. "I asked him what he thought the prospects were," Taylor says. "He said he had no idea how things would develop but that we should just play it by ear for the time. I played it by ear for the next twenty years."

Now there was the matter of more permanent and more prestigious quarters for the revived London office, and the search began. Taylor states:

> Chuck Grinnell thought we should be in the West End or in the vicinity of Saint Paul's. He felt that a situation like this would impress visiting mill men and their wives. But, as a result of extensive bomb damage and long delays in rebuilding, office space was at a premium.
>
> We were just at the point of signing a contract for rooms in Grand Buildings, an old hotel block overlooking Trafalgar Square, covered in pigeon droppings, when Bill McAdam, Agent General for B.C., told us of some sublet space available in B.C. House. This, of course, was an ideal address for Seaboard. Soon after we became sub-tenants of Westinghouse Electric in three rooms on the third floor, later moving to the fourth floor. Ultimately we obtained a lease for that floor.
>
> The old regime was changing. In the years following decontrol, the number of Seaboard agents was gradually shrinking like the ten little Indians. I cannot remember the exact number when I joined; about thirteen I think. We shed them one-by-one including Churchill & Sim, Alfred Dobell, Pharoah Gane, Balfour, Williamson until we stabilized with four consisting of Brandts', Leary's, Munro's and Foy's. This last agent came to us when Alaska Pine joined Seaboard.

Of all the changes occurring at that time, and those to occur to the end of the sixties, George Taylor would remain a solid contributor until his retirement in 1972. Perhaps the most important single change occurred in mid-spring of 1953 when Charles Grinnell, with little warning, decided to take early retirement.

Charles Grinnell's replacement, logically enough, was Claude Effinger. He had been with Grinnell from the beginning and had been in direct contact with the markets at all times, starting with the United Kingdom where he managed Seaboard's office and continuing with frequent organizational and exploratory trips worldwide on behalf of the company. His enthusiasm for the pursuit of new markets was in marked contrast to Grinnell's strengths, which were best applied from the head office.

Grinnell, an American by birth, had always inclined towards the U.S. market, and Seaboard started in business from that base. Although he was concerned with every export market, his familiarity with the U.S. market caused him to be more at ease in that sales environment. Effinger, on the other hand, had advanced through a more eclectic set of sales experiences in the United Kingdom, Europe, the Middle East and the Far East. For a time he had been in charge of sales to South Africa, the West Indies and South America. He had been Seaboard's secretary since 1946. As a result he was able to step into Charles Grinnell's position with little or no disruption and to deal with his new and larger responsibilities with relative ease.

At the same time, Harry Berry was appointed company secretary in addition to his regular duties as comptroller. Harry O'Hagan was promoted from manager of U.S. Sales to sales manager, and Bob Edgett stepped from manager of U.K. Sales to assistant sales manager.

Effinger did not assume his new post in salubrious times. In the first four months of 1953, exports to the traditional offshore markets declined by 25 per cent. Bottlenecks still existed in the United Kingdom, in spite of the removal of Timber Control. It was not until November 1953 that Bob Edgett was able to report the lifting of consumer licences in the U.K., warning at the same time that plywood sales would not be deregulated for at least another ten months.

In anticipation of the decontrol of plywood, the decision was made to prepare for the promotion and sale of this product in the U.K. The first practical move had been made with the hiring of Douglas Reid in 1952. Reid had no previous experience in wood product sales but was known by Bob Edgett to possess excellent sales techniques. His first assignment was to spend several months in the plants and sales offices of Seaboard's plywood manufacturing members, and while he was undergoing a thorough indoctrination, Bob Edgett went to the U.K. accompanied by P. H. (Spike) Brown, Pacific Veneer's sales promotion manager, to generate an interest in plywood and improve the climate for sales.

The first two weeks of the visit were uniformly discouraging. Neither the agents nor the plywood importers were interested in Douglas-fir plywood. In fact, many of them had a preconceived opinion of the product, stating that it was not versatile, that it was difficult to paint and varnish and that it could not compare with the birch plywood to which they were accustomed. Some went so far as to damn plywood, declaring that it was an unreliable product that would fall apart as soon as it was subjected to moisture.

Edgett and Brown were faced with a formidable selling job. They had to convince both agents and importers that plywood had come a long way since the prewar years when its glued laminations were indeed vulnerable to moisture. In a fifteen-year period plywood had been developed into a completely waterproof product suitable for use indoors and out, and was even being used in North America as a boat-building material. Furthermore, a wide selection of decorative plywoods had been developed offering a variety of surface textures and paint and stain finishes applied at the factory. In North America, Douglas-fir plywood had become a standard and essential building material, while in the U.K. it continued to suffer from its past reputation.

No amount of persuasion on Edgett's part could alter the opinion of the plywood importers. "Brown and I were becoming desperate," he states. "Finally I decided that we must try a new approach. We would avoid using the word 'plywood' and talk about a new, improved form of softwood boards, and we decided to make our presentation, in company with a large plywood importer, directly to a large buyer of softwood boards in the United Kingdom—General Motors."

GM's director of purchasing became interested when Edgett told him he had a strong, waterproof softwood product that could be delivered in sheets eight feet long and four feet wide, ideal for the construction of large crates. "We never mentioned plywood," Edgett states, "and the General Motors man couldn't have been more receptive. His logic was that GM purchased its glass and steel in sheet form, why not buy softwood the same way?

"That meeting gave us the leverage we needed with the agents and lumber importers," Edgett relates. "We had given up on the plywood importers who were suffering from hopeless tunnel vision. What we did now was to persuade the lumber importers to get into the plywood business, and of course the plywood importers then followed suit. Plywood was better than lumber in every way as a concrete forming material. The trip was a great success after all and we went back to Vancouver in high spirits, knowing we had found a market for plywood."

In 1954, as Edgett had predicted, the U.K. eased import restrictions on plywood, permitting its entry under conditions of "open individual trading" for the first time in fifteen years. Price-setting controls were a thing of the past. Within five days of the announcement of the removal of plywood import restrictions, Seaboard's Douglas Reid and W. E. (Pat) Burns, representing Canadian Forest Products' Pacific Veneer, were in the United Kingdom meeting with agents and importers to capitalize on Edgett's initial effort. At that time, Seaboard began to sell plywood through Flatau Dick, who were Pacific Veneer's plywood agent. Plywood was also sold through Leary and Brandts. However, as plywood sales developed, requiring more specialized attention, Flatau Dick, under the direction of Charles Hatfield, became Seaboard's primary plywood agent.

In that same year, in expectation of a growing demand for plywood in the United Kingdom and elsewhere, Canadian Collieries (Dunsmuir) constructed a plywood mill, and Canadian Western expanded its already large plant. At Seaboard, Douglas Reid was elevated to manager of a flourishing plywood sales department.

During Claude Effinger's first months as general manager of the company, his concerns were not only for the general decline in overseas sales but also for a serious drop in prices created in large part by the competitive tactics of Russian, Scandinavian and Baltic exporters. It was not wise to be complacent even though sales and prices were better close to home. Canada's increase in domestic demand and an upswing in U.S. business helped to alleviate what could have been extremely troubling times for the mills, but these two markets enabled production to remain high. One other lifesaver presented itself at the beginning of the year when Pakistan, working under the provisions of the Colombo Plan, placed an order for 10,775,000 feet of railway sleepers. Seaboard received a substantial part of this business. The sleepers, consisting of both Douglas-fir and Pacific hemlock, were pressure creosoted by Timber Preservers and Canada Creosoting Company Ltd. This substantial order was not completed until March 1954.

Seaboard House, circa 1953

Charles Grinnell was a man of system and self-discipline, qualities which he encouraged in his managers and staff. In his capacity as Seaboard's managing director, his presence and authority were felt in all aspects of the company's operations, ranging from the efficient performance of every employee to each employee's personal welfare. In his dealings with personnel he was patriarchal both in terms of the discipline he imposed and the assistance he extended.

Unless travel or some unusual business commitment prevented it, he was in his office at door opening each morning. More often than not he was at work well before business hours began, taking time from his desk after all staff arrived to make the first of his two daily tours of the entire Seaboard House complex.

He began with a quiet word with the two receptionist/switchboard operators. The board opened an hour before the sales staff arrived and a long list of calls would be waiting by the time the business day commenced. Grace Eccleston, senior board operator—a position she held for thirty-five years—earned an international reputation as a remarkable manipulator of the keyboard system of the day. Not only was her proficiency in placing and receiving calls impressive but her ability to recognize a voice issuing from her headphones from anywhere on earth approached the legendary. She needed only to hear a customer's voice once, coupled with the name of the caller, to remember that voice for all time. Grace Eccleston was known and respected by countless callers over the years, most of whom knew her only by telephone.

Beside her sat Audrey Galbraith, an especially capable switchboard operator/receptionist drawn from the ranks of B.C. Telephone's long-distance staff. Grinnell's habit was to question both women at the opening of the day. If an overseas or New York emergency was building, they would be aware of it.

Forewarned and forearmed with this informal resumé, Charles Grinnell would now proceed down the left side of the office, the large general sales office to his right and the offices of department and market managers to the left. First there was Douglas Reid, head of the plywood and hardboard departments for all markets. Reid was a relative newcomer, placed in charge of these wood commodities now beginning to make an impact in world markets.

Next was Bill Whiles, another recent appointee, taking over Caribbean, South Seas and miscellaneous markets. The office next to his was occupied by Dick Dobell, son of Temple Dobell who had headed up one of Seaboard's principal agencies in the United Kingdom before the demise of Seagents.

Dick Dobell was being groomed for larger duties in the Seaboard organization. Like a number of other young men with aspirations in the lumber trade, he had been sent to British Columbia to learn the manufacturing and grading processes in Seaboard member sawmills. Following an indoctrination period in Seaboard House, the "trainee" either returned to one of the Seaboard agencies in the U.K. or remained at Seaboard in a sales or shipping capacity. Dobell was one of those selected to stay at Seaboard House, as was Jack Brigden, at the moment working in the United Kingdom sales department under the management of Bob Edgett.

Next down the corridor was Tom Ferris, trimly moustached and invariably of jovial countenance, guiding the sales performance of the South Africa sales department. Beyond him was the office of Dick Silbernagel, manager of the Australia and New Zealand sales department; and beyond him again, Harry O'Hagan, manager of the United States sales department, whose extroverted and ebullient performances on the long-distance telephone were memorable.

In the final office on the left-hand side of the corridor was the desk of Claude Effinger, unoccupied much of the time because of his frequent business trips.

On the far right-hand side of Seaboard's main floor was the office of Bob Edgett, recently appointed manager of the United Kingdom sales department. He, like Harry O'Hagan, had a powerful voice and a persuasive sales manner. When the two were on their telephones—which was usually the case—taking orders from their markets or placing orders with the mills, the dual performance was impressive, even behind closed doors.

As Grinnell returned down the right-hand side of Seaboard House's main floor each morning, he first passed the offices of the traffic department headed by H. Lloyd Ford, his assistant traffic manager Douglas Diamond, and department personnel John McLaughlin, Jim Ceperley, Bill Schofield and Kim Thomson.

Farther along, sharing offices, were Len Spratley, in charge of Seaboard's claims department, and Ernie Perrault, whose responsibility it was to conduct a program of corporate public relations including editing company publications and conducting mill tours for visitors from Seaboard's markets.

Continuing to the front of the main floor, Grinnell would encounter Tommy Thompson poring over sheaves of sales statistics in order to extract sales patterns for the afternoon's sales meeting, and would pass the office boy in his cubby-hole busy with scales and postage machines.

Adjacent to Grinnell's own office at the front of Seaboard House was that of Harry Berry, the chief accountant/comptroller. Berry had been with Seaboard since 1938, hired by the then chief accountant for the Shipping Company, John McKenzie, who had since retired. Accounting procedures were divided into two in his time: shipping and sales, with Stewart Slater as manager of sales accounting. Berry's duties included day-to-day office management and administration. Between his and Charles Grinnell's office was the desk of executive secretary Mitzi McCulloch, ministering to the needs of the two men and keeping a keen eye on the performance of the secretarial staff.

And in the large general office area, within the perimeter of management and department head offices, were the desks of aspiring sales assistants and the secretarial force supporting the entire sales operation. Many of the young sales staff, each attached to one of the major sales departments, would advance and in later years become department heads or the heads of overseas Seaboard offices. Others would move to sales positions with member mills.

In this pool, labouring to gain experience and advance themselves up the ladder, were such stalwarts as Gordon Cowan, Herbert Stacey, Al Gardner, Bill Kelsberg, Rich Clefstad, Jack Brigden, Don Moffett, Jack Hanna, Hugh MacMillan, Allan Clapp, Dave Clarke, Jack Devereaux, Bud Roberts, Bill Sparling, and others whose names have not been recorded or have been lost to memory.

Climbing the stairs to the second floor, Grinnell would begin his first survey of the day in this area. It was a crowded and busy place at any time, dominated by the staff of Seaboard Shipping managed by Hap Solloway. Second-in-command was Murray Mather who combined solid shipping experience with an inexhaustible repertoire of anecdotes. He had a talent, known throughout the trade, for producing a brilliantly delivered joke to suit any occasion from black disaster to signal success.

Others in the Shipping Company were the dispatcher, Jack Lewis, and the marine superintendent, Capt. William Rion. Rion had been the first master hired for Seaboard's fleet of Park vessels. When they were sold he stayed on with Seaboard to devise and supervise the systematic loading plan for vessels and, in general, to oversee the movements and seaworthiness of the vessels shuttling between B.C. ports to pick up Seaboard lumber. The main loading points were Vancouver, North Vancouver and New Westminster on the mainland and Victoria, Nanaimo and Crofton on Vancouver Island. Captain Rion was on the move to one of these ports almost every day of the year.

At the same time, Seaboard's supercargo group assumed responsibility for overseeing the actual loading of each vessel according to Rion's plan, and exchanging proper documents with ships' masters before vessels departed for their destinations. This group included Ken Milton, Jack Cunningham, Jack Tolhurst and Dick Witts.

The accounting department for the Shipping Company was managed by Dudley Darling, who had been hired in 1939 directly upon graduation from the University of British Columbia. Vassall Forrester, newly appointed manager of the Shipping Company, had brought him into the organization on the recommendation of then chief accountant John Mackenzie. Darling's group consisted of Bill Thomson, shipping documents manager, Stanley Prokop, Katherine Fyvie, Phil Bond, Dorothy McLean and Edward Riera.

The Seaboard Lumber Sales documents department was on the second floor as well, managed by Gordon Landahl and supported by Minerva Potter, John Roberts, Norman Brown and Patricia Sagris.

The accounting department, by now combining the work of both the Shipping and Sales Companies, was overseen by Comptroller Harry Berry, directing the activities of Ella Sim, Eleanor Tuffley and Charles Grinnell Jr.

A man with a roving commission was Arthur Fullman, whose unenviable task it was to conduct frequent visits to all the member mills to inspect the quality of production and ensure that grading standards were maintained. Not only did he stand guard over quality control but he was also expected to look for such details as the proper end marking of the Seaboard symbol on lumber consignments, proper anti-stain treatment and any other potential deficiency in a lumber order which might result in a protest or a claim being imposed by the agent or buyer. By agreement, he arrived at the mills unannounced, conducted his inspections without fear or favour, and submitted candid and objective reports. There is no doubt that he saved Seaboard a fortune in potential claims over the years.

In addition, an echelon of stenographers and other support staff at Seaboard kept the adding machines rattling and documents moving through a battery of typewriters, all part of the business of sending as much as a billion feet of lumber annually to U.S. and overseas markets. This was the organization which Charles Grinnell, to a substantial extent, had built to this level of achievement.

Grinnell's habit, when touring Seaboard House, was to carry with him one or two softcover books—fiction and nonfiction titles which he considered to be good reading. If he saw a staff member, particularly a junior sales or shipping employee, gazing ahead into space, he construed this to be the result of a lack of work. Seldom did Grinnell accuse anyone of wasting time or slacking off. His attitude was that lulls could occur in any of the departments, and when this happened the employees should invest their time in some useful manner. The books he carried were for those who had not come equipped for recesses in the workday. He would distribute them with a few words describing the contents, and then pass on to the next point in his office tour.

It was Grinnell's nature to take a personal interest in the people who worked for him. If he was aware of a staff member stricken with serious illness and without a personal physician, he would summon the best medical care. When, for instance, Bill Whiles was afflicted suddenly with an acute eye infection during a business trip to Texas, Charles Grinnell arranged for the best eye specialist available to save his sight. This patriarchal concern extended to the families of employees as well, and beyond. Learning that a seaman aboard a vessel carrying Seaboard lumber to Japan had suffered an attack of acute appendicitis, he arranged for a seaplane to rendezvous with the ship many miles off the West Coast to pick up the man and transport him to hospital for essential surgery.

His daily sales meetings, held every afternoon in a small board room adjacent to his office, were a combination of hardnosed, no-nonsense business and good-humoured camaraderie. Each department head in turn would report on the current sales position and the mill supply positions. Hap Solloway would present the latest update on freight rates and space positions. Invariably, Grinnell was able to add new information, demonstrating that he was in at least as close contact with all markets and the shipping scene as were his managers. He took nothing for granted, exhibiting sharp impatience with guesstimates and conjecture based on secondhand information.

One of the half-serious games he played with his managers was to conduct running wagers with them on the rise and fall of the markets. This was a contest they did not take too lightly because real money was involved, and Grinnell was more often a winner than a loser.

The general assessment of all those who remember him is that he ran a tight, efficient ship, was a fair man and remained willingly and voluntarily involved in all levels of Seaboard's structure. His titles during the Seaboard years ranged from manager (1928–32), to secretary (1935–36), to secretary-treasurer (1937), to vice-president (1938), to vice-president and general manager (1939–46), to vice-president and managing director from 1947 to his retirement. Whatever his title, he had been at the management helm from the beginning, influencing every move and decision the company made.

In June 1953, twenty-five years after the formation of the first Seaboard, he quietly cleaned his desk and retired from the scene. He was a few years short of official retirement age, but his health had been deteriorating and he was ready for a more leisurely way of life. He moved with his wife to Vachon Island near Seattle and seems to have been able to disassociate himself completely from Seaboard involvement.

We have singled out 1953 because it marked a peak in a time of change for Seaboard: the passing of mills and the gaining of mills; the retirement of key management and the accession of new managers. Seaboard was mounting to a higher plateau, drawn there by the compelling forces of changing technology and mounting competition in the export markets.

It was a time of change in the United Kingdom too. Queen Elizabeth II ascended to the throne. As their tribute to the event, seven of Seaboard's mills presented the new monarch with a Douglas-fir maypole forty-five feet tall cut by Timberland. Donors were Alaska Pine, B.C. Manufacturing, Brownsville Sawmills, Canadian Western, Pacific Pine, Timberland and Timber Preservers. It was erected in London in front of St. Mary le Strand Church.

·TWELVE·

THE EFFINGER YEARS

As we have implied, a transition was occurring in the lumber industry which included the export business in its scope. Large corporations, often American-based, were becoming more actively involved. The Harvard School of Business attitude was beginning to make itself felt, and business administration was becoming more of an exact science. Where personalities like Grinnell, Humbird, McConville and Mackin had been the principal arbiters and policy makers up until now, working from their own experience and established methods of doing business, others had come into the member mill complex with new approaches to administration, sales and accounting. At the same time, individual mills, where they could afford it, were retooling and modernizing in an effort to keep pace with technological developments and the need for a more efficient and complete utilization of the forest harvest.

Issues of the *British Columbia Lumberman* profiled many of the mills in the early fifties, recording the growth and transformation of Seaboard. Canadian Forest Products, the *Lumberman* noted, claimed 100 per cent utilization of the log in their three Eburne Division mills. These plants handled everything from logs seven feet in diameter to waste wood which was converted into either woodchips or hog fuel. Peeler logs went to their Pacific Veneer and Plywood Division, and wood waste went to Bellingham to be converted into pulp and paper. Soon the company would be supplying its own pulp mill. Alaska Pine was highly integrated with a combination of sawmills, shingle mills and pulp mills which enabled maximum utilization of the log supply. Even smaller mills like L & K Lumber worked to achieve greater log utilization as economically as possible. When the mill burned down in 1952, a new one rose from the ashes equipped with the latest in electrically powered gangsaws and provision for advanced barking and chipping machinery. In truth, the established mills had no other recourse but to modernize if they wanted to stay in business.

While Seaboard was not a producer, it depended entirely on the productive capabilities of its member mills and on the prices they must charge to cover the cost of modernization, the increase in the cost of logs and the wage demands of the labour force. All these factors were unavoidably reflected in costs. For instance, a more complete utilization of the log affected the levy of stumpage fees. L. L. G. Bentley, president of the B.C. Lumber Manufacturers Association in 1954, commented in his annual report: "This new utilization has undoubtedly raised the value of logs and the price of stumpage received by the government very materially. It is always risky to mention figures, but I would conservatively estimate that hemlock logs on the Vancouver market would have to sell for at least $8 less—and fir logs about $6 less per thousand feet without this new development."

And labour costs were rising dramatically. Wages for loggers had increased by more than 90 per cent since the mid-forties. Sawmill workers' wages had increased by well over 100 per cent in that same time period. The cost of export lumber went up accordingly, making the B.C. product increasingly vulnerable to competition from offshore suppliers. Seaboard's member mills were obliged to accept the slimmest possible profit margins, and were often reduced to selling at cost or at a loss in order to keep the saws operating.

The U.S. market, with its national housing program at a peak, was more amenable to price increases than was the U.K. and the other overseas markets. In testimony to this was the Seaboard cargo that went to the U.S. Eastern Seaboard in 1954 headlined as "the biggest individual cargo in the history of Vancouver." Eleven million feet of lumber sailed on the S.S. *Ceres* on 23 March. On the same newspaper page was a story on the *Elias G. Kulukundis* under charter to Seaboard, carrying a deck cargo of 1,033,000 feet loaded 12½ feet high forward, 8 feet high amidships and 12 feet high aft. This ship was headed for the United Kingdom.

It was at this time that market development took place in Puerto Rico. Bill Whiles appointed Arturo Geigel's Pacific Agencies to be Seaboard's agent in March 1954. This rather unheralded market has quietly become one of Seaboard's reliable mainstays, and this agency is still active today after thirty-one years under the direction of Arturo Geigel's son, Pucho, and his sons. In 1973 the Dominican Republic was added to their market coverage.

Russian, Scandinavian and Baltic competition provided the strongest possible motivation for British Columbia forest products manufacturers to deliver top quality, even if they were hard-pressed to compete in price. The appearance of lumber parcels and individual pieces of lumber was improved markedly. Stringent application of Pacific Lumber Inspection Bureau rules in the mills was largely responsible for this. Graders were encouraged to scrutinize the mill product with uncompromising eyes.

Anti-stain treatment was becoming standard practice. Many established mills at first balked at the strong suggestion that they adopt such programs. At a time when every mill was searching for ways to cut manufacturing costs, the introduction of anti-stain treatment was a troubling imposition. The grudging concession of some mills was to assign an employee to sprinkle anti-stain solution onto stacked piles of lumber, using an ordinary garden watering can for the purpose. This lumber went overseas and arrived in the buyers' hands as discoloured and unattractive as ever.

Once buyers knew that anti-stain treatment was in effect and that lumber parcels could be preserved unblemished, they were even less forgiving than before, exercising their right to file claims without hesitation. When the British Columbia mills, Seaboard members included, realized that stained lumber was resulting in expensive penalties, they proceeded with alacrity to install proper anti-stain equipment. Experiments were conducted with various types of stain inhibitors and different techniques for the efficient application of anti-stain solutions. A number of mills went to the considerable expense of constructing dry kilns. Properly dried lumber virtually eliminated any risk of staining— and was undoubtedly the best way to treat hemlock, as the Koerners had proven at Alaska Pine.

Thus British Columbia lumber was arriving in the export markets, for the most part well graded, bright in appearance, and carrying Seaboard's mark as well as the symbols of the supplying mills. A frustrating problem remained, however. Although in 1938 the United Kingdom had agreed to accept the scant sizes of lumber provided by B.C. mills, in practice scant size acceptance was disappointingly small. In the postwar

period, almost no scant sawn lumber was purchased in the U.K. although regulations permitted it to be imported without restriction.
Buyers were accustomed to full sawn lumber, and no amount of logic or
persuasion had been able to change their ways.

In the early fifties, the B.C. Lumber Manufacturers Association renewed its efforts to change what it regarded as an outdated British
"fashion." Their difficult task was to communicate with sufficient persuasion the advantages of scant sizes. Both Canada and the United
States used these sizes, having received the permission and approval of
all government construction authorities. Obviously it was to the advantage of the B.C. manufacturers to provide one size of product to all
markets, in particular markets where the lumber cargo was waterborne.
Scant sawn lumber occupies less space, thereby saving on freight costs.

In 1956 the BCLMA succeeded in winning a contract to build twenty-
two houses for RCAF servicemen at Langor, near Nottingham. The
framing material to be used was dressed (scant sawn and planed)
softwood lumber. G. C. Edgett, the BCLMA's timber development director, expressed his confidence that this would be the beginning of the
general acceptance of scant sizes in the construction of timber frame
houses. He felt that it was just a matter of time before the U.K. buyers
realized that scant sizes and the resulting reduction in bulk meant a
decrease in transportation costs. Rounded edges on the lumber meant
easier handling, and the smooth, dimensionally precise lumber eliminated the need for shimming or, as it was referred to in the United
Kingdom, "thicknessing" or "firring out."

At the same time, the BCLMA was working with the U.K. Timber
Development Association to popularize timber frame housing construction in that market. The U.K. association co-operated by establishing a
design service to assist builders in adopting and adapting to the use of
scant lumber. After their successful promotion in Canada, Trend
Houses were displayed in the U.K. in 1957 utilizing scant sawn hemlock
for framing, western red cedar for cladding and roofing, and B.C.
plywood for interior walls and decorative finish.

These product improvements, technological transformations and
marketing strategies naturally had their effect on Seaboard, influencing
its actions and calling for swift sales and shipping management reflexes
in response to the idiosyncrasies of a dozen world markets. Claude
Effinger was Seaboard's helmsman through all this. In retrospect he
looks on his period of office with satisfaction: "My period as vice-
president and managing director extended from 1953 to 1963," he said.
"We increased our shipments every year and earned excellent money for
the member mills."

Although true, Effinger has allowed time to simplify and soften his observation. World events were causing considerable turbulence in the marketplace and in the area of shipping. Where shipping was concerned, Effinger was determined to draw Vassall Forrester back into the organization. H. E. (Hap) Solloway was manager of Seaboard Shipping, but he was having health problems, and because the United States Eastern Seaboard market was flourishing, Claude Effinger's thoughts turned to Forrester.

Forrester had not come back to Seaboard after the war, the most generally accepted reason being that he and Charles Grinnell had suffered a difference of opinion on matters of shipping policy. Grinnell guarded the paramount position of Seaboard Sales to the end, insisting that the Shipping Company serve and follow.

"I had no axe to grind with Vassall Forrester," Effinger relates. "We had always worked well together. It was just a matter of time before Hap Solloway would throw in the towel; we all knew that. Vassall Forrester was the best possible choice to take over the shipping company and I went after him."

Claude Effinger's first attempt to coerce Forrester into returning was in 1953, shortly after he had taken over as vice-president. Forrester was in New York, having opened an office in that city for Eggar, Forrester and Verner in 1945. Concurrently he started his own company, American and Overseas Shipbrokerage, of which he was president. Functioning in the heart of a burgeoning U.S. lumber market and thoroughly conversant with the intricacies of the shipping and freight play, he was a good man to have on Seaboard's side.

"I went to New York specifically to bring Forrester back," Effinger recalls. "Our meetings were friendly enough, but nothing I could say or offer was enough to take him away from his own business. He was adamant, and I returned to Vancouver without so much as his promise to consider our offer."

In 1955 Hap Solloway resigned his position as manager of Shipping, another of the Seaboard pioneers who had been with the company from the beginning through the good times and the bad. Seaboard's management and the member mills saw him into retirement with genuine regret, and then turned to the task of finding his successor. Effinger renewed his campaign to recruit Forrester, creating a suitable opportunity during a winter holiday in Palm Springs. "I had a feeling that I had softened his attitude somewhat on that occasion," he said. "I told him that I would not take 'no' for an answer and that I would persist. He went back to New York with a great deal to think about."

Later that spring, Claude Effinger travelled to New York once more, intent on securing Forrester's services. He describes their meeting: "In the dining room on the roof of the St. Regis Hotel, I made him a renewed offer in the presence of his wife, Betty. In fact I think I tried as hard to persuade her as I did him. This time I was successful. Vassall countered my offer with a few additional provisos, and I returned to Vancouver to get the approval of Henry Mackin and the Board of Directors. Mackin's attitude was that if I thought it was a fair deal we should telephone Forrester and confirm his appointment as manager of Seaboard Shipping. It was done."

Almost immediately Vassall Forrester found himself contending with violent fluctuations in freight rates. Just as U.K. buyers began to react favourably to the marketing efforts of the B.C. Lumber Manufacturers Association, and at the moment when mortgage money in the U.K. began to ease for the construction of timber houses, aided by a Building Societies agreement to advance 75 per cent of the necessary funding, the Suez crisis occurred. This resulted in a sharp jump in freight rates and instability in the chartering business which in turn dealt B.C.'s lumber export trade a severe blow. The impact was felt most acutely in the United Kingdom where importers reduced orders in 1956 to 50 per cent of the total for 1955. Figures had not been this low since 1950.

Trying to anticipate and keep pace with the freight rates was like riding a wild horse. In June 1957 rates had plummeted in search of trade. Absence of grain and coal bookings pushed freight rates far down. Overnight the trans-Atlantic coal rate dropped to one-fifth of its previous rate per ton. The irony was that although Seaboard Shipping had predicted a decrease and had allowed for it, there was no way it could capitalize on freight advantages in selling to the United Kingdom. The government of that domain chose that year to release its Strategic Reserve Stock of lumber, 50 per cent of which was high grade Canadian stock. The British Board of Trade was careful to demand fair and current prices for these reserves rather than dumping them on the market, but the existence of all this prime lumber in place in the U.K. and ready for sale put a severe dent in British Columbia's lumber sales to that country.

An increase in wage rates in British Columbia did not help matters. Production costs increased and so did the cost of lumber. A passage in *Empire of Wood* describes it this way: "The year 1957 had been difficult. . . . MacMillan & Bloedel found itself producing dear and selling cheap, as costs rose and product prices fell. Wages had risen without any increase in hourly production. Taxes . . . had increased threefold." The B.C. coastal forest industry, which accounted for 30 per cent of the province's total income, reported the lowest earnings in a decade.

Seaboard continued to make gestures intended to maintain and strengthen its relations with the trade and the builders in the U.K. One of these gestures generated wide publicity in 1955–56. As usual, Timberland was in the forefront of this special event, supplying three masts and several spars for a replica of the *Mayflower*. The vessel sailed from Plymouth, England, on 4 July 1956, its sails billowing from its masts and spars, generating worldwide publicity not only for an authentic re-enactment of history but also for Timberland and its sales arm, Seaboard.

This was J. G. Robson's last international public relations gesture for Seaboard. He resigned as a vice-president in April of the same year, and shortly thereafter he sold Timberland to Canadian Collieries (Dunsmuir), having been unable to interest his sons in continuing with the company. Robson was one of the original members of Seaboard; Timberland, which was one of Seaboard's most prestigious mills, had been under his ownership since 1918. It was said of J. G. Robson that his heart and soul were part and parcel of his mill. He died in 1959.

The *Mayflower* episode was virtually the only encouraging event occurring on Seaboard's behalf during that period. And matters were not improved when, in May 1958, Montague L. Meyer Ltd., the close ally of H. R. MacMillan in the United Kingdom, purchased the remainder of the Strategic Reserve Stock from the government (an amount estimated at 45,000 standards or 90 million feet).

Some felt that this move was for the ultimate good of the B.C. industry, reasoning that Meyer would dispose of the lumber in the shortest period of time and open the way for improved business with B.C. An article in *British Columbia Lumberman* that same month stated: "The takeover was a bold stroke and the firm concerned has the goodwill of friends and competitors." But Seaboard was not entirely comfortable with Meyer's acquisition since, if collusion existed between Meyer and MacMillan, the huge reserve of lumber could be used to their mutual advantage and to the detriment of Seaboard.

While the ultimate effects of Meyer's cornering of a large, landed lumber supply were difficult to measure, there could be no misinterpretation of the action taken by the government of Finland in the summer of 1958. The Finnmark was devalued sharply, making its lumber the cheapest in the international marketplace. At the same time Britain increased its bank rate to 7 per cent, the highest since 1920. The result was to stifle the activities of the country's lumber importers. With Finnish lumber prices at a new low and U.K. importers caught behind an interest barrier, Seaboard's expectations of business in that market were slim indeed.

The legitimate question to ask then is why did Claude Effinger describe his tenure from 1953 to 1963 as a period of considerable profit for the member mills? The answer, of course, lies in the flourishing state of the United States lumber market in that same time frame. Housing starts in the U.S. were running at well over 1 million units annually with lumber prices ranging from $75 to $90 per thousand (as compared to $50 per thousand in the U.K.). In Canada an industrial boom was absorbing large quantities of lumber at comparable prices. And best of all, prices were holding steady with no sign of future weakness.

This happy situation more than compensated for the sad state of affairs in the U.K. The B.C. industry was able to come to grips with the increased wage demands of the IWA, and, just as important, it had the financial resources to penetrate forest reserves which until now had been uneconomic to harvest. It was this economically healthy environment that acted like a magnet to draw more big investors north.

*   *   *

Soaring construction in the United States and the stability of the economy in that country were the main motivating forces that attracted large U.S. corporations to move into the British Columbia forest industry. Here in this corner of the Northwest were the largest stands of timber remaining in North America, in combination with mills willing to discuss consolidation.

We have described earlier the alliance of Alaska Pine and Canadian Western with U.S. interests. In 1950 Canadian Western, in partnership with Pacific Mills, a Canadian subsidiary of Crown Zellerbach, built a large and modern pulp and paper plant at Elk Falls on Vancouver Island. In 1953 Canadian Western Lumber Company, through an exchange of shares, became a division of Crown Zellerbach Canada Ltd., which in turn was to become the largest single unit in the international holdings of Crown Zellerbach Corporation of San Francisco.

What this meant was that one of British Columbia's longest-established, largest and most productive mills had become the holding of a United States corporation. Canadian Western, in its heyday, had been called the largest sawmill complex in the British Commonwealth. Certainly it was the largest in British Columbia, employing up to 2000 people at a time, owning or leasing more timber than any other company, operating the largest mileage of logging railways, owning and operating its own fleet of tug boats, and owning and operating one of the largest plywood plants and shingle mills in the province.

When Henry Mackin, vice-president and managing director of Canadian Western, announced the merger he stated that the principal reason was to "achieve complete and more efficient utilization of forest resources and sawmill waste for both companies." Henry Mackin and his directors, it is to be supposed, were convinced that the arrangement with Crown Zellerbach made good business sense. There is little indication that the company was in straitened circumstances which would have obliged it to merge with a larger entity. In any event, Mackin became a vice-president of Crown Zellerbach Canada, and continued on as president of Seaboard Lumber Sales.

The incursion of the United States multinationals continued. Alaska Pine & Cellulose, which began its expansion in alliance with Abitibi Power & Paper in 1950, entered into negotiations with Rayonier Inc., New York, in 1954. The outcome was Rayonier's acquisition of 80 per cent of the Alaska Pine company. Three years later Rayonier completed the transaction with the purchase of the balance of the common shares of Alaska Pine & Cellulose, and in 1959 the company name was changed to Rayonier Canada Limited, first appearing on Seaboard's member list in 1960. T. Lloyd Roberts was the company's representative on the Seaboard board of directors, later to become a vice-president.

The corporate evolution was not yet complete, and we move out of the time frame of this chapter for a moment to bring the Alaska Pine episode to a conclusion. In 1968, Rayonier Inc. merged into ITT Rayonier Inc. At that time International Telephone Corporation acquired all the shares of Rayonier, the understanding being that the company thus formed, while a subsidiary of ITT, would continue to function as a separate entity with a large degree of management autonomy. Needless to say, the management techniques and business principles subscribed to by companies of this magnitude were somewhat more professional than those by which Seaboard was accustomed to operate.

One more corporate merger must be related here, not only because it resulted in the formation of the largest forest industries complex in British Columbia but also because once more Seaboard lost a major member. The story of this merger, which has been described by some participants and close observers as a takeover, albeit elaborate and convoluted, was something of a cause célèbre, which even today can generate animated discussions and arguments.

It is not our purpose to attempt an account of the formation of MacMillan, Bloedel and Powell River Limited. Other writers have dealt with the incident at length, some expertly and objectively, others with varying degrees of emotionally charged bias. We have described earlier how the Powell River Company, one of the province's longest-established and most successful enterprises founded on pulp and paper production, had expanded its sawmilling involvement with the purchase of Westminster Shook Mills, British Columbia Manufacturing and Maple Ridge Lumber Company, all of which were Seaboard members. This was in line with Powell River's policy to assemble a more completely integrated forest industry complex, as well as to ensure an adequate and continuing source of residual wood supply for pulp production. President of the company was Harold Foley, joined in 1948 by his brother, Joseph Foley, who became executive vice-president. These two men and their management team successfully administered the operations of the world's largest manufacturer of newsprint.

The company town at Powell River was a five-hundred-home model community with a reputation for high employee morale that could be traced back to the Foleys' management style—an effective combination of paternalism, absolute fairness at every level of the operation, an insistence on good internal communications and, of course, an ability to produce and sell newsprint to a world market.

Although the Powell River Company was able to announce profits each year substantially higher than the average for the industry, competition began to be felt in the early fifties from the southwestern United States where newsprint manufacturers, aided by new technology, had combined the advantages of cheap, readily available oil with the fast-growing characteristics of southern pine. They were challenging the traditionally secure positions of the pulp and paper mills to the north.

The Foleys had to consider other factors as well: a depression in the U.S. market for newsprint forced the Powell River mill to reduce its output; an industry-wide pulp and paper strike created further problems; MacMillan & Bloedel installed a more modern and efficient newsprint machine at Port Alberni. The advantages of a merger with another large company were becoming attractive.

Several possible mergers were considered, involving both Canadian and U.S. corporations; but finally Harold Foley, having discovered that MacMillan & Bloedel were receptive, engaged in a first round of discussions with that company's management. This was in 1957, and the initial decision of the Powell River board was to reject amalgamation with MacMillan & Bloedel on the basis that the disparate management philosophies of the two companies would lead to ultimate conflict.

Talks were renewed again in 1958, escalating to serious negotiations between Harold Foley and MacMillan & Bloedel's president, J. V. Clyne, in early 1959. In January 1960, following rumours and counter rumours, and in a market frenzy that saw the shares of both companies escalate astronomically, the formal announcement was made that Powell River Company and MacMillan & Bloedel had joined forces. The name of the new company would be MacMillan, Bloedel & Powell River Limited. On the surface, the merger was presented as a happy marriage. H. R. MacMillan is quoted in *Empire of Wood* on the occasion of a reception to celebrate the amalgamation: "Between the MacMillan & Bloedel and the Powell River companies there has always been warm friendship and affinity," he said. "The new company has not been created just to be big, although that is important now to meet competition on an equal footing, but it was created to do a better job for the community, the country, employees and shareholders, on whom we all depend for the large amounts of capital without which beneficial expansions are impossible."

J. V. Clyne was chairman of the board; Harold Foley was vice-chairman and Joseph Foley was president. Powell River's representation appeared to be equitable, and efforts to integrate the management of the two companies continued apace. Yet within a year, differences of opinion and management dissension had spread like a plague. Most of Powell River's management had been persuaded or had elected to depart. Joseph Foley submitted his resignation, an action which Harold Foley emulated shortly after. The opinion of Powell River's board back in 1957 had proven to be correct: the management philosophies of the two companies were incompatible in the extreme, and the MacMillan & Bloedel faction possessed the power within the merger to gain absolute control.

All of which is incidental to the continuing affairs of Seaboard Lumber Sales, except to indicate that, with the passing of the Powell River Company went three of Seaboard's member mills.

In 1958 Henry Mackin resigned as chairman and president of Seaboard, having served in these capacities through much of the corporate transition when Canadian Western became part of the Crown Zellerbach corporate structure. He had been one of Seaboard's founders and had remained prominent in its management and the decision-making processes that had enabled it to survive and thrive. While he was a lumberman of the old school, he had been one of the first of that generation to be persuaded that a new wind was blowing through the industry and that only strong, well-financed and highly integrated companies could hope to succeed in the new forest industries environment.

He had been manager of Canadian Western Lumber Company since 1914, and vice-president and managing director since 1935. In 1932 he had headed the British Columbia delegation to the United Kingdom which had been instrumental in expanding lumber sales to that market. He had served terms as head of the B.C. Lumber and Shingle Manufac-

turers Association, as well as serving actively on virtually every important committee concerned with the manufacture and marketing of
forest products both domestically and in the export markets. By all
measures, Henry Mackin was dedicated to and totally immersed in the
lumber industry.

He had been a vice-president of the new Seaboard since its formation
in 1935, becoming president in 1951 after the untimely resignation of
Bruce Farris. There is no doubt that he had distinguished himself during
that period, particularly in his seven-year presidential tenure. His replacement would have to extend himself to measure up to Mackin's
performance. These duties fell to L. L. G. Bentley, a senior executive of
Canadian Forest Products, whose capabilities, success patterns and
forthright approach to the forest products industry were well known
and respected by all of the Seaboard members. He had been a member
of the executive committee and a director of Seaboard since 1953, and
thus was thoroughly prepared to take over as chairman and president.

His installation coincided with both bad and good events in the
industry. A month-long strike of dock workers in 1958 played havoc
with Seaboard's shipping operations and, by extension, its sale performance. Inventories piled up in the mill yards, and Seaboard was obliged
to extend loans to member mills in trouble. Vassall Forrester, into his
third year as manager of Seaboard Shipping, was hard-pressed to deal
with the paralysis caused by the strike.

The good news materialized in 1959 with the beginning of a substantial boom in the United Kingdom. At last the economic floodgates were
opened; employment was on the rise, housing rentals were decontrolled
and housing starts began to escalate in an atmosphere of revived prosperity. And British Columbia shared in this sudden demand for lumber.

It is illuminating to note, however, that British Columbia and Canada
were far from being exclusive suppliers of lumber to the U.K. The
following comparative figures show a partial breakdown of United
Kingdom lumber contracts for 1959 and make it clearly evident that
Canada was trading in stiff competition:

Finland	836 million feet
Russia	690 million feet
Sweden	682 million feet
Canada	352 million feet

Canada's disadvantage was price. Finland, the top supplier, was selling
a good lumber product at prices considerably lower than those the
British Columbia mills were obliged to charge.

The industry cast about anxiously for ways and means to improve its competitive position in the U.K. and elsewhere. Quality of product had to be maintained, product education had to be increased and, wherever possible, costs of manufacture and delivery of lumber had to be reduced. In 1959 a breakthrough occurred in the handling of lumber. During the previous year, a mill near Prince George in British Columbia's interior had been courageous enough to experiment with unit packaging. B.C. Spruce Sales' method was to assemble lumber packages for customers and bind them with steel bands for shipment by rail. While this is the first account of the use of packaged lumber in British Columbia, Vassall Forrester states that Weyerhaeuser had been shipping packaged lumber at least a year before. He notes that "Seaboard was first to ship packaged lumber to the U.K." The results could not have been more encouraging. Even with the unspecialized lifting equipment of the day, the ship was loaded and unloaded in less than half the time it would take for a conventional, loose-stowed lumber cargo. This dramatic saving of time could be equated with an appreciable saving in cost.

An idea of the degree of labour dispensed with when lumber packaging was introduced is revealed in an interview with longshoreman Pat McFeely, published in the October 1962 issue of *Western Business and Industry:*

> He recalled the former days of the pick-em-up and lay-em-down method of loading lumber on ships. "Took twice as long, and twice the aches in the back," he mused. In the pick-em-up days Pat reflected on, lumber was slung into the holds in loose bundles and laid out piece by piece by crews of men darting back and forth across piles of lumber below decks. This was necessary because, with engines amid-ships, there was a tunnel running through the after holds of the ship to carry the propeller shaft, and a level floor had to be built around it. With the new engines-aft ships, the holds are flat bottomed.

By 1962, 50 per cent of British Columbia's ocean-shipped lumber was transported in packaged form. The mills were swift to install the necessary equipment for steel-strapping their lumber parcels; new ships were designed to receive and stow this packaged cargo more efficiently, and equipment at the shipping terminals was designed or modified to handle the bundled lumber with maximum dispatch. Seaboard secured two vessels on long-term charter, the *Fenix* and the *Judith Ann,* to carry packaged lumber, and was the first to construct a vessel for this purpose. The *Tiha* was another open-hatched bulk carrier designed to accommodate the steel-strapped bundles of lumber.

Charles Grinnell had tended to worry about the status of the shipping company, and had exerted his influence to ensure that it remained a service arm of the sales company rather than a profit centre in its own right. Suddenly shipping was becoming the key to the profitable operation of Seaboard Lumber Sales. The company's lumber prices were barely competitive in the overseas markets, and it fell to the shipping company to overcome this disadvantage by means of cost cutting wherever this could be achieved.

Conversion to packaged lumber shipping was one part of the formula. The use of large container vessels equipped with powerful gantries, and driven by engines that enabled greater speeds at lower fuel costs, completed the equation. Seaboard contracted with the Johnson Line in 1972 for the long-term charter of two modern, dual-purpose carriers, the *Suecia* and the *Pacific*. These 22,000-ton vessels were designed with special "trays" or platforms to carry automobiles from Sweden to the Pacific Coast of North America. On their return voyages to Europe, these same trays carried packaged lumber. Seaboard representatives worked with the naval architects to ensure that a maximum lumber cargo could be transported in this manner.

Equipped with large gantries or shipboard cranes, ships like this could load or discharge twice as much cargo as a conventional lumber carrier in four or five days, as compared to from ten to fourteen days. Faster loading meant faster turnaround time and less demurrage; faster cruising speeds meant less time at sea; faster unloading again meant faster turnaround time. The resulting savings were such that lumber prices could be brought more in line with those of the Russians and Scandinavians.

However, competition with these countries remained keen in spite of this minor shipping revolution, and in spite of the enthusiastic response British Columbian and Canadian lumber products received in the United Kingdom's boom year of 1960. The Canada Trend House on display at the Olympia exhibit in London was inspected by some 250,000 visitors, and comparable numbers viewed the *Woman's Journal* "House of the Year" constructed predominantly of B.C. wood products in Liverpool. People applauded the use of B.C. wood, as well as the attractive architecture—but they walked away, depressed by the price.

In August 1960 a United Kingdom delegation of buyers and government officials visited British Columbia and spent three busy weeks inspecting all aspects of the industry and conferring on a multitude of subjects related to the export trade. The hospitality of the B.C. lumber fraternity and the provincial government could not be faulted;

cameraderie was the order of each day. But under all this was the serious concern the entire delegation felt for the high Canadian lumber prices.

The visitors were sympathetic, but they were also intent on discovering ways and means to lower prices and thus increase British Columbia's lumber trade with the U.K. Furthermore, there were many diehards among them who still pressed for rough rather than scant dimension lumber. The Europeans, they pointed out, were not only selling lumber at lower prices but they were also happy to supply a full-size product. The delegation departed for home wishing the B.C. manufacturers well, and leaving them with much to think about.

In October 1960 Jack McConville, the grand old man of British Columbia's lumber trade, died. Even in his final, failing year, he must have shaken his head in wry amusement as he heard the arguments still hotly conducted, after twenty-five years, on the subject of scant versus full dimension lumber. His passing in many ways marked the end of British Columbia's individualist, owner/manager regime. He was a mill man through-and-through. An article in the mid-1920s, appearing in the *Shipping Register,* describes him thus: ". . . A man who likes lumber so well that he keeps a jar of freshcut sawdust in his office so he can always retain in his nostrils the tang of the forests and their products." Seaboard's official tribute to Jack McConville on his retirement was to honour him with a dinner attended by all of the mill members. Included in the tribute paid him was the statement that he "had done more than anyone else to stabilize lumber export values during the past quarter century."

McConville had started with Astexo, the first organization to attempt to assemble the forces of the individual mills. By 1920 he was its manager and saw the gradual move of strength from Astexo to Seaboard, having difficulty through most of that period in accepting the transition from an organization that sold the product of its mills to local exporters to an organization that exported the products of its member mills. When the last vestiges of Astexo disappeared in 1938, he was drawn into the Seaboard organization as manager of the Australian, New Zealand and South Seas markets, with Dick Silbernagel as his second-in-command. When he retired in 1946, Silbernagel took over his position.

* * *

While the fifties leading into the early sixties was a period of intense preoccupation with the United Kingdom and United States markets, close attention was directed to a number of other offshore markets in a concerted effort to balance the depressions in one area with the up-swings in others. A market surge in Japan in 1961 was just such an example of a balancing upswing.

In that year Japan received its first shipment of logs since the 1930s, giving rise immediately to a hot controversy as to the wisdom of allow-ing whole logs to go to this market. Log export had been restricted since just before World War II, the rationale being to encourage the manufac-ture of lumber in British Columbia. Opponents of log export warned darkly that the logs shipped to Japan would return to British Columbia as furniture and other manufactured goods, while British Columbia and Canada would remain nothing more than the suppliers of a primary product where the least profit was extracted.

This argument might have succeeded once more in the curtailment of log exports were it not for the fact that Japan increased its demand for lumber as well, and was quite prepared to take grades and dimensions less acceptable to other markets. Almost overnight that country became British Columbia's fastest-growing market as indicated by the export figure for two consecutive years recorded by the Pacific Lumber Inspec-tion Bureau: in 1960 lumber exports to Japan were 1,607,274 feet; for the first eight months of 1961 they were 84,662,275 feet. This encourag-ing upturn in business to Japan more than justified the trip Harry O'Hagan and Bill Whiles took to that country in 1961 to familiarize themselves and Seaboard with building customs, and to reinforce busi-ness and agent contacts.

Shortly after this visit, Thorleif Monsen persuaded Seaboard to per-mit him to set up a lumber sales agency department within his shipping organization, Aall & Company (which had a close relationship with Seaboard, having been its shipping agent since the late 1940s), which continues to this day. Bill Whiles worked with Mr. Fujisawa at Aall & Company to rebuild this market from virtually nothing to over 100 million feet in the early 1970s, thus becoming one of Seaboard's major market areas.

While the United States continued to be British Columbia's largest lumber buyer as 1961 came to a close, purchasing 1266 million feet that year, the United Kingdom was demonstrating more activity, with im-ports of 423 million feet. Japan was the third largest importer, taking 155.5 million feet, the largest amount it had purchased since 1929. Even British Columbia's lumber exports to Europe had improved by 1961. A forest industries trade report published in 1956 showed the following Canadian lumber exports in FBMs to European markets for that year: Eire, 20 million; Holland, 3.6 million; Benelux, 8 million; France, 2 million; Italy, 1.2 million; West Germany, 200,000, for a total of 35 million.

In 1961 British Columbia's lumber exports alone to the European markets were 68 million feet, and hemlock had gained the ascendancy over Douglas-fir for the second consecutive year. Coast production in 1961 was a record-breaking 2950 million feet of which 40.5 per cent was hemlock and 36.6 per cent was fir. These figures make it clear that hemlock was no longer the poor cousin in the forests of the Pacific Northwest.

·THIRTEEN·

OUT WITH THE OLD
IN WITH THE NEW

From 1960 to 1970 new management winds began to sweep through the Seaboard structure. The era of the family-owned and managed mill was going into eclipse, overshadowed by the large public companies we know today. The buoyant economies and the buoyant sellers' markets Seaboard had experienced in the late fifties would take a sudden and disconcerting turn by the end of the sixties, calling for immediate strategies to cope with a buyers' market.

New technology in the mills, the shipping and the administration of the business called for the ability to adapt to change; new hardware and software became essential tools for the efficient conduct of business. Hemlock was gaining ascendancy over fir. The leap in the production of pulp and paper had placed growing value on the total log regardless of size. This, in turn, was reflected in increased lumber costs and further escalated by increasing labour costs. Plywood was coming into its own as an important timber product. In 1961 Seaboard exported 41 million square feet, more than doubling this amount in 1962 and 1963. In 1964 the total had risen to 169 million square feet; by 1968 the total plywood shipped was 243 million square feet, the majority of it going to the United Kingdom.

Bob Edgett, joined by Doug Reid, had done much to introduce plywood in overseas markets, and Reid as manager of plywood sales would continue to promote the product in a manner that won him the respect and confidence of the overseas trade. He gained additional strength in 1963 when Richmond Plywood Corporation became a Seaboard member. A key figure in that company was H. E. (Ed) Manning, a sales executive who had done much to build the softwood plywood market in Canada. The head of his own sales company, he acquired the exclusive sales rights for the Richmond Plywood Corporation, and in 1968 became that company's Seaboard director. He worked closely with Reid in the late sixties and early seventies to expand plywood sales overseas, travelling with him to most of the plywood markets. He was elected to Seaboard's executive committee in 1970 and remained in that capacity until retirement in 1983.

As the 1960s began, Seaboard's directorate consisted of the following: chairman and president was L. L. G. Bentley supported by eight vice-presidents, as the directors were then called, making up the company's executive committee. These included: T. L. Roberts (first vice-president), S. Heller, R. H. Ellison, R. S. McDonald, W. S. Moore, A. D. Anderson, H. Stone, D. R. Schmidt and C. Effinger. The representation ran the gamut from one of Seaboard's oldest mills, Hillcrest (now represented by Carlton Stone's son, Hector) to newcomers and integrated forest giants such as Alaska Pine, now a part of Rayonier, and Canadian Western, now absorbed by Crown Zellerbach. T. L. Roberts, representing Rayonier, and D. R. Schmidt, representing Crown Zellerbach, brought large corporation attitudes into this administrative mélange. Claude Effinger, also a member of the executive committee, was vice-president and managing director of both lumber sales and shipping. Vassall Forrester was general manager of the shipping company, and Harry Berry functioned as secretary of both companies.

There were thirty-two mills on the membership roster, down from thirty-nine in 1959, the result of a damaging International Woodworkers of America strike that had worked havoc with marginal mills. In the export markets, Seaboard maintained offices in New York, Boston, Johannesburg and Sydney; Geneva, Switzerland, was added in 1961 when Kit Candler was sent there to manage the company's business on the European continent.

Claude Effinger's tenure as vice-president was coming to an end, as were a range of responsibilities that he and Charles Grinnell had been assigned. Even before he departed the company, the management position had been removed from his shoulders when, in 1961, Harry O'Hagan was appointed general manager and Bob Edgett was named sales manager. These changes were the most obvious signs of a growing effort to adapt administrative procedures to the times.

Claude Effinger in his final years—he retired in 1962—was much involved in an exchange of trade missions to and from British Columbia, the object being to further stimulate trade with the United Kingdom and the Continent, and to continue to press the educational process in the use of B.C. timber. In 1960 a thirty-four man delegation, led by William E. Vesey, president of the Timber Trade Federation of the United Kingdom, arrived in British Columbia as guests of the provincial government. They were formally escorted from Britain by Maj. Gen. B. M. Hoffmeister, Agent General for British Columbia in London (and a former president of MacMillan Bloedel Ltd.).

Seaboard's role in the entertainment and edification of this timber delegation was considerable. In three tightly organized weeks the mission of buyers and government agency representatives examined virtually every phase of the forest products industry, from logging operations to the manufacture of a full range of timber products and their use in timber construction. They visited Seaboard member mills, lumber yards and shipping facilities, and were shown the anti-stain treatment techniques currently in use. Sessions were held with architects, builders and authorities on timber technology in an effort to demonstrate new and better ways to employ wood in construction.

The following year British Columbia sent a twenty-two member mission to the United Kingdom to follow up on the educational and sales process. Bob Edgett represented Seaboard's management; Robert MacMillan, one of Canadian Western's rising executives, and Hershell Smith, head of Sooke Forest Products, were there to represent the Seaboard mill members' interests. The delegation was headed up by Robert W. Bonner, British Columbia's Minister of Industrial Development, Trade and Commerce.

While one of the mission's concerns was to obtain as much new information as possible on British building habits and preferences, the main strategy was directed towards convincing the building trade, insurance companies, mortgage lenders and county councils that the almost universal use of brick, stone and masonry in the U.K. could be combined advantageously with timber. One of the recommendations was that the traditional materials could enclose an entire timber frame interior. Another was that Britain's popular Tudor-style residences could be replicated making use of British Columbia timber and plywood in conjunction with stucco. Every member of the delegation was an emissary delivering the message that timber frame construction was faster than building with traditional materials, warmer both aesthetically and in terms of insulation factors, designed to conceal wiring and central heating ducts and, if properly erected, as permanent as brick or masonry.

In May 1962 Claude Effinger was official Seaboard host to the last visiting timber trade contingent in his tenure when a group of timber specialists from West Germany, Holland, France, Belgium and Italy arrived in Vancouver as guests of the government of British Columbia; and once more Seaboard and its member mills were prominent in a three-week tour of indoctrination.

Effinger's days with Seaboard were drawing to a close. There remained only the delayed tribute payed him in 1962 by the Timber Trades Federation of Scotland. He was invited to Edinburgh to address the Federation's annual convention, the first Canadian to be so honoured. Effinger remembers the occasion fondly. "It was a formal and elegant affair," he recalls, "and I don't mind admitting that I was excited by it all. When I rented my white tie and tails from Moss Brothers, one of the U.S.S.R. timber trade representatives was there being fitted for the same occasion. What I didn't realize was that I was witnessing the beginning of a small disaster."

On the evening of the dinner, James Edmiston Forrest, president of Scotland's Timber Trade Federation, introduced Effinger as ". . . the Canadian who saved the United Kingdom," referring to the efforts Claude Effinger had made to keep lumber moving to the British Isles throughout the war years. "I thought the introduction was far too extravagant, and I said so," Effinger relates. "I can't remember exactly what else I said now, but I recall that it seemed to be appropriate. For me the evening was a tremendous experience, but I am afraid it was quite the opposite for the poor Russian trade representative. He had disregarded his country's rule which forbade wearing formal clothes at official events. I heard later that he was sent back to Russia within a few days."

Effinger had weathered his years with Seaboard well. His ten-year term as vice-president and managing director, measured across all the markets, had been profitable for the company. One of the company's tributes to him was to appoint him an honorary director of Seaboard Lumber Sales Company Limited.

The executive committee had a difficult decision to make upon Effinger's departure. His logical successor would be one of two capable and highly eligible men: Bob Edgett and Harry O'Hagan. Both were dynamic and aggressive sales executives with excellent records of achievement in the several departments and divisions they had managed; both had proven their total dedication to the welfare of the company. Some are of the opinion that Charles Grinnell deliberately fostered a brisk rivalry between the two, encouraging them to outdo one another in the achievement of sales objectives, thus extending their capabilities to the limit.

At the time, by far the largest portion of Seaboard's business was with the United States Eastern Seaboard, a market which was managed by Harry O'Hagan in his high-energy style. Over the years he had developed a reliable instinct for the movement of the U.S. market, and was also a shrewd observer of the wholesalers with whom he dealt. At the beginning of the sixties the United States was a buoyant seller's market. The mills were more than happy with the situation, and O'Hagan's reputation and performance were held in high esteem.

Seaboard's second largest market was the United Kingdom and European continent, managed by Bob Edgett in a manner no less effective than O'Hagan's, though conditions far beyond his control prevented him from generating sales comparable to those enjoyed by his counterpart in the U.S. Competition from the Scandinavian countries and the U.S.S.R. was fierce and unremitting. British Columbia lumber prices were unattractive to many U.K. importers; grades and dimensions were not always to the buyers' liking, and timber frame construction was not accepted to the same extent that it was in North America.

A further impediment to Edgett's greater sales success in the United Kingdom was the internecine competition now openly practised among Seaboard's lumber agents which worked to Seaboard's disadvantage. In the late fifties four Seaboard lumber agents—Brandts, C. Leary, Munro, Brice and Foy, Morgan—were in pursuit of approximately 100 major importers and other buyers. As Bob Edgett today describes the scene: "The significance of this was that we had a handful of agents in the U.K. all chasing the same accounts. The agents were vying with each other for a firm counter-offer against every quote, and this was seriously affecting Seaboard's ability to obtain a proper price in the market."

Edgett had a reputation for resourcefulness and innovation which did not always meet with the approval of the member mills. The mills were predominantly conservative in their outlook, choosing to remain with the status quo unless conditions in the marketplace reached alarming proportions. Even then their tendency was to attempt to make adjustments within the established systems to which they were accustomed. When the Seaboard agents began to damage Seaboard's trading ability in the United Kingdom, Edgett searched for ways to correct the problem, pressing strongly for the creation of a central selling organization which would eliminate the dangers inherent in competition between agents. "The only condition we put on the scheme," Edgett says, "was that we would retain the right to name the managing director."

Brandts was in favour of the plan, but the other three agents were actively opposed and let their feelings be known to Seaboard's executive committee. Leary later agreed to a central selling agency provided that Seaboard's agents were reduced to two, of which Leary would be one. This was not acceptable either to the agents who were likely to be eliminated or to Seaboard. Finally Peter Morgan of Foy, Morgan was able to sell a compromise to the other agents and to Seaboard which split the accounts among the agents.

Edgett opposed the plan, "but Poldi Bentley liked the idea," he states, "and Claude Effinger would not oppose Bentley. The accounts were divided among the agents and I made a point of predicting that this arrangement was doomed to failure."

Edgett's forthright opinions did not always work in his favour, and his frankness may have been taken into account when Claude Effinger's successor was chosen. Harry O'Hagan was appointed vice-president and managing director of Seaboard in January 1963, and Bob Edgett was appointed general sales manager with Harry Berry as secretary-treasurer.

While Harry O'Hagan was very much preoccupied with the two major market areas, the U.S. East Coast and the United Kingdom, he nevertheless closely monitored activity in other markets. In 1964, for example, he travelled to Italy with Tom Ferris and Cliff Glover to examine sales activity. At that time, J. G. Schmidt in Genoa was Seaboard's agent. While in Italy, O'Hagan appointed an agency in Naples for southern Italy, Dr. Giovanni Traversa, to provide better market coverage. The following year, the Schmidt agency was terminated and Messrs. Sylvander were appointed to handle plywood in the north. Under the capable direction of Enrico Traversa, the agency prospered and was awarded in 1970 an exclusive for the entire Italian market. In 1973 the agency moved its offices to Rome and changed its name to ETT Agenzia Legnami S.p.a. Today, the agency continues under the direction of Mia Traversa, the widow of Enrico, who tragically died in 1982.

In the meanwhile the search continued for ways and means either to lower Seaboard's lumber prices in the United Kingdom and on the Continent, or to discover new or more efficient ways to manufacture and deliver lumber to the export markets and thus compensate for higher lumber prices. For some time Vassall Forrester had been recommending the acquisition of a stevedoring company, an idea first suggested and researched by Dudley Darling, then head of the shipping company's accounting department. Forrester states that British Columbia's stevedoring companies were causing difficulties for the exporters at that time: "They had joined forces and they had increased their rates to the limit. It made sense for us to have our own stevedoring company if only to keep ship loading costs at a reasonable level. Dudley Darling and I did some investigating and learned of a stevedoring company going through troubled times because of low volume and management deficiencies. I recommended in 1960 that we make an offer to purchase." In spite of his urgings, the executive committee resisted and took no action until 1962 when, after careful study, the decision was made to purchase a 45 per cent share in Western Stevedoring Company.

It was a measure of Seaboard's caution that it did not purchase the entire company at that time. A few years later, when Western Stevedoring had returned an unfailing profit, and showed every sign of continuing to do so, Seaboard's management expressed regret that it had not made an outright purchase when the opportunity presented itself.

In the United Kingdom the Seaboard agents' new arrangement was not working satisfactorily. Niel Morison, representing Seaboard's interests, was able to apply a certain amount of pressure to keep the agents in line. But there was always the danger that two or more of the agents could come to private agreement on price, and there were regular complaints launched by individual agents that Seaboard was favouring one to the exclusion of the others. Morison commanded the agents' respect, but there was little he could do when instinct for profit overcame loyalty to Seaboard's interests.

In 1962, shortly before Claude Effinger's departure, Morison was obliged to retire because of ill health. When he made his retirement decision known, Seaboard sent Tom Ferris to join him in the London office for a period of indoctrination; and when Morison departed, Ferris picked up the reins, strongly supported by George Taylor, who provided valuable liaison and continuity gained from twelve years with Associated Seaboard Agents and Seaboard Lumber Sales.

Morison, by reason of long, personal association with the agents, and because of his intimate knowledge of the "local scene," had been able to command a reasonably reliable performance. Ferris, notwithstanding his proven capabilities as a lumber marketing practitioner, was an outsider in an unfamiliar environment. The best he could do was to conduct a watching brief, protect Seaboard's interests to the extent of his ability, and work on the development of a stronger liaison with the importers and other buyers of Seaboard lumber. His role was similar to that of a trade ambassador working on behalf of Seaboard.

From time to time Seaboard pressed the idea of forming a consortium of agents which would constitute a central selling agency headed by Seaboard. The agents countered with the argument that a central selling structure managed by a non-British company would be unacceptable to United Kingdom buyers. No buyer, they said, would relinquish the traditional way of doing business and purchase direct from an overseas company. No one would co-operate on financing. The tendency to complain and to criticize product would accelerate and lead to costly delays and claims. The concept, so the agents counselled, would be just too complex and difficult to execute. They spoke from a position of long-entrenched power, confident apparently that Seaboard would not supplant them, and that at best the breaking of an agency contract would be unsporting. Were it not for the initiative provided by MacMillan, Bloedel and Powell River in 1963, Seaboard might have resigned itself indefinitely to its existing arrangement with its agents.

MacMillan, Bloedel had decided that the time had come to evaluate its organization not only in the domestic market but also overseas in order to adapt to changing technological and economic conditions. To this end they retained the firm of McKinsey and Company to conduct an exhaustive study of the forest company's marketing and production techniques. After months of observation and survey, the McKinsey group submitted a report which in due course resulted in radical changes throughout MacMillan, Bloedel's entire operation. Of particular interest to Seaboard was the initiation of a joint venture company in the United Kingdom, which brought together the MacMillan interests with Montague L. Meyer, H. R. MacMillan's friend and business associate of many years. The company—MacMillan Bloedel Meyer Ltd.—was established to sell direct to importers and other buyers and users of lumber products. Forthwith, all agent contracts were cancelled. Seaboard, a most interested observer, waited and watched for the repercussions to rock the industry. There were none of any consequence.

The total number of importers doing business in the United Kingdom in the mid-sixties was 412 of which Seaboard sold to 240. Only a few of these were true importers; most, in fact, were large merchants supplying to smaller clientele, and most were not substantial or regular buyers. In fact, more than 50 per cent of Seaboard's sales were to no more than 18 importers.

Among the advantages of using an agent network was the willingness of the agents to guarantee the solvency of the buyers. In addition, and as a matter of course, they insured credit risks, extended bill terms up to four months (usually at 1 per cent over bank rate), and limited bill terms to a maximum of 7½ per cent. Seaboard's agents also acted as brokers, arranging sales to importers for which they received a commission. The importers, in turn, resold to two general buyer categories: merchants and smaller importers, and large industrial consumers. Seaboard had relied on this chain of distribution to conduct its sales in the United Kingdom from the first day it went into business. It would be difficult indeed to cast the system adrift.

And yet MacMillan, Bloedel, in a startling move, had eliminated all agency arrangements in exchange for an association with the United Kingdom's largest importer, Montague L. Meyer. From that day on, all sales in the U.K. would be made by MacMillan Bloedel Meyer Limited. Furthermore the new company had acquired large terminals at Newport, Hull and a twenty-acre terminal at Tilbury—Berth 42.

The new company's stated intention was to import and carry stock at these terminals for resale to importers on an FOT* basis at the terminals, or delivered according to the buyer's instructions. Iconoclastic though all of this might have seemed, the sky did not fall. Examining its own position in the light of the new MacMillan, Bloedel system, Seaboard judged itself to be at a disadvantage.

Servicing too many small buyers in too many discharge ports was resulting in small orders and demanded a large sales staff. Preparation and packaging of small parcels and the attendant documentation and exchange of communication were inordinately expensive. Interestingly, Bob Edgett had been pressing for a consolidation and streamlining of Seaboard's U.K. operations for some time, and now some of his observations came into focus. As long as the agents were the intermediaries, Seaboard had no direct control over the sales force and could never be certain that its directives were accurately communicated by the agents. It was difficult to build close customer relationships and strong distribution services from a secondary position removed from the buyer.

Then there was the matter of agent allegiance. Seaboard's agents did not provide exclusive service; they divided their resources between Seaboard's sales requirements and those of a number of other countries. For instance, Brandts' total annual sales consisted of 45 per cent Seaboard lumber, 25 per cent Russian, 10 per cent Finnish, 10 per cent Swedish and 5 per cent East German. Foy's annual imports broke down this way: 20 per cent Seaboard, 30 per cent Russian, 20 per cent Finnish, 15 per cent Swedish, 7½ per cent East Germany and 2½ per cent Brazil. A report distributed to the Seaboard directors on 16 May 1966 concluded that "our present trade structure is costly and our current system is non-competitive with MacMillan Bloedel/Montague Meyer"—an observation bound to cause uneasiness.

Adding to Seaboard's uneasiness was the corroborated information

---

* A price quoted up to and including the loading of lumber from mill onto truck or from ship onto truck.

received in July of the same year that MacMillan, Bloedel had made an offer to acquire one of the United States' largest lumber importers, Blanchard Lumber Company. Was the scenario with Montague Meyer in the U.K. now about to be played again with Blanchard's in the U.S.?

In Harry O'Hagan's opinion the implications of this move were nothing to be too worried about; Seaboard's U.S. customer relations were not endangered. Nevertheless, Poldi Bentley himself asked if Seaboard should make a counter move, a measure which O'Hagan judged unnecessary. He was more concerned about the Australian market and the Continent where he felt Seaboard should take a stronger and more direct stand. It had been learned that MacMillan, Bloedel was planning to set up its own sales agency in Australia.

Chairman of the executive committee L. L. G. Bentley, addressing a meeting of the committee on 27 May 1966, advised the gathering that he had discussed with the chief executive officers of Crown Zellerbach and Rayonier the repositioning of Seaboard as a marketing leader rather than a follower. A study of the situation was recommended, leading to long- and short-range planning. Out of this study new marketing concepts must emerge. It was the first recorded evidence of Seaboard's wakening realization that a new era had dawned and that the company was still in the shadows.

It was unanimously agreed at the same meeting that the agents should be warned that unless Seaboard remained competitive in the U.K. market their services would have to be dispensed with. However, the minutes also show the influence the agents continued to have on the Seaboard shareholders. There was a cautious note observing that Seaboard had a moral obligation to continue to use the agents if at all possible, and it was decided that nothing more could be done until they had been briefed and their response received.

Within a matter of days Seaboard launched a search for a suitable U.K. survey organization, finally settling on the British-based Economic Intelligence Unit and summoning their representative to Vancouver for thorough briefing and the establishment of guidelines. Now that the principle of short- and long-range planning had been accepted, and the analytical process had assumed top priority, it was decided to appoint a market analyst specializing in the lumber trade and assign him to develop and oversee the company's ongoing marketing strategies. At an executive committee meeting held on 13 October 1966, Harry O'Hagan advised the members that an analyst had been hired and would take up his duties within a month. The successful candidate was Reg L. Barclay. His training and experience were of particular interest to Seaboard because he was attracted from the ranks of MacMillan, Bloedel's or-

ganization where he had been associated with the restructuring of that
company's marketing systems.

Barclay, Victoria-born, had trained for a career in the forestry industry, influenced perhaps by his grandfather who had been inspector of
royalties for the Provincial Department of Forestry. He had a degree in
forestry from the University of Washington and had acquired professional experience first with the B.C. Forest Service and then with Bay
Lumber Company, a Seaboard member. In 1957 he joined MacMillan
& Bloedel, starting with the Vancouver Plywood Division and then
joining the company's Wood Products Marketing Division to work in
market research and planning. When he joined Seaboard he was made
Manager of Market Planning.

As a further indication of the company's intention to improve the
organization at every level, it was decided late in 1966 to rotate the
members of the executive committee in order to involve every mill
member over a period of time. This action was generated by L. L. G.
Bentley. Today he regards it to have been a most effective tactic. "Up
until then, the majority of the mill members played quite a passive
role," he said. "Many of them felt, for one reason or another, that they
were not qualified to make top policy decisions. Perhaps they felt overshadowed by the larger Seaboard mills. In any event, we proceeded to
involve all of them as active members of the executive committee. Their
understanding and co-operation increased remarkably."

Any feeling built up over the years that decisions were made by a
powerful few in some inner Seaboard circle was eliminated in this manner. The Economic Intelligence Unit report, for instance, delivered in
February 1967, in other times might have been considered top secret
and beyond the pale for the smaller member mills. Under the new
arrangement every member knew that he would be privy to the contents
of the report in due course.

The E.I.C. report was not born easily. A first draft studied by the
committee revealed a lack of understanding on the part of the consultants, and Bob Edgett and Reg Barclay travelled to London to oversee
the drafting of a final report. The marketing strategy emerging from the
lengthy study was capsulized in a sentence—"to market a planned portion of annual lumber volume in a suitable specification, confirmed by
member mills and supplied on a regular basis to each market at the
highest possible average annual mill return."

Expanded on in the full report was the proposition that Seaboard's
future sales policy should be directed to serving approximately twenty
or thirty major importers in the United Kingdom. Added to this list
would be a lesser number of smaller accounts supplying specific trades.

The reasoning behind this recommendation was that this cross-section of the trade accounted for more than 50 per cent of British Columbia's total lumber exports, and this was the group as well that preferred to purchase lumber on a forward shipment basis. It was estimated that 80 per cent of Seaboard's business with this assembly of importers could be done on a presold basis.

Except in special circumstances, Seaboard should not sell to small buyers; the key list of major importers would have the opportunity to resell to smaller importers. It was further recommended that Seaboard should negotiate directly with this key list in order to build better customer relations and stronger distributor connections.

This, of course, meant that Seaboard would assume responsibility for all sales negotiations and customer service, thus eliminating the agents' sales function. It was thought that the one remaining connection with the agents might be in the area of financing with the agents assuming the credit risk in return for the standard commission; and there would be no objection to the agents acting as brokers between Seaboard's key importers and smaller importers.

Furthermore, if the confident estimate was that, under this new arrangement, Seaboard could presell 80 per cent of its export total, there was every good reason to establish at least one major bulk carrier terminal in the U.K. where lumber could be assembled and stockpiled for future delivery to or purchase by the key importers.

The formal report and the recommended strategy were compiled by Reg Barclay in consultation with Bob Edgett, both of whom made significant contributions. It is interesting to note that while the findings of the Economic Intelligence Unit were taken into the account, not all of their advice was incorporated in the final document.

On 23 February 1967 the report was presented to the executive committee by Edgett and Barclay.

When all the pieces were finally in position, a firm proposal was placed before Seaboard's member mills calling for the formation of a subsidiary to market lumber products in the United Kingdom. The alternative would be to enter into a joint venture with the agents, and Bob Edgett among others was no longer in favour of that. His strong support went to a Seaboard subsidiary because it would have the advantage of independence—no agent strings attached and no suspicion of customer favouritism.

Edgett saw the subsidiary as a way to invest Seaboard with a degree of autonomy rather than to retain the image of an "employee" of the member mills. Among Seaboard's management were several who, like Edgett, felt that the company had never been given the credit or the

status it deserved as a full-scale, successful operating entity. The acquisition of a sales subsidiary would be a positive step towards a stronger
corporate identity.

O'Hagan was not adamantly opposed to the concept, but neither was
he keenly interested, largely because of his preoccupation with the turbulent U.S. market and the need for new strategies in that area. He was
not particularly comfortable with the prospect of having to set up a
formal subsidiary structure, and shared some of Poldi Bentley's feelings
that a subsidiary was going to mean expensive new overhead. Bentley
was in favour of the tried and true agency system, arguing that "agents
are best because you only pay them when you use them. No need to be
burdened with fixed costs."

Put to a vote, the subsidiary concept won the day both with the
executive committee and at the board of directors' level. On 13 April
1967 Harry O'Hagan advised the executive committee that Seaboard
had incorporated two subsidiary companies: Seaboard International
(Timber & Plywood) Limited, and Seaboard Shipping Services Limited.
He also reported that contracts with Seaboard's three remaining lumber
agents—Brandts, Foy, Morgan, and Flatau Dick—had been cancelled,
and Seaboard's agent liaison office in London would be closed, to be
supplanted as soon as possible with the offices of Seaboard International.

Tom Ferris, in his semi-trade ambassadorial role, would remain in
London for as long as it took to effect the transition, and a search for
suitable management and staff would commence immediately. It was
agreed that the first choice of a managing director for Seaboard International should be an experienced marketing practitioner resident in the
United Kingdom. This man's familiarity with the U.K. trade and traders
would be a distinct advantage. The position was offered first to John
Brandt, whose uncle headed up Brandts, one of Seaboard's recently
deposed agencies. Brandt chose to stay with the family business, and
Seaboard was obliged to look elsewhere.

Subsequently the post was offered to R. R. Dobell, son of the owner
of one of Seaboard's former agencies, a long-time employee of Seaboard, and at the time United Kingdom sales manager in the company's
head office in Vancouver.

Dobell had been raised in England, was well-connected through his
family with the U.K. timber trade, and was thoroughly familiar with
Seaboard's procedures and policies in that market. O'Hagan announced in May 1967 that Dobell was considering the position and that
it was expected he would accept. As well, he advised the executive
committee that other staff members were being hired to man the Sea-

board International office in London. In that same month Vassall Forrester was authorized to begin negotiations with the Port of London Authority to obtain Berth 46 at Tilbury.

By July Dick Dobell had agreed to take on the position of managing director of Seaboard International on the private understanding that he would not serve in that position for more than five or six years, after which he would return to Seaboard's head office as second in command to Harry O'Hagan. Three others joined him from Vancouver: William G. McCallion, who served as technical advisor for the plywood sales staff; E. A. (Ted) Cameron, who would be responsible for cedar and lumber specialty sales as well as developing new business, and Peter Appleby, a junior sales executive assigned to general lumber sales.

Dobell lost little time in setting up offices in London. Although the new company would not begin business until January 1968, Dobell was in place by November 1967, holding a press conference for the business trades shortly after his arrival. His statements generated considerable editorial coverage. The *Timber Trades Journal* reported:

> Seaboard Lumber Sales Company Ltd., the export marketing organization of 34 independent producers in the British Columbia forest industry, has formed a United Kingdom subsidiary to serve the British market more efficiently by bulk deliveries of packaged wood products.
>
> Mr. Richard R. Dobell, managing director of Seaboard International (Timber and Plywood) Ltd., the new subsidiary, said that the annual worldwide turnover of the parent company is over $150 million on a delivered basis, with the British market accounting for more than 20 per cent.
>
> Mr. Dobell said that at any one time 270,000 tons of shipping was on charter, with 40 or 50 per cent serving the United Kingdom.
>
> This move is a sign of our faith in the continued strength of the British market for our timber and plywood.

Dobell allayed fears among U.K. timber importers that the new company's marketing operation might mean direct selling to consumers by stating that Seaboard would rely on the import trade to perform this function.

Since negotiations to secure Berth 46 at Tilbury were continuing satisfactorily, Dobell was able to announce at the same press conference the formation of another company, Seaboard Shipping Services Ltd., which would work with the appointed U.K. delivery agents, Eggar, Forrester, to distribute lumber to the customers. Seaboard Shipping Services in turn had formed Seaboard Pioneer Terminals Ltd., which would be responsible for terminal operations at Tilbury. The ownership of Berth 46 would be shared equally by Seaboard and the Reid Paper Group. "It is expected that this 18-acre terminal will be fully operational by the end of 1968," Dobell said. "Other public terminal facilities or ports capable of handling bulk carriers will be used if inducement of volume and price is offered."

Today Vassall Forrester describes the opening of the Tilbury terminal as one of the most harrowing experiences of his life. "I was responsible for the choice of the terminal," he states. "I had convinced Seaboard that Berth 46 was the best possible location, and I had put considerable time and effort into the design of a first-class facility intended to improve Seaboard's competitive edge. No sooner did we open the terminal when the longshoremen went on strike. It was a six-month strike that seemed like six years to me. The issue had to do with the handling of containers and did not involve us in any way—except that we couldn't use our own terminal. I did not feel well-liked by the Seaboard member mills during that period."

Dobell and his colleagues had been given the assignment to familiarize themselves with the U.K. market, to learn the full range of existing end uses for lumber and plywood, to develop new uses and new markets, and to put Seaboard in a stronger position with industrial accounts. An additional mandate was to hire and train a sales force, seeking out people who had experience in selling Canadian wood. The decision to hire salesmen from each market region proved to be a good one. Almost without exception, the members of this sales force were able to concentrate their full attention on Seaboard's sales objectives to an extent that had not been possible under the old agency system.

One of the sales candidates interviewed and hired by Dick Dobell was an employee of Edward Chaloner, a long-established London agent. His name was Clive D. G. Roberts and he had been sales director with Chaloner since 1961. While his familiarity with Canadian wood products was not great, he came highly recommended as an aggressive and energetic sales executive. Within six months Dobell put him in charge of plywood sales—which was a considerable challenge since Roberts possessed small knowledge of this product and was called upon to learn all he could about it in short order. Time and circumstance conspired to change Clive Roberts's destiny considerably in the years to come.

While Seaboard had been ushered into a new marketing era in the United Kingdom by something of an organizational revolution, the transition had been remarkably lacking in discord. Fears of agency reprisals were groundless, and the dire warnings that British buyers would refuse to deal direct with overseas interests did not materialize except in a few isolated and inconsequential cases. There was no turbulence to speak of, whereas in the United States the first eddies of an approaching storm were making themselves felt as the sixties marched to their conclusion.

·FOURTEEN·

FEAST & FAMINE & SOME SOLUTIONS

Partly because of the incentive provided by MacMillan Bloedel to remain competitive, partly because of suggestions and observations made by the Economic Intelligence Unit and the new market analyst, Reg Barclay, and partly as well because of the influence and insistence of mill members such as Crown Zellerbach and Rayonier, Seaboard was reaching in every direction, both in the marketplaces and internally, seeking ways to improve, streamline and economize.

In July 1967 the company began to advertise for a transportation economist whose main assignment would be to work out more efficient methods of transporting lumber from mill to ship, and of discharging at destination. In that same month the decision was made to install a computer system capable of recording and controlling inventory, accelerating the accounting processes, and storing and supplying information to management for purposes of control and planning.

Following the lead of member mills on the coast who were now looking to British Columbia's interior for a continuing supply of timber, and recognizing the growing importance of interior mills and the increasing value of western white spruce, Seaboard opened an office in Prince George in 1965 with Richmond Clefstad as manager. Three interior mills—Carrier Lumber Ltd., Dunkley Lumber Ltd. and Rustad Brothers Ltd.—joined forces to create Overseas Spruce Sales Ltd. Clefstad's responsibility was to see to the sales and shipment of product generated by this company.

Corporate soul-searching reached to the top management echelon. The new thinking was that the best efforts of owner/managers were no longer sufficient in themselves to cope with the competitive forces evolving in the marketplace. L. L. G. Bentley, president and chairman of the board of Seaboard Sales and Shipping since 1958, was an owner/manager par excellence. His company was Canadian Forest Products, and one of Seaboard's principal flagships. He was in the tradition of John Humbird and H. J. Mackin, both of whom had tended to regard their companies and Seaboard as fiefdoms over which they presided with a degree of benign autocracy. These men made genuine efforts to defer to the opinions or the expressed anxieties of the entire mill membership, but their strength of personality and their undisputed personal success were powerful forces not easily overcome. For many years this kind of leadership worked.

In testimony to Bentley's earnest wish to encourage every mill member to avail himself of the democratic processes was his action, reported previously, to place every member on the executive committee on a rotating basis. To be a member of the executive committee was one thing; to override or question Poldi Bentley's policies and recommendations was quite another.

Bentley was admired and respected by most, and he influenced not a few. Dudley Darling tells the story of J. E. Feigl, president of Bay Forest Products, who was one of Bentley's admirers and unquestioning supporters. "I was at a meeting of the executive committee where Poldi Bentley spoke very persuasively on an issue concerning all of the mills," Darling recalls. "Bentley's opinion was that the members should go for it, and Feigl was one of the first to agree. The following day I received a call from Feigl. 'Tell me, Dudley,' he said, 'explain to me what I agreed to yesterday, will you.' "

Within the ranks of Seaboard's own management there were degrees of resentment that the member mills, as represented by leaders like Bentley, should make or influence decisions which were more sensibly their concern. In some opinions the mill members were downgrading Seaboard's expertise and experience in export trade. Harry O'Hagan was less sensitive to Seaboard's perceived second-class status. His activities as a consummate salesman, and his close rapport with Poldi Bentley, compensated for any concern he may have had over possible subordination. Others, like Edgett, felt that their effectiveness was dampened by the overriding influence of the member mills. In various ways these men made their feelings known wherever they could find a sympathetic ear. And there were those among the new mill members who were quite prepared to listen.

In the ranks of the executive committee and the board of directors were representatives of the new breed of manager who not only subscribed to modern management techniques but who also practised them with success in their own companies. Crown Zellerbach and Rayonier, in particular, endorsed the utilization of professional management in lieu of the old owner/management system. When men like Gordon L. Draeseke and T. L. Roberts of Rayonier and D. S. Denman and R. G. Rogers of Crown Zellerbach made their opinions known in the executive committee, they spoke both from positions of experience with the new management systems and with the authority invested in them by reason of the size and success of their companies. In this very real sense, Poldi Bentley was addressed by his peers.

On 18 January 1968, preliminary discussions having been held between Bentley and members of the executive committee, it was resolved that Harry O'Hagan should become president of Seaboard Lumber Sales and Seaboard Shipping while Poldi Bentley would retain the title of chairman of the two companies. This announcement was interpreted by most as a vote of confidence in Seaboard's management capabilities.

At the same time, Seaboard's new corporate symbol and logo were displayed for approval. A public relations consultant, Reginald Meek, working with artist George Smith, had designed a new graphic device in keeping with Seaboard's updated corporate image. The stylized tree incorporating the ancient symbols for wood and water and joined with the "Seaboard" logotype remain the company's identifying mark to this day.

While Harry O'Hagan now held the position of president, with the implicit autonomy that title should convey, the executive committee, perhaps unwittingly, had introduced a check and balance factor at the same time. Four advisory committees were appointed from the ranks of the member mills: one to work with the president, and the others to be available to Seaboard's lumber, plywood and shipping managers respectively.

Each committee was comprised of four members who would serve as advisors and consultants at the call of Seaboard's managers. Although Bob Edgett might have been expected to resent what could be interpreted as a continuing intrusion by the mill members, he apparently did not. The lumber committee consisted of Robert McMillan (Crown Zellerbach), Noel Harrison (Rayonier), Mike Robson (Canadian Forest

Products) and Bryce Page (Weldwood), a group which soon came to be known as "The Four Horsemen." All of them were in favour of careful planning and market projections, which was Edgett's attitude as well.

On the other hand O'Hagan was *not* comfortable with his president's advisory committee and availed himself of their services as little as possible, an understandable reaction in light of O'Hagan's preference for running his own organization. He was good at what he did and was not accustomed to making decisions by committee. He and his telephone could solve problems and close sales across a continent in minutes. In this manner he had achieved remarkable results for Seaboard over the years, and he saw his advisory committee as an unnecessary encumbrance.

Even in his position as president, which placed upon him the responsibility for Seaboard's activities in all markets, he remained close to the U.S. market. Its unpredictable action seemed to suit his powerful style. When it came to U.S. sales negotiations, he operated almost by instinct, using his experience and employing the leverage of his many contacts to react to market fluctuations quickly and usually correctly. In the sellers' market, which prevailed until the late 1960s, O'Hagan's record of performance was virtually flawless, and he saw little reason for long-range planning in such a volatile market.

He was comfortable with Seaboard's physical presence on the East Coast. Seaboard had established a branch office in New York well before the war, managed effectively by Harry Martin until his death in 1948. His replacement was Ken Sloat, a good friend of O'Hagan's. Later Sloat was joined by Charles Grinnell's son James, a move which was not regarded favourably by many of the Seaboard contingent since it had the strong appearance of nepotism. Ultimately James resigned from the company, and his position in New York was taken over by Laird Wilson, who had manned the Boston office since 1950. William Kelsberg was sent from Vancouver to fill the Boston vacancy. With these people in place, O'Hagan could work the U.S. East Coast market in his own inimitable way.

Business was done by telephone and telegraph. The Seaboard branch managers would phone customers to inform them that lumber in certain specifications was available for purchase in Vancouver. The customers would indicate interest in particular quantities and specifications. This information was sent by telex to Vancouver each evening. The Vancouver office would put together a firm agreement and send a reply the following morning. (Seaboard's U.S. branch offices were never referred to as sales offices and, in fact, never actually sold anything; they functioned as intermediaries, with Harry O'Hagan and his staff in

Vancouver doing the actual selling and the placement of orders with the member mills.)

During the fifties and into the mid-sixties Seaboard enjoyed a feast of sales in the United States. Business was so good and the demand so great that Seaboard's customers competed hotly for the available lumber supply. In 1961, for instance, 43 per cent of Seaboard's total exports went to the United States. During this time, Seaboard succeeded in selling 500 million board feet annually to the U.S. with a minimum of effort on the part of manager Ken Sloat in New York.

In the summer of 1966, when MacMillan Bloedel purchased the largest of the U.S. wholesale lumber dealers, Blanchard Lumber Company, gaining access to all of that company's U.S. retail outlets, Seaboard was engrossed in the reformation of its marketing strategies. For a brief moment, when MacMillan was negotiating for Blanchard, Seaboard was tempted to make a counter offer, but this was soon controlled in the knowledge that Seaboard's customer list in the U.S. was more than ample. True, Blanchard had been a good customer and would now be lost to MacMillan Bloedel, but Seaboard's remaining firm customers would more than compensate.

In fact, Seaboard had the opportunity a few months later to purchase another large wholesaler, A. C. Dutton, one of its large importers. It was decided not to accept the offer, even though it would have placed Seaboard in a position comparable to MacMillan Bloedel. The fact that A. C. Dutton was prepared to sell out was reason enough to ask questions. Was the company experiencing trouble which had not yet revealed itself in the trade? If this was true, then Dutton's asking price was too high. There was a rumour circulating as well that MacMillan Bloedel had been seduced into paying an inflated price for Blanchard, and there was a real danger that other U.S. wholesalers might sue MacMillan for usurping their positions. Would Seaboard suffer the same attrition if it purchased Dutton? In spite of the fact that comparable potential dangers had concerned it needlessly when it established Seaboard International in the U.K., Seaboard's decision was not to take over Dutton but to continue with the established trading system.

Seaboard had always done a large business with cargo wholesalers in the United States. In its first years, when it was exporting exclusively to the U.S. East Coast, many wholesalers with their own fleets of ships bought lumber cargoes from Seaboard. Over the years business with cargo wholesalers was mainly with four majors: A. C. Dutton, Timberlane Lumber Company, Furman Lumber Company and Weyerhaeuser Timber Company. Of these, Weyerhaeuser, one of Seaboard's earliest customers, was considerably the largest, taking half of Seaboard's U.S.

exports most years. The rapport between the two companies could scarcely have been stronger, and it was this long, close and lucrative relationship with Weyerhaeuser, more than any other factor, that enabled Seaboard to brush off MacMillan Bloedel's competitive moves.

Weyerhaeuser made Seaboard's marketing efforts gratifyingly simple. The big American company was a multiport wholesale distributor with head offices in Tacoma. Its buying system was centralized in that office and it had been accustomed for years to deal direct with Seaboard's Vancouver office for all of its import needs. Another of Weyerhaeuser's advantages was that it gave Seaboard access to five major distribution terminals on the U.S. East Coast, thus economizing shipping and distribution logistics substantially.

Under the circumstances, Harry O'Hagan's satisfaction with the marketing system in the United States was quite understandable. It was difficult to see how Seaboard's position could have been rendered stronger, even though there were some among the Seaboard members who were concerned that the company might have too many eggs in one trading basket. If, by some remote chance, the bottom fell out, there were few compensating trade affiliations to turn to.

These reservations were expressed to Harry O'Hagan and to others on the executive committee, but the arrangements with Weyerhaeuser possessed so many advantages, and O'Hagan's long-time friendship with manager Ken Sloat was so firm, that it did not seem to justify the effort required to introduce new and more aggressive systems into the New York office. In the final years of 1960, up to three-quarters of Seaboard's sales to the United States were handled directly out of Vancouver, and Weyerhaeuser accounted for the largest part of this.

In January 1969, in response to the addition of professional management staff and the new computer system and staff, O'Hagan announced at the annual meeting that the Seaboard office would undergo a 5000-square-foot expansion at a cost of $200,000. There were no objections, nor would there have been good reason for any; no one could argue that these changes were not neccessary in order to remain competitive. A few months later the bottom dropped out of Seaboard's U.S. basket.

For some years the company's importers had been accustomed to order ahead of the market in confident anticipation of a continuing national housing and general construction program that seemed to see no end. Almost overnight a series of events occurred that inflicted grievous wounds on the lumber traders. An oversupply of lumber coincided with a crippling strike on the Atlantic coast. At the same time the United States government, in an attempt to combat an incipient inflationary trend, imposed general credit restrictions and established high interest rates which immediately brought housing starts and other construction projects to a halt.

Mountains of lumber were stockpiled in the terminals, with little prospect of sales at the current prices—or at any price. Weyerhaeuser, without warning to any of its suppliers, decided to reduce its inventories, dropping its price per thousand by $25 in one day and continuing to reduce prices to find a sales level. Two-by-four lumber selling for $140 per thousand in March was down to $124 by April, and had plummeted to $74 by late summer. Other wholesalers, many of them in precarious cash flow positions, were outraged by Weyerhaeuser's precipitate move and were in a panic to unload their stockpiles, knowing full well that they would be extremely fortunate to break even. All of them had bought high and now were attempting to sell in a rock bottom market. For instance, Timberlane owed Seaboard $521,238 for delivered but unsold stock and had few prospects of selling its inventory for even half that amount. Other Seaboard buyers were in similar if not more precarious situations. The disaster has been called the "Crash of '69," and Seaboard was not spared from punishment.

As long as panic and dumping prevailed, prices would continue to spiral downward, and the only thing Seaboard could do to attempt to prevent the price drop was to take back its lumber and refund the buyers' money, or a reasonable portion thereof. Harry O'Hagan, addressing a directors' meeting on 14 August 1969, spelled out the alternatives. He explained that unless Seaboard took back the buyers' inventories, they would be threatened with bankruptcy and would fight in the courts with all the means at their disposal to prevent their companies from failing. In the event of litigation Seaboard was extremely vulnerable as a Canadian company in an American political environment. Furthermore, he contended, Seaboard had a certain obligation to assist the buyers. He felt the original cargo prices charged them had been too high, particularly when U.S. rail prices were falling. He argued that U.S. freight had been subsidizing U.K. freight for years and now it was time to compensate for that subsidy. He reported that the Timberlane Company must be regarded as a salvage situation. The company could not pay fully for more than 14 million feet of delivered lumber and would have to dump it on the market, to the further distress of all other buyers. Seaboard's only recourse was to take back the lumber.

Bentley, chairing the directors' meeting, put the motion "that the ex-gratia allowances be charged to all the lumber producing mills based on their shipments to all markets in 1969." The motion was passed with one dissenting vote cast by a member mill in financial difficulties. The meeting was also advised that the freight refund for the year, together with the commission refund, which would have totalled approximately $4.5 million, would have to be reduced by approximately $2 million to pay back U.S. buyers and to rescue the Timberlane Lumber Company. O'Hagan was hopeful that Timberlane would be able to pay all or a portion of its delinquent account in the future.

It was not a happy day for the directors, and it marked the turning point in the habitual attitude of the mills to engage in a kind of opportunistic lumber trading based heavily on one customer. The realization was beginning to permeate their thinking that the days of "cut now and sell later" were over, and that more reasoned processes must be introduced. Even when, within six months, the U.S. market turned around again and prices began to move upward, the Seaboard mills retained their cautious stance. The balmy days of a sellers' market were over, not because sellers' markets would not occur again, but because Seaboard never again could allow itself the luxury of relaxation in a fluctuating market.

In the past, good luck or pure circumstance had almost invariably come to Seaboard's rescue at times of single market crises. When one market was depressed, one or more of the other markets would be strong enough to compensate for the weak trading area. The buoyant market in the United States through the fifties and well into the sixties had more than balanced out Seaboard's modest trade and lower prices in the United Kingdom and other countries. This time, when the U.S. floundered for an interval, there was no alternative market to take over.

In the United Kingdom, housing starts were showing the effects of tight money, high interest rates and poor building weather. In Australia, Weyerhaeuser and other U.S. lumber manufacturers were scrambling to place their production, with a resulting lowering of price even though there was little business to be had. The same was true in South Africa where, for example, Seaboard lost business to one of the smaller American exporters who came in with prices much lower than anything Seaboard could afford. In Japan, absolutely no interest was being shown in B.C. lumber. The Japanese were closely attuned to the events occurring in the U.S. and placed their orders when prices bottomed out. Seaboard could not compete.

As for Seaboard's trading position in the United States, it was hollow comfort to know that, in co-operating with the distressed importers, they had retained their goodwill and a strong degree of allegiance. Timberlane was in serious trouble and would take months to sort out its affairs, if ever. Dutton had suffered severe damage but possessed sufficient resources to survive. The other buyers on the Seaboard roster

were experiencing varying degrees of difficulty in their efforts to re-
cover, and some had gone under.

In addition, British Columbia's interior sawmills and Eastern Canada's mills were beginning to compete by rail with Seaboard and Mac-
Millan Bloedel for the U.S. market, and had made substantial inroads in
the period leading up to the "crash." They could be expected to re-enter
that market as soon as the demand and the price warranted.

A representative survey of U.S. Atlantic Coast wholesalers conducted
by Reg Barclay gave Seaboard some indication of the direction it should
take to maintain a competitive stance. Seaboard was in immediate need
of an interim strategy that called for solid member mill commitment.
Going beyond that, a long-range plan must be in position and ready for
launch no later than the spring of 1971.

While the elements of a long-range plan were far from clear at this
stage, it seemed that the company must control its inventory on the
Atlantic Coast. It was no longer sufficient to be a trading organization
engaged primarily in selling documents and contracts; the company
must enter the marketplace and sell goods. Consideration should be
given to selling directly to stocking wholesalers under the terms of an
annual contract, while office wholesalers should buy from an inventory
held by Seaboard on the Atlantic Coast. These were just a few of the
more significant observations and opinions which were reported to the
executive committee as a preliminary to action.

*   *   *

Just as packaging of lumber had enabled Seaboard to remain price
competitive with Russian and Scandinavian suppliers a few years previously, further innovations in the handling and shipping of lumber
yielded substantial advantages in the final years of the sixties.

Better methods of lumber handling occupied considerable time and
attention. The first written record of this important subject appears in
the executive committee minutes of 15 February 1968, when president
and managing director of Sooke Forest Products, Hershell Smith, raised
a number of questions, echoing opinions first generated by Bob Edgett.
He pointed out that MacMillan Bloedel was now making extensive use
of bulk carriers in conjunction with loading from one port wherever
possible, and he wondered why Seaboard was not considering a similar
system. He felt that the company was moving too slowly in any attempt
to create savings by loading from one or two assembly wharves, instead
of from a multitude of mill wharves, and he requested that Seaboard
supply him with the cost of assembling lumber from the Island mills at
two points: Cowichan Bay and Victoria.

Vanguard to the Present

1 Seaboard's executive committee, 1976. *Left to right:* L. J. Martin; H. A. Berry, senior vice-president; L. R. Ridenour, v.p. finance; R. C. MacMillan; C. D. G. Roberts, president and c.e.o.; P. J. G. Bentley, chairman; T. A. Buell, vice-chairman; R. R. Ogilvie; E. Sonner; H. B. Urquhart; G. M. Lyttle.

2

2

Claude Effinger (*l*) entertains visitors Donald
Wright of C. Leary & Company, Mrs. Niel
Morison, Charles Dodd of C. Leary & Company,
and Niel Morison.

3

In 1965 Seaboard sent a delegation to the U.K. on a
"spruce mission" to promote the merits of B.C.
interior spruce, pine and fir. At London's Café
Royal are (*l to r*) Len Park, Park Timber; Peter
Morgan, Foy, Morgan; Clifford Glover, Seaboard;
Henry and John Brandt of Wm. Brandt; Paul
Cantwell, Canadian Forest Products; (*behind
Cantwell*) Brian Thomson, Wm. Brandt; Claude
Parish, Buck River Timber; Mel Rustad, Rustad
Bros.; Robert Thorsen, Northwood; John Wright,
Foy, Morgan.

4

4
L. L. G. (Poldi) Bentley, president and chairman from 1959
to 1969.
5
Gary S. J. Bowell, chairman, 1970, 1971 and 1972.
6
Robert G. Rogers, chairman, 1973, 1974 and 1975.
7
Peter J. G. Bentley, chairman, 1976 and 1977.
8
Thomas A. Buell, chairman, 1978 and 1979.
9
Thomas G. Rust, chairman, 1980 and 1981.
10
William L. Sauder, chairman, 1982 and 1983.

6

7

8

9

10

11

11
At the stern of M.V. *Skaugran,* 1979, watching lumber being loaded are (*l to r*) Clive Roberts, Brynjulf Skaugen, Capt. Leif Lysuik (ship's master) and Clyde Jacobs.

12
Seaboard Lumber Sales received a Government of Canada Export Award in 1983 for its achievement in developing new export markets. Displaying the export award flag are (*l to r*) Clive Roberts, Reginald Barclay, Clifford Glover, Larry Ridenour, Ted Cameron, Clyde Jacobs (regional office) and Government of Canada representatives Don Wismer and Robin Dodson.

13
The maiden voyage of M.V. *Nordpol,* 1974. *Left to right:* Jurgen Falkensteen, Norden Ltd.; Capt. A. Mortensen; Clyde Jacobs, and Jurgen Kruhl, Norden Ltd.

14
Seaboard's present managment committee (*l to r*): Colin Brock, E. A. (Ted) Cameron, Larry R. Ridenour, Clive D. G. Roberts, Reg Barclay, Clyde Jacobs.

12

13

14

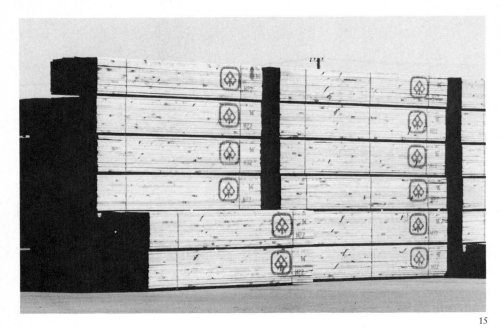

15
Seaboard lumber, red end-sealed and Sea
Brited for protection during the voyage,
marked with the corporate symbol.
16
Mr. Aida of Nissha-Iwai Canada Ltd.
presents an original watercolour to Clive
Roberts at the opening of Seaboard's new
office in the Oceanic Plaza, 1978.

Shortly thereafter a technical committee was formed to study the feasibility of a dock assembly system in the Vancouver area. The committee was comprised of P. Hall, J. McWilliams, R. Vallance, H. Homewood, R. Ogilvie and K. Rymer representing the member mills while R. Murray Mather, G. Dudley Darling and Peter J. Raven represented Seaboard, and Vassall Forrester conducted a watching brief. Dudley Darling, as manager of distribution for Seaboard Shipping, as well as a director of Seaboard Pioneer Terminals, was deeply involved in all aspects of the study. Peter Raven, hired because of his training and expertise in transportation systems, was able to focus the latest methodology on the project to test feasibility and perform comparative surveys.

Early in November 1969 the committee presented a report and a set of recommendations for a dock assembly system, indicating that such a system should provide ample berthage in good depth of water, thus reducing or eliminating ships' waiting time, as well as speeding up the loading operation. Better loading would mean better and quicker discharge at destination, and would reduce cargo damage to a minimum.

A discussion was held on the best place to locate the assembly facility. The port of Vancouver seemed to be the best choice, but Roberts Bank at the mouth of the Fraser River was a distinct possibility. Vassall Forrester assured the committee that Vancouver Harbour would be the best location for at least the next ten years, and pointed out that it made little difference to an owner where his ships loaded as long as the facilities were amenable to safety and quick turnaround.

Crown Zellerbach, represented by W. O. Beaton and Victor Vallance, expressed concern for the company's situation. Crown Zellerbach had its own deep-sea berth at Fraser Mills and there seemed nothing to gain by committing to Seaboard's dock assembly facility. Chairman of the executive committee G. S. J. Bowell stated firmly that it was pointless to consider an assembly facility if any mill stood to be penalized, and it was agreed that more study would be put into the estimate of financial return from the facility. Harry O'Hagan assured the assembly that no commitment would be solicited from any member mill until every mill was satisfied as to the advantages of the dock assembly system. In the meantime it was agreed that Seaboard could negotiate with the National Harbours Board in a search for the best choice of locations for the facility.

The search for an appropriate waterfront location took some time and was conducted concurrent with ongoing feasibility studies to establish conclusively that loading from a terminal was less costly and more efficient than the traditional method of loading from scows. Engineering consultants, naval architects and computer technologists were assigned to the project. Time and motion studies were carried out even to the extent of trial shipments to determine the cost and time expended to move some 4500 tons of lumber and plywood to wharfside and the same amount into a ship every working day. It was determined beyond doubt that the dock assembly system was best in all respects.

The requirements laid down for a suitable location were that it possess a large back storage area for lumber and plywood awaiting shipment. Sufficient draft at any tide was essential, and there must be enough berth space to load three ships simultaneously as well as room to unload scows.

It was also important that the assembly wharf facility be central to the member mills and easily accessible to ships and to parcels of lumber and plywood delivered by scow, truck or rail. Companies like Crown Zellerbach, with their own deep-sea berths, would have to be satisfied as to the advantages of a Seaboard assembly wharf. In the end, member mill consensus was achieved and the project moved into its final stages.

A location was found in Vancouver Harbour on the north shore, just west of the Second Narrows bridge, not far from the last vestigial remains of some of British Columbia's earliest mills. A multimillion dollar construction program began on the development of fifty-five acres of land capable of accommodating up to 100 million board feet of lumber awaiting shipment at any given time. The entire area was asphalt paved, rail lines were installed and a large plywood warehouse was erected adjacent to the offices for the terminal management. The result was the largest wood products assembly and loading facility of its kind in the world, equipped with the latest in loading and unloading equipment.

Lumber-laden scows arriving from the mills could be discharged by forklift to the assembly area via floating barge ramps which rise and fall with the tide. The large size of the assembly area allowed lumber shipments, whether they arrived by scow, rail or truck, to be positioned adjacent to the wharf edge. The entire system was engineered to provide not only for the efficient use of conventional equipment and ship's gear but also for new types of ships and equipment, in particular the specialized vessels then coming into use, featuring gantry cranes and roll-on/roll-off capabilities. These systems are still operative today.

While all this was approaching completion, Seaboard turned its attention to the adequate manning of the facility. The company had acquired a substantial share of Western Stevedoring Company in 1962, a move which had proved to be both a more reliable way to handle lumber shipments and a steady source of revenue. Now the opportunity presented itself to purchase Associated Stevedoring, a company which, after a number of years of operation, had encountered serious financial difficulties. The ailing company first asked Western Stevedoring to provide management assistance and, in a few months, elected to sell out to Western, thus strengthening Seaboard's stevedoring resources considerably as well as expanding a profit centre. When Seaboard's dock assembly facility went into operation in August 1971, Western Stevedoring, augmented by Associated Stevedoring, was charged with the responsibility of loading and unloading.

It must be noted that Seaboard's undertakings were not always unanimously endorsed by the directors. Sooke Forest Products' president Hershell Smith, who had been among the first to urge the establishment of a lumber assembly terminal, was one of a minority who were unhappy with the physical location of Seaboard International Terminal. From the outset he had wanted an assembly terminal for the mills on Vancouver Island where his own plant was located. When the dissenting minority finally agreed to the terminal's North Vancouver location, Hershell Smith remained in opposition and became further alienated when Seaboard's stevedoring business was not put out to tender. In his estimation all the stevedoring companies should have equal access to Seaboard's business on a bidding basis. The final outcome was that he withdrew his mill from Seaboard and for some time associated himself with MacMillan, Bloedel. In 1976 he returned to Seaboard claiming that he felt more at ease conducting his export business in that environment.

The first vessel to arrive at the new facility, formally designated the Seaboard International Terminal, was one of the new lumber carrier types. The M. V. *Pacific*, 29,000 tons deadweight and 604 feet in length, was on long-term charter to Seaboard Shipping. Owned by the Johnson Line and constructed in Finland, it was one the first vessels to be designed specifically to carry automobiles (from Sweden) to North America's West Coast, and to carry specially stowed lumber back to the United Kingdom and the Continent. The vessel was equipped with gantry cranes for handling packaged lumber and plywood in specially designed flat racks. The system for stowing lumber worked out by Johnson Line in collaboration with Seaboard was twice as fast as that using conventional vessels and equipment.

Package size is standardized at 4 feet wide by 2 feet high, and to this Seaboard added another refinement—"stickers." Conceived by Bill Schofield and effectively promoted by Dudley Darling, this basically simple concept contributed another degree of effectiveness and cost savings to the handling of lumber. The member mills were persuaded,

and financed where neccessary, to install equipment for attaching stickers to each package of lumber. Three four-feet-long stickers are attached by steel straps to the underside of each package, providing a
space to accept the forks of a forklift machine. In a matter of seconds, a
machine can wheel into place, position its forks under the package and
carry it within reach of a ship's crane, eliminating the need to handle
blocks on the terminal.

In the case of the M. V. *Pacific* and her sister ship the M. V. *Suecia*,
the packaged lumber was placed on flat racks, two packages wide, two
packages high and 32 feet in length. A gantry crane can lift up to 18 tons
of lumber or plywood on each platform, lowering it into the ship's hold
where it slides along guides into its allocated space. The *Pacific* had a
carrying capacity of 13 million board feet or the equivalent. Its first
cargo was destined for delivery to Seaboard Pioneer Terminal at Tilbury
in London. Actually the vessel had anticipated the formal opening of
Seaboard International Terminal in Vancouver by three months. Final
stages of construction were under way when she arrived. When the
terminal received its official inauguration in November, the *Suecia*
marked the event, her maiden voyage taking place in the same period.
Seaboard's schedule for the two vessels called for ten voyages annually,
comprising five round trips for each, an arrangement which, in spite of
the large investment, was a positive step forward for Seaboard in its
never-ending search for competitive advantages.

The search, directed once more to Seaboard's operations in the U.S.
market, was stimulated both by the need to deal with specific problems
such as the financial distress of Timberlane, and the obvious overall
need for a strategy tailored to the new demands and changing characteristics of the market. In the case of Timberlane, there was great cause
for concern. The company had not earned a profit since 1 June 1969.
Now, better than a year later, no part of its indebtedness to Seaboard
had been paid. Something had to be done to receive regular payments
even if they could not be linked to profits. H. A. Berry was instructed to
begin negotiations along these lines.

The company's first objective was to activate an interim strategy
which would satisfy the U.S. buyers until long-range strategy could be
devised. In October 1970 Seaboard offered its U.S. buyers an annual
contract incorporating a price-adjusting formula with additional com-
pensation for holding stock during the winter months. The annual
purchase agreement would be for a specified monthly volume incorporating a form of differential pricing for stock holding, the effect of
which was not to exceed $1 per thousand feet on total purchases. The

alternative to the customer would be open trading with no supply or purchase commitment.

In order to make the interim marketing strategy work, the member mills were asked to commit to Seaboard at least 80 per cent of the total projected exports to the U.S. in 1971. On the buyers' side, they were asked to cover 50 per cent of the total projected volume with annual purchase agreements which would be backed up by firm supply contracts with the member mills. Seaboard frankly acknowledged that situations might arise which would prevent buyers from taking their monthly allocated quantity, and it was prepared to accept this position.

Psychologically, Seaboard's interim efforts to put the buyers' minds at ease were well-directed because they demonstrated an earnest attempt to co-operate and maintain a mutually viable sales structure. However, buyers' purchasing power was still suffering from the destructive events of 1969 and they were disinclined to commit themselves to any plan, no matter how attractive it might appear, and sales to the U.S. continued to be depressed.

At the same time that the interim marketing strategy was placed in position, work began on the preparation of a long-range marketing plan. The Boston Consulting Group was commissioned to conduct an in-depth study of Seaboard's situation on the U.S. East Coast.

The group noted that although markets change inevitably, organizational behavior often does not, failing or refusing to adapt to changing conditions. Specifically they proposed to focus on "the near term problem at the wholesale level of distribution." Part of their study method was to interview both retailers and wholesalers, concentrating on an area extending from Boston to Baltimore within 100 miles of the Atlantic coastline. Response from these two groups was positive and cooperative, since they recognized that anything Seaboard could do to solve a growing competitive problem would work to the advantage of all.

It is interesting to note that Weyerhaeuser declined to take part in these interviews for reasons that were not clearly stated, and in spite of the fact that they remained Seaboard's largest U.S. buyer. The 1969 sales debacle, undoubtedly triggered by Weyerhaeuser, could not be regarded by Seaboard as a maliciously contrived strategy. The big American buyer had simply done what was neccessary to survive in a falling market.

Weyerhaeuser was large enough and financially strong enough to withstand the attrition of the crash, and when the market regained a sufficient degree of stability, its trading relationship with Seaboard continued as before, serving as the mainstay in the U.S. market. Seaboard's other principal buyers at that time, in various stages of recovery and solvency, were: A. C. Dutton, a long established, family-run company with a strong sales force but with a dwindling management base; Furman Lumber Company, with marginal capitalization but an aggressive sales force and strong middle management; Timberlane Lumber Company, a company that had enjoyed success as a rail wholesaler, only to founder badly in the cargo business; Shepard and Morse, a smaller, old-line New England firm with an older staff and conservative approaches, and a list of Brooklyn wholesalers serving metro New York. One of these, Abe Meltzer, would spread his wings in later years and become a millowner in British Columbia. Another company dealing with Seaboard in a small way, Futter Lumber Company Limited, was destined to figure more significantly in the U.S. East Coast customer mix.

In 1970 A. C. Dutton gave Seaboard the opportunity to purchase it outright, an offer which Seaboard decided to forgo. Timberlane, although in financial distress and possessed of limited free equity, was under long-term contract to Seaboard. The Brooklyn wholesalers would deal with Seaboard if the price was right, but many of them did most of their business with MacMillan Bloedel.

The changing nature of the distribution system was key to Seaboard's success or failure in the U.S. market after 1969. The number of lumber retailers had been declining for the better part of a decade. Figures from the U.S. Department of Commerce reveal that 34,867 lumber retailers registered in 1958 had been reduced to 24,296 by 1967. The greatest decline was among the ranks of the smaller in-city yards, referred to traditionally as the "spot buyers," who purchased lumber from wholesalers' inventory when they needed it. Further inland, and also reduced in numbers, were the large framing yards, accustomed to carry large inventories because of their distance from the Atlantic Coast ports.

After 1969, partly because of the losses incurred at that time which made the assembly of large inventories difficult and worrisome, and principally because Blanchard and Weyerhaeuser carried large inventories, marketed aggressively and were prepared to deliver off the dock, the retail operators ceased to deal with their previously favoured wholesalers. The result was that the wholesalers had to strike out in other directions or go out of business. A few, in fact, did suffer bankruptcy. Others adopted a cautious stance and reduced inventories drastically or switched from cargo business to rail, attracted by lower rail rates and a growing number of Canadian mills electing to ship by this method.

Seaboard found itself the target of open suspicion aimed by wholesalers who stated that Seaboard must be favouring Weyerhaeuser with prices so low that the American company could sell retail at the wholesaler's purchase price. Seaboard's efforts to persuade them that Weyerhaeuser, as usual, was simply determined to maintain market share at any cost, was anything but comforting. How could any conventional wholesaler cope with this kind of competition?

Blanchard, for instance, proved its willingness to take large losses in the short term in order to attract retailers away from their long-time wholesale suppliers. The Boston Consulting Group's advice was that Blanchard's aggressive marketing strategy on behalf of MacMillan Bloedel must be matched by Weyerhaeuser's similar efforts on behalf of Seaboard. The comparison, of course, was not accurate. MacMillan Bloedel owned Blanchard; Seaboard did not own Weyerhaeuser, nor was there any possibility that it would. And the price Seaboard would have to pay for an aggressive alliance with Weyerhaeuser would be, at least, the commitment of a larger share of Seaboard lumber.

In the opinion of the Boston Consulting Group, Seaboard had three options: one was to continue with its established system, with the expectation that its market share would continue to decline and distribution outlets would continue to diminish (Dutton and Furman let it be known that under these circumstances they would withdraw from the cargo business entirely); to form a wholesale company, which would place Seaboard in direct competition with Weyerhaeuser, or to introduce policies to reduce the wholesalers' perceived risks. These would include formalized price rollbacks, with Seaboard prepared to absorb losses during market depressions, and the introduction of a variable commission formula, which would oblige Seaboard to revise prices on all invoices and subsidize the wholesalers' inventory stocking costs.

Of the three courses of action, the consulting group recommended the second, to be phased in gradually, starting with the existing system and adding a price protection plan, accumulating an inventory of unsold lumber, and establishing a marketing office to sell it. Following this, a joint venture marketing organization would be established, supplanting the present system and offering long-term price and supply agreements. Finally, a selling force would be placed in position to market unsold inventory to retailers.

The report was presented to Seaboard's member mills and management in May 1970, and it is interesting to observe that, as with the case of the survey and report conducted by the United Kingdom consultants, the response of Seaboard and its members was far from positive. The general consensus was that the consultants had adopted an unduly pessimistic stance.

From the consultants' point of view Seaboard's members shared an unfounded conviction that there was a major backlog in demand for housing in the U.S., in particular the Eastern Seaboard. A wry observation was that Seaboard's confidence in the possibility of this kind of an upturn was considerably stronger than that felt on the East Coast. Their stated reasons for a more cautious attitude were based on the expressed commitment of the U.S. Department of Housing and Urban Development to nonwood construction, coupled with the likelihood of continuing high interest rates and the changing pattern of residential construction, which was moving out to the U.S. suburbs and away from the ports and the inner city areas.

Nevertheless, Seaboard's decision was that it should not be unduly influenced by the report of the Boston Consulting Group, but regard it as information input from which the company could draw if neccessary. In the meantime it was recommended that Ted Cameron, who had by now transferred to the New York office, work with Reg Barclay on the assembly of a long-term U.S. strategy report.

We have dealt at some length with the introduction of Seaboard's short- and long-range plans because their devising and application are indicative of the company's difficult but essential struggle to replace old and comfortable thinking with new and unfamiliar approaches. It was a time of administrative and marketing revolution without which process Seaboard might conceivably have been reduced to a much weakened force, if not consigned to gradual oblivion. Following this, the company entered a period where the incompatibility between established management and new strategies manifested itself as a prelude to Seaboard's present modus operandi. The time of rugged individualism and intelligent guesstimates was over. The successful management of companies and corporations was becoming more of an exact science subject to measurable checks and balances served by new technological tools which included the computer. Presidents and managers were less likely to be mill men of the old school and more likely to be honours graduates in business administration with several years of successful experience behind them.

FIFTEEN

THE TURBULENT
SEVENTIES

When L. L. G. Bentley retired as Seaboard's chairman in 1970, he removed from Harry O'Hagan's side the strength and support of a persuasive, like-thinking ally with an acknowledged flair for individual decision making. Bentley's position was taken over by Gary S. J. Bowell, a man of a considerably different stripe and background. Bowell, a Rhodes scholar, was president of Weldwood of Canada, with his experience in the British Columbia forest products industry reaching back into the top ranks of the Mac-Millan Bloedel organization.

One of the recommendations made by the McKinsey group in 1962, when it examined MacMillan, Bloedel and Powell River's production and administration procedures, was that the huge organization should be consolidated into four principal groups, each virtually autonomous and a profit centre in its own right. Bowell, because of his training and experience as a marketing specialist, was selected to become vice-president and general manager of the pulp and paper group. He was closely acquainted with the organizational changes inspired by the McKinsey consultants, and had an opportunity to observe the operation of the new principles before he was attracted to Weldwood with the offer of top management responsiblities. He was marketing oriented in the most contemporary sense.

At Seaboard's annual meeting in January 1971, Bowell and O'Hagan held forth. Harry O'Hagan reported sales well below normal for the second year in a row, and also stated that weaker prices had resulted in a decrease in value of sales from $175 million to $160 million. He pointed out that the U.S. government move to reduce inflation had caused a scarcity of housing money and lowered the demand for construction materials. With the U.S. market representing 45 per cent of Seaboard's total exports, any decline there must be regarded with concern. Bowell, in his first statement as chairman, expressed hope that the company would improve its situation in the coming year. He felt that 1971 would be a year of recovery, but not a bonanza by any means.

The B.C. lumber industry had been hurt by a succession of labour disputes starting with a longshoremen's strike early in 1970, followed by a six-week towboat strike, then a pulp and paper workers' strike and protracted negotiations with the International Woodworkers during which the danger of a strike loomed large. Added to labour problems was the unpredicted escalation of shipping charter rates, soaring in 1970 to the highest level since the Korean war. Sales to Japan had come to a virtual halt; and the heaviest blow of all was the revaluation of Canadian currency in June 1970, when an increase in the value of the Canadian dollar took up to 8 per cent from the company's annual returns.

In the United Kingdom the sales performance had been somewhat better. Seaboard International Limited had enjoyed an improvement of 71 per cent over the previous year although at unattractive prices compared to those commanded in the United States. Dick Dobell and his management and sales team were directing all their energies to the increase of existing business and to the acquisition of new buyers. Clive Roberts was demonstrating an impressive talent for sales performance as head of the plywood sales department.

Meanwhile, O'Hagan's and Bowell's expressed hope for recovery in 1971 was hardly realized. At the annual meeting in January 1972, O'Hagan had to report no increase in sales over 1971, in spite of a minimum of labour disturbances. The ongoing campaign to gain the support and the co-operation of the member mills for new marketing strategies remained a confidential matter to which the news media were not privy.

The executive committee was pressing strenuously for commitment to a plan devised jointly by Bob Edgett and Reg Barclay in collaboration with the lumber advisory committee. Having established a planned export lumber volume by product and market for each mill, Seaboard would ask each mill to commit for sale specific quantities and specifications for agreed shipping periods. These commitments would be made on the basis of the established or customary buying pattern for the product and market. In the East Coast market, for example, the normal buying pattern was monthly, thirty to sixty days prior to the month of shipment. Under the new plan, mills would be asked to commit their planned U.S. volume ninety days prior to the month of shipment, and the lumber would be offered for sale at the competitive price levels prevailing or expected to prevail for the shipment offered. However, in the case of the U.S. market, it was anticipated that a significant portion, up to 50 per cent of the annual volume, would be distributed under annual purchase agreements, calling for Seaboard to guarantee supply at competitive prices for a year ahead. In this case the mills would be asked to back up such arrangements with supply commitments for the coming year. Pricing would be monthly, in line with the prevailing competitive market, and the mills would be expected to adhere to their commitment even if they did not consider the price to be attractive.

Specifically, each mill was asked to supply a planned volume of lumber annually to each overseas market it chose to serve, specifying species, grades and dimensions. This, in effect, would be the mill's annual export marketing plan, and it would be arrived at in close co-operation with Seaboard's supply division. Seaboard's reasonable argument for projecting this plan was that it was in a position at all times to seek out and secure the best prevailing price for its members.

Each overseas market was subject to its own array of external and internal forces and methods of buying and selling. In the United Kingdom, for instance, Scandinavia and Russia were stern competitors; shipping patterns and pricing methods differed radically from those in the United States market. Seaboard was keenly aware of all this and professionally staffed to deal with the vagaries of each market—but only if it had the freedom and authority to do so.

With few exceptions the mills were not prepared to accept the principle of committing specific quantities of lumber to specific markets except on a firm order. From Seaboard's inception, the member mills had always exercised their rights to decide when to sell, how much to sell and for what shipping period. They could also accept or reject an order on the basis of price; and they could withhold supply or change their product or their market mix.

The mills had the right, under their sale agreements, to second-guess Seaboard on timing of sales, on volumes, on shipping positions and specifications ... and they did not hesitate to exercise that right

whenever it seemed advantageous to do so. Under this arrangement
Seaboard was vulnerable to the individual judgement calls of the entire
mill membership. What Seaboard now wanted in essence was for the
mills to relinquish a number of their traditional rights and responsibilities and place them in the hands of Seaboard.

There was much to be said for a system that allowed for advanced
production planning, better inventory control, a regular flow of shipments, an efficient and co-ordinated sales effort in every market and
substantial savings in shipping. There was built-in protection against
cyclical price swings; and it appeared that the mills could expect a
better average annual return. Certainly the plan would secure good
market share positions.

On the other hand, and this was a matter of strong concern, the mills
would relinquish part of their time-honoured right to trade individually
for the highest price. Some of their freedom and flexibility would be
removed. And, of course, another administrative task would be imposed on them: the need to plan meticulously and to gear mill production to long-range scheduled commitments.

Even if they did subscribe to the plan and lived up to its requirements,
would Seaboard be able to deliver the accurate forecasting called for?
Was the company as professionally capable as it purported to be? Seaboard was asking for an unaccustomed degree of autonomy and freedom of action, not the least of which was the right to establish the
selling price in any market. Price was the sacred prerogative of the mill;
that is the way it had always been. Some of the larger Seaboard mills
such as Crown Zellerbach and Rayonier went on record as supporting
the plan as early as January 1971, but the majority of the member mills
needed to weigh the odds. The ferment surrounding the development of
long-range marketing strategy remained vigorous.

One of the inducements used to persuade Dobell to become the first
manager of Seaboard International had been an unofficial understanding that as soon as the U.K. company was on a solid operating basis, he
would return to Vancouver as the ultimate successor to Harry O'Hagan. This arrangement may have appeared to be unfair to Bob Edgett,
who had laboured long and effectively on behalf of the company, but
from a long-range administrative point-of-view, Edgett had age working against him no matter how vigorous and forward-reaching his performance continued to be. Today he states that he never had any presidential expectations. "The presidential succession was set back in
1953," he says. "Harry O'Hagan was senior in service and position. We
worked well together under Claude's management, and I had no unrealistic ambitions as to my ultimate position with the company."

Edgett was an energetic innovator, always prepared to relinquish outmoded systems and replace them with better strategies. In fact he often demonstrated his impatience by taking the initiative in the exploration of innovative marketing techniques. O'Hagan, on the other hand, revealed a strong tendency to remain with tried and true methodology. What had worked before would continue to work, in spite of temporary setbacks. It is generally acknowledged that he resisted with considerable stubbornness the urgings and the opinions of his president's committee regarding long-range marketing strategy. He gave small encouragement to those who wished to depart from the status quo. This attitude did much to stalemate the completion of a long-range marketing plan.

Also, while his mandate as president was for the company's worldwide operations, he spent a large proportion of time dealing with the problems of the U.S. market. This can be understood if we remember that this was the market he was most familiar with, and which he had built into Seaboard's single largest buyer. He identified with its current dilemmas perhaps to the disadvantage of Seaboard's other markets. Still, he was president. He had earned the loyalty of the member mills, most of which remained supportive even in the troubled period of the 1969 crash. In 1972, had his effectiveness been put to a vote, there is little doubt that he would have received the endorsement of the majority.

Dick Dobell felt obliged to align himself with the person most likely to advance his position with the company. Under the circumstances it seemed apparent that O'Hagan, because of his official position, and because he had the ear of the member mills, was the man to cultivate, this in spite of the fact that most of Dobell's day-to-day dealings were with Bob Edgett. When Edgett's policies were not in accord with O'Hagan's, Dobell acceded to the latter. As 1972 came to a close, Dobell was summoned back from the United Kingdom and given the position of general manager, Seaboard lumber and shingle/shake sales. Edgett remained vice-president, marketing.

In the United Kingdom, Clive Roberts took over as managing director of Seaboard International, having performed with evident success as director for plywood sales. Very early he proved to be a self-starter accustomed to conceiving new sales ideas and pressing them aggressively. "I was pleased to have been given management of Seaboard International," he states today, "and I must admit that I wasn't too surprised; I felt that I was in line for the position, and I had quite definite ideas as to what I proposed to do with the organization. One was to strengthen the sales force."

Seaboard International consisted of some fifty individuals, sales personnel principally working out of the head office in London and a branch office in Liverpool. Among them was the venerable George Taylor, now at the end of his working years and positioned as a director of the company in charge of industrial sales. In Roberts's opinion, while Taylor's presence with SIL was constructive and building, the same could not be said for all of those employed in SIL's formative years. "Seaboard attempted to fill the ranks of Seaboard International by hiring or appointing from the companies that had once been its agents—as an act of appeasement perhaps. It didn't always work. In my estimation the criterion in building a sales force must be proven experience and performance, and you track down the best talent available wherever you can find it."

Whatever Clive Roberts's intentions might have been to further improve the performance of Seaboard International, he had little opportunity to do so. A series of events was destined to change the lives of several including Roberts himself. As Seaboard entered 1973, O'Hagan's annual report to the directors was far from salutary. The hoped-for upswing in U.S. sales had not occurred, nor were there any firm signs of resurgence that he could point to in the immediate future. Sales in the other export markets were not compensating for this depressed condition either in volume or price. In fact, while Seaboard's competitors had succeeded in filling contracts with Japan for the first two quarters of 1973, Seaboard was still in the process of selling for the first quarter. "It was quite apparent," Clive Roberts says, "that Seaboard was losing its share of the market, and there didn't seem to be any plan in place to turn this situation around. The long-range U.S. marketing strategy was not yet formulated and, in the minds of many of the directors, this was long overdue. Management was not acting in a decisive manner, and frustration amongst the mills was spreading."

In January of that year Seaboard, whose success depended on the largest possible mill membership, lost ten mills for a variety of reasons: Acorn Forest Products, Swanson Lumber Company, Pacific Pine Company, McKay & Flanagan Bros. Lumber Mill, Evans Products Company, R. B. McLean Lumber Company, and Timber Preservers. While very few of these left because of disenchantment with Seaboard, their departure was still worrisome.

In February 1973 G. S. J. Bowell stepped down as chairman of Seaboard and his position was filled by R. G. Rogers, chief executive officer of Crown Zellerbach, later to become the lieutenant governor of British Columbia. He was a very experienced executive, keenly concerned to extricate Seaboard from threatening paralysis and determined to take positive action. He was willing to take considered and intelligent advice from any authoritative source, and the president's advisory committee constituted just such a resource.

The committee, consisting of Robert McMillan (Crown Zellerbach), Bryce P. Page (Weldwood), Noel Harrison (Rayonier) and Mike Robson (Canadian Forest Products), was hampered in its efforts to work in tandem with Harry O'Hagan, no matter how constructive the intentions. O'Hagan was simply unaccustomed to operating in this fashion. He regarded the presence of a president's committee as an unnecessary interference and an encroachment on his authority, and was unable to satisfy them that he was making or would make critical decision calls. The situation was stalemated.

Then the unexpected happened once more, and once more Weyerhaeuser was the instigator. While O'Hagan listened to those directors who worried over Seaboard's vulnerability vis à vis Weyerhaeuser, his inclination was to change nothing even though he is on record, on the eve of the unexpected ultimatum, as feeling that a large commitment to Weyerhaeuser placed Seaboard in danger.   On 27 June 1973 Weyerhaeuser announced that, in order to continue in the cargo buying business, it would have to ask for substantial discounts in lumber prices; otherwise it would be obliged to discontinue cargo in favour of rail. While Weyerhaeuser might have had a moral commitment to continue to purchase large volumes from Seaboard, and while Seaboard had already committed large volumes in advance to Weyerhaeuser at prices it was now asked to discount, the ultimatum was firm and irrevocable.

Seaboard could not, and would not, yield to Weyerhaeuser's demand and, in due course, Weyerhaeuser ceased to engage in cargo business, leaving Seaboard with thousands of feet of lumber unshipped to the Eastern Seaboard unpaid for and without a buyer in sight. In the short term Seaboard had to withhold payment from the member mills who had supplied the U.S. lumber. Only the smaller, marginal mills received payment in order to keep them in business until Seaboard could restore some balance in the U.S. market and arrange for bank financing to survive the crisis.

It was a dark period for Seaboard and one from which O'Hagan failed to emerge. In August Harry O'Hagan submitted his resignation, generous arrangements having been made for his early retirement. In retrospect it can be said that a superb sales executive became the victim of changing times and unpredictable circumstances.

That same month Clive Roberts arrived in Vancouver to attend a plywood symposium organized by Seaboard's member plywood mills.

Within a day of his arrival, Bob McMillan, representing the advisory committee, asked him to attend a meeting in the office of Seaboard's chairman, R. G. Rogers. "At the time it posed difficulties for me," Roberts admits. "Harry O'Hagan wanted me at a management meeting at the same time. As far as I was concerned he was president and I had no reason to believe otherwise. Bob McMillan and Bob Edgett managed to extricate me from Harry's meeting, and I went over to Roger's office, wondering what could be sufficiently important to call for my attendance."

Arrived in the chairman's office, Roberts found himself in the company of Rogers and Crown Zellerbach's executive vice-president, Richard Nelson, who engaged him in a friendly conversation to no apparent purpose. "I think we may have started with a discussion of the weather," Roberts states. "Later they got around to my activities with Seaboard International, asked my opinion on certain aspects of the U.K. market and talked about business in general. When the meeting concluded I was still quite in the dark. As I stood to go, Rogers asked me to remain behind for a moment. Privately he told me that Harry O'Hagan was resigning and that I was being offered the position of president of Seaboard. I couldn't have been more surprised."

Roberts accepted the offer before week's end, and Seaboard management was informed of the appointment. For Dick Dobell it was a shocking revelation to find that the man he had hired as an employee of Seaboard International was about to become the president of Seaboard, the position to which he had aspired.

Clive Roberts returned to the United Kingdom to put his affairs in order and to gather his family and possessions together for the move to Vancouver. This took the better part of two months, during which time Harry Berry served as Seaboard's interim president. On 10 September 1973 Harry O'Hagan's resignation was accepted, and in October Clive Roberts returned to Vancouver to assume the responsibilities of president and chief executive officer of Seaboard Lumber Sales and Seaboard Shipping.

*   *   *

The choice of Clive Roberts as president of Seaboard came as a surprise to many. It had become accepted procedure for Seaboard presidents to earn or inherit the position by reason of long tenure and proven performance within the organization. Claude Effinger had succeeded Charles Grinnell; Harry O'Hagan had taken over from Effinger by right of earned succession. Bob Edgett, qualified in terms of length of tenure, and management performance, was eliminated by time, and had made it known that he wished to retire at the age of sixty.

Clive Roberts was a relative newcomer, familiar with Seaboard's operational procedures but sufficiently detached from the old guard to be able to be objective in his decision making. He had not had time to become immersed in Seaboard's established operational procedures and therefore would have less difficulty in discarding any procedure that had become redundant or unproductive. His own performance with Seaboard International had been impressive, revealing a talent for innovation and a willingness to take initiative. He had served in the Royal Navy and had been appointed Lieutenant Commander in the Royal Naval Reserve, Active List in 1966, a position that attested to leadership qualities. If Seaboard was going to find a president within its own organization, Clive Roberts appeared to be the best choice. Failing that, a search would begin outside the company. "When Rogers offered me the presidency," Roberts says, "he stated that if I was unable to accept they would look beyond Seaboard for a suitable person. In terms of familiarity with Seaboard, I felt that I had a head start on anyone they might find."

While Claude Effinger and Harry O'Hagan had taken up their presidential positions in relatively buoyant times untroubled by crises of any significant proportion, Roberts stepped into a more complicated scene. To begin with, there was the matter of top management. His lieutenants were all senior people close to retirement and divided in their allegiances and attitudes. Vassall Forrester, general manager of Seaboard Shipping since 1956, and vice-president since 1968, went into retirement 1 January 1973 to be succeeded by his second-in-command during that entire period, Murray Mather. Mather himself was only two years away from retirement.

Harry Berry was due to retire in September 1976, Dick Silbernagel in January 1974, Tom Ferris in December 1975 and Bill Whiles in April 1976. If nothing else was changing Seaboard, time was. Very quickly Roberts made his first appointments. Harry Berry was made senior vice-president and secretary of the company. Dick Dobell accepted the post of vice-president, lumber; Doug Reid remained vice-president, plywood, and Bob Edgett took over as managing director of Seaboard International in the United Kingdom, choosing this rather than vice-president, marketing second to Clive Roberts in Vancouver. Obviously a number of these appointments would not last long, but they gave Roberts the time he needed to find successors.

An administrative overhaul was not the only issue to occupy

Roberts's attention. In October 1973 the shipping world was hit by a fuel crisis which did not exclude Seaboard in any respect. Roberts and his colleagues at that time are not likely to forget the experience. "The OPEC nations created instant chaos," he recalls. "The price of bunkers went from $3 a barrel to $26 a barrel overnight. Our order file was based on oil at the old rates and everyone was scrambling to find existing supplies. At one time we were literally unable to find enough oil to get our ships across the Pacific." Seaboard's executive committee minutes of 21 November 1973 record that the company would have five ships in Japan without fuel by December, and that the decision was made not to take any new or outside business until the world fuel crisis had levelled off.

Seaboard, like every other similar company, was forced to search every corner of the world to secure oil supplies while struggling to anticipate and allow for price fluctuations. At one point Seaboard considered purchasing an old tanker, sending it wherever bunkers were to be had, and filling it up to serve as a floating reservoir for the company's vessels. This plan was sidelined when British Columbia's Council of Forest Industries established an oil group to secure oil supplies through the concerted influence of the entire industry, which helped to assuage the situation. Seaboard received additional assistance through the efforts of Esso, B.C., whose manager, J. Leyland, extended himself tirelessly on Seaboard's behalf.

In an interview with the business editor of the *Province* in February 1974, Roberts stated that higher costs generated principally by the oil crisis had added $8 per thousand board feet to the cost of lumber delivered to the United States, and $12 per thousand to United Kingdom and continental exports. The company exported 907 million board feet in 1973 compared to 935 million in the previous year. On the other hand plywood sales increased to 280 million square feet compared to 250 million in 1972 and 185 million in 1971. He pointed out that in spite of the serious problems created by the escalation of oil costs, Seaboard had not missed a shipment.

In April 1974, when Seaboard's president issued his annual report, he was able to announce the company's highest sales dollar volume ever, for 1973, in excess of $200 million. In spite of this, the returns to the member mills were down because of sharply rising costs.

Roberts stated that one of his principal objectives was to increase Seaboard's membership and thus the volume of lumber available for export, citing this as one of the strengths the company had to offer. He stressed his determination to introduce a long-range marketing plan at the earliest moment possible. At the time of the February interview Seaboard had sixteen member companies on its list: Bay Forest Products Ltd., Brownsville Sawmills Ltd., Canadian Forest Products Ltd., Crown Zellerbach Canada Ltd., Eurocan Pulp and Paper Company Ltd., Field Sawmills Ltd., L & K Lumber (North Shore) Ltd., McDonald Cedar Products Ltd., Overseas Spruce Sales Ltd., Plumper Bay Sawmills Ltd., Raven Lumber Ltd., Rayonier Canada (B.C.) Ltd., Richmond Plywood Corporation Ltd, Weldwood of Canada Ltd, Western Forest Industries Ltd., and Whonnock Lumber Company Ltd.

Early in 1974 Roberts began to make top management changes, starting with the appointment of a new shipping manager in the person of Clyde Jacobs. Murray Mather was due for retirement in September and Roberts wanted to have his successor in position for a period of indoctrination in company with Mather; as a result, Jacobs took up his duties as vice-president, shipping in May. He was not elevated from Seaboard's ranks but was chosen from candidates outside the company. He received his early schooling in Yakima, Washington, going on to the U.S. Merchant Marine Academy in New York where he obtained his Bachelor of Science in Marine Transportation. Practical experience was gained as a chief mate sailing in the U.S. Merchant Marine, and he proceeded from there to the U.S. Navy during the Korean war, serving with the rank of Lieutenant Commander U.S.N.R. In 1955 he joined Crown Zellerbach Corporation in San Francisco, learning all facets of that company's traffic and transportation systems. By 1973 he was in charge of traffic and transportation; and in that year he formed his own consulting company, heading it for one year before coming to Seaboard.

At the same time, an executive who had joined Seaboard Lumber Sales in 1968 as office manager was appointed vice-president, finance. L. R. (Larry) Ridenour began his career in 1962 as a chartered accountant with Peat, Marwick, Mitchell & Company in Vancouver, continuing his studies towards a Master of Business Administration, a degree he completed in 1973. Familiarity with the forest products industry was gained with Columbia Cellulose Company Ltd. (now B.C. Timber Ltd.) in Vancouver. He joined that company in 1966 as supervisor of accounting and treasury assistant. At Seaboard he advanced steadily, becoming divisional controller in 1969, corporate controller in 1971, treasurer in 1973 and vice-president, finance in 1974.

Rounding out the management team as it exists today, E. A. (Ted) Cameron, a British Columbian born into a forest products family and with a Bachelor of Commerce degree (Forestry Option) from the University of British Columbia, came straight to Seaboard from the university in 1962, starting in the plywood division under Doug Reid. A year later he was placed in charge of interior spruce sales for all markets, proceeding from there to western red cedar sales for all markets. In 1966 he moved to market planning, working with Reg Barclay on market research. When Seaboard International was formed in 1967, he joined Dick Dobell, handling sales development and research and in 1971 moved to the New York office. He returned to Vancouver in late 1974, after Ken Sloat retired and the New York office was closed, to work on the implementation plan for the U.S. strategy.

In 1975, he was appointed vice-president, lumber sales, the position held by Dick Dobell. Bob Edgett, managing director of Seaboard International, was one year removed from retirement, and Clive Roberts offered Dobell the opportunity to take over from Edgett. Dobell, feeling the move to be retrogressive, chose to phase out of the company, taking early retirement.

When Harry Berry's retirement day occurred in September 1976, Reg Barclay was appointed corporate secretary for both Seaboard Lumber Sales and Seaboard Shipping. Dudley Darling was appointed general manager, distribution, reporting to Clyde Jacobs.

Doug Reid continued as vice-president, plywood sales until his untimely death 24 December 1978. He had distinguished himself in his years in plywood sales, and had been largely instrumental in the accelerating sales of that product in the world markets.

His successor, Colin Brock, was born in England and received his first experience in lumber products sales with Denny, Mott & Dickson in London. His years with this large and prestigious importer of lumber and plywood familiarized him thoroughly with both importing and selling to the U.K. trade. He emigrated to Vancouver in 1957 where he commenced a business administration course at the University of British Columbia, combining this with employment at Seaboard in September of the same year. After a short period in the documents department he was transferred to the plywood division as assistant to Doug Reid. Except for a six-month period in 1962, when he went to Seaboard's London office as plywood representative pending the establishment of Seaboard International, he worked with Seaboard's plywood division, becoming sales manager upon Reid's demise, and receiving the promotion to vice-president, plywood sales in 1980.

These six—Reg Barclay, Colin Brock, Ted Cameron, Dudley Darling, Clyde Jacobs and Larry Ridenour—together with Clive Roberts constituted Seaboard's senior management group. In company with Seaboard's executive committee and the lumber, plywood and shingle consulting committees drawn from the ranks of the member mills, they enacted the changes that have occurred in Seaboard's organization since 1973.

The restructuring of Seaboard's overseas organization began shortly after Clive Roberts took office. The studies and surveys conducted by the Boston Consulting Group and Barclay, Cameron and Edgett were drawn upon, refined, modified and tailored to conditions specific to each market. In 1973 Seaboard's sales office in Sydney, Australia, was made a wholly owned subsidiary, with a staff of three headed by Alan Gardner. Gardner had succeeded Frank Solloway in the Sydney office in 1957. Now he became managing director of the Seaboard subsidiary, a position he held until he was replaced by Ron A. McLaine in 1977.

The trend to replace agencies and sales offices with subsidiaries, first demonstrated with the formation of Seaboard International in the United Kingdom, and now in Australia, would continue as the opportunities presented themselves. South Africa was an exception.

From its beginning, Seaboard had worked energetically to develop healthy trade relations with that country, competing with the Baltic and Scandinavian exporters who were the traditional suppliers. The executive committee minutes of 10 February 1948 record Tom Ferris's report of eleven months spent in South Africa studying the market and developing business. The company appointed an agency to represent its interests: African & Overseas Traders (Pty.) Ltd., Capetown. Managing director of that company was E. C. (Kit) Candler, an experienced lumber sales executive. For the next few years Candler dedicated himself to the promotion of Seaboard's British Columbia lumber products to the extent that he was offered and accepted the position as Seaboard's sales representative and manager of the Seaboard office in Johannesburg, which the company set up in 1954. While Tom Ferris directed South Africa sales from the Vancouver office, Candler processed the business and at the same time opened a branch office in Capetown. By 1955 Ferris was able to report a marked improvement in sales. In his opinion the branch office method of selling was much superior to selling through an agency.

Kit Candler managed Seaboard's affairs in South Africa until 1962 when he opened a Seaboard office in Geneva, Switzerland. His position in South Africa was filled by A. P. L. Tottenham, who continued to do business under increasingly difficult conditions, impeded by import controls, monetary restrictions, keen competition from the European exporters and slow acceptance of B.C. wood species. Added to this was the growing success of South Africa's forestry program; domestic plantations were beginning to supply much of the country's forest products needs.

In 1974 Seaboard attempted to improve its situation by setting up a subsidiary staffed with a sales force authorized to deal directly with all categories of buyers. At the same time, emulating the successful introduction of a new product started by Clive Roberts while with Seaboard International, a line of Far East hardwoods was added to Seaboard's South Africa inventory—to small avail. When Tottenham died suddenly in 1976, Seaboard had little incentive to continue in business in that market. All offices were closed summarily, and Seaboard has done relatively little business with South Africa since that time.

The decision to establish a wholly owned sales subsidiary in the United States, first considered back in 1970 in the aftermath of the '69 crash, was made finally in November 1974 when Seaboard International Lumber and Plywood, Inc. came into being. R. W. Kirkham, formerly vice-president of Triangle Pacific Corporation, was appointed president, and he continued expanding the buyers' list in every category and replacing and increasing business once provided by Weyerhaeuser and the other cargo buyers.

Clive Roberts, determined to extricate Seaboard from its market planning impasse, had much to do with the formation of the United States sales subsidiary. Using this as ammunition, he embarked on a vigorous program of mill recruitment with two objectives in mind: one, to compensate for attrition in the ranks of the member mills, and the other, to increase Seaboard's export volume.

In 1975, there were twenty-one members of Seaboard: Ainsworth Lumber, Brownsville Sawmills, Canadian Forest Products, Bay Forest, Carrier Lumber, Crown Zellerbach Canada, Dunkley Lumber, Eurocan Pulp & Paper, Gregory Industries, L & K Lumber, McDonald Cedar Products, Northwest Shake, Plumper Bay, Prince Rupert Forest Products, Raven Lumber, Rayonier Canada (B.C.), Richmond Plywood, Rustad Brothers, Weldwood of Canada, Western Forest Industries and Whonnock Lumber. The roster had increased by four since February 1974. Between 1975 and 1981 eight companies joined Seaboard: Clearwater Timber Products, Imp-Pac Lumber, Jacobson Bros. Forest Products, Lignum, Orion Bowman, Pacific Forest Products, Slocan Forest Products and Sooke Forest Products (returned in 1976). Of these, five were companies that owned interior mills.

(Within this mill line-up, a series of acquisitions serves to point up the complexity of Seaboard's member relationships. Whonnock Lumber Company Limited had joined Seaboard in 1952 as a medium-sized mill.

Pacific Pine Company Limited became a member of Seaboard in 1945. When New York wholesaler Abe Meltzer broadened his empire to include home construction, he formed a company called Triangle Pacific Forest Products Limited. In order to safeguard his source of lumber supply in British Columbia, he purchased the Pacific Pine Sawmill in 1970, withdrawing it from Seaboard membership in 1973. Meanwhile, Whonnock Lumber Company had been purchased by Whonnock Industries Limited, and this company proceeded to expand its holdings further with the acquisition of Holding Lumber Company Limited, a B.C. interior mill, and the purchase of Pacific Pine from Meltzer in 1976. In 1977 Sauder Industries Limited acquired controlling interest in Whonnock Industries, contingent on Whonnock's purchase of McDonald Cedar Products and Bay Forest Products, two of Seaboard's established members. Chester A. Johnson, who had been one of the prime movers in Whonnock Industries, was a Seaboard director from 1977 to 1979 and served on the executive committee. In 1980 W. L. Sauder became Whonnock Industries' Seaboard director and a member of the executive committee, positions which he holds at present. As a result of these acquisitions, Whonnock Industries is at the moment Seaboard's single largest shareholder.)

Seaboard's agent in Japan was the next focus of Roberts's attention. Until June 1974 the firm of Aall & Company had represented Seaboard's interests in Japan, a function it performed with considerable success. While Seaboard's inclination in this period of reformation was to dispense with agents in favour of sales subsidiaries, a different formula was tried in the case of Japan. Aall & Company were offered participation in a joint venture with Seaboard, an opportunity which they decided to forgo. Seaboard advised them that their services would be dispensed with in ninety days and began the process of establishing a subsidiary company.

The timing was opportune since changes in the Japanese building code had just occurred bringing it in line with Canada's national grading rule. The significance of this to British Columbia's lumber industry was that it could now begin to introduce Japanese buyers and builders to the use of dressed lumber and finished lumber products. Up until this time Japan had been interested almost exclusively in "baby squares"— timbers 4 inches square—and in medium squares—timbers 12 inches square. Dressed lumber represented a mere 5 per cent of the market. The change in code cleared the way for an intensive selling program and justified the formation of a sales subsidiary. Seaboard Timber & Plywood Asia Ltd. opened its doors in November 1974 under the direction of Steven Kaufman.

Before joining Seaboard, Kaufman had been first commercial secretary for the Canadian government in Hong Kong and then in Tokyo. Well-equipped for his new task, he spoke two Chinese dialects as well as fluent Japanese, and had worked closely with the Japanese Ministry of Construction to set up an education program on Canadian construction methods, particularly woodframe construction as specified by British Columbia's Council of Forest Industries. In Kaufman's opinion the Japanese market would remain static until Canadian lumber products were upgraded, and he pressed for quality production from Seaboard's member mills.

The year 1975 was not a banner one either for Seaboard or for the B.C. lumber industry. Ted Cameron in an interview with *B.C. Business Magazine* in March 1976 stated that 1975 was the worst year in recent history for lumber sales, an admission which Clive Roberts corroborated in April when he gave his annual report. He observed that sales and shipments of lumber and plywood from the B.C. coast reached a thirteen-year low in 1975.

The report revealed that because of strikes in British Columbia and depressed demand for lumber in the overseas markets, the value of wood products shipments handled by Seaboard had been reduced to $145 million, compared to $231 million in 1974. Nevertheless, Seaboard succeeded in increasing its share of all B.C. waterborne shipments to 40 per cent, the largest single amount of any lumber exporting entity. As well, it was able to maintain 60 per cent of all plywood shipments. Many of Seaboard's shareholder members suffered losses, though Seaboard itself was able to claim a marginal surplus on shipments of 518 million board feet of lumber, 26,000 squares of shingles and shakes and 183 million square feet of plywood. The value of shipments declined by 37 per cent.

Much of this was the legacy of the oil crisis which had generated a fear of inflation, which in turn created a rush to start housing and construction projects before prices went up. Housing starts increased, creating a demand for lumber, whereupon prices and interest rates escalated to the point that prospective house buyers backed off and the wild spiral collapsed, working severe punishment on the lumber industry, Seaboard included.

SIXTEEN

STARTING THE EIGHTIES

The arrival of Clive Roberts, coinciding as it did with the introduction of new marketing strategies, business methodology and personnel moves, impressed on the years from 1974 into the eighties an atmosphere of calculated innovation and change reaching into every aspect of Seaboard's operations and organization.

British Columbia's lumber industry, which had relied from its beginning almost entirely on the timber of the coastal forests and the mills that manufactured from this resource, was experiencing an increasingly strong challenge from mills in the province's interior, manufacturing from stands of interior spruce, fir and pine. Some of Seaboard's established member mills were purchasing plants or establishing subsidiaries in this region, while Seaboard directed considerable energy to draw interior mills into its membership.

At the outset the recruiting effort was not entirely successful. Many of the interior mills relied almost entirely on domestic and U.S. trade, and made use of rail to deliver their product. In 1965 Seaboard had set up an office in Prince George to sell the export production of member mills in that region. In May 1974 this effort was extended when Chester Cotter was appointed northern representative for Seaboard Lumber

Sales Company Ltd. He opened an office in Quesnel and from there proceeded to direct and develop sales for Canadian Lumber Standard interior spruce, fir and pine. It was a fortuitous decision which resulted in an increase in sales for these products, particularly when overseas buyers became accustomed to them.

Ever on the search for ways to counter increasing costs with greater efficiencies and new profit centres, Seaboard International Terminal, now under the management of Dave Barker, formerly a senior manager at B.C. Forest Products, made its facilities available for the loading and discharge of non-Seaboard cargoes, and appointed Don Des Lauriers sales manager of this operation in August 1974.

Shipping, as usual, was an area where savings could be introduced and profits generated if the right decisions could be made—not an easy accomplishment in one of the world's most mercurial industries. Accordingly, the shipping company proceeded to develop a shipping strategy for approval by the board of directors, which recommended acquisition of vessels on long-term charter, representing about 60 per cent of the company's anticipated requirements. Early in 1974 the decision was approved to charter three bulk carriers in the 30,000- to 35,000-ton range. This size was deemed the most practical for a number of reasons, not the least of which was the capacity of the Panama Canal. Other vessels were added throughout the seventies as it was once again decided that the company should hedge its exposure in the ocean freight market which constituted a significant percentage of the delivered price.

The first charter was signed in March 1974 with the Norden Company of Copenhagen, and in October the M.V. *Nordpol* arrived in Vancouver on its maiden voyage from Japan. A 33,740-ton bulk carrier, she was under ten years' charter, the longest ever undertaken by Seaboard. The previous July Seaboard committed to the charter of two similar bulk carriers, and in December 1974 the *Pacific* and the *Suecia* had their charters extended for five years. At the end of that period, in 1979, Seaboard entered into another long-range charter for these carriers, at the same time calling for their modification. The car-carrying racks were eliminated to produce all-hatch bulk carriers capable of taking dry cargo. The ships were renamed *Pacific Lumberman* and *Pacific Forester*.

In January 1977 Clyde Jacobs recommended the acquisition by charter of two roll-on/roll-off vessels. In June of the same year Seaboard and I. M. Skaugen Norway signed a somewhat unusual charter party which included a purchase option. The charter period is for twelve years, at the end of which time Seaboard will own 50 per cent of each ship. After the fifth year through the tenth year Seaboard has an option to purchase one or both of the vessels.

In an interview with *British Columbia Business* in 1980, Clive Roberts explained the company decision to choose Ro/Ro vessels, as they are called in the shipping business. Seaboard's eyes were on the expansion of business with Japan, a market which consumes enormous quantities of raw materials while exporting equally large quantities of manufactured goods. "We saw an opportunity to develop the backhaul markets for ships carrying our products to Japan," Roberts said. "The Ro/Ro's enabled us to go after the backhaul in addition to which our lumber cargoes arrived in better condition." The effect was to reduce the cost of shipping Seaboard's lumber. Before the first ship was delivered, Seaboard had concluded contracts with two Japanese car manufacturers to backhaul cars for the North American market.

In the same period negotiations were conducted with Trans Atlantic, the principals of Pacific Australia Direct Line (PAD) and German ship owners to charter a Ro/Ro vessel, *Lillooet,* for use between the Pacific Northwest and Australia starting in December 1978. Seaboard shares the charter through a related long-term arrangement by giving access to four of PAD's vessels. The immediate advantages were that Seaboard had guaranteed Ro/Ro space as a preferred shipper to Australia on a bi-weekly service.

The second of Seaboard's bulk carriers, the 26,103-ton *Eastern Venture,* was commissioned in June 1975, working on a ten-year charter. And one year later another bulk carrier, M.V. *Nordkap,* arrived and began work on an eleven-year charter. In the meantime, the two Ro/Ro vessels *Skaugran* and *Skaubord,* delivered on schedule, immediately generated such a gratifying profit that Clyde Jacobs's proposal to charter a third one for the Japanese trade was approved in November 1980 for delivery in 1982.

Seaboard's executive committee continued to function as the ultimate seat of authority in the decision-making process. Policies developed at this level always go to the board of directors for a formal vote and final adoption, and only rarely are there differences of opinion between the committee and the board. However, even the executive committee was subject to revision in the last years of the seventies.

Humbird, Mackin and Bentley, in their terms of office as chairmen of what became the executive committee, had served for up to ten years each. When Gary Bowell replaced Poldi Bentley in 1970, his tenure was considerably shorter, not by official decree but by reason of his own company responsibilities to which he owed first allegiance. The same applied to Bob Rogers who succeeded him in 1973. Rogers served effectively as chairman until 1975, at which time Peter J. G. Bentley assumed the office. The son of Poldi Bentley and the president and chief executive officer of Canadian Forest Products, he had worked through the ranks of that company and had equipped himself academically to take over the reins from his father at the appropriate time. He was thoroughly conversant with Seaboard's background and function and was able to perform the chairman's role from a background of familiarity born and bred.

In his first year as chairman of the executive committee, his committee members were: George M. Lyttle, L & K Lumber (North Shore); Howard B. Urquhart, Rayonier Canada (B.C.); Eric Sonner, Bay Forest Products; Thomas A. Buell, Weldwood of Canada; Thomas G. Rust, Crown Zellerbach (Canada); L. J. (Pat) Martin, Raven Lumber; H. Edward Manning, Richmond Plywood Corporation; Ronald R. Ogilvy, Whonnock Industries, and Clive Roberts of Seaboard. Other personnel were invited depending on the nature of the business agenda.

Peter Bentley remained chairman until 1977, but in that year a review of the organizational structure of the executive committee was initiated. It was ruled that as of March 1978 the committee, in addition to Seaboard's president, would consist of a total of eight mill members, each of whom must be the president and chief executive officer of his company. These members would be chosen from large and small members to ensure broad representation of the membership. In addition, the chairman's term of office would be two years. Thomas Buell, chairman, president and chief executive officer of Weldwood of Canada, was elected chairman. When his term was completed in 1979, Thomas Rust, president and chief executive officer of Crown Zellerbach (Canada), took his place, to be followed by William Sauder, president and chief executive officer of Whonnock Industries in 1982 and 1983.

Both at a mill level and within Seaboard's own organization, modern marketing techniques were now playing a critical role. Time and circumstance had supplanted traditional management with a new breed of chief executive thoroughly versed in the subtleties of contemporary business administration and finance. At the same time, Seaboard's steady pressure over the years to obtain a greater degree of autonomy had finally resulted in substantial concessions from the mills, as evidenced by Seaboard's freedom to establish subsidiaries wherever their superiority over the agent system could be demonstrated. Specific to Seaboard's business on the Continent, the first move towards a subsidiary system was made in July 1974 when Rut De Bruyn Kops was appointed out of Seaboard International in London to become sales representative for Holland and Belgium, working from a branch office in Utrecht.

When, in 1978, Ingemar Nordin, Seaboard's agent in France since 1954, announced his decision to retire, the opportunity presented itself to move one step closer to a subsidiary system. In June of that year Clive Roberts recommended the establishment of a continental subsidiary agency company to be in charge of sales in France, Benelux and Germany. His target date for the initiation of this system was January 1979.

In Germany, news of Seaboard's intention was not well received. Seaboard's agent in that country since 1961 was Jacob Juergensen, an established firm long accustomed to a comfortable working relationship with Seaboard. Herbert Franke asked for at least three or four more years of representation or, alternatively, a joint venture arrangement, but Seaboard's final decision was to terminate, and Jacob Juergensen was given an extension until June 1980 to phase out.

On schedule, 1 January 1979 Seaboard's European sales subsidiary went into operation under the name of Seaboard Timber & Plywood Europe Ltd. The offices in Utrecht and Paris, managed by Rut De Bruyn Kops and Jean Lemut respectively, were responsible for sales in France, the Netherlands, Belgium and Luxembourg. Both Jean and Rut were very experienced in Seaboard's products. Jean had worked for Nordin on the Seaboard account. Rut had been the Seaboard salesman for Altius & Company until 1974 and then represented Seaboard to 1979, reporting to SIL London. Later Germany was included, and an office was opened in Hamburg, managed by Cornelius Grimm, which also covered Denmark, Sweden and Norway.

The march into the eighties saw the reawakening of business with South America, the development of which was under area sales manager, Laird Wilson. An agent was named in Venezuela, Pedro J. Coll, and replaced in 1977 by Gepavenca C. A., Caracas. And in that same year a cargo of lumber was delivered to Cumana, Venezuela, the first from Seaboard in twenty years.

In England, Bob Edgett's retirement was imminent and the time had come to decide on a replacement for him as managing director of Seaboard International. The final choice was John Ingle, a lumber sales executive who had joined SIL in 1968 as manager of the company's Liverpool branch office. In 1972 he was transferred to the London office as director of lumber sales where he had three years to familiarize himself with the workings of the United Kingdom subsidiary before taking over from Edgett. Bob Edgett remained chairman of SIL until the end of 1975 and then returned to Vancouver.

His official retirement date was 1 May 1976, bringing to a close forty-one years with the company, most of that time in top management positions. His talents as a sales executive combined with his unwavering allegiance to Seaboard and its objectives had been an invaluable asset, and his influence had been felt in the constructive evolution of the organization. Harry Berry's retirement came four months later on 1 September and a joint retirement reception was held for the two long-time Seaboard executives at which both Seaboard mill directors and Seaboard staff paid sincere tribute.

In March 1976 one of Vancouver's major developers approached Seaboard with an offer to purchase Seaboard House. In due course the offer was accepted, and the following October third the company moved to two floors in Oceanic Plaza at 1066 Hastings Street where ample space enabled efficiencies not possible in the old location.

In the first part of 1977 Clive Roberts visited Japan, mainland China, Hong Kong and Singapore, meeting with customers, representatives of the lumber and plywood trade and the shipping business, and government and trade associations. It was more than a goodwill visit; he wanted to observe first hand the potential for British Columbia wood products, and to identify new areas of trade. In particular he saw the People's Republic of China as the largest remaining new market opportunity, an opinion which he confirmed later in 1980 during a visit to China as a member of a Canada-China Trade Council mission.

On the Japan leg of his 1977 visit, Roberts was hosted by his vice-president of Seaboard Asia, Steve Kaufman, who brought him together with key representatives of the lumber trade and government. Roberts's message to the trade was that Seaboard would strengthen its Japan office, introduce a regular shipping service, and produce wood products specific to Japan's construction needs in terms of species, sizes and quality. All of these commitments have since been fulfilled.

In October 1977 Steve Kaufman relinquished his post as vice-president and general manager of Seaboard Asia and returned to Seaboard's Vancouver office, there to assist Doug Reid in the Plywood Division. His position in Tokyo was taken over by Akira Ishikawa, who had joined Seaboard Asia in 1975 as manager of the Tokyo office. At the same time two others joined Seaboard Asia, a clear indication of Roberts's intention to strengthen Seaboard's identity in Japan. Seiji Omote was appointed market development co-ordinator and Akira Takahashi became manager of traditional lumber specifications.

Seaboard entered 1980 with five sales subsidiaries and eleven sales agents/distributors: Seaboard (Timber & Plywood) Australia Pty. Ltd. in Sydney was managed by Ron McLaine and Mike Bartlett, director of sales. In New York, Seaboard International Lumber & Plywood Inc. was presided over by Bob Kirkham, with Mike Davis in the position of sales manager and Tom Kiritsis as controller; Seaboard Timber & Plywood Asia Ltd. was headed by Akira Ishikawa, supported by Haruo Gunji as sales manager, and Kiyoshi Nakajima, manager of ship operations; John Ingle was managing director of Seaboard International (Timber & Plywood) Ltd. in London, with his management team consisting of Michael Paul, director of lumber sales, Dennis Ray, director of ship operations and distribution, John Miller, director of administration, Mike Cowan, director of agency plywood imports, and Ed Annan as associate director of North American plywood and specialty products; manager of Seaboard Timber & Plywood Europe Limited in Utrecht was Rut De Bruyn Kops, in Paris was Jean Lemut and in Hamburg was Cornelius Grimm.

Agents/distributors were: T. Geddes Grant (Barbados), Bridgetown, Barbados; in Cyprus, Pan Vouros, Nicosia; in Germany, Jacob Juergensen, Hamburg (soon to be phased out); in Greece, N. M. Sitaras & Company, Athens; in Italy, Ett Agenzia Legnami S.p.a., Rome; in Norway, S. C. Heyerdahl Plywood A/S, Oslo; in Puerto Rico and the Dominican Republic, Pacific Agencies Inc., San Juan; in Spain, J. V. Lang S.A., Madrid; in South Africa, C. E. Westergaard (Pty.) Limited, Marshalltown; in Trinidad and Tobago, T. Geddes Grant (Trinidad) Ltd., Port of Spain, and in Venezuela, Gepavenca C. A., Caracas.

In Ireland the firm of Belwood Limited, Dublin, under the direction of Michael Raben, had been appointed as resident representatives for Seaboard, and in Scotland a sales force had been organized to handle the sale of wood products, working through the London and Liverpool offices of Seaboard International.

Beginning in 1976 Seaboard's fortunes improved considerably. Lumber shipments were 807 million FBM as compared to 518 million in 1975. The CIF value of all shipments was $223 million as compared to $145 million in the previous year and in the United States, Seaboard's largest single market, the company's market share increased to 28 per cent. (In 1975 it had been 20 per cent.) Shipments to the United Kingdom increased 88 per cent, making Seaboard the largest Canadian supplier in the market. Export volumes to France doubled over the previous year, yielding Seaboard 50 per cent of the market share, the leading position. In Germany sales were up substantially.

The U.S. subsidiary, Seaboard International Lumber & Plywood,

Inc., New York, completed its first full year of operations with a sales performance exceeding expectations. There was no doubt that it had succeeded in establishing itself as a major supplier to independent wholesalers, and that the sale of product from stockpiled inventories landed in U.S. ports was meeting with broad acceptance.

The roles of the independent wholesalers and buyers continued to change in that market. Futter Lumber Company, for instance, had been a modest buyer of Seaboard Lumber for a number of years. A relatively small wholesale company with offices in downtown New York, its purchases in the early seventies rarely exceeded 3 or 4 per cent of Seaboard's annual shipments to that market. However, in 1975, when other wholesalers were responding slowly to Seaboard's new marketing strategy, Futter began to move significant volumes of lumber for Seaboard, amounting to approximately half of its U.S. sales. Until 1980 Futter remained the largest single customer of Seaboard's New York sales organization.

Other buyers included the new with the old, among them A. C. Dutton, Dant & Russell, Georgia Pacific, Weyerhaeuser, Slaughter Bros., Woodtex, Sherwood, Mid-Atlantic, McCoy Lumber, Timberlane and Furman Lumber.

Seaboard Shipping sent fifty-six vessels to forty-four different ports in 1976, carrying a total of 1.25 million long tons of wood products. The company's largest shipment ever, 23.9 million FBM of lumber and plywood, was carried aboard the M.S. *Bianca* to the United Kingdom; and the largest recorded Australian shipment was delivered by the M.S. *Leda,* which represented a substantial portion of Seaboard's 70 per cent sales increase to Australia that year. Seaboard International Terminal showed a profit of $166,781 compared to a loss of $645,048 in 1975. A substantial portion of the new revenue was earned from the loading and discharge of non-Seaboard cargoes.

In the United Kingdom, Seaboard established a Ship Agency Department to handle the movement of vessels to U.K. and European ports. Eggar Forrester had been doing this for the company since the incorporation of Seaboard International, but the formation of an in-house agency was a distinct economy. Eggar Forrester continued to act as Seaboard's principal ship broker.

In 1977 Clive Roberts was able to report a marked sales improvement over 1976. Lumber shipments amounted to 981 million FBM, plus plywood exports of 214 million square feet. Plywood sales, in fact, were the highest since 1973. The total CIF value of all wood products was $308 million. The United States once more accounted for the largest volume, with the European Common Market including the U.K. next, followed by Japan, which showed a sales increase of 25 per cent over the previous year. Sales to Australia, Puerto Rico and other Caribbean markets were up, and new markets had opened in Venezuela, Iran and Morocco. In this year Seaboard was the largest supplier of softwood plywood to the European market, improving the market further with an entrée to Italy through the port of Trieste. In line with this increase in business, Seaboard Shipping deployed sixty-one vessels to fifty-nine ports, carrying 1.8 million long tons of wood product cargo. The fleet of long-term chartered vessels totalled ten vessels, including four Ro/Ro's scheduled for delivery between 1979 and 1982.

The market had not peaked yet. In 1978 lumber shipments totalled 1041 million FBM together with 256 million square feet of plywood; this represented a total CIF value of $383 million. The United States market continued to lead in sales, but Japan had now climbed to second position with sales of 191 million FBM. The steady increase of sales to Japan was accounted for by Seaboard's concerted effort to supply wood products specifically designed for building needs in that country, both in species and sizes. In addition, the company's subsidiary sales force was having increasing success in promoting the use of Canadian Standard dimensions in lieu of logs and squares for remanufacture in Japan. Sales increased over 1977 on the Continent and in the Mediterranean, Australia, the Caribbean and South America. In the United Kingdom, however, sales were slow for the better part of the year. By the time the market was ready to purchase, much of Seaboard's supply had been committed to other buyers.

There seemed to be no end to the escalation of business. Sales in the year 1979 topped those of 1978 with a 21 per cent increase in volume. The total of lumber exported was 1242 million FBM together with 260 million feet of plywood, representing total sales of $594,000,000 CIF. Japan showed a dramatic increase in sales over the previous year, and sales to France, Germany and Italy combined revealed a 32 per cent increase. Sales to Australia were up, assisted substantially by the introduction of a regularly scheduled Ro/Ro service in conjunction with Pacific Australia Direct Line. Sales to New Zealand, Venezuela, Argentina and Algeria remained steady and, for the first time, a shipment of lumber was delivered to Hungary.

Long-term charter vessels like the *Skaugran* and the *Skaubord* (the largest Ro/Ro vessels in the world at 42,000 tons), the *Lillooet,* the *Pacific Forester* and the *Pacific Lumberman* were now in service, enabling the transportation of 8 per cent more cargo per ship on the average.

In 1979 sixty-four vessels delivered wood products to fifty-four ports, moving in a relatively strong charter market that worked to Seaboard's advantage in minimized freight costs.

In five years of continuously escalating sales, the CIF value of Seaboard's shipments had multiplied by four times, from $144,870,135 in 1975 to $594,571,071 in 1979. The year 1980, however, revealed the first evidences that sales had peaked. Clive Roberts described 1980 as a difficult year. Undoubtedly it was, although an export volume of 1010 million FBM of lumber and 221 million square feet of plywood could not be regarded as disastrous. The difficulties could be attributed to the recession beginning to cripple the United States, and the repercussions of this downturn in other markets of the world.

Seaboard's exports to the United States dropped by 50 per cent over 1979. Reduced demand in this and other markets, combined with increased competition, motivated Seaboard to redirect export production to other areas of the world. Severe curtailment of shipping to the U.S. East Coast led to the redeployment of long-term charters to Europe, the Middle East and Japan—an action which helped to compensate for the drastic reduction in sales in the U.S.

Sales to the United Kingdom did not help; a weak market and fierce competition from Scandinavia, the Baltic and the United States depleted Seaboard's sales. On the Continent, however, sales were considerably better, showing an increase of 46 per cent in France, 44 per cent in Benelux and 53 per cent in Italy. Construction slowdowns in Germany and the Netherlands depressed those markets, but shipments to Africa and the Middle East increased by 50 per cent over the previous year. The company recorded a shipment to Egypt and another to the People's Republic of China, this latter described by Roberts as a breakthrough for both Seaboard and the B.C. forest industry. Sales to Puerto Rico and Australia were up moderately, and Japan was a strong market until the fourth quarter of the year when business dropped alarmingly. An oversupply of logs and lumber together with a reduction in construction demand in that country put a halt to sales.

Seaboard Shipping handled fifty-six ships in 1980, contending with a 30 per cent increase in fuel oil prices. Notwithstanding the recession clouds massing in the U.S. and the resulting economic turbulence in the rest of the world, negotiations were concluded for a third Ro/Ro vessel, *Skeena,* in the same class as the *Skaugran* and the *Skaubord,* scheduled to go into service to Japan in 1982.

In 1980, as well, the decision was made to construct a terminal in San Juan, Puerto Rico, to serve the markets in that part of the world. General Manager of Distribution Dudley Darling was placed in charge of the project with a mandate to develop a six-acre property in the port of San Juan capable of accommodating 75 million FBM of lumber. Tentative date for completion of the terminal was March 1981. The actual inaugural date was December 1981, marking Seaboard's twenty-eighth year as an exporter to that market.

Clive Roberts and his executive committee had cause for concern as the final months of 1980 approached. The year had started with the first inroads of recession in the United States, worsening as time moved on. All the signs pointed to the emergence of a cyclical downturn of far-reaching proportions. World economic recovery was not expected to be swift, and Seaboard, in keeping with the entire British Columbia forest industry, could only hope that interest rates would lower to a point where construction activity could begin again. The key market in this recovery would be the United States and would spin off to other countries.

On 31 October 1980, as a further indication of an old era passing and a new era beginning, Grace Eccleston, the "voice of Seaboard," closed her switchboard for the last time, after thirty-two years of day-to-day contact with mill members, agents, buyers and overseas representatives who had come and gone through Seaboard's good and bad times. Her place was taken by Irene Fredrickson.

There were a few more to follow: Dudley Darling, who had been actively involved in distribution planning since the late 1960s, and general manager of distribution since 1975, took his retirement in May 1981, having played a leading role in the establishment of Seaboard Pioneer Terminals at Tilbury, Seaboard International Terminal in North Vancouver and Seaboard Caribbean Terminal Inc. in San Juan. Most of his duties were taken over by Al McLean, general manager of chartering. Laird Wilson retired on the same day, after thirty-four years with the company, beginning in the U.S. East Coast market before returning to Seaboard in 1961 as sales development manager for the U.S. East Coast, and later as manager of Japan sales. Al Gardner, who had once managed Seaboard's Australian operations, passed away in 1981. He had joined Seaboard in 1947.

Much had been achieved in the period following Clive Roberts's appointment as president. From the forest industry recession cycle in 1975 the company had reorganized, introducing marketing strategies that had gone far in maximizing mill returns and earning profits. The change in shipping strategy had proved to be profitable.

In the period leading up to the oil supply crisis in 1974, Seaboard had relied mostly on spot-charters to ship its products, but the very strong freight market in the early seventies resulted in Seaboard becoming

uncompetitive compared with other B.C. shippers. Conversely, Mac-
Millan Bloedel's Canadian Transport shipping company, which had
several long-term charter vessels, benefited until the freight market collapsed following the oil crisis in 1974–75.

In an interview with *B. C. Business* in 1980, Roberts, referring to the
aftermath of the 1974 oil crisis and a failing market, stated: "It became
apparent it would be prudent to have a number of long-term charter
ships as a hedge against inflation and the freight market. We were
fortunate the charter market was at a low point. It was a good time to
make a move. We knew we would always have a base value of products
to be shipped, and it is always more difficult to obtain suitable ships at a
time when you need them. After all, when you are in the market you
pay the current market price."

Seaboard's decision to arrange charters for up to fifteen years led to
the long-term chartering of ten vessels by 1980. These carriers accounted for 60 per cent of the company's export, in anticipation of
rising markets, with spot-market charters used for less predictable sales.
In this manner the company was able to gain an advantage in the
intensifying international competition and developed significant shipping profits for the members.

As the company proceeded into the eighties, the perpetual search for
competitive strategies went on. Innovative shipping tactics could not be
relied on as the sole means of maintaining a competitive position.
Roberts stated that the search for new markets must continue unabated,
and that the development of new product and the improvement of
existing product must be given high priority. He stressed the importance of increasing the list of shareholder mills and said that the company would proceed with its recruitment campaign. In this respect, he
was able to announce that, in 1980, shipments of interior spruce-pine-
fir had increased by 102 per cent over 1979, due in part to the enlistment
of additional B.C. interior shareholder mills, and due as well to continuing acceptance of these interior wood products.

Seaboard, in company with the entire B.C. forest industry, was entering a period of growing stress. The consortium, as it approached its
fiftieth year, consisted of twenty-two shareholders controlling the export production of sixty-eight coastal and interior mills, these employing in excess of 18,000 individuals. As Clive Roberts observed, the
decade of the eighties would present formidable challenges, but great
opportunities as well. Grasping those opportunities and turning them to
advantage would call for all the human and technological resources
Seaboard could muster.

EPILOGUE

The preceding pages have rendered an account of fifty years in the life of Seaboard Lumber Sales Company Limited and Seaboard Shipping Company Limited, in the process of which considerable attention has been focussed on the entire British Columbia lumber export business, the efforts these companies made to gain entrée to world markets, and the strategies they have employed to secure and maintain a significant position.

The foregoing chapters make evident that change has been the constant factor and the greatest challenge: change in economies, change in the legislation of nations, change in technologies, change in attitudes towards wood products, changes in ships and shipping. The process of change continues unabated today. Even as these words are written Seaboard and the British Columbia lumber industry are examining the portents of change and preparing to adapt to an increasingly competitive export market in a difficult world economy. The next chapters could prove more significant than any that have gone before.

SELECTED REFERENCES

Baptie, Sue. *First Growth*. Vancouver: British Columbia Forest Products, 1975.
British Columbia Department of Industrial Development, Trade and Commerce.
        "Principal Statistics of the Forest Industry in British Columbia
           1946–1957." Queen's Printer, 1958.
        "Statistical Record of Lumber in British Columbia 1950–1965."
           Queen's Printer, 1966.
British Columbia Forest Industries Yearbook 1965–66.
British Columbia Lumberman. 1924–present.
  In particular: "A Great Timber Exporting Organization."
        September 1939, pp. 57–59.
        "B.C. Mills form Atlantic Marketing Organization."
           June 1928, p. 24.
        "New Organization to Handle U.K. Export Sales."
           April 1935, p. 31.
        "The Work of Associated Timber Exporters of B.C. (Astexo)."
           September 1934, pp. 36–37.
British Columbia Lumber Manufacturer's Association Annual Reports 1932–1966.
British Columbia. *Royal Commission of Inquiry on Timber & Forestry 1909–1910.*
  Ottawa, 1910.
Cameron, Jamie. "Cameron Brothers Pioneered Island Timber Industry." *Daily Colonist,* January 5, 1969, pp. 10–11.
Canada. Royal Commission on Canada's Economic Prospects. *The Outlook for the Canadian Forest Industries.* Prepared by Davis, Best, Lachance, Pringle, Smith and Wilson. Ottawa, 1957.

————. *Royal Commission on Corporate Concentration — MacMillan Bloedel.* Prepared by R. Schwindt. 1977.

Dixon, L. B. "The Birth of the Lumber Industry." In *British Columbia Lumberman,* Bound edition. Nov. 1955—Sept. 1956.

"Forest Ships try New Tack." *Province,* November 23, 1977.

Francis, Robert J. "Analysis of B.C. Lumber Shipments 1947—1957." Unpublished thesis, University of British Columbia, 1957.

"Grinnell: American Who Spent Lifetime Selling B.C. Lumber Never Regretted His Choice." *The Lumberman,* June 1953, pp. 92—93.

Humbird diaries. Private collection.

Humbird papers. Special Collections, University of British Columbia.

Lamb, W. Kaye. "Early Lumbering on Vancouver Island." *British Columbia Historical Quarterly* 2, 1 (1938): 31—53.

Lawrence, Joseph C. "Markets and Capital: A History of the Lumber Industry of British Columbia (1778—1952)." M.A. Thesis, University of British Columbia, 1957.

"Lumber Terminal World's Largest."*Province,* 8 September 1971.

MacKay, Donald. *Empire of Wood.* Vancouver: Douglas & McIntyre, 1982.

Newman, Peter C. *The Canadian Establishment.* Toronto: McClelland & Stewart, 1975.

Ormsby, Margaret. *British Columbia: A History.* Toronto: Macmillan, 1958.

Pethick, Derek. *Men of British Columbia.* Vancouver: Hancock House, 1975.

"Recent Visit of Sir James Ball and Montague Meyer to B.C." *Pacific Coast Lumberman,* June 1919, pp. 24—26.

Rohmer, Richard. *E. P. Taylor.* Toronto: McClelland & Stewart, 1978.

"Seaboard Announces Tokyo Office." *Business in B.C.* 1—2, Nov./Dec. 1974, pp. 30—31.

"Seaboard Lumber: Order Files are back to Normal." *B.C. Business Magazine,* March 1976, p. 15.

Seaboard Lumber Sales Company Limited. Annual Reports.

————. Executive Committee Minutes.

"Seaboard Member Mills cut half Timber Sawn Annually in B.C." *B.C. Journal of Commerce Weekly.* 31 Jan. 1953, p. 12.

"Seaboard Outlook for Lumber Market." *Harbour & Shipping,* May 1975, pp. 22—25.

Seaboard Shipping Company. Annual Reports.

————. Executive Committee Minutes.

"Stone Family Pioneered Logging in Cowichan." *Daily Colonist,* 21 July 1968. pp. 12—13.

Taylor, Geoffrey W. *Timber: A History of the Forest Industry in British Columbia.* Vancouver: J. J. Douglas, 1975.

SELECTED MILL ARTICLES IN *B.C. LUMBERMAN*

"Alaska Pine Joins Seaboard." March 1952, p. 63.

"Bay Lumber Company: A 7-Year Pioneer." May 1953, pp. 75, 82.

"59 Years Ago - $60 Contract: That was the Start of Moore-Whittington." March 1952, pp. 35—36, 120.

"Hillcrest is a Family Mill." March 1953, p. 77.

"Maple Ridge: Story of 50 Years." Dec. 1954, pp. 72—73.

"M.B. King Lumber - Abreast of the Times." Aug. 1954, pp. 73—74.

"Modern Plywood Production." (Pacific Veneer, division of B.C.F.P.) Oct. 1954, pp. 54—56.

"Mohawk Handle Wood Scraps for Increased Revenue." May 1956, pp. 71–73.

"New Mills for Old." (L & K Lumber) Sept. 1953, pp. 71–76.

"1900–1950 Golden Jubilee: B.C. Manufacturing Company, Pioneers in Kiln Dried Pacific Coast Hemlock." April 1950, pp. 77–79, 83.

"100% Utilization Aim of Eburne Sawmills." March 1949, pp. 96–97, 101.

"Photo Visit to New Seaboard Member." (McDonald Cedar Products) July 1953, p. 74.

"River Mill moves with the Times." (Whonnock) Nov. 1954, p. 72.

"This is a Family Affair." (Hillcrest) Jan. 1957, pp. 42–43.

Appendix A

SEABOARD LUMBER SALES COMPANY
& SEABOARD SHIPPING COMPANY

MANAGEMENT TEAM, SEPTEMBER 1939

J. A. Humbird	*President*
J. G. McConville	*Vice-president*
C. H. Grinnell	*General Manager and vice-president*
H. V. Simpson	*Secretary*
V. Forrester	*Manager, Seaboard Shipping*
H. E. Solloway	*Assistant Manager, Seaboard Shipping*
J. P. O'Hagan	*Manager, Astexo* FAS *Department*
C. Crispin	*Manager, U.K. Department*
F. G. Solloway	*Assistant Manager, U.K. Department*
A. A. Head	*Manager, Sydney Office*
C. N. Effinger	*Manager, London Office*
G. D. Anderson	*Manager, New York Office*
H. L. Martin	*Assistant Manager, New York Office*
H. P. O'Hagan	*Manager, Montreal Office (closed Aug.1939)*
C. D. Schultz	*Manager, Caribbean Office*
R. H. Edgett	*Cedar & Misc. Accumulations, U.K.*

Appendix B

SEABOARD LUMBER SALES COMPANY

MEMBER MILLS, 1938

Alberni Pacific Lumber Company (Alberni)
Alberta Lumber Company Ltd. (Vancouver)
B.C. Manufacturing Company Ltd. (New Westminster)
Bloedel, Stewart & Welch Ltd. (Port Alberni)
Burke Lumber Company Ltd. (Vancouver)
Cameron Lumber Company Ltd. (Victoria)
Canadian Robert Dollar Company Ltd. (North Vancouver)
Canadian Western Lumber Company Ltd. (Fraser Mills)
Cedar-Cove Sash and Door Company Ltd. (Vancouver)
Crofton Export Company Ltd. (Crofton)
Eburne Sawmills Ltd. (Vancouver)
False Creek Lumber Company Ltd. (Vancouver)
Glaspie Lumber Company Ltd. (North Vancouver)
Goodwin-Johnson Ltd. (Vancouver)
Hillcrest Lumber Company Ltd. (Duncan)
Hammond Cedar Company Ltd. (Hammond)
Industrial Timber Mills Ltd. (Youbou)
Inlet Timber Company Ltd. (Vancouver)
International Wood Products Company (?)
Lemon-Gonnason Company Ltd. (Victoria)
Maple Ridge Lumber Company Ltd. (Port Haney)
Mohawk Lumber Company Ltd. (New Westminster)
Moore-Whittington Lumber Company Ltd. (Victoria)
Manning Lumber Mills Ltd. (Victoria)
Nelson Spencer Ltd. (Vancouver)
Pacific Lime Company Ltd. (Blubber Bay)
P. Bain (Mission City)
Port Mellon Operating Company Ltd. (Port Mellon)
R. B. MacLean Lumber Company Ltd. (Alberni)
Robertson & Hackett Sawmill Company Ltd. (Vancouver)
Shawnigan Lake Lumber Company Ltd. (Shawnigan Lake)
Sterling Lumber Ltd. (Vancouver)
Sproat Lake Sawmills Ltd. (Kleecoot)
Straits Lumber Company Ltd. (Red Gap)
Timberland Lumber Company Ltd. (New Westminster)
Victoria Lumber & Mfg. Company Ltd. (Chemainus)
Westminster Shook Mills Ltd. (New Westminster)
Wood & English Ltd. (Englewood)

Appendix C

SEABOARD WARTIME "PARENTS"

J. H. Bloedel

D. O. Cameron

C. J. Culter

Norman English

Fred Fearman

D. A. Gatus

C. H. Grinnell

J. A. Humbird

J. G. McConville

R. G. McDonald

A. R. Macfarlane

R. B. McRae

Fred Manning

A. W. Millar

Brooks Pendleton

Wayne Pendleton

H. V. Simpson

C. Stone

William Burke

J. O. Cameron

J. M. Edwards

B. M. Farris

Vassall Forrester

E. S. Glaspie

G. R. Hackett

Goodwin Johnson

J. H. McDonald

Robert McDonald

H. J. Mackin

F. A. E. Manning

Harold Manning

J. R. Murray

F. R. Pendleton

J. G. Robson

Nelson Spencer

T. H. Wilkinson

Appendix D

BRITISH TIMBER CONTROL CONTRACT NEGOTIATIONS

On Sunday February 11th which was the day after our arrival in London, Mr. MacMillan advised us that he had sold the Control a total quantity of 150,000 standards with the Control's option to reduce to 120,000 standards, for shipment during the period APRIL/SEPTEMBER. Prices at $2.00 per 1000 fbm more than the September order.

Mr. Humbird and Mr. Grinnell then came to Bristol and saw Mr. David and Mr. Williams on Tuesday 13th and also saw Major Harris, Mr. Powell and Mr. David on Wednesday 14th, which was followed by a discussion with Mr. Williams by Messrs. Humbird, Grinnell, Effinger and Williams.

In the cable which Mr. Humbird had received from Mr. MacMillan in Paris, Mr. MacMillan had stated that he had closed the above order with the Control on their undertaking that they would make us the same offer. When we saw the Control on Tuesday 13th February, they offered us a quantity of 100,000 standards with their option to reduce to 75,000 standards, for shipment over the period JUNE/SEPTEMBER inclusive. Mr. Humbird called Mr. MacMillan in London on Tuesday evening and asked Mr. MacMillan who it was at the Control who had given the undertaking of which he advised us in his cable to Mr. Humbird in Paris. Mr. MacMillan stated that Major Harris had given him the undertaking.

As a result of that advice, Mr. Humbird and Mr. Grinnell saw Major Harris, Mr. Powell and Mr. David on Wednesday noon and when Major Harris denied ever having given any such undertaking to Mr. MacMillan on our behalf, we went through our arrangements with MacMillan right from the start. At that meeting Mr. Powell made the suggestion that we should arrange with MacMillan to give us part of his order. Major Harris said he would be agreeable to it being handled in that way. Therefore, Mr. Humbird and Mr. Grinnell went to London on Thursday morning, 15th February and met Mr. MacMillan there at 4.30 in the same afternoon. Messrs. Humbird, Grinnell and MacMillan returned to Bristol on Friday morning, together with Messrs. Woolrich and Shaw upon the undertaking of Mr. MacMillan that he would be agreeable to dividing his order up with us. Mr. MacMillan saw Major Harris and Mr. Powell on Friday noon and at 2.30 in the afternoon Messrs. Humbird, Grinnell and Effinger were shown terms and conditions without any indication of increasing the quantity offered us the previous week, viz. a maximum of 100,000 standards, minimum 75,000 standards, for shipment over period JUNE/SEPTEMBER.

We then went to the Hotel and Messrs. David and Williams met Messrs. MacMillan, Woolrich and Shaw. Then at about 7 o'clock Messrs. David and Williams met with Messrs. Humbird, Grinnell, Effinger and Wilson and they proposed a contract on the following terms:—

Shipping dates. April/September on contract, but it is understood that no tonnage will be furnished before June.

General. Whilst the Control will do its utmost to lift cargoes evenly throughout the months mentioned above, it must be understood by Sellers that the control's efforts in this direction are governed entirely by the amount of tonnage allocated to it by the Ministry of Shipping. In order therefore to avoid unnecessary accumulation and congestion being caused by an absence of tonnage the following to be agreed:

1) The Control to give Sellers one calendar month's notice of the quantity it expects to be able to ship during the ensuing month.

2) Notwithstanding this Sellers may, to suit their own purposes during the first three months of the contract period, or before, cut pro rata to the minimum quantity and specification.

3) At the end of three months (i.e. on July 1st) a balance to be struck. The Control at that time to declare whether it will take the total minimum quantity, or total maximum quantity, or alternatively to state a figure between the two. In the event of the Control being unable to decide the question at that date, some subsequent date for the decision to be mutually agreed.

4) Quantity to be cut during the remaining three months of the contract period to be in accordance with instructions from the Control as near as possible prorata to specification, such instructions to be given one month in advance of each production month.

5) At the expiry of the shipping period, the unshipped balances to be dealt with as follows:

   a) Any cut lumber to be increased in price by one dollar per 1000 ft., for the first month and by 25 cents for each subsequent month the goods remain unpaid for, and at the risk and expense of the Sellers.

   b) On any uncut lumber, the Control to have the option of cancelling or of treating in the manner prescribed under the above heading "a".

They suggested that Clause "B" be changed as follows:

"On any uncut lumber either the Control or Sellers to have the option of cancelling but in the event of Sellers not electing to cancel, the Control to have the option of treating in the manner prescribed under the above heading 'a'."

They then left us to consider the matter and they went to see Messrs. MacMillan, Woolrich and Shaw. They shortly returned to our room and we asked if we could consider the matter over-night which they said we could. Therefore we all went to dinner.

Late on Friday afternoon Mr. Humbird talked to Mr. MacMillan and obtained Mr. MacMillan's definite consent to Seaboard receiving 60% of the total business placed and MacMillan receiving 40% of the total business placed. It was agreed between Messrs. Humbird and MacMillan at that time that if Dollar does not get any Control business, a proportionate amount of business would be given to Dollar from Seaboard and MacMillan in the ratio of 60% Seaboard, 40% MacMillan.

On Saturday, 17th February Mr. Humbird talked with Mr. MacMillan and it was agreed that Messrs. Humbird, Grinnell and Effinger should see Messrs. David and Williams and try to get away from the terms suggested by Mr. Williams and Mr. David on Friday evening particularly insofar as their option to stop cutting at the end of June and also to endeavour to get away from the option which they had included which gave the Control the option of cancelling any uncut portion of the order.

This meeting was held at 10 o'clock without any success and we therefore told Mr. David and Mr. Williams that we would accept the 100,000 standards with their option to reduce to 75,000 standards on the basis of the terms which they had proposed on

Friday night. It is understood that Clause "B" will be changed as per above.

We then returned to the Hotel; Mr. Humbird met Mr. MacMillan and it was agreed that they two should return to meet Mr. David and Mr. Williams to arrange for the Control to give Seaboard 60% of the order which MacMillan had closed with them and to give to MacMillan 40% of the order which the Control had placed with Seaboard. Messrs. Humbird and MacMillan went to see the Control first, with Messrs. Grinnell, Effinger, Woolrich and Shaw following and remaining on call at the Control. At about 12 o'clock we were all called to Mr. David's office and everything seemed to be in agreement and Mr. MacMillan outlined it in the presence of Messrs. David, Williams, Humbird, Grinnell, Effinger, Woolrich and Shaw as follows:

1) As regards final payment of any cut and unshipped portion of either contract, payment will be made on January 31st, 1941 against Control's form of Bank Guarantee, the property then to remain at the risk of the Buyers, the Sellers to waive any storage, handling or rental charges after January 31st.

2) Messrs. Seaboard and MacMillan to prepare a joint memorandum towards the elimination of the interest charges on drafts under the present system, which would be presented to Mr. Gelcken of the Control who would take the matter up with the Treasury Department to see if anything could be accomplished towards the elimination of these interest charges on drafts.

3) Any cut lumber to be increased in price by $1.00 per 1000 ft. if lifted during October, and by an additional 25 cents per 1000 ft. if lifted during November, an additional 25 cents per 1000 ft. if lifted during December, and an additional 25 cents per 1000 ft. if lifted during January, in all instances Bill of Lading date to decide. The maximum increase, therefore, if cut goods are held at the end of January over the contract price is $1.75 per 1000 ft.

4) On January 31st the documents required for payment of cut goods would be:
    usual invoice
    P.L.I.B. certificate that goods are
    actually in existence, and
    Bank Guarantee

5) Reference the option of cancellation, and this also refers to Control's attitude towards exercise of their option of minimum quantity, both Mr. David and Mr. Williams said that neither the cancellation clause nor the option of the minimum quantity would ever be used in relation to the market price, that they would be guided in respect to cancellation or minimum quantities solely by freights. They clearly stated that it would never be used in case the market goes down and that they will not cancel nor use the minimum quantities of our contracts and place an equivalent amount of business elsewhere. Mr. Williams stated that they would put a clause in the contract that any quantity cancelled or reduced would be held in abeyance for us and we be given first refusal on that quantity before any purchases would be made elsewhere.

6) Mr. MacMillan then said that he and Mr. Humbird, also Mr. David and Williams were agreeable that 60% of the order which MacMillan had sold to the Control would be placed with Seaboard, and 40% which Seaboard had sold to the Control would be placed with MacMillan, actually four orders would be placed by the Control, two with Seaboard and two with MacMillan. The total quantity of the four orders will be 195,000 standards, and the maximum will be 250,000 standards. *Therefore the total of MacMillan's orders will be 78,000 standards minimum, 100,000 standards maximum, and the total of Seaboard's orders will be 117,000 standards minimum, 150,000 standards maximum.* [Humbird's emphasis]

As regards SPECIFICATIONS, Messrs. David and Williams have agreed to meet with Mr. Effinger, Wilson, Woolrich and Shaw on Wednesday, 21st February at 11 o'clock to arrive at specifications to the extent of 90% of the order, which is to be along the lines of the specifications submitted to the Control by Price & Pierce on January 1st, of which Mr. Williams let us view a copy of Friday 16th February and of which Mr. Effinger holds a copy. 10% of the specification will not be given at the present time, but will be held in abeyance by the Control, however prices will be agreed upon at this time and at the time orders are placed for this 10% the quantities and specifications will be subject to mutual consent of both the Control and the Sellers."

Appendix E

AVAILABILITY OF LUMBER TO BRITISH TIMBER CONTROL, 1945

	Reasonably sure delivery *standards*	Possible delivery *standards*
Swedish	240,000	400,000
Russian	25,000	50,000
Finland	-------	165,000
Eastern Canada	90,000	125,000
British Columbia	250,000	400,000
U.K. grown	200,000	200,000

Appendix F

OFFICERS OF SEABOARD LUMBER SALES COMPANY

See notes on p. 298.

1935
President	J. A. Humbird
1st Vice-President	C. McRae
Vice-President &	
General Manager	C. H. Grinnell
Secretary	C. H. Grinnell
Treasurer	C. H. Grinnell

1936
President	J. A. Humbird
1st Vice-President	J. G. Robson
Vice-President	B. M. Farris
	H. J. Mackin
Secretary	C. H. Grinnell
Treasurer	C. J. Culter

1937
*President	J. A. Humbird
*1st Vice-President	J. G. Robson
*Vice-President	B. M. Farris
	H. J. Mackin
	C. J. Culter
	J. H. McDonald
	A. R. McFarlane
	F. R. Pendleton
	Carlton Stone
Secretary	C. H. Grinnell
Treasurer	C. H. Grinnell

1938
*President	J. A. Humbird
*1st Vice-President	J. G. Robson
*Vice-President	B. M. Farris
	H. J. Mackin
	C. J. Culter
	J. H. McDonald
	A. R. McFarlane
	F. R. Pendleton
	Carlton Stone
	C. H. Grinnell
Secretary	H. V. Simpson

1939
*President	J. A. Humbird
*1st Vice-President	C. J. Culter
*Vice-President	B. M. Farris
	H. J. Mackin
	J. G. Robson
	J. H. McDonald
	A. R. McFarlane
	Brooks Pendleton
	Goodwin Johnson
*Vice-President &	
General Manager	C. H. Grinnell
Secretary	H. V. Simpson

1940
*President	J. A. Humbird
*1st Vice-President	C. J. Culter
*Vice-President	B. M. Farris
	H. J. Mackin
	J. G. Robson
	J. H. McDonald
	A. R. McFarlane
	Wayne Pendleton
	Carlton Stone
	Goodwin Johnson
*Vice-President &	
General Manager	C. H. Grinnell
Secretary	H. V. Simpson

1941
*President	J. A. Humbird
*1st Vice-President	C. J. Culter
*Vice-President	B. M. Farris
	H. J. Mackin
	J. G. Robson
	J. H. McDonald
	E. S. Glaspie
	Brooks Pendleton
	Carlton Stone
	Goodwin Johnson
	J. G. McConville

* Vice-President &
    General Manager   C. H. Grinnell
  Secretary   H. V. Simpson

1942
* President   J. A. Humbird
* 1st Vice-President   C. J. Culter
* Vice-President   B. M. Farris
                        H. J. Mackin
                        J. G. Robson
                        J. H. McDonald
                        R. B. McRae
                        Wayne Pendleton
                        Carlton Stone
                        Goodwin Johnson
                        J. G. McConville

* Vice-President &
    General Manager   C. H. Grinnell
  Secretary   H. V. Simpson

1943
* President   J. A. Humbird
* 1st Vice-President   C. J. Culter
* Vice-President   B. M. Farris
                        H. J. Mackin
                        J. G. Robson
                        J. H. McDonald
                        E. S. Glaspie
                        Brooks Pendleton
                        Carlton Stone
                        G. R. Hackett

* Vice-President &
    General Manager   C. H. Grinnell
  Secretary   C. H. Grinnell

1944
* President   J. A. Humbird
* 1st Vice-President   C. J. Culter
* Vice-President   B. M. Farris
                        H. J. Mackin
                        J. G. Robson
                        J. H. McDonald
                        R. B. McRae
                        L. L. G. Bentley
                        Carlton Stone
                        A. W. Millar

* Vice-President &
    General Manager   C. H. Grinnell
  Secretary   C. H. Grinnell

1945
* President   J. A. Humbird

* 1st Vice-President   C. J. Culter
* Vice-President   B. M. Farris
                        H. J. Mackin
                        J. G. Robson
                        J. H. McDonald
                        Brooks Pendleton
                        L. L. G. Bentley
                        Carlton Stone
                        E. S. Glaspie

* Vice-President &
    General Manager   C. H. Grinnell
  Secretary   C. H. Grinnell

1946
* President   J. A. Humbird
* 1st Vice-President   B. M. Farris
* Vice-President   M. B. King
                        H. J. Mackin
                        J. G. Robson
                        J. H. McDonald
                        C. J. Culter
                        L. L. G. Bentley
                        Carlton Stone
                        A. W. Millar

* Vice-President &
    General Manager   C. H. Grinnell
  Secretary   C. N. Effinger

1947
* President   B. M. Farris
* 1st Vice-President   H. J. Mackin
* Vice-President   M. B. King
                        F. A. E. Manning
                        J. G. Robson
                        J. M. Edwards
                        Brooks Pendleton
                        L. L. G. Bentley
                        Carlton Stone

* Vice-President &
    Managing
    Director   C. H. Grinnell
  Secretary   C. N. Effinger

1948
* President   B. M. Farris
* 1st Vice-President   H. J. Mackin
* Vice-President   M. B. King
                        E. S. Glaspie
                        J. G. Robson
                        R. S. McDonald
                        G. R. Hackett
                        L. L. G. Bentley
                        Carlton Stone

* Vice-President &
  Managing
  Director　　　　　C. H. Grinnell
Secretary　　　　　C. N. Effinger

1949
* President　　　　　　B. M. Farris
* 1st Vice-President　　H. J. Mackin
* Vice-President　　　　M. B. King
　　　　　　　　　　　Samuel Heller
　　　　　　　　　　　J. G. Robson
　　　　　　　　　　　W. S. Moore
　　　　　　　　　　　J. M. Edwards
　　　　　　　　　　　L. L. G. Bentley
　　　　　　　　　　　Carlton Stone

* Vice-President &
  Managing
  Director　　　　　C. H. Grinnell
Secretary　　　　　C. N. Effinger

1950
* President　　　　　　B. M. Farris
* 1st Vice-President　　H. J. Mackin
* Vice-President　　　　M. B. King
　　　　　　　　　　　E. S. Glaspie
　　　　　　　　　　　J. G. Robson
　　　　　　　　　　　R. S. McDonald
　　　　　　　　　　　Brooks
　　　　　　　　　　　　Pendleton
　　　　　　　　　　　L. L. G. Bentley
　　　　　　　　　　　Carlton Stone

* Vice-President &
  General Manager　C. H. Grinnell
Secretary　　　　　C. N. Effinger

1951
* President　　　　　　B. M. Farris
　　　　　　　　　　　(resigned 19
　　　　　　　　　　　Oct.)
　　　　　　　　　　　H. J. Mackin
* 1st Vice-President　　H. J. Mackin
* Vice-President　　　　M. B. King
　　　　　　　　　　　Samuel Heller
　　　　　　　　　　　J. G. Robson
　　　　　　　　　　　W. S. Moore
　　　　　　　　　　　R. S. McDonald
　　　　　　　　　　　L. L. G. Bentley
　　　　　　　　　　　J. A. C. Drew

* Vice-President &
  Managing
  Director　　　　　C. H. Grinnell

Assistant Manager
  & Secretary　　　C. N. Effinger

1952
* President　　　　　　H. J. Mackin
* 1st Vice-President　　J. G. Robson
* Vice-President　　　　M. B. King
　　　　　　　　　　　Samuel Heller
　　　　　　　　　　　J. P. O'Hagan
　　　　　　　　　　　W. C. Koerner
　　　　　　　　　　　R. S. McDonald
　　　　　　　　　　　L. L. G. Bentley
　　　　　　　　　　　J. A. C. Drew
　　　　　　　　　　　H. A. Renwick

* Vice-President &
  Managing
  Director　　　　　C. H. Grinnell
Assistant Manager
  & Secretary　　　C. N. Effinger

1953
* President　　　　　　H. J. Mackin
* 1st Vice-President　　L. L. G. Bentley
* Vice-President　　　　M. B. King
　　　　　　　　　　　Samuel Heller
　　　　　　　　　　　W. S. Moore
　　　　　　　　　　　W. C. Koerner
　　　　　　　　　　　J. G. Robson
　　　　　　　　　　　H. A. Renwick
　　　　　　　　　　　J. A. C. Drew

* Vice-President &
  Managing
  Director　　　　　C. H. Grinnell
　　　　　　　　　　　(resigned 30
　　　　　　　　　　　June)
　　　　　　　　　　　C. N. Effinger

Assistant Manager
  & Secretary　　　C. N. Effinger

1954
* President　　　　　　H. J. Mackin
* 1st Vice-President　　L. L. G. Bentley
* Vice-President　　　　A. D. Anderson
　　　　　　　　　　　Samuel Heller
　　　　　　　　　　　W. S. Moore
　　　　　　　　　　　W. C. Koerner
　　　　　　　　　　　J. G. Robson
　　　　　　　　　　　H. A. Renwick
　　　　　　　　　　　J. A. C. Drew

* Vice-President &
  Managing
  Director　　　　　C. N. Effinger
Secretary　　　　　H. A. Berry

1955
* Chairman &
 President — H. J. Mackin
* 1st Vice-President — L. L. G. Bentley
* Vice-President — A. D. Anderson
 Samuel Heller
 J. P. O'Hagan
 W. C. Koerner
 J. G. Robson
 H. A. Renwick
 H. Stone

* Vice-President &
 Managing
 Director — C. N. Effinger
 Secretary — H. A. Berry

1956
* Chairman &
 President — H. J. Mackin
* 1st Vice-President — L. L. G. Bentley
* Vice-President — A. D. Anderson
 Samuel Heller
 J. P. O'Hagan
 T. L. Roberts
 J. G. Robson
 H. A. Renwick
 H. Stone

* Vice-President &
 Managing
 Director — C. N. Effinger
 Secretary — H. A. Berry

1957
* Chairman &
 President — H. J. Mackin
* 1st Vice-President — L. L. G. Bentley
* Vice-President — A. D. Anderson
 Samuel Heller
 W. S. Moore
 T. L. Roberts
 A. L. Lyttle
 H. A. Renwick
 H. C. Stone

* Vice-President &
 Managing
 Director — C. N. Effinger
 Secretary — H. A. Berry

1958
* Chairman &
 President — H. J. Mackin
 (resigned 17 Dec.)

* 1st Vice-President — L. L. G. Bentley
* Vice-President — D. R. Schmidt
 Samuel Heller
 W. S. Moore
 T. L. Roberts
 A. L. Lyttle
 H. A. Renwick
 H. C. Stone

* Vice-President &
 Managing
 Director — C. N. Effinger
 Secretary — H. A. Berry

1959
* Chairman &
 President — L. L. G. Bentley
* 1st Vice-President — T. L. Roberts
* Vice-President — D. R. Schmidt
 Samuel Heller
 W. S. Moore
 R. S. McDonald
 A. L. Lyttle
 H. A. Renwick
 H. C. Stone

* Vice-President &
 Managing
 Director — C. N. Effinger
 Secretary — H. A. Berry

1960
* Chairman &
 President — L. L. G. Bentley
* 1st Vice-President — T. L. Roberts
* Vice-President — D. R. Schmidt
 Samuel Heller
 W. S. Moore
 R. S. McDonald
 R. H. Ellison
 A. D. Anderson
 H. C. Stone

* Vice-President &
 Managing
 Director — C. N. Effinger
 Secretary — H. A. Berry

1961
* Chairman &
 President — L. L. G. Bentley
* 1st Vice-President — T. L. Roberts
* Vice-President — D. G. Allison
 Samuel Heller
 W. S. Moore

R. G. Rogers
R. H. Ellison
A. D. Anderson
H. C. Stone

* Vice-President &
  Managing
  Director — C. N. Effinger
Secretary — H. A. Berry
General Manager — H. P. O'Hagan
Sales Manager — R. H. Edgett

1962
* Chairman &
  President — L. L. G. Bentley
* Vice-President — D. G. Allison
Samuel Heller
J. P. O'Hagan
R. G. Rogers
T. L. Roberts
A. D. Anderson
H. C. Stone
F. H. Pendleton

* Vice-President &
  Managing
  Director — C. N. Effinger
Secretary — H. A. Berry
General Manager — H. P. O'Hagan

1963
* Chairman &
  President — L. L. G. Bentley
* Vice-President — H. A. Smith
Samuel Heller
R. H. Ellison
R. G. Rogers
T. L. Roberts
A. D. Anderson
H. C. Stone
F. H. Pendleton

* Vice-President &
  Managing
  Director — H. P. O'Hagan
Secretary-Treasurer — H. A. Berry
General Sales
  Manager — R. H. Edgett

1964
* Chairman &
  President — L. L. G. Bentley
* Vice-President — D. G. Allison
Samuel Heller
R. H. Ellison

R. G. Rogers
T. L. Roberts
H. A. Smith
J. E. Feigl
A. O. Sauer

* Vice-President &
  Managing
  Director — H. P. O'Hagan
Secretary-Treasurer — H. A. Berry
General Sales
  Manager — R. H. Edgett

1965
* Chairman &
  President — L. L. G. Bentley
* Vice-President — D. G. Allison
F. C. Brooks
W. Guy Flavelle
D. S. Denman
C. R. Matthison
H. A. Smith
J. E. Feigl
G. L. Draeseke

* Vice-President &
  Managing
  Director — H. P. O'Hagan
Secretary-Treasurer — H. A. Berry
General Sales
  Manager — R. H. Edgett

1966
* Chairman &
  President — L. L. G. Bentley
* Vice-President — J. W. Buchanan
F. C. Brooks
G. M. Lyttle
D. S. Denman
J. D. Cameron
H. C. Stone
J. E. Feigl
G. L. Draeseke

* Vice-President &
  Managing
  Director — H. P. O'Hagan
Secretary-Treasurer — H. A. Berry
General Sales
  Manager — R. H. Edgett

1967
* Chairman &
  President — L. L. G. Bentley

* Vice-President

| J. W. Buchanan |
| F. H. Pendleton |
| G. M. Lyttle |
| D. S. Denman |
| W. R. McCutcheon |
| H. C. Stone |
| J. P. O'Hagan |
| G. L. Draeseke |

* Vice-President &
  Managing
  Director — H. P. O'Hagan
Secretary-Treasurer — H. A. Berry
General Sales
  Manager — R. H. Edgett

1968
* Chairman — L. L. G. Bentley
* Vice-Chairman — D. S. Denman
* Vice-President — D. E. Cluck

| Samuel Heller |
| G. M. Lyttle |
| H. A. Smith |
| J. P. O'Hagan |
| J. E. Feigl |
| G. L. Draeseke |

* President &
  Managing
  Director — H. P. O'Hagan
Secretary &
  Vice-President,
  Finance — H. A. Berry
Vice-President,
  Marketing — R. H. Edgett

1969
* Chairman — L. L. G. Bentley
* Vice-Chairman — G. S. J. Bowell
* Vice-President — D. E. Cluck

| Samuel Heller |
| W. O. Beaton |
| H. A. Smith |
| C. R. Matthison |
| J. E. Feigl |
| D. G. Allison |

* President &
  Managing
  Director — H. P. O'Hagan
Secretary &
  Vice-President,
  Finance — H. A. Berry
Vice-President,
  Marketing — R. H. Edgett

1970
* Chairman — G. S. J. Bowell
* Vice-Chairman — R. C. McMillan
* Executive Director — D. E. Cluck

| R. R. Ogilvy |
| G. M. Lyttle |
| L. L. G. Bentley |
| H. E. Manning |
| J. E. Feigl |
| G. L. Malpass |

*President &
  Managing
  Director — H. P. O'Hagan
Secretary &
  Vice-President,
  Finance — H. A. Berry
Vice-President,
  Marketing — R. H. Edgett

1971
* Chairman — G. S. J. Bowell
* Vice-Chairman — R. C. McMillan
* Executive Director — C. R. Matthison

| R. R. Ogilvy |
| G. M. Lyttle |
| L. L. G. Bentley |
| H. E. Manning |
| J. E. Feigl |
| H. B. Urquhart |

* President &
  Managing
  Director — H. P. O'Hagan
Secretary &
  Vice-President,
  Finance — H. A. Berry
Vice-President,
  Marketing — R. H. Edgett

1972
* Chairman — G. S. J. Bowell
* Vice-Chairman — R. C. McMillan
* Executive Director — C. R. Matthison

| R. R. Ogilvy |
| G. M. Lyttle |
| L. L. G. Bentley |
| H. E. Manning |
| J. E. Feigl |
| H. B. Urquhart |

* President &
  Managing
  Director — H. P. O'Hagan

Secretary &
  Vice-President,
  Finance   H. A. Berry
Vice-President,
  Marketing   R. H. Edgett

1973
* Chairman   R. G. Rogers
* Vice-Chairman R. C. McMillan
* Executive Director C. R. Matthison
              R. R. Ogilvy
              G. M. Lyttle
              L. L. G. Bentley
              H. E. Manning
              E. Sonner
              H. B. Urquhart
              G. S. J. Bowell
* President &
  Managing
  Director   H. P. O'Hagan
              (resigned 23
              Aug.)
              C. D. G. Roberts
Secretary &
  Vice-President,
  Finance   H. A. Berry
Vice-President,
  Marketing   R. H. Edgett

1974
* Chairman   R. G. Rogers
* Vice-Chairman R. C. McMillan
* Executive Director C. R. Matthison
            R. R. Ogilvy
            G. M. Lyttle
            L. L. G. Bentley
            H. E. Manning
            E. Sonner
            H. B. Urquhart
            G. S. J. Bowell
* President &
  Managing
  Director   C. D. G. Roberts
Senior Vice-
  President   H. A. Berry
Secretary   H. A. Berry
Vice-President,
  Lumber &
  Shingle Sales R. R. Dobell
Vice-President,
  Sheet Material
  Sales   R. D. Reid
Vice-President,
  Finance   L. R. Ridenour

1975
* Chairman   R. G. Rogers
* Vice-Chairman P. J. G. Bentley
* Executive Director C. R. Matthison
           R. R. Ogilvy
           G. M. Lyttle
           R. C. McMillan
           H. E. Manning
           E. Sonner
           H. B. Urquhart
           T. A. Buell
* President & Chief
  Executive Officer C. D. G. Roberts
Senior Vice-
  President   H. A. Berry
Secretary   R. L. Barclay
Vice-President,
  Lumber &
  Shingle Sales E. A. Cameron
Vice-President,
  Sheet Material
  Sales   R. D. Reid
Vice-President,
  Development &
  Administration L. R. Ridenour

1976
* Chairman   P. J. G. Bentley
* Vice-Chairman T. A. Buell
* Executive Director L. J. Martin
           R. R. Ogilvy
           G. M. Lyttle
           R. G. Rogers
           H. E. Manning
           E. Sonner
           H. B. Urquhart
* President & Chief
  Executive Officer C. D. G. Roberts
Senior Vice-
  President   H. A. Berry
Secretary   R. L. Barclay
Vice-President,
  Lumber &
  Shingle Sales E. A. Cameron
Vice-President,
  Sheet Material
  Sales   R. D. Reid
Vice-President,
  Development &
  Administration L. R. Ridenour

1977
* Chairman   P. J. G. Bentley
* Vice-Chairman   T. A. Buell
* Executive Director   J. L. Buttar
                           C. A. Johnson
                           G. M. Lyttle
                           H. E. Manning
                           L. J. Martin
                           T. G. Rust
                           E. Sonner

* President & Chief
     Executive Officer   C. D. G. Roberts
  Secretary   R. L. Barclay
  Vice-President,
     Lumber   E. A. Cameron
  Vice-President,
     Plywood   R. D. Reid
  Vice-President,
     Finance   L. R. Ridenour

1978
* Chairman   T. A. Buell
* Vice-Chairman   T. G. Rust
* Executive Director   J. L. Buttar
                           C. A. Johnson
                           G. M. Lyttle
                           H. E. Manning
                           L. J. Martin
                           E. Sonner
                           P. J. G. Bentley

* President & Chief
     Executive Officer   C. D. G. Roberts
  Secretary   R. L. Barclay
  Vice-President,
     Lumber   E. A. Cameron
  Vice-President,
     Plywood   R. D. Reid
  Vice-President,
     Finance   L. R. Ridenour

1979
* Chairman   T. A. Buell
* Vice-Chairman   T. G. Rust
* Executive Director   J. L. Buttar
                           C. A. Johnson
                           G. M. Lyttle
                           H. E. Manning
                           L. J. Martin
                           P. J. G. Bentley

* President & Chief
     Executive Officer   C. D. G. Roberts

  Secretary   R. L. Barclay
  Vice-President,
     Lumber   E. A. Cameron
  Vice-President,
     Finance   L. R. Ridenour

1980
* Chairman   T. G. Rust
* Vice-Chairman   W. L. Sauder
* Executive Director   J. L. Buttar
                           J. M. Rustad
                           G. M. Lyttle
                           H. E. Manning
                           T. E. Buell
                           P. J. G. Bentley
                           W. M. Sloan

  President & Chief
     Executive Officer   C. D. G. Roberts
  Secretary   R. L. Barclay
  Vice-President,
     Lumber   E. A. Cameron
  Vice-President,
     Plywood   C. Brock
  Vice-President,
     Finance   L. R. Ridenour

1981
* Chairman   T. G. Rust
* Vice-Chairman   W. L. Sauder
* Director   J. L. Buttar
                           J. M. Rustad
                           G. M. Lyttle
                           H. E. Manning
                           T. A. Buell
                           P. J. G. Bentley
                           W. M. Sloan

* President & Chief
     Executive Officer   C. D. G. Roberts
  Corporate Secretary   R. L. Barclay
  Senior
     Vice-President,
     Lumber   E. A. Cameron
  Vice-President,
     Plywood   C. Brock
  Vice-President,
     Finance   L. R. Ridenour

1982
* Chairman   W. L. Sauder
* Vice-Chairman   P. J. G. Bentley

* Director | D. Ainsworth
| T. A. Buell
| G. M. Lyttle
| H. E. Manning
| T. G. Rust
| W. M. Sloan

* President & Chief
  Executive Officer | C. D. G. Roberts
Corporate Secretary | R. L. Barclay
Senior
  Vice-President,
  Lumber | E. A. Cameron
Vice-President,
  Plywood | C. Brock
Vice-President,
  Finance | L. R. Ridenour

1983
* Chairman | W. L. Sauder
* Vice-Chairman | P. J. G. Bentley
* Director | D. Ainsworth
| T. A. Buell
| G. M. Lyttle
| H. E. Manning
| T. G. Rust
| W. M. Sloan

* President & Chief
  Executive Officer | C. D. G. Roberts
Corporate Secretary | R. L. Barclay

Senior
  Vice-President,
  Lumber | E. A. Cameron
Vice-President,
  Plywood | C. Brock
Vice-President,
  Finance | L. R. Ridenour

1984
* Chairman | P. J. G. Bentley
* Vice-Chairman | T. A. Buell
* Director | D. Ainsworth
| L. C. Ryan
| W. L. Sauder
| W. M. Sloan
| H. A. Smith

* President & Chief
  Executive Officer | C. D. G. Roberts
Corporate Secretary | R. L. Barclay
Senior
  Vice-President,
  Lumber | E. A. Cameron
Vice-President,
  Plywood | C. Brock
Vice-President,
  Finance | L. R. Ridenour

* Executive Committee

From 1980, Directors were not Officers but were members of the Executive Committee. The Executive Committee of Seaboard Shipping Company is the same.

Appendix G

OFFICERS OF SEABOARD SHIPPING COMPANY

1936
President — J. A. Humbird
1st Vice-President — J. G. Robson
Vice-President — B. M. Farris
H. J. Mackin
Secretary — C. H. Grinnell
Treasurer — C. J. Culter

1937
President — J. A. Humbird
1st Vice-President — J. G. Robson
Vice-President — B. M. Farris
H. J. Mackin
C. J. Culter
J. H. McDonald
A. R. McFarlane
F. R. Pendleton
Carlton Stone
Secretary — C. H. Grinnell
Treasurer — C. H. Grinnell

1938
President — J. A. Humbird
1st Vice-President — J. G. Robson
Vice-President — B. M. Farris
H. J. Mackin
C. J. Culter
J. H. McDonald
A. R. McFarlane
F. R. Pendleton
Carlton Stone
C. H. Grinnell
Secretary — H. V. Simpson

1939
President — J. A. Humbird
1st Vice-President — C. J. Culter
Vice-President — B. M. Farris
H. J. Mackin
J. G. Robson
J. H. McDonald
A. R. McFarlane
Brooks Pendleton
Goodwin Johnson
C. H. Grinnell
Secretary — H. V. Simpson

1940
President — J. A. Humbird
1st Vice-President — C. J. Culter
Vice-President — B. M. Farris
H. J. Mackin
J. G. Robson
J. H. McDonald
A. R. McFarlane
Wayne Pendleton
Carlton Stone
Goodwin Johnson
C. H. Grinnell
Secretary — H. V. Simpson

1941
President — J. A. Humbird
1st Vice-President — C. J. Culter
Vice-President — B. M. Farris
H. J. Mackin
J. G. Robson
J. H. McDonald
E. S. Glaspie
Brooks Pendleton
Carlton Stone
Goodwin Johnson
C. H. Grinnell
Secretary — H. V. Simpson

1942
President — J. A. Humbird
1st Vice-President — C. J. Culter
Vice-President — B. M. Farris
H. J. Mackin
J. G. Robson
J. H. McDonald
R. B. McRae
Wayne Pendleton

	Carlton Stone	Secretary & General	
	Goodwin Johnson	Manager	W. L. Hurford
	C. H. Grinnell		(resigned 11 Jan)
Secretary	H. V. Simpson		H. E. Solloway

1943

President	J. A. Humbird
1st Vice-President	C. J. Culter
Secretary	C. H. Grinnell

1944

President	J. A. Humbird
1st Vice-President	C. J. Culter
Vice-President	C. H. Grinnell
Secretary	C. H. Grinnell

1945

President	J. A. Humbird
1st Vice-President	C. J. Culter
Secretary	C. H. Grinnell

1946

President	J. A. Humbird
1st Vice-President	B. M. Farris
Vice-President	C. H. Grinnell
Secretary	W. L. Hurford

1947

President	B. M. Farris
1st Vice-President	H. J. Mackin
Vice-President	C. H. Grinnell
Secretary & General Manager	W. L. Hurford

1948

President	B. M. Farris
1st Vice-President	H. J. Mackin
Vice-President	C. H. Grinnell
Secretary & General Manager	W. L. Hurford

1949

President	B. M. Farris
1st Vice-President	H. J. Mackin
Vice-President	C. H. Grinnell
Secretary & General Manager	W. L. Hurford

1950

President	B. M. Farris
1st Vice-President	H. J. Mackin
Vice-President	C. H. Grinnell

1951

President	B. M. Farris
	(resigned 19 Oct)
	H. J. Mackin
1st Vice-President	H. J. Mackin
Vice-President & Managing Director	C. H. Grinnell
Secretary & General Manager	H. E. Solloway

1952

President	H. J. Mackin
1st Vice-President	J. G. Robson
Vice-President & Managing Director	C. H. Grinnell
Secretary & General Manager	H. E. Solloway

1953

President	H. J. Mackin
1st Vice-President	L. L. G. Bentley
Vice-President & Managing Director	C. H. Grinnell (resigned 30 June)
	C. N. Effinger
Secretary & General Manager	H. E. Solloway

1954

President	H. J. Mackin
1st Vice-President	L. L. G. Bentley
Vice-President & Managing Director	C. N. Effinger
Secretary	H. A. Berry
General Manager	H. E. Solloway

1955

Chairman & President	H. J. Mackin
1st Vice-President	L. L. G. Bentley
Vice-President & Managing Director	C. N. Effinger

Secretary H. A. Berry
General Manager H. E. Solloway
(resigned 30
June)
V. G. B. Forrester

1956
Chairman &
President H. J. Mackin
1st Vice-President L. L. G. Bentley
Vice-President &
Managing
Director C. N. Effinger
Secretary H. A. Berry
General Manager V. G. B. Forrester

1957
Chairman &
President H. J. Mackin
1st Vice-President L. L. G. Bentley
Vice-President &
Managing
Director C. N. Effinger
Secretary H. A. Berry
General Manager V. G. B. Forrester

1958
Chairman &
President H. J. Mackin
(resigned 17
Dec)
1st Vice-President L. L. G. Bentley
Vice-President &
Managing
Director C. N. Effinger
Secretary H. A. Berry
General Manager V. G. B. Forrester

1959
Chairman &
President L. L. G. Bentley
1st Vice-President T. L. Roberts
Vice-President &
Managing
Director C. N. Effinger
Secretary H. A. Berry
General Manager V. G. B. Forrester

1960
Chairman &
President L. L. G. Bentley
1st Vice-President T. L. Roberts

Vice-President &
Managing
Director C. N. Effinger
Secretary H. A. Berry
General Manager V. G. B. Forrester

1961
Chairman &
President L. L. G. Bentley
1st Vice-President T. L. Roberts
Vice-President &
Managing
Director C. N. Effinger
Secretary H. A. Berry
General Manager V. G. B. Forrester

1962
Chairman &
President L. L. G. Bentley
Vice-President &
Managing
Director C. N. Effinger
Secretary H. A. Berry
General Manager V. G. B. Forrester

1963
Chairman &
President L. L. G. Bentley
Vice-President &
Managing
Director H. P. O'Hagan
Secretary-Treasurer H. A. Berry
General Manager V. G. B. Forrester

1964
Chairman &
President L. L. G. Bentley
Vice-President &
Managing
Director H. P. O'Hagan
Secretary-Treasurer H. A. Berry
General Manager V. G. B. Forrester

1965
Chairman &
President L. L. G. Bentley
Vice-President &
Managing
Director H. P. O'Hagan
Secretary-Treasurer H. A. Berry
General Manager V. G. B. Forrester

1966
Chairman &
  President   L. L. G. Bentley
Vice-President &
  Managing
  Director   H. P. O'Hagan
Secretary-Treasurer   H. A. Berry
General Manager   V. G. B. Forrester

1967
Chairman &
  President   L. L. G. Bentley
Vice-President &
  Managing
  Director   H. P. O'Hagan
Secretary-Treasurer   H. A. Berry
General Manager   V. G. B. Forrester

1968
Chairman   L. L. G. Bentley
Vice-Chairman   D. S. Denman
President &
  Managing
  Director   H. P. O'Hagan
Secretary &
  Vice-President,
  Finance   H. A. Berry
Vice-President &
  General
  Manager   V. G. B. Forrester

1969
Chairman   L. L. G. Bentley
Vice-Chairman   G. S. J. Bowell
President &
  Managing
  Director   H. P. O'Hagan
Secretary &
  Vice-President,
  Finance   H. A. Berry
Vice-President &
  General Manager   V. G. B. Forrester

1970
Chairman   G. S. J. Bowell
Vice-Chairman   R. C. McMillan
President &
  Managing
  Director   H. P. O'Hagan
Secretary &
  Vice-President,
  Finance   H. A. Berry

Vice-President &
  General Manager   R. M. Mather

1971
Chairman   G. S. J. Bowell
Vice-Chairman   R. C. McMillan
President &
  Managing
  Director   H. P. O'Hagan
Secretary &
  Vice-President,
  Finance   H. A. Berry
Vice-President &
  General Manager   R. M. Mather

1972
Chairman   G. S. J. Bowell
Vice-Chairman   R. C. McMillan
President &
  Managing
  Director   H. P. O'Hagan
Secretary &
  Vice-President,
  Finance   H. A. Berry
Vice-President &
  General Manager   R. M. Mather

1973
Chairman   R. G. Rogers
Vice-Chairman   R. C. McMillan
President &   H. P. O'Hagan
  Managing   (resigned 23
  Director   Aug.)
                           C. D. G. Roberts
Secretary &
  Vice-President,
  Finance   H. A. Berry
Vice-President &
  General
  Manager   R. M. Mather

1974
Chairman   R. G. Rogers
Vice-Chairman   R. C. McMillan
President &
  Managing
  Director   C. D. G. Roberts
Secretary &
  Vice-President,
  Finance   H. A. Berry
Vice-President &
  General Manager   R. M. Mather

1975

Chairman	R. G. Rogers
Vice-Chairman	P. J. G. Bentley
President & Chief Executive Officer	C. D. G. Roberts
Senior Vice-President	H. A. Berry
Vice-President & General Manager	C. L. Jacobs
Vice President, Development & Administration	L. R. Ridenour
Secretary	R. L. Barclay
General Manager, Distribution	G. D. Darling

1976

Chairman	P. J. G. Bentley
Vice-Chairman	T. A. Buell
President & Chief Executive Officer	C. D. G. Roberts
Senior Vice-President	H. A. Berry
Vice-President & General Manager	C. L. Jacobs
Vice-President, Development & Administration	L. R. Ridenour
Secretary	R. L. Barclay
General Manager, Distribution	G. D. Darling
Executive Director	G. M. Lyttle
	H. E. Manning
	L. J. Martin
	R. R. Ogilvy
	R. G. Rogers
	E. Sonner
	J. L. Buttar

1977

Chairman	P. J. G. Bentley
Vice-Chairman	T. A. Buell
President & Chief Executive Officer	C. D. G. Roberts
Vice-President & General Manager	C. L. Jacobs
Vice-President, Finance	L. R. Ridenour
Secretary	R. L. Barclay
General Manager, Distribution	G. D. Darling
Executive Director	H. E. Manning
	L. J. Martin
	T. G. Rust
	E. Sonner
	J. L. Buttar
	C. A. Johnson
	G. M. Lyttle

1978

Chairman	T. A. Buell
Vice-Chairman	T. G. Rust
President & Chief Executive Officer	C. D. G. Roberts
Vice-President & General Manager	C. L. Jacobs
Vice-President, Finance	L. R. Ridenour
Secretary	R. L. Barclay
General Manager, Distribution	G. D. Darling
Executive Director	J. L. Buttar
	C. A. Johnson
	G. M. Lyttle
	H. E. Manning
	L. J. Martin
	E. Sonner
	P. J. G. Bentley

1979

Chairman	T. A. Buell
Vice-Chairman	T. G. Rust
President & Chief Executive Officer	C. D. G. Roberts
Vice-President & General Manager	C. L. Jacobs
Vice-President, Finance	L. R. Ridenour
Secretary	R. L. Barclay
General Manager, Distribution	G. D. Darling
Executive Director	J. L. Buttar
	C. A. Johnson
	G. M. Lyttle
	H. E. Manning
	L. J. Martin
	P. J. G. Bentley

1980

Chairman	T. G. Rust
Vice-Chairman	W. L. Sauder
President & Chief Executive Officer	C. D. G. Roberts

Vice-President &	
General Manager	C. L. Jacobs
Vice-President,	
Finance	L. R. Ridenour
Secretary	R. L. Barclay
General Manager,	
Distribution	G. D. Darling
Executive Director	J. L. Buttar
	J. M. Rustad
	G. M. Lyttle
	H. E. Manning
	T. A. Buell
	P. J. G. Bentley
	W. M. Sloan

1981

Chairman	T. G. Rust
Vice-Chairman	W. L. Sauder
President & Chief	
Executive Officer	C. D. G. Roberts
Vice-President &	
General Manager	C. L. Jacobs
Vice-President,	
Finance	L. R. Ridenour
Corporate Secretary	R. L. Barclay
Executive Director	J. L. Buttar
	J. M. Rustad
	G. M. Lyttle
	H. E. Manning
	T. A. Buell
	P. J. G. Bentley
	W. M. Sloan

1982

Chairman	W. L. Sauder
Vice-Chairman	P. J. G. Bentley
President & Chief	
Executive Officer	C. D. G. Roberts
Vice-President &	
General Manager	C. L. Jacobs
Vice-President,	
Finance	L. R. Ridenour

Corporate Secretary	R. L. Barclay
Director	D. Ainsworth
	T. A. Buell
	G. M. Lyttle
	H. E. Manning
	T. G. Rust
	W. M. Sloan

1983

Chairman	W. L. Sauder
Vice-Chairman	P. J. G. Bentley
President & Chief	
Executive Officer	C. D. G. Roberts
Vice-President &	
General Manager	C. L. Jacobs
Vice-President,	
Finance	L. R. Ridenour
Corporate Secretary	R. L. Barclay
Director	D. Ainsworth
	T. A. Buell
	G. M. Lyttle
	H. E. Manning
	T. G. Rust
	W. M. Sloan

1984

Chairman	P. J. G. Bentley
Vice-Chairman	T. A. Buell
President & Chief	
Executive Officer	C. D. G. Roberts
Vice-President &	
General Manager	C. L. Jacobs
Vice-President,	
Finance	L. R. Ridenour
Corporate Secretary	R. L. Barclay
Director	D. Ainsworth
	L. C. Ryan
	W. L. Sauder
	W. M. Sloan
	H. A. Smith

Appendix H

SEABOARD LUMBER COMPANY SHAREHOLDER COMPANIES

Note: "Present" is 31 December 1984

Acorn Forest Products Ltd.	1964–1973
Ainsworth Lumber Co. Ltd.	1961–present
Alaska Pine Co. Ltd.	1952–1961
Alberni Pacific Lumber Co.	1935–1938
Alberta Lumber Co. Ltd.	1935–1960
Anderson Bros. Lumber Co. Ltd.	1945–1974
Anglo-Canadian Timber Products Ltd.	1954–1969
(division of Vanwest Logging)	
Admiral Forest Products	1983–present
Bay Lumber Co. Ltd.	1953–1979
(name changed to Bay Forest Products in 1964)	
(acquired by Whonnock Industries in 1979)	
Bloedel, Stewart and Welch Ltd.	1935–1952
B.C. Fir and Cedar Lumber Co. Ltd.	1942–1954
B.C. Manufacturing Co. Ltd.	1935–1957
(acquired by Powell River Lumber Co. Ltd. in 1958)	
Brownsville Sawmills Ltd.	1944–1977
Burke Lumber Co. Ltd.	1935–1974
Cameron Lumber Co. Ltd.	1935–1946
Canadian Collieries (Dunsmuir) Ltd.	1955–1965
(acquired by Weldwood of Canada Ltd. in 1965)	
Canadian Forest Products Ltd.	1944–present
Canadian Plywood Corp. Ltd.	1967–1968
Canadian Robert Dollar Co. Ltd.	1935–1938
Canadian Western Lumber Co. Ltd.	1935–1960
(acquired by Crown Zellerbach Building Materials Ltd. in 1960)	
Canyon Creek Forest Products Ltd.	1980
(acquired by Clearwater Timber Products Ltd. in 1980)	
Carrier Lumber Co. Ltd.	1975–present
Cattermole Timber Ltd.	1978
Cedar Cove Sash and Door Co. Ltd.	1937–1966
(name changed to Cedar Cove Mills Ltd. in 1944)	
Celgar Ltd.	1965–1966

Clearwater Timber Products Ltd.	1981–present
Collins-Macken Lumber Company	1952–1968
Cooke Lumber Co. Ltd.	1965–1967
(acquired by Northwood Mills Ltd.)	
Cowichan Bay Forest Products Ltd.	1968–1969
Crofton Export Co. Ltd.	1938–1942
Crown Zellerbach Building Materials Ltd.	1961–1983
(named changed to Crown Forest Industries Ltd. in 1983)	
Crown Forest Industries Ltd.	1983–present
Dunkley Lumber Ltd.	1975–present
Eburne Sawmills Ltd.	1935–1944
(acquired by Canadian Forest Products in 1944)	
Eureka Sawmills (1956) Ltd.	1956
(acquired by Anglo-Canadian Timber Products in 1956)	
Eurocan Pulp and Paper Co. Ltd.	1968–present
Evans Products Co.	1961–1973
False Creek Lumber Co. Ltd.	1935–1939
Farris Lumber Co. Ltd.	1952–1964
Field Sawmills Ltd.	1968–1974
Glaspie Lumber Co. Ltd.	1939–1954
Goodwin-Johnson Ltd.	1937–1945
Gregory Industries Ltd.	1974–1980
Charles Grinnell	1937–1954
Hammond Cedar Co. Ltd.	1938–1947
Hillcrest Lumber Co. Ltd.	1935–1969
John Humbird	1944–1948
Imp-Pac Lumber Ltd.	1977–1980
(acquired by Whonnock Industries in 1980)	
Industrial Timber Mills Ltd.	1935–1947
Inlet Timber Co. Ltd.	1935–1939
International Woods Products Co.	1938–1940
Jacobson Bros. Forest Products Ltd.	1977–present
Keeley Lumber Co. Ltd.	1960–1961
(acquired by Canadian Collieries in 1961)	
M. B. King Lumber Co. Ltd.	1944–1973
(becomes division of Fullerton Lumber in 1950)	
L&K Lumber (North Shore) Ltd.	1952–present
(name changed to L.& K. Lumber Ltd. in 1982)	
Lake Logging Co. Ltd.	1941–1944

Lamford Cedar Ltd.   1960–1970
   (acquired by Sooke Forest Products in 1970)
Langley Sawmills Ltd.   1948–1952
   (acquired by McDonald Cedar Products in 1952)
Lemon-Gonnason Co. Ltd.   1937–1960
Lignum Ltd.   1980–1983
Lions Gate Lumber Co.   1945–1973

McDonald Cedar Products Ltd.   1952–1978
   (acquired by Whonnock Industries in 1978)
McKay and Flanagan Bros. Lumber Mill Ltd.   1948–1973
Manning Lumber Mills   1938–1960
   (name changed to Manning Timber Products in 1947)
Maple Ridge Lumber Co.   1935–1963
   (name changed to Maple Ridge Lumber Co. (1954) Ltd.)
Mohawk Lumber Co. Ltd.   1935–1954
Moore-Whittington Lumber Co. Ltd.   1938–1964

Nanaimo Sawmills Ltd.   1950–1954
Nelson Spencer Ltd.   1938–1946
North Shore Lumber Corp. Ltd.   1944–1954
Northwest Shake Ltd.   1974–1983
Northwood Mills Ltd.   1963–1968

Oak Bay Lumber Ltd.   1952–1961
   (amalg. with Goodridge Sawmills to become Sooke
   Forest Products Ltd. in 1961)
Orion Bowman and Sons Ltd.   1977–1980
Overseas Spruce Sales Ltd.   1962–1975

Pacific Lime Co. Ltd.   1938–1940
Pacific Logging Co. Ltd.   1979–1980
   (name changed to Pacific Forest Products Ltd. in 1980)
Pacific Forest Products Ltd.   1980–1984
   (name changed to CIP Forest Products Inc. in 1984)
Pacific Pine Co. Ltd.   1945–1973
   (acquired by Triangle Pacific Forest Products Ltd.
   in 1970)
P. Bain   1935–1938
Plumper Bay Sawmills   1963–1983
   (acquired by Admiral Forest Products in 1983)
Port Mellon Operating Co. Ltd.   1937–1943
Powell River Lumber Co. Ltd.   1958–1960
Prince Rupert Forest Products Ltd.   1974–1980
Prince Rupert Sawmills Ltd.   1965–1966
Raven Lumber Ltd.   1968–present
Rayonier Canada (B.C.) Ltd.   1960–1980
   (acquired by Western Forest Products in 1980)

R. B. McLean Lumber Co.	1935–1973
Richmond Plywood Corp. Ltd.	1963–present
Robert McNair Shingle Co. Ltd.	1948–1952
Robertson and Hackett Sawmills Co. Ltd.	1935–1953
Royal City Sawmills	1942–1963
R. S. Stulz	1936–1937
Rustad Bros. Co. Ltd.	1975–present
Savona Timber Co. Ltd.	1965–1973
Shawnigan Lake Lumber Co. Ltd.	1938–1946
Silvertree Sawmills Ltd.	1952–1968
(acquired by Rayonier Canada (B.C.) Ltd. in 1968)	
Simson-Trethewey Lumber Ltd.	1947–1952
Slocan Forest Products Ltd.	1981–present
Sooke Forest Products Ltd.	1961–1970,
	1976–present
Sooke Lake Lumber Ltd.	1948–1960
(name changed to Victoria Plywood Ltd. in 1961)	
Sproat Lake Sawmills Ltd.	1935–1952
Sterling Lumber Ltd.	1938–1945
Straits Lumber Co. Ltd.	1935–1944
Swanson Lumber Co. Ltd.	1965–1973
Timber Preservers Ltd.	1942–1973
(changed name to TPL Industries Ltd. in 1967)	
Timberland Lumber Co. Ltd.	1935–1954
(acquired by Canadian Collieries in 1954)	
Universal Lumber Box Co. Ltd.	1952–1957
Vancouver Kraft Corp.	1942
Victoria Lumber and Manufacturing Co. Ltd.	1935–1946
Victoria Plywood Ltd.	1961–1969
Weldwood of Canada Ltd.	1964–1981
Western Forest Industries Ltd.	1952–1981
Western Forest Products Ltd.	1980–1981
(⅓ interest owned by Whonnock Industries Ltd.)	
Western Plywood Co. Ltd.	1961–1964
(acquired by Weldwood of Canada Ltd. in 1964)	
Whonnock Industries Ltd.	1974–present
Whonnock Lumber Co. Ltd.	1952–1974
(acquired by Whonnock Industries Ltd. in 1974)	
Westminster Shook Mills Ltd.	1935–1958
(acquired by Powell River Lumber Co. Ltd.)	

Wood and English Ltd. 1937–1946
  (name changed to Beaver Cove in 1945; acquired by
  Canadian Collieries in 1946)

Yukon Lumber Co. Ltd. 1964–1968

Appendix I

SEABOARD SHIPPING COMPANY SHAREHOLDER COMPANIES
1936—1981

Shareholders in Shipping Company are identical to those in Lumber Company
(Appendix H), except for Alberni Pacific Lumber Co. (1935—1938), Canadian Robert
Dollar (1935—1938) and P. Bain (1935—1938), which are not shareholders.
Alberta Lumber Co. Ltd. does not become a shareholder until 1938.

Appendix J

SEABOARD LUMBER SALES COMPANY
SEABOARD SHIPPING COMPANY

DIRECTORS 1935—1984

Grainger, M.A.	1935–1936	†Millar, Alex W.	1942–1946
Pendleton, Ross	1935–1936	Gadd, T. Howard	1942–1952
Bain, P.	1935–1936	Strike, A. I.	1942–1944
Manning, F. C.	1935–1936	†O'Hagan, James P.	1942, 1951–1971
†McRae, Chris	1935–1936	Crowe, H. F.	1942, 1948
Dollar, H. B.	1935–1937	Leitch, A. K.	1942–1945
‡*Humbird, John A.	1935–1946	Nichols, W. Kimball	1942–1950
†McDonald, John H.	1935–1946	Brown, Fred B.	1943–1944
*Farris, Bruce M.	1935–1952	Burley, Norman G. B.	1944–1952
*Mackin, Henry J.	1935–1958	†King, M. Donald B.	1943–1955
†Hackett, G. Robin	1935–1952	Gonnason, Carl S.	1944–1947,
†Pendleton, Frank R.	1935–1942		1949–1958
Lamb, Thomas A.	1935–1939	Edgett, Lloyd W.	1942–1944
†Stone, Carlton	1935–1950	McLennan, Roderick D.	1944–1946
†Pendleton, Brooks L.	1935–1951	Nalos, Richard G.	1944–1945
Cameron, James O.	1935–1941	*Bentley, L. L. G.	1945–1974
†MacFarlane, Adelbert R.	1935–1941	Spencer, W. A.	1945
†Anderson, Arthur D.	1935–1939,	†Allison, Douglas G.	1945–1971
	1945–1971	†Heller, Samuel	1945–1970
†Culter, Carl J.	1935–1946	Plant, Ralph S.	1945–1948
Fearman, Frederick W.	1935–1952	Nichols, W. K. Jr.	1946–1972
†Edwards, John M.	1935–1951	†McDonald, Robert S.	1946–1961
†‡Robson, James G.	1935–1956	Morgan, Thomas E.	1946–1955
Burke, William T.	1935–1973	Simson, W. C.	1947–1952
Manning, Harold A.	1937–1946	Manning, Albert H.	1947–1950
McConville, Jack G.	1937–1946	McLennan, W. A.	1948–1952
†‡Grinnell, Charles H.	1937–1953	McNair, J. Earl	1948, 1951–1952
English, Norman	1937–1941	†Cameron, Newton D.	1948–1968
Weeks, Ernest E.	1937–1941	Lewall, R. A.	1948–1952
Airth, Harry C.	1938–1939	Flanagan, W. H.	1949–1954
†Moore, W. Stanley	1938–1964	Riggs, Thomas	1949–1950
Munsie, William H.	1938–1941	Fairburn, J. H.	1949, 1951–1952
Cherry, Robert B.	1938–1941	Fladgate, D. G.	1950–1951
Hunter, Harold W.	1938–1941	Shelly, H. E.	1950–1952
†Johnson, Goodwin	1938–1944	†Drew, J. A. C.	1951–1954,
Spencer, Nelson	1938–1943		1969–1971
Hanbury, Lawrence M.	1938–1941	Brooks, Frank C.	1951–1967
†McRae, Roderick B.	1939–1958	Pendleton, F. S.	1952
†Manning, Frederick A. E.	1939–1949	Vaughan, R. C.	1952–1957
†Glaspie, Elmer S.	1939–1950	†Renwick, H. A.	1952–1959
†Pendleton, Wayne	1940–1943	†Koerner, W. C.	1952–1955

Gattie, B. B.	1952–1961	Rolston, Eugene	1964–1965
McLean, H. A.	1952–1971	†Denman, Dennis S.	1965–1968
Farris, Richard H.	1952–1957,	†O'Hagan, Harry P.	1965–1972
	1967–1975	Sidhu, Ajaib	1965–1966
†Sauer, Albert O.	1952–1965	Winspear, W. W.	1965–1969
†Roberts, T. Lloyd	1952–1964	Garside, C.	1965–1967
Macken, W. L.	1953–1967	Monson, Ira N.	1965–1967
†Lyttle, A. L.	1953–1959	†Flavelle, W. G.	1965
†Smith, Hershell A.	1953–1970,	Tarling, Frank	1965
	1976–1984	Black, R. N.	1966–1969
†Feigl, John E.	1953–1972	Moss, D.	1966–1969
†‡Effinger, Claude N.	1953–1963	Cooke, E.	1966
Mackin, W. J.	1954–1955	†Buchanan, John W.	1966–1967
Edwards, D. A.	1954–1962	Nichol, Richard	1966–1967
Sloan, Peter	1955–1957	†McCutcheon, W. R.	1967
†Stone, Hector C.	1955–1968	Zinck, Errol B.	1967–1973
Seidler, S.	1955–1965	Armstrong, J. B.	1968
Drumb, F. A.	1955–1957	†Manning, H. Edward	1968–1984
King, G. G. C.	1956, 1965–1967	Gerrard, W. G.	1968–1969
Douglas, G. C.	1956–1958	Newell, R. F.	1968
Sahlin, Carl	1956	†Cluck, Donald E.	1968–1970
McGeachie, A. Gordon E.	1956–1959	Gill, S.	1968
Johnston, R. M.	1956–1958	Skogster, M.	1968
Robinson, W.	1957–1961	Grant, G. W.	1968
†Schmidt, D. R.	1957–1960	*Bowell, Gary S. J.	1968–1975
Seidler, Irving	1958–1965	†Ainsworth, David	1968–1972,
Ruttan, C. H.	1958–1959		1976–1984
†Ellison, R. H.	1959–1965	†Beaton, W. O.	1968–1969
†Lyttle, George M.	1959–1984	Hastings, Earl	1968
†Pendleton, F. H.	1959–1968	Dunn, R. A.	1968–1971
Biggs, J. C.	1960–1970	Hammond, Donald F.	1969–1981
Keeley, B. J.	1960–1962	†Martin, L. J.	1969–1984
*Rogers, Robert G.	1960–1964,	Henri, Herbert L.	1969–1971
	1973–1976	†Malpass, George L.	1969–1971,
Tullidge, G. H.	1960–1966		1976–1980
McKay, Gordon R.	1961–1965	Ford, D. L.	1969–1971
Battle, W. F. Tucker	1961–1968	Schwarzfeld, A.	1969–1972
†Sonner, Eric	1962–1968,	Montgomery, E. R.	1969
	1976–1978	†Ogilvy, Ronald R.	1970–1977
Harrison, G. Noel	1962–1968	†McMillan, Robert C.	1970–1975
Frewer, P. G.	1962–1967	†Urquhart, Howard B.	1971–1976
McDonald, I. W.	1962–1963	Van Allen, A. M.	1972–1973
Stothers, J. G.	1962–1968	Drake, J. R.	1972
Rustad, M. E.	1963–1973	†Roberts, Clive D. G.	1973–1984
Johl, Peary S.	1963–1975	†Rustad, James M.	1974–1984
Porritt, R. V.	1963	*Bentley, Peter J. G.	1975–1984
Zimmerman, A. H.	1963–1967	Dunkley, William	1975–1977
†Matthison, C. Rann	1964–1977	Manning, Norman B.	1975–1976
†Draeseke, Gordon L.	1964–1968	Noel, Leo	1975–1980
Gregory, Peter J.	1964–1967	Potter, James R.	1975

Isaacson, Roy	1975	Montgomery, John	1979–1981
Wrede, C. L-H.	1975–1983	†Sloan, William M.	1979–1984
White, John W.	1976–1984	*Sauder, William L.	1980–1984
Lovick, A. Kent	1976	Schine, D.	1980–1981
*Buell, Thomas A.	1976–1984	Dunkley, David	1980–1982
Kordyban, William W.	1976–1984	Kerr, John C.	1981–1983
*Rust, Thomas G.	1976–1983	Noel, Frank	1981–1982
†Buttar, James L.	1976–1981	Swanson, Robert W.	1982–1984
McWilliams, James F.	1977–1978	Barber, Irving K.	1982–1984
†Johnson, Chester A.	1977–1979	Novak, Henry	1983–1984
Jacobson, Harold M.	1977–1984	Fisher, Robert W.	1984
Gardner, S.	1977	Jones, William D.	1984
Culley, G. W.	1977–1978	†Ryan, L. Carl	1984
Cattermole, Robert S.	1977–1979	Suopanki, Kari J.	1984
Novak, Anton	1978–1979		

*Past Chairman
†Executive Committee
‡Honorary Director

INDEX